GOTHIC STAINED GLASS

1200~1300

Louis Grodecki and Catherine Brisac

GOTHIC STAINED GLASS

1200~1300

Cornell University Press
Ithaca, New York

Translated from the French:
Le Vitrail gothique au XIIIᵉ siècle

Copyright © 1984, Office du Livre S.A.,
Fribourg, Switzerland

English translation: Copyright © 1985 Office du Livre S.A.
All rights reserved. Except for brief quotations in a review, this book, or parts thereof, must
not be reproduced in any form without permission in writing from the publisher.
For information address Cornell University Press,
124 Roberts Place, Ithaca, New York 14850
English edition published 1985 by Cornell University Press

Library of Congress Cataloging in Publication Data
Grodecki, Louis, 1910-
    Gothic stained glass, 1200–1300
    Translation of: Le vitrail gothique au XIIIᵉ siècle.
    Bibliography: p.
    Includes index.
    1. Glass painting and staining, Gothic—France.
2. Glass painting and staining—France. I. Brisac,
Catherine. II. Title.
NK5349.A1G7613 1985   748.59'02   85-71277
ISBN 0-8014-1809-7

Printed and bound in Switzerland

Contents

Preface

When Louis Grodecki died on March 22, 1982, the Introduction and the first three chapters of this book, begun eighteen months before his death, were already written; moreover, we had already organized the last two chapters, prepared the catalogue and chosen some of the illustrations. His widow, Madame Catherine Grodecki, our publisher Jean Hirschen and I felt that the completion and publication of this book would be the finest honor that could be paid to the scholar who trained so many French and foreign art historians in the study of medieval stained glass.

Without the support and confidence of many medievalists, especially historians of stained glass, this work could not have been brought to completion. I would especially like to thank Catherine Grodecki; Jean-Jacques Gruber, who introduced me to the art of stained glass; Marie-Madeleine Gauthier, who conceived the idea for this book; Anne Prache and Jean Taralon, directors of the French committee of the *Corpus Vitrearum Medii Aevi*; Willibald Sauerländer, Director of the Zentralinstitut für Kunstgeschichte in Munich; Eva Frodl-Kraft, President of the International Committee of the *Corpus Vitrearum Medii Aevi*, and its vice-presidents, Madeline Caviness and Rüdiger Becksmann.

Also of great assistance were Catherine de Maupeou and Jean-Marie Bettembourg, Director and Head, respectively, of the *Vitrail* section at the Research Laboratory of the Monuments Historiques, Champs-sur-Marne; Claudine Lautier, engineer at the CNRS *(Corpus Vitrearum Medii Aevi)* as well as Véronique Chaussé and Françoise Gatouillat, researchers in stained glass at the Inventaire général des Monuments et Richesses artistiques de la France; Julia Fritsch, researcher at the Ile-de-France secretariat of the Inventaire général; Jane Hayward, President of the American committee of the *Corpus Vitrearum Medii Aevi*; Michael Cothren, Meredith Lillich, Helen Zakin, Linda Papanicolaou and Virginia Raguin, members of the American committee of the *Corpus Vitrearum Medii Aevi* and Dr. Erhard Drachenberg, Secretary of the committee of the *Corpus Vitrearum Medii Aevi* in the German Democratic Republic.

I am equally grateful to the master glaziers who welcomed me into their workshops and shared their experiences with me, especially to Didier Alliou in Le Mans, Sylvie Gaudin in Paris, Gérard Hermet and Mireille Juteau in Chartres, Benoît Marcq in Reims and Jean Mauret in Saint-Hilaire-en-Lignières (Cher). I am also indebted to Chantal Bouchon, curator at the Bibliothèque centrale des Arts Décoratifs, to Jean Ancien and to Jean Rollet. The affection and humor of my children have provided daily stimulus throughout this undertaking and helped me to bring it to fruition.

The publication of this book is due to collaboration between the authors and the energetic staff of Office du Livre: Dominique Guisan, who was the coordinator; Alain Le Coultre, editorial secretary; Ronald Sautebin, the designer; Marcel Berger, who oversaw the production and Ingrid de Kalbermatten, who was responsible for the illustrations. I would like to thank them personally for their very efficient work.

Catherine Brisac
May 25, 1984

Introduction

This volume is a sequel to *Le Vitrail roman,* published in 1977. Though inspired by the same methodological approach, it is conceived in a very different manner for reasons that become obvious when the vast quantity of Gothic material is compared to surviving Romanesque stained glass. A different scale of presentation was required for the stylistic problems, the relationships to architecture and the iconography. There are more than a thousand windows to be considered when selecting those to be discussed, often presenting idiosyncratic and complex problems. Many had never been studied; indeed, they have scarcely been mentioned or drawn, and were poorly photographed. For certain countries, like France, the advancement of research is still insufficient despite the efforts of the *Corpus Vitrearum* (a complete census of stained glass), undertaken twenty-five years ago at the initiative of Hans R. Hahnloser, and the *Recensement général des vitraux anciens de France,* begun in 1972; this is especially true for the condition of the glass. There are a number of monographic or general works on the most famous series of Gothic stained glass; however, many of these works are uncertain in their method and hypothetical in their conclusions.

The authors of the present work, though motivated to improve upon the work of their predecessors, have often been able to present only second-hand information, hypotheses, and personal or summary judgments. With the exception of certain English and Scandinavian glass, we have seen almost all the windows of the thirteenth and early fourteenth centuries that are preserved in Europe, and most of those in the United States. It does not necessarily follow that we perceived, noted or remembered all we should. The problem of choosing significant works and eliminating secondary ones often arose, and the solution may not always seem judicious.

The second difference between *Le Vitrail roman* and this volume is the plan and arrangement of chapters. Romanesque works were grouped primarily according to artistic regions, often coinciding with political ones in the western medieval world. Clear stylistic differences, however, separate these regions, only occasionally mitigated by sporadic contacts between them. A similar division of "Gothic" trends is not possible. From the beginning of the thirteenth century, common traits appeared in regions at some distance from each other—England and the Ile-de-France, northern France and Berry for instance. The same phenomenon can be seen in the development of architecture and manuscript illumination after 1200. Local traditions did not check this common progression, which reached the Rhineland as early as 1230. Of course, the "Late Romanesque" style had a tenacious hold in the Holy Roman Empire, and definitive "Gothicization" was not evident until after the middle of the thirteenth century. Consequently, it is the evolution of Gothic stained glass and its various phases that must serve as the principal framework for this volume, rather than local peculiarities, however numerous and significant they may be. Shortly after 1900, Emile Mâle[1] presented this evolution in a schematized form that subsequent historians have often adopted. The essential aspects of glass production in the twelfth century, with the exception of those in the Champagne region, were seen to derive from Saint-Denis, that is, from Paris. There, workshops of Notre Dame Cathedral (under construction from 1162) dominated the formation of Gothic stained glass. When other major sites opened in the north of France at the beginning of the thirteenth century—at Bourges as well as at Chartres—a homogeneous style established itself everywhere, proving its common origin.

Developments of the period from the beginning of the century up to about 1240 were best represented at the cathedral of Chartres, from where workshops dispersed throughout France. Proof of this was found at the cathedral of Rouen, where a *Clemens vitrearius carnotensis* signed a window in the ambulatory. The iconography, the general conception of the windows (lower windows with complex armatures and numerous scenes, upper windows with large figures), the compositional types and the palette were seen to be the same everywhere—at Chartres, Bourges, Laon, Soissons, Sens and Auxerre. The windows in the apse at Lyons constituted the only exception to this rule of uniformity, otherwise explainable by the unity of the Parisian source and by Chartrain expansion.

After the "Chartrain period" came a period around 1240 dominated by Parisian art, best defined by works in the Sainte Chapelle in the Palais de Justice. According to Emile Mâle, everything changed at that time. Palettes became darker; compositions more stereotyped and simplified because of the narrowness of the divisions in the lancet windows. Even the figural style became more slender and mannered, following the general evolution in Gothic painting and sculpture. The large ensembles in the choirs of the cathedrals at Le Mans and Tours or the windows in the cathedral of Clermont-Ferrand belong to this expansion of Parisian art between 1240 and 1245. Stained glass from the end of the thirteenth century—with which Mâle was less concerned—followed Parisian tendencies and developed them in another formal context; the introduction of grisaille panels modified the monumental effect and thus the relationship of windows to architecture.

Despite its great advantage of placing the principal French ensembles in a coherent order, a synthesis this simple—even simplistic—no longer accords with present exigencies nor with the state of documentation, which is infinitely greater than what Emile Mâle had at his disposal. Many major questions concerning this development have been posed and resolved. In 1928, Jean-Jacques Gruber analyzed the importance of the decades around 1300.[2] Jean Lafond studied the stained glass of Normandy dating after 1250,[3] while Louis Grodecki studied regional groups from the beginning of the thirteenth century.[4] New problems concerning the evolution of architecture and art, in France as well as in other countries, were clearly presented: the "1200 Style," the formation and affirmation of the Rayonnant style, the "Saint Louis" style.[5] In 1958, following the exhibition of stained glass at the Musée des Arts Décoratifs in Paris, a volume taking into account the most recent research was published.[6] Grodecki wrote a number of chapters in that book, notably the one on thirteenth-century glass. More than twenty years later, it is clear that this out-of-date text needs to be reappraised.

The authors of this book have personally contributed to the broadening of knowledge of stained glass through the publication of monographs and articles. Graduate work, often unpublished, has also contributed. In France this included studies of the windows at Clermont-Ferrand, Evreux, Lyons and Toul, Saint Sulpice at Favières and Saint Pierre at Dreux. In other countries, especially the United States, graduate research focused on the windows in the cathedrals at Auxerre, Tours, Beauvais and in the former abbey church of Saint Pierre at Chartres. All this research is cited in the bibliographies or catalogue entries of the present work.

Our principal focus is, necessarily, on the windows in France—the most numerous and, with few exceptions, the most important of the time. However one cannot judge the art of the 1200s without taking into account the renewal of western art along the Rhine and in England at the beginning of the thirteenth century. The essentially Germanic creation of a "Late Romanesque" art that is simultaneously "proto-Gothic" provided some of the most impelling and original masterpieces of stained glass of the century. It is true that French influence, through the impulse of Gothic architecture, penetrated across the Rhine, the English Channel and the Pyrenees from the middle of the thirteenth century. However, this influence was not decisive, and compromises were made with earlier local traditions. Regional, almost national, reactions modified the French Gothic style. The results enriched Gothic art—architecture and sculpture, as well as stained glass—reaching beyond the formal models provided by the French Gothic style. To determine the state of the question for the areas, numerous fairly early works can be consulted such as those by Read, Wentzel and Ainaud de Lasarte. More recent publications include the *Corpus Vitrearum Medii Aevi* for Italy by G. Marchini and the works by H. Rode, R. Becksmann and, finally, E. Drachenberg and K. J. Maercker (Germany), as well as those by Eva Frodl-Kraft and E. Bächer (Austria) and by M. Caviness, P. Newton and N. Morgan (England). We are acquainted with these publications and have discussed our ideas with these scholars, who are our friends. This book is, therefore, the result of long personal reflection, but also of extensive reading, many conversations and much advice over the years. At its beginning, then, we must thank all our friends—specialists in stained glass—some of whom are unfortunately deceased. While they do not bear the responsibility for this work, it is the result of a collective effort by many art historians, in which we participated, but from which we also profited.

1 Chartres, cathedral of Notre Dame, back of the west facade, (from left to right): Passion, Childhood of Christ, Tree of Jesse; ca. 1145–1150.

Definition of Gothic Stained Glass in the Thirteenth Century

The art of stained glass in the thirteenth century—often considered the time of its most perfect flowering—was determined by the role it played in architecture. Similarly, Romanesque stained glass of the eleventh century and a large part of the twelfth was determined by its position in the building: the high windows of the cathedral at Augsburg come to mind, and one can imagine how the French Romanesque windows in Le Mans Cathedral or the nave of Saint Remi at Reims must have looked. Today these works are largely altered but can be reconstituted; originally, stained glass windows were placed in bays that pierced thick walls in which the windows were but small openings. Surrounded by a vast wall surface, the stained glass acquired luminous power and colorful fascination, attracting the gaze of the faithful and condensing the spiritual significance of the image. However, this was not the sole architectural use of stained glass in the twelfth century. In that period, there were broad, tall openings in the great monumental compositions adorning west facades, chevets or even transept arms; they spilled their generous light within and provided grandiose interpretations of the fundamental subjects of Christian iconography. Very little remains of these grand compositions. There is enough to provide an idea, however, in the flat chevet of the cathedral at Poitiers or in the three bays of the facade at Chartres. There stained glass windows are, or were, essential because of the scope of the iconographic program and the extent of the luminous, colored surfaces. Even today, the nave of Chartres Cathedral is essentially lit by its three immense western windows, and the almost lyrical effect obtained inside is due to their illumination. At Poitiers, the edifice is illuminated by the large Crucifixion in the chevet, which justifies, in itself, the architectural formula of the monument. A third type of thirteenth-century window could be interpreted as the result of the inception of Gothic art, for instance, in Saint Denis at the gates of Paris: it involves the multiplication of windows and their enlargement into series of compositions, varied in subject, in radiating chapels or ambulatories. In their formal elaboration, these windows are precious, yet coherent in their effect as an ensemble. A similar effect was probably sought in other buildings—in the Romanesque cathedral at Châlons-sur-Marne,[1] in the apse of the abbey church at Arnstein (whose windows are preserved today in the Landesmuseum at Münster in Westphalia)[2] or in the ambulatory of Trinity Chapel in Canterbury Cathedral, where the great masterpiece of this form of translucent decoration can be seen.

Are there common denominators among these formulae predating the so-called Gothic Age? Firstly, whether the window was small or large, whether there were few openings or many, stained glass played the same role in relation to architecture: the windows always separated by a solid wall, which isolates them from each other yet affirms their independence and individual value. The entire luminous effect, in opposition to the purely architectural effect of a building, is captured and shaped by glazing. The exception to this is in some Cistercian formulae, where the use of entirely colorless grisaille panels, or of slightly colored ones, intensifies the light inside the building and negates the characteristic effect of painted glass. Few examples of such a formula survive (Obazine or Bénissons-Dieu), and one can only reconstruct the effect in a few more recent examples from the thirteenth century that we shall discuss later.

A second common trait of twelfth-century glass, entirely opposed to Gothic stained glass, is the extraordinary elaboration of painting technique in Romanesque windows.[3] The detailing emphasizes the plasticity of the borders, which abound in intertwining forms, foliated scrolls or even figures such as griffins. Braids with substantial beading more often frame the scenes; the backgrounds are decorated with geometric 'mosaic', damask, or even rinceaux designs (at Champ-près-Froges, Canterbury or Arnstein). The colored and luminous radiance of all these elements contributes to the decorative effect and increases the appearance of preciousness, such that the glass seems to parallel goldsmith's work or

2   Paris, Musée de Cluny: Saint Timothy, panel from the former abbey church of Saint Pierre et Saint Paul at Neuwiller-lès-Savern (Bas-Rhin); 1145–1150.

▷
3   Canterbury, cathedral, nave and chevet.

manuscript illumination in its richness. The same preciousness can be discerned in the handling of figures; in the overly ornate drapery at Augsburg, Saint Denis or Le Mans; in the interpretation of individuals such as Saint Timothy from Neuwiller (now in the Musée de   2 Cluny) and in the fragments preserved at Bourges Cathedral; or in anatomy, for instance, in the Saint Vincent spread on the grill in a medallion from Saint Denis. In the art of the thirteenth century, these subtleties would be eliminated by a more energetic and summary painting technique.

The third common denominator of twelfth-century glass as opposed to that of the next century is again derived from its relationship to architecture; however, it is of an iconographic or spiritual nature. Certainly some vast monumental programs of stained glass were conceived as early as the beginning of the twelfth century. This can be seen at Augsburg, where prophets and apostles may have surrounded the Virgin, probably a little later in the

4   Chartres, church of Saint Pierre, chevet; ca. 1220.

▷
5   Chartres, cathedral of Notre Dame, ambulatory,
bay 5: Life of Saint James the Greater; ca. 1220–1225.

Genealogy of Christ in Saint Remi at Reims and finally in the upper windows of Canterbury
Cathedral, where the entire ancestry of Christ since Adam was planned and carried out after 3
1175.[4]

The last example already encroaches upon the history of thirteenth-century glass, however.
In general, twelfth-century iconographic programs were restrained in development but extraordinarily profound in intent. They most often addressed the essential themes of faith—
Redemption and the path to it, the symbolism of the Virgin Mary and the intercession of
certain patron saints, chosen among the major figures of the Church and the Christian
religion. The iconography and spirituality of thirteenth-century glass went beyond these
subjects, keeping only a few themes from the preceding age, and introduced great cosmic
and eschatological themes, lives of the saints in the widest sense of the term or even the
history of the world as told in Scripture. All the prior traits were a consequence of the
relatively restrained place reserved for windows in proto-Gothic architecture.

The reconstruction of the cathedral of Chartres after the fire of 1193/1194 imposed a new
esthetic for stained glass. The architects were able to increase the size of the windows to
proportions never attained before: they multiplied the openings to the point of practically
eliminating the wall surfaces. The new techniques in stained glass were a corollary to the 4
new architectural esthetic. A new interpretation of the translucent decoration of religious

buildings was elaborated in iconographic programs and influenced the general significance of stained glass.

Within a quarter of a century, the evolution seen at Chartres produced a whole series of major Gothic monuments in northern France. Stained glass occupied an ever larger proportion of the wall surface and, consequently, affected the amount of light transmitted into the nave. It is possible, as some authors have suggested, that this evolution was accompanied by a specific modification of the windows, since they were beginning to take the place of wall surfaces.[5] Because of the size of the bays, the windows had to have multiple compartments, which were assembled according to increasingly complex schemes, and it became necessary to give them coloristic and formal consistency.

The windows of Chartres between 1200 and 1210 (the probable dates of the nave windows) have sometimes been considered the first examples of this type of design. In fact, however, this compositional development had taken place even earlier, and the new type had already been used with virtuosity at Canterbury.[6] The division of windows into multiple compartments also provoked the development of backgrounds—multicolored mosaics set in the spandrels of panels or even occupying entire panels placed between scenes. The borders that had played such a large role in the composition of Romanesque windows gradually became narrower and more restricted in motifs and execution. The range of colors was also modified, stronger tones—reds, blues, purples and greens—coming into use. Light colors played only a secondary role, giving value to figures or as separations between compartments in the form of smooth or pearled fillets. This first manifestation of Gothic glazing produced masterpieces of remarkable formal invention: compositions in circles, quadrants and stars, where the combination of mosaics and ornamental motifs such as *fermaillets* ("ornamental bosses") linked the historiated compartments together. Whether the ornamental motifs were abstract or vegetal, they gave a formal richness and decorative elaboration to the stained glass of the first quarter of the thirteenth century that would not be continued in Gothic painting except in rare instances. Obviously these large windows of the later period retain earlier compositional elements—rectilinear arrangement, generous floral borders, simplified mosaic backgrounds—but, in the main, this period both benefited from the impetus of the great English and French building campaigns at the end of the twelfth century and engaged in multiple new experiments.

Architecture and Gothic Stained Glass

From the first quarter of the thirteenth century, the evolution of architecture brought about a rapid metamorphosis in stained glass. The tall windows at Chartres, consisting of two lancets separated by a substantial trumeau and surmounted by a rose, already show a tendency to create double windows and to try to achieve a unified effect within an ensemble composed of multiple openings. At the cathedral of Reims and at Amiens (about 1220), the separation between the two lancets was no longer a solid trumeau but a narrow mullion. The master glazier had to take this new situation into account and fully develop the principle of window *cloisons*, or compartments, to take the place of wall surfaces. From 1225 or 1230, the enlargement of the Gothic window—which was subdivided into two, three and then four lights at the cathedral of Troyes or at the abbey of Saint Denis—instituted an absolutely new order of composition with which the master glazier had to comply. No longer were the openings over 2 meters wide as in the cathedrals of Chartres or Bourges; windows were now composed of narrow lights, 1 to 1 1/2 meters in width, assembled in architecturally unified compositions.

Beyond all question, the masterpiece of "Rayonnant" architecture is the Sainte Chapelle in the Palais de Justice in Paris (1242/43–1248). The narrowness of the window's lights, fifteen times higher than they are wide, is astonishing; they are decorated with a multiplicity of superimposed scenes, all small in scale. When four lights are assembled under Rayonnant tracery within the same window, the composition is subdivided into figurative and decorative panels to such an extent that the eye is distracted and unable to follow the images in sequence. In buildings of the mid-thirteenth century (in the choir of the cathedral at

6   Chartres, cathedral of Notre Dame, ambulatory, 1st north radiating chapel; ca. 1220–1225.

▷
7   Paris, Sainte Chapelle in the Palais de Justice (formerly a royal palace), upper chapel; between 1242 and 1248. Cf. cat. 57.

Troyes, in the inner ambulatory of the cathedral at Le Mans and then at Tours), these immense stained glass compositions, made up of small scenes, give a very strange impression of the religious art of this period. In a sense, the painted image seems to have lost its deeper purposes: the representation of the sacred and the education of the faithful. The biblical stories in the Sainte Chapelle are essentially incomprehensible. To try to recount the story of Esther and Ahasuerus in one hundred and twenty-nine scenes is to assume the verbosity of a serial novel. Hagiography also lent itself to this sort of "dilution" and to repetitions that are often meaningless. Of course, the earlier, alternative formula—large figures decorating the upper windows—was preserved until the middle of the thirteenth century. In this way large figures of Christ, the Virgin Mary, prophets, apostles and patron

8   Bourges, cathedral of Saint Etienne, chevet clerestory, bays 200, 201 and 202: Virgin and Child and
Saint Stephen in the axial windows, flanked by David
and Saint John the Baptist in the left windows, and
Saint Peter and Saint Paul in the right ones; ca. 1220–
1225.

saints of the Church could be represented in accordance with hagiographic programs that
were often very interesting, e.g. the choir clerestory in the cathedrals at Reims or Le Mans.
However, in these instances, darkening of the palette and simplification of the abundant
ornament take away from the admirable legibility of the large figures from the beginning of
the century at Chartres and Bourges. Because of the size of the bays, the tradition of 8
depicting a single large figure per window was often replaced by depicting superimposed
figures, or even by the insertion of entire scenes in the clerestory.

   Thus, the evolution of architecture after 1225–1230 brought about a change in stained
glass that could not have been anticipated around 1200–1210. A kind of opposition, or even
rivalry, developed between the glass painter and the architect: the more the architect pierced
the walls to bring light into the building, the more the glass painter tried to employ the
increasingly large surfaces offered to him, enriching them by his own means and cultivating
the effect of strong and sustained colors.

   Around 1260 this formula reached a critical impasse: the bays could not be enlarged 9
further, the wall surface having been reduced to a structural minimum, and the glass painter,
having reached the point of saturation in the vividness of his color range, could also go no
further. The previous formula was then totally reversed: very large, grisaille panels were
employed with full-colored figural panels of various sizes (in the Canons windows at Loches

9 Troyes, church of Saint Urbain, chevet and choir, south side; ca. 1270. Cf. cat. 94.

27 and the Archbishops window at the cathedral of Tours or in the great masterpiece of this new formula—Saint Urbain at Troyes). This tendency was not a completely new invention but rather the generalized use of an earlier system that can be seen in uncolored Cistercian glass from the beginning of the twelfth century.

During the first half of the thirteenth century, whether through economic necessity or through the need to finish glazing rapidly, white glass had been made; sometimes colored elements such as fillets, borders or "brooches" were included. Examples are the upper nave 43 at Bourges, very probably that of Notre Dame in Paris and of the abbey church at Orbais in Champagne, where there remains some very beautiful glass with just a trace of coloring. Two particularly rich formulae for glazing appeared toward the middle of the century. The first used grisaille lights and colored lights placed side by side. The second innovation was 10 the band-window, in which large horizontal bands of colored figural glass were set between registers of grisaille. This expedient was partially adopted at Tours around 1260.[7] Other formulae, rarer and without real consequence, can also be mentioned: at the cathedral of Auxerre, large borders of grisaille surrounded figural panels; in the chapel of Saint Jean 48 jouxte les fonts in Rouen Cathedral, completely colored figural panels were set and mounted 59 in grisaille windows; and in Sainte Radegonde at Poitiers, vividly colored figures were placed directly against a grisaille background.

21

10   Chartres, church of Saint Pierre, choir clerestory, south side, bay 213: Old Testament figures and grisaille lights; ca. 1270.

▷

11   Chartres, cathedral of Notre Dame, south transept arm, ensemble donated by the Dreux-Bretagne family: (above the donors) the Virgin and Child flanked by four tall prophets carrying an Evangelist; (in the rose) Christ with the Elders of the Apocalypse; 1221–1230. Cf. cat. 30.

As Jean-Jacques Gruber pointed out in a noteworthy study,[8] the overall effect of these new tendencies was not only to transform profoundly lighting conditions within churches but also to make a complete change in the pictorial style and iconography used in stained glass. Nothing could be more logical than this solution to the crisis of the years 1260 to 1270. Rayonnant architecture, in France above all, but also in the countries affected by the French Gothic style, developed such subtle building proportions and outlines, such refinement in decoration and an almost manneristic conception of space that its effects would have been invisible without very abundant lighting. The vibrant light provided by grisaille glass regrouped and underlined the building's inner volumes, perhaps making them purer. In the upper story of the cathedral at Beauvais, where colorless glass was employed before the collapse of the vaults in 1272, the architecture is displayed with almost unbearable rigidity by the light. In the same way, both Saint Urbain at Troyes and Saint Nazaire at Carcassonne—the great masterpieces of the last quarter of the century—were built to receive uncolored glazing. Gruber has observed that, whatever the subtlety of grisaille (which was often strewn with points of color at this time), full-color windows would appear too dark in radiant light if the opaque palette of 1240–1250 continued in use. Artists had to lighten their palettes, seeking out light blues, less violent reds and paler purples. Likewise, it is at this time in Normandy (most probably in the cathedral at Evreux) that the first applications of silver stain (yellow) made their appearance, lightening the color range and adding new brilliancy to the art of glass painting. Painting style began to be oriented toward a more nuanced representation of reality, in accordance with contemporary tendencies in Parisian and English miniature painting; the authority of line-work was abandoned in favor of modeling. Iconography was necessarily restricted to a limited number of scenes, and the overabundant narrative of the preceding epoch was abandoned, making the scenes clearer and more legible. In an attempt to produce novel spatial effects, scenes were neatly balanced in rectangular compartments or medallions, and figures were juxtaposed to provide new depth.

Spiritual and Iconographic Meanings

These few observations on the transformations of iconography certainly do not take into account the spiritual function of Gothic stained glass. It is well known that stained glass retains the basic symbolism of Christian art. This symbolism is already contained in sacred writings of the fourth and fifth centuries, where God is compared to light and the penetration of light into a building compared to the visible action of God. We have stressed this symbolism elsewhere;[9] it was concretized much more fully during the Middle Ages than during the Early Christian and pre-Romanesque periods. During the Romanesque period, some authors evoked the idea of a building with walls of light, like the Heavenly Jerusalem of the Apocalypse, built of translucent precious stones; however, such an edifice was impossible to build because of the structural system then in use. A desire to attain this goal is manifest in the west facade at Chartres and the chevet at Poitiers, where the light from the very large glazed openings adds to lighting within the building. The advent of Gothic means of construction enabled grandiose structures to be built such as the nave and choir at Chartres and, later, the Sainte Chapelle in Paris. Thus, it is not surprising that some thirteenth-century writers, like Durand de Mende, evoked the symbolism of the Heavenly Jerusalem when speaking of the windows in Christian churches. These authors speak from actual experience, having seen with their own eyes buildings in which the walls seemed to be replaced by luminous screens of glass in dazzling colors.[10] The explanation of the ancient Christian symbolism had never before attained such force and clarity.

The significance of stained glass became much more general and universal once it went beyond Romanesque aspirations. The spectator's fascination with a window in a Romanesque bay that captured and shaped the light gave way to a fascination of another order, in which the spectator came under the thrall of the glazing as a whole, without being able to fix his attention on individual parts of the ensemble. Because of corrosion, the overall effect of Gothic stained glass has lost much of its resonance in modern times, leaving dimmed these marvelous translucent walls that play with the sunlight and seem different each hour of the day. In some monuments where, fortunately, much ancient glass has been preserved, the mobility of light and color produced by the stained glass calls to mind magnificent

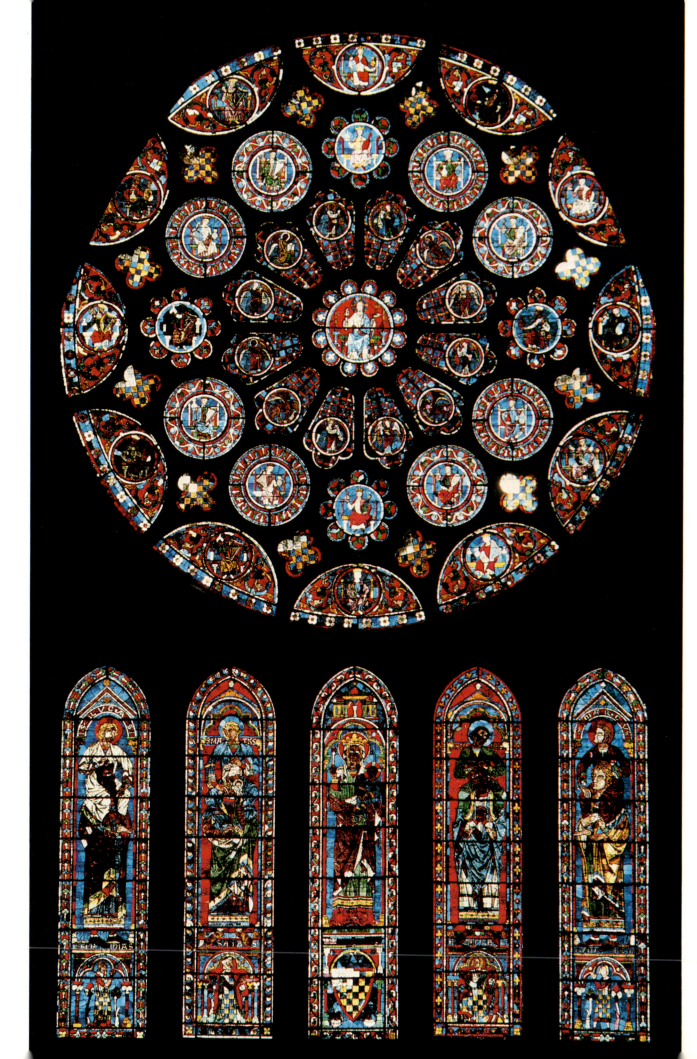

comparisons with the *lapides vivi*, the living rocks on which the Church is built, a theme developed by medieval writers. A modern author, J.K. Huysmans, was particularly sensitive to all these meanings when he wrote about the cathedral of Chartres at the beginning of this century.

For nonspecialists, or for a visitor not armed with strong binoculars, the great windows of the thirteenth century have become illegible, and the particular significance of each of them is now obscure. Was it the same in the Middle Ages? Paul Claudel, in an essay on stained glass, has suggested that a guide explained to the faithful the meaning of each of the scenes.[11] This is simply pure fantasy in our opinion. As in the case of the sculpture on the facades of great cathedrals (Reims, for example), where the figures are placed too high to see details or where they are too difficult to interpret precisely, the medieval viewer—like today's—was overcome by the expressive force of the ensemble rather than by an analysis of details. The instructive value of thirteenth-century glass, that "catechism for illiterates," was probably not extensive and did not go beyond the few isolated images or those placed for favorable view.

It is true that there are some privileged locations in the great buildings of the thirteenth and fourteenth centuries: the terminal walls of the transept arms, the back of the facade and, sometimes, the chevet. There, the architectural composition contributed to the creation of formal programs to which the glass responded or that it had helped to create. Examples are the rose windows at Chartres, Paris and Lausanne, the west facade at Mantes and the eastern ensemble at Laon.

The evolution of rose windows was slow during the twelfth century; in the thirteenth century, however, rose windows developed rapidly. They increased in size in each decade, attaining a diameter of 13 meters at Notre Dame in Paris. The openings were subdivided by increasingly complicated tracery, above all in Rayonnant architecture after 1230.

What subjects could be more appropriate for such "encyclicals" than the Creation, the Last Judgment, God or the Blessed Virgin in Glory? In these compositions, all the complementary scenes were grouped around the spiritual center of the ensemble. Alternatively, at Lausanne, the cosmological *Mundus*, or world, was represented. Other possibilities were the Signs of the Zodiac, or the moral world with the Virtues and the Vices as at Laon.

One can easily understand the marvelous effect that these immense radiating flowers of glass produced and how they intrigued the spectator into trying to understand their meaning. Placed high up under the vault, these compositions required, at their base, a series of openings to complete their message. The five enormous bays of the south transept at Chartres have one of the most wonderful iconographic programs—Ecclesia flanked by the major prophets carrying the Evangelists. There too, however, illegibility quickly sets in, as it does in the rose windows of Notre Dame in Paris. Another system for emphasizing exceptional compositions in stained glass makes use of the eastern end of a building, for example the chevet in the cathedral of Laon whose Marian rose surmounts three theological and hagiographical windows. A further example is the sequence of several windows, which can be seen together at a glance, in the back of the choir at Bourges or at Reims. The central bay contains a subject of major importance—the Coronation of the Virgin Mary, the Virgin and Child or the patron saint of the edifice—and is accompanied by figures of prophets or apostles, often identified by large inscriptions. By contrast, it is next to impossible to read the upper windows of the choir at Chartres or Tours.

Nevertheless, large, coherent iconographic programs for cathedrals were more successful in the thirteenth century than in the twelfth; however, almost no program from this first period survives intact. At best, at Canterbury or in Saint Remi at Reims, they can be reconstructed with some certainty. The much more substantial number of preserved works enables us to recognize thirteenth-century masters' efforts to organize coherent, if not logical, iconographic programs. Occasionally it seems that their plans were thwarted by the particular devotions or the choices of the windows' donors, the nave and ambulatory windows at Chartres being one of the best examples. It is rare to find intact a unified iconographic program inspired by a single directing thought. This was the case at the end of the twelfth century in Trinity Chapel at Canterbury Cathedral and, at the beginning of the thirteenth century, in the ambulatory and radiating chapels at Bourges. Obviously the apogee of this tendency is the Sainte Chapelle in Paris, where the stories of Christ and of the two Saint Johns are set between the main chapters of the Old Testament that lead from the Creation to the Redemption, from there to the History of the Relics of the Passion and to

12 Laon, former cathedral of Notre Dame: in the lights of the lower level (from left to right), Life and Martyrdom of Saint Stephen and Legend of Theophilus, Passion of Christ, Life of the Virgin and Childhood of Christ with typological figures; (in the rose) the Glorification of the Virgin Mary; 1210–1215. Cf. cat. 40, 41.

13 London, Victoria and Albert Museum: panel with foliated scrolls from a window in Trinity Chapel, Canterbury Cathedral, dedicated to the Life of Thomas Becket (bay 15 or IV); 1190–1205. Cf. cat. 99.

▷
14 Chartres, cathedral of Notre Dame, nave, north aisle, bay 43: Life of Saint Eustace (detail); Saint Placidas Hunting; ca. 1210. Cf. cat. 27.

the End of the World. Programs that are now incomplete but can be easily reconstructed must also be borne in mind. Examples are the upper choir in Reims Cathedral (all the churches in the diocese of Reims placed around the Virgin Mary and the apostles); Lyons with its Coronation of the Blessed Virgin in the center and the nave clerestory at Strasbourg with its immense procession of saints, the women in the south windows and the men in the north ones. These developments are the counterpart of the visual illegibility and overall effect discussed above. Once again, after 1260, the new spirit in glazing would bring an end to this contradiction with the luminous program in Saint Urbain at Troyes and, later, in Saint Ouen at Rouen.

Another important characteristic of thirteenth-century glass, which derives in part from the Romanesque esthetic but is more accentuated and reaches a greater degree of expression later, is the preciosity of stained glass, the fragmentation of its colors and the juxtaposition of pieces of vividly colored glass to resemble a mosaic of precious gems. Contemporary secular and religious literary texts confirm that the association between colored glass and precious stones was in the forefront of many minds and that much of the emotive power of stained glass came from this comparison. Despite the increasing window surface in thirteenth-century buildings, the scale of ornamentation was not conceived with monumental effects in mind. On the contrary, the goal was to multiply the play of backgrounds composed of pieces cut very small and studded with pearling and multicolored fillets. Even the borders—which narrowed, especially after 1200—reached a new level of invention and decorative fantasy, surpassing the superabundance of the Romanesque period.

Distinctive forms of border ornament include the rinceaux, or foliated-scroll, backgrounds that resulted in extraordinary floral effects in the spandrels and frames of glazed panels (cf. Canterbury, Sens and a few windows at Chartres). The use of rinceaux necessitated meticulous work on the part of the glass cutter and the glazier, for they were at the limits of what was technically possible. This complicated process was quickly abandoned in favor of the more expeditious means of cutting rectilinear backgrounds.

The second means of enhancing borders was the introduction of heraldic elements in an age when the evolution of feudal society brought about the increasingly frequent use of coats of arms and emblems. In England and in France, these motifs appeared from the first quarter of the thirteenth century; the truly widespread popularity of this decoration occurred between 1240 and 1260, when the fleur-de-lis (symbol of France) and the three-towered castle (representing Castile) filled the borders and backgrounds of windows in the Sainte Chapelle as well as in many other places in France and abroad (though with no valid historical basis abroad). The juxtaposition of red or blue backgrounds and golden-yellow motifs enriched the colors of thirteenth-century windows, while reducing the admirable ornamental efforts of the first third of the century. At the end of the century, the renewed use of this formula was rare, with the exception of the surprising borders in Saint Urbain at Troyes that displayed the arms of the Champagne region and of Pope Urban IV.

From the beginning of the fourteenth century, a new figurative fancy took hold in border decoration with the introduction of lively shapes such as birds, animals and people (for instance in the Lady Chapel of the cathedral at Rouen).

The evolution of architectural motifs in stained glass must also be emphasized. Romanesque art had already made use of such multicolored elements in the Rhineland and in France.[12] Complex canopies, veritable "cities on arcades,"[13] which can be seen in the upper windows at Chartres and at Reims,[14] gave way to increasingly extensive frames that created, above the figures, systems derived from the art of building—colonnettes, arcades and gables within which the figures move, all surmounted by increasingly fantastic, fictive architecture. Since this architecture was purely imaginative, no limits were placed on the glass painters, who seized this opportunity to build their painted architecture skyward over many panels. In eastern France and Germany, the success of this type of decoration was much greater than that of the band-window, which was never as widely utilized there, where the tops of windows were given over to these airy structures.[15] There was also, as in the earlier types of decoration we have discussed, a willingness to create an imaginary world—to set this architecture of dreams within real architecture. This produced a new contradiction within the art of stained glass, in its relationship to architecture and iconography. Nothing in the formal or spiritual sphere justified such bypassing of the principles that Gothic art seemed to impose on the interpretation of reality. Architectural logic, which had become law in the thirteenth century, was being totally denied.

Relationships with Other Techniques

Is it possible to define the styles of figuration in Gothic stained glass? Again one must start by going back to the diversity of Romanesque figural styles. In that period, strong relationships often existed between stained glass and manuscript illumination or wall painting in western France, the Champagne or even in the Auvergne region.[16] Stained glass seems to have taken some of its inspiration from these nontranslucent techniques of painting. Other relationships can be discerned between stained glass and the decorative arts that employed precious metals—goldsmith's work and enameling—for instance at Saint-Denis. Stained glass appears to have played a role in the evolution of Romanesque styles and to have depended on it to a certain extent.

It has long been known that, in the thirteenth century, the relationships among the various artistic techniques was just the opposite:[17] in thirteenth-century manuscript illumination, the use of gold-leaf backgrounds seems to be an attempt to reproduce the effect of light that can only really be achieved in stained glass. Even the formal line-work and the sharp silhouetting with increasingly marked outlines strikingly resemble the effect produced in stained glass by leading. Furthermore, the use of color in manuscripts (and in thirteenth-century painting in general) is similar to the exultation of contrasting colors natural to glass painting. It is as if the subtleties of modeling and the pictorial techniques used in the twelfth century were forgotten or simplified. Moreover, in the compositions of certain thirteenth-century illuminations and paintings, groupings with superimposed medallions are reutilized along with complex arrangements and cropped panels derived from the insertion of stained glass into compartments in the armature. Examples are the Psalter of Blanche of Castile, now in the Bibliothèque de l'Arsenal (ms. 1186) or the later *Bibles moralisées* ("Moralized Bibles"), in which figurative medallions are set against mosaic grounds identical to those found in stained glass. Thus, for several decades of the thirteenth century, the dominant esthetic in painting was derived from stained glass and not from manuscript illumination.

Obviously such a simplistic view must be qualified. The figurative style of the Romanesque period and of the "1200s" was defined principally in techniques other than stained glass, and they continued to exert their influence on glass painting for some time; this was the case of the stained glass at Laon, Soissons and in the Rhineland, where the Romanesque style survived for a long time.[18] These relationships, however, were far from constant.

From the mid-thirteenth century, and above all at its end, miniature painting evolved more rapidly and decisively than stained glass toward a kind of formal mannerism. Works such as the Second Evangelary of the Sainte Chapelle (Paris, Bibl. Nat., ms. lat. 8892)[19] or the group of *Sommes le Roi* manuscripts pared down forms, refining them in a manner appropriate to the smallness of that medium. Mannerist stained glass in Saint Urbain at Troyes and in La Trinité at Fécamp in Normandy seems to be derived from this pictorial tendency rather than to have created it. Early in the fourteenth century, Parisian and English miniatures inspired the glass painters in Saint Ouen at Rouen and in the cathedral of Evreux.

Another problem is the relationship of stained glass to sculpture, which is considered the dominant technique of monumental Gothic art. A number of precise relationships between the two mediums can be seen at Laon and Chartres, perhaps at Sens, and certainly in Saint Urbain at Troyes, as we shall see. But what of the general relationship between these two most representative figurative arts of the thirteenth century?

The birth of the Gothic portal multiplied the examples of a constantly evolving style that had an extraordinary impact on artistic vision and imagination: first with its column-statues, then with its splay statues, its voussoirs and bases. The porches of the transept at Chartres and the facades at Amiens or Reims define the stages in a stylistic development that goes from the elegance of the "1200 Style" to the almost Cubist severity of formal treatment in the years from 1225 to 1240. After the Sainte Chapelle, a new, almost mannerist softening is evident in Parisian art, which led to the expressive exaggerations of the end of the century: twisted silhouettes, complicated axes and monumental values undermined by narrative or picturesque detail. Though it is difficult to prove with a sufficient number of specific examples, the art of French stained glass surely evolved in a similar way through many variations—sometimes behind the sculptural trends, sometimes ahead of them. These evolutionary schemes are not applicable to German and English art, however, nor to the few Italian and Spanish works of stained glass from the thirteenth and early fourteenth centuries.

15 Champs-sur-Marne, castle, storage depot of the Monuments Historiques: border of birds with confronted heads, panel from a window devoted to the Acts of the Apostles, formerly in the cathedral at Amiens; ca. 1240. Cf. cat. 12.

16 Paris, Bibliothèque Nationale: ms. lat. 11560, *Bible moralisée* ("Moralized Bible"), fol. 83ᵛ; ca. 1220.

17 Paris, Bibliothèque Nationale: ms. lat. 8892, Evangelary of the Sainte Chapelle, fol. 6; ca. 1250.

Artists and Patrons

The question of who created the stained glass windows of the Middle Ages remains, and perhaps it is unanswerable. Despite the existence of texts and signatures, there is little solid information. Undoubtedly the glazier was held in high esteem from the twelfth century: Abbot Suger, describing the windows at Saint-Denis, spoke of the *"manus exquisita… multorum magistrorum de diversis nationibus"*;[20] and Gerlachus, the master glazier of

18   Rouen, cathedral of Notre Dame, ambulatory, bay 11: Story of the Patriarch Joseph (detail), signature of Clement of Chartres; ca. 1235. Cf. cat. 68.

Arnstein, signed a window declaring himself *clarus*—"famous".[21] As these and other texts attest, these men were "master glaziers,"—artists recognized for their talent and not simple craftsmen working under the supervision of a master architect.

Stained glass windows were expensive, very expensive: at Saint-Denis, it is thought that they may have cost as much as the entire choir to build, though this has not been proven.[22] At the beginning of the thirteenth century, a large window in the cathedral of Soissons was made possible by a royal donation of 40 pounds—a considerable sum at the time. Mention is made in the thirteenth-century register of the Grande Commanderie of Saint Denis of a *vitrearius* in 1228 or 1229, who was responsible for the upkeep of the abbey's windows. The man received an annual payment of 8 pounds, in addition to all expenses for glass, lead and iron.[23] At the end of the thirteenth century (beginning in 1284), there are a series of references, with figures, to the glass and lead purchased for the maintenance of, or for additional work on, the windows in the abbey. Such work often involved considerable expense—35 pounds one year, 39 another, and so on. Master glazier Guillaume was paid 16 pounds a year and received additional "bonuses" for himself and his assistants. Other sums were given to him to pay for his house and clothing.[24] There are annual accounts available for Saint Denis for each year through the beginning of the fourteenth century. Consequently, it is very probable that many master glaziers worked directly for the owners of major buildings. This was the case at the Sainte Chapelle, where King Louis IX created the job of custodian of glass, responsible for repairing the windows.

Was it always so? Certainly during the rapid creation of large ensembles of stained glass such as those at Chartres, Le Mans or the Sainte Chapelle, it was necessary to call on a number of master craftsmen, who sometimes came from great distances.[25] Each workshop must have consisted of a varying number of helpers and apprentices working under the direction of the master. Later we shall discuss how stylistic study demonstrates that, at Bourges for instance, at least three important workshops can be distinguished.[26] However, a single name is known to us thanks to a very vague document: *Stephanus, vitrearius*—who lived in a canonical house in Bourges around 1220. Journeying masters must have been numerous, making the study of contacts among various regions difficult but fascinating. One

of these men signed a window in the ambulatory of the cathedral at Rouen: *Clemens vitrearius carnotensis*, indicating his Chartrain roots.[27] (The signature *Bartholomeus* in the cathedral at Auxerre seems now to be of doubtful authenticity.) At the Sainte Chapelle in Paris, at least three master glaziers were at work; yet to complete the extensive glazing program in five to seven years, a minimum of forty to fifty specialized workers would have been needed to cut the glass, to paint it, to lead it, and so forth.

Shrouded in anonymity as they are, these artists—some of them very great masters—have not gone entirely unrecognized, for, as we shall see later, we can define their originality and their genius.

Our knowledge of commissions for stained glass is often much more complete. Sometimes an entire ensemble was commissioned (the Sainte Chapelle in Paris, a royal edifice, or Saint Urbain in Troyes, a collegiate church richly endowed by a pope). But most often, in the thirteenth century, the expense of constructing and decorating a huge edifice far surpassed the financial means of a cathedral chapter or of an abbey, regardless of its wealth. Therefore, it was necessary to solicit gifts or donations far and wide.

The generous result of these efforts can best be seen at Chartres.[28] Kings, princes, noblemen, canons and the city's guilds offered windows of varying size, "signing" them with a representation of their professional activity or with a "portrait" at the bottom of the window, where the figure, often kneeling,[29] sometimes held a small model of the window in his hands. There were also inscriptions signaling the name and rank of the donor or identifying feudal insignia in the windows.[30] Even so, surviving information is not sufficient to allow us to reconstruct all the circumstances under which the masterpieces of stained glass were created during the Middle Ages. Admittedly, information about these men—masters and workmen—and these donors, even when they were famous, remains insufficient. For example, did Saint Louis conceive the glazing program for the Sainte Chapelle himself? Did he really think about the stained glass? Did the humble water carriers of Chartres and the vintners of Le Mans, who arrived too late for the consecration of the new choir in the cathedral on April 20, 1254, realize the value of their gift?

To our eyes, these windows are not only the legacy of a civilization but also a reflection of a special kind of spirit, where religious sentiment was allied to a collective esthetic, created by a generation of artists who had an incomparable mastery of technique.

19 Le Mans, cathedral of Saint Julien, choir clerestory, bay 209, left light, lower register: the donor Jean de Fresnay giving a window; ca. 1260.

The First Quarter of the Thirteenth Century in France

The "1200 Style" and Its Expansion

Obviously, it was not in the year 1200, exactly, that Gothic stained glass began to be made in France. A number of experiences in the twelfth century, beginning with the abbey church of Saint Denis and continuing through the entire second half of that century, had already suggested new formal and iconographic ideas. These were taken up in the thirteenth century, with changes that were more or less decisive for the future of the style: compositions with superimposed medallions, with half-medallions flanking a central compartment and with complex ensembles using bars shaped to the medallions[1] gradually increased. In the ambulatory at Canterbury Cathedral, these changes reached a profusion that could well be thought of as already appropriate to the thirteenth century. Similarly, the new conception for upper windows (large figures under a canopy, or sometimes in tiers in a single light) can be seen in Saint Remi at Reims as early as the last decades of the twelfth century.

Even in drawing and painting styles, there are formal elements and general characteristics that can be distinguished from Romanesque stylization. Their inspiration was drawn from archaizing or Mosan sources or even from the final flowering of Byzantine art in Sicily and southern Italy. We now know that, in the last quarter of the twelfth century, a style neither Romanesque nor Gothic was prevalent in much of Europe: in England, France, the Meuse and Rhine valleys and in Italy. Designated the "1200 Style," it was shaped in part by the art of stained glass, which contains some of its finest masterpieces. We shall leave aside discussion of the "Master of Methuselah" at Canterbury and his archaizing style, as well as discussion of the Troyes glass of 1170–1180 (now dispersed), which is so close to Mosan miniatures. We shall, however, focus on an important region for the "1200 Style"—northern France and such centers as Reims, Soissons, Laon and Saint-Quentin.

The Laon-Soissons Group

Important glass painting traditions already existed in this region in the twelfth century. The upper choir windows in Saint Remi at Reims can be viewed as "proto-Gothic" models for the Soissons, Laon and Vermand areas.

Most likely it was also in this region that important illuminated manuscripts were created in the years just before 1200. The Ingeborg Psalter (Chantilly, Musée Condé, ms. 1695)[2] is one of the most important examples of this style; it combines archaizing and even Byzantinizing qualities with an almost naturalistic character that is in opposition to Romanesque art and, in certain respects, prefigures Gothic style. The miniatures in the Ingeborg Psalter have, with good reason, been compared to stained glass, especially to the windows in the cathedral at Laon. In a masterful manner, that monument, on which construction began around 1160, defined the style of the "first Gothic architecture": multiple stories, and the compact rhythm of successive bays and openings. The north transept rose (only the iconographic program of the Liberal Arts and some original medallions remain) was probably created just before 1200 (1185–1195?). All the monumental grandeur of the architecture seems to be echoed in the figural style seen there—the ample silhouettes gathering their strength, the abundance of soft yet firmly rendered drapery, the large scale of modeling in faces and bodies. Next to work in Saint Remi at Reims, these characteristics provide a second "proto-Gothic" model for glass painting. This figural style can also be compared to the reliefs on the left portal of Laon's west facade, for instance the Erythraen Sibyl.[3]

20 Laon, former cathedral of Notre Dame, west facade, left portal, voussoir: figure; 1195–1205 (casting, before restoration, Paris, Musée des Monuments français).

22

20

21 Laon, former cathedral of Notre Dame, lower chevet level, bay 2, right light: Childhood of Christ with Typological Scenes (detail), The Flight into Egypt; 1210–1215. Cf. cat. 41.

22 Chantilly, Musée Condé: ms. 1695, The Ingeborg Psalter, fol. 18ᵛ, lower register: The Flight into Egypt; between 1193 and 1213.

▷
23 Laon, former cathedral of Notre Dame, lower chevet level: (from left to right), Life and Martyrdom of Saint Stephen and Legend of Theophilus, Passion of Christ, Life of the Virgin Mary and Childhood of Christ with typological figures; 1210–1215. Cf. cat. 40, 41.

In the beginning of the thirteenth century (probably after 1205), the chevet in Laon 23 Cathedral was rebuilt and enlarged. As part of this reconstruction, a magnificent composition was created: a flat wall, pierced by a tall, three-light window and surmounted by a large rose. The windows in the three bays portrayed (at the center) the Passion of Christ; His Childhood and symbolic figures (to the south) and, oddly enough, the Martyrdom of Saint Stephen and the Legend of Deacon Theophilus (to the north). Since the iconographic program is not unified, it has been assumed that windows from the earlier ambulatory were reused. (The ambulatory was demolished at the beginning of the thirteenth century to make way for the present flat chevet.)

There are evident stylistic parallels between the Passion and the Childhood windows and the large north rose just mentioned. Iconographic parallels to the Ingeborg Psalter are also to be found in the Childhood scenes; therefore, it must come from the same tradition—the same 1200 Style —and perhaps it is a more recent work of the same workshop by the same artists who were responsible for the transept rose.

Because of the legendary focus of these windows, however, the artists had to reduce their scale and multiply the number of figures. Consequently, the windows are not as monumental as those in the north rose. Unfortunately, these three legendary windows are much restored, but where the best scenes do retain their monumental nature, this is due either to the density of the composition (which can also be seen in reliefs on the Gothic tympana at Laon), or to the open and widely spaced compositions such as the Carrying of the Cross or even the Flight into Egypt. The more evolved and refined drapery style is close to that of the north rose. The types of faces vary, with features accentuated by strong modeling, which helps reestablish a kind of "classicism" due to the economy of the scenes, the harmony in the rendering of silhouettes and postures, and the clarity and precision of the pictorial treatment. With the fullness of their silhouettes and their sweeping gestures, the two censing angels at the top of the central bay evoke the masterpieces of the 1200 Style in the work of Nicholas of Verdun, in the Ingeborg Psalter and in Chartrain sculpture around 1210.

The three windows in the chevet at Laon are not of comparable quality. The Saint Stephen and the Deacon Theophilus window is by a different hand and does not define Laon style at the beginning of the thirteenth century with the same clarity and ease as the other windows.

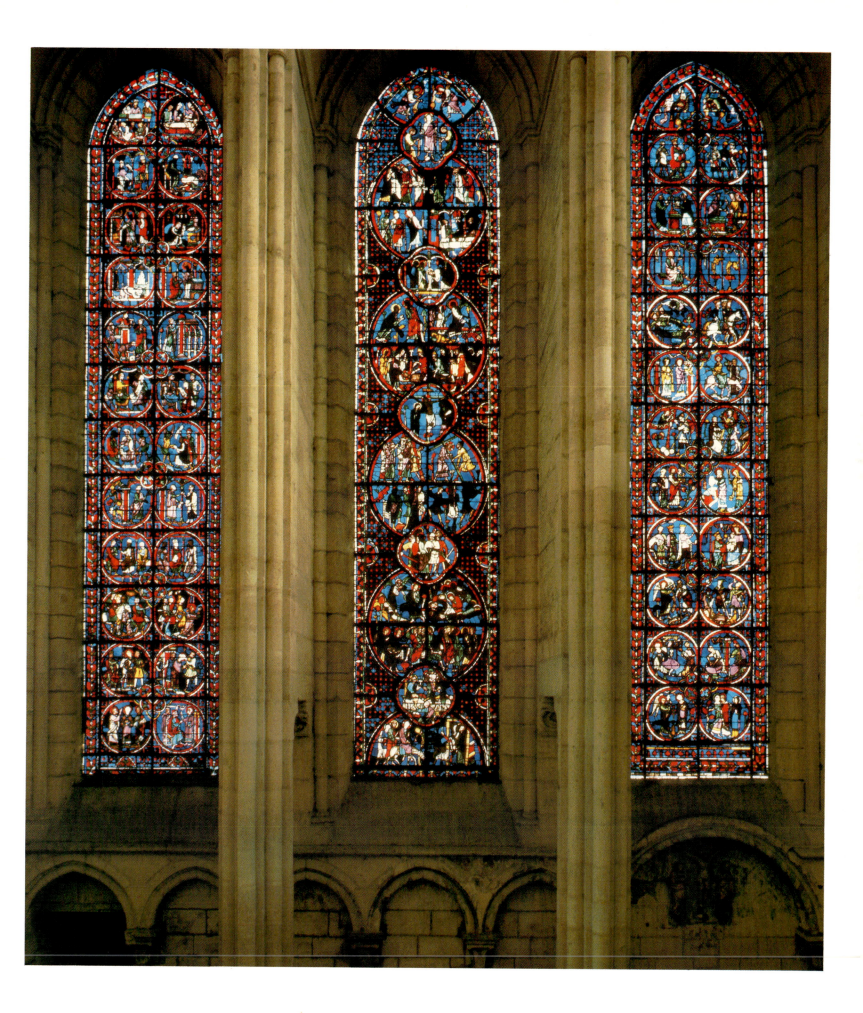

24 Laon, former cathedral of Notre Dame, chevet clerestory, bay 100, rose: (detail), an Elder of the Apocalypse; 1210–1215.

▷
25 Bryn Athyn, Pennsylvania, The Glencairn Museum: Ancestor-King, panel from the Jesse Tree window in the cathedral of Soissons; ca. 1200–1210. Cf. cat. 83.

The rose crowning this ensemble is dedicated to the Blessed Virgin. Placed at its center, surrounded by the twelve apostles and the twenty-four elders of the Apocalypse, she also represents Ecclesia. The style of this composition (less restored than the three legendary windows) is essentially the same as that of the Passion and the Childhood windows. The image of the Mother of God is characterized, above all, by its extraordinary "classical" purity, which represents the ultimate stage in the development of Laon's style that began with the Liberal Arts window in the north rose. This style is very close to the works (probably close to 1220) at Saint-Quentin and at Baye, which are discussed below. This rose was certainly glazed after 1205 and perhaps around 1215, at the time the chevet was completed. The fact that the rose came from the same workshop as the three historiated windows—which are heirs to the style of the north rose—points to remarkable activity at Laon for a minimum of three decades. This phenomenon is paralleled at Soissons, Saint-Quentin, Baye and, outside this region, in Champagne and the Ile-de-France.

Close geographically and chronologically to the windows at Laon are those in the cathedral of Saint Gervais et Saint Protais at Soissons. The south transept at Soissons was erected at the end of the twelfth century, and the choir (already following the example of Chartres in its construction) was begun soon after 1195. Unfortunately the cathedral windows at Soissons have been badly damaged over the centuries, particularly by the explosion of two nearby powder magazines in 1815. Moreover, the glass underwent considerable restoration in the second half of the nineteenth century, which provoked new losses. During the

38

First World War, much of the glass that was not protected in time suffered from artillery fire. Consequently, it is difficult today to appreciate the importance of the Soissons workshops without taking into account the numerous examples of their output preserved for the most part in museums and collections outside France.[4]

The principal window in the upper choir is known from a textual reference to have been donated by King Philip Augustus. It must, therefore, date before 1223 but could have been given as early as 1210 or 1215, when the upper choir was already nearly finished. This window, representing the Tree of Jesse, retains beautiful original glass in the figures of the prophets and of Christ. The Virgin Mary, in the collection of the Kunstgewerbemuseum in Berlin from 1908, was destroyed in the Second World War. Another panel, representing one of Christ's Ancestor-Kings, is in the Pitcairn Collection (The Glencairn Museum, Bryn 25 Athyn, Pennsylvania). These figures must be considered among the finest masterpieces of the 1200 Style: impressive, monumental ease in the figures, beautiful rendering of drapery and faces, and strong confident painting.

The windows that flank this work—the Creation of Adam and Eve, and the Last Judgment—are far inferior in quality. Both have undergone serious and very obvious restoration. The first is composed of wide registers with large figures, the second of compartments that form a star, inspired by the system of the legendary bays. Several characteristics of the great Soissons style can be recognized, however. Two historiated windows complete the decoration of the apse hemicycle. The south window depicts the Death and the Coronation of the Virgin in large oval medallions extending over three divisions of the window. In the second window, around four of Christ's ancestors, is a strange mixture of small medallions representing the Signs of the Zodiac and the Liberal Arts. The Death and the Coronation of the Virgin are certainly no longer in their original positions. Here the style becomes heavier and bulkier, lacking the beauty of works from the major workshop. As for the combined window facing these in the north, it was probably not even originally in the cathedral. Some indications point to a provenance from the abbey church of Saint Yved at Braine, about 15 kilometers from Soissons. The encyclopedic program of the small medallions may indicate that they come from one or more multifoil roses, for they recall the layout of the north rose at Laon.

In the ambulatory chapels, little remains from the period when the chevet was constructed. This is, in large part, the fault of restorers, who literally pillaged the original panels: at Soissons itself, only two windows relating to Saint Crispin and Saint Crispinian remain in the first radiating chapel to the south. Despite appalling additions, it is simple to recognize the characteristics already observed in the bays of the upper choir. The other ambulatory windows, devoted to the lives of Saints Sixtus and Sinice, Saint Giles, Saints Gervase and Protase (patrons of the cathedral) and to Saint Lawrence, are relatively successful modern substitutions, with some insignificant reuse of original glass. It seems that most of the original pieces were still at Soissons during the first half of the nineteenth century but were subsequently dispersed for sale on the art market.[5] The Musée du Louvre retains one part of a window from the Legends of Saint Nicasius and his sister, Saint Eutropia. (The other part of this window is in the Isabella Stewart Gardner Museum in Boston.) Several hagi- 26 ographical scenes relating to Saint Crispin, Saint Crispinian and Saint Blaise are now in the Corcoran Gallery of Art in Washington, D.C.,[6] and two panels from the Life of Saint Blaise belong to the Musée Marmottan in Paris.

The most beautiful of these dispersed works—notably the two panels in Boston—are really wonderful, comparable to the best creations in the chevet at Laon or to the Jesse Tree at Soissons. In the People of Reims Witnessing a Miracle by Saint Nicasius, the composition, drapery style and features of the figures have been characterized as truly "antique"; and yet all the ambulatory windows must be attributed to the first two decades of the thirteenth century.

The high quality of these works can also be seen in two panels from a Life of Saint 27, Nicholas, shown for the first time at an exhibition of the Raymond Pitcairn Collection held at The Cloisters in New York in 1982. The two scenes illustrate an episode rarely shown in windows of this period devoted to that saint: Saint Nicholas intervening to plead for the life of an innocent man condemned to death by a Roman consul. The attribution of the glass to the cathedral of Soissons cannot be verified by archeological information. No local commentary, not even Baron François de Guilhermy, ever mentioned a window or panels from a window about Saint Nicholas. On the other hand, the second radiating chapel south of the axis was

26 Boston, Isabella Stewart Gardner Museum: The People of Reims (?), panel from the Saint Nicasius window in the cathedral of Soissons; ca. 1215.

dedicated to the saint up to 1768, and one of the bays could well have been glazed with a window dedicated to its patron. These panels have been attributed to Soissons purely through stylistic analysis. The composition—notably the position of the characters in relation to one another, their stature, the calm, determined expressions on their faces and the precision in the fluid trace-line of the folds—show that these two panels belong to the fiefdom of Soissons as defined by its best examples, preserved in the United States at the Corcoran Gallery of Art in Washington, D.C. and at the Isabella Stewart Gardner Museum in Boston.

▷ ▷

27, 28 New York, The Metropolitan Museum of Art, The Cloisters Collection: Heads, details of two panels from a window depicting the Legend of Saint Nicholas from the cathedral of Soissons (?); 1210–1215. Cf. cat. 84.

29 Saint-Quentin (Aisne), former collegiate church of Saint Quentin, chevet, apse, axial chapel, bay 2: Glorification of the Virgin Mary (detail of the upper register), Censing Angels; ca. 1220.

The windows at Saint-Quentin and in the chapel of the castle at Baye are similar in style and belong to about the same period.

The collegiate church at Saint-Quentin, one of the largest and most beautiful Gothic buildings in Picardy and the whole of northern France, is poorly dated because of a lack of specific texts before 1228. Archeological study of the monument seems to demonstrate that construction began with the western tower and the chevet at the beginning of the thirteenth century, at the same time as work began on Beauvais Cathedral, or perhaps a little before. The choir, with its five radiating chapels of equal size, must have been used for religious services like the precincts of the chevet, before 1228 and probably prior to 1225. It is not within the scope of this work to decide whether the choir at Saint-Quentin is the prototype for, or an imitation of, the choir at Beauvais Cathedral.[7] Strong influence from the Champagne region apparent in this part of the building suggests that Saint-Quentin is earlier.

The most interesting windows in the glazing program are those in the central chapel of the ambulatory, dedicated to the Virgin Mary, and several figures remaining in the upper choir. In the Lady Chapel are two windows from the first quarter of the thirteenth century, representing the Childhood of Christ and the Glorification of the Virgin; they flank a Tree of Jesse made by Edouard Didron the Younger around 1880. A number of compartments in these two windows have been very extensively restored or even entirely remade in the nineteenth century. The original glass—the middle and upper zones of the two windows—is among the masterpieces of glass painting from this period. The compositions are identical in the two bays: figurative half-medallions set around compartments shaped like canted squares. While this format is very rare, it can be compared to some arrangements at Canterbury and at Chartres. The ornamentation in the borders and the backgrounds between the figurative compartments are of exceptional quality and based on plant forms derived from acanthus

◁ 30 Saint-Quentin (Aisne), former collegiate church of Saint Quentin, chevet, apse, axial chapel, bay 1: The Childhood of Christ (detail), The Nativity; ca. 1220. Cf. cat. 74.

scrolls. These scenes clearly belong to the Laon-Soissons style; however, there is an almost mannered refinement of gesture, silhouette and expression. The "classical" breadth of the Laon style has been diluted, perhaps due to the small scale of the scenes, but the fluidity of the lines and the harmony of the compositions have been retained and new softness added to modeling and color. The colors—dominated by greens and purples—are relatively cool, in contrast to the stronger, warmer tonalities used at Chartres and Bourges. The Saint Eustace window in the cathedral at Chartres, which we believe is in the same style and perhaps by the same hand as the windows at Saint-Quentin, stands in contrast to the windows that surround it, with its blue tones.

As for iconography, the two windows at Saint-Quentin have certain analogies with the Marian windows at Canterbury and at Laon and with the illuminations in the Ingeborg Psalter. The iconography of the Flight into Egypt, where a serving maid accompanies the Holy Family in a formula close to Byzantine sources, has been particularly stressed. There are, however, also very beautiful details in the Nativity and the Adoration of the Magi. Compositions such as the Annunciation or the Coronation of the Virgin, simple and devoid of superfluous detail, go beyond the models provided by twelfth-century painting or early Gothic sculpture.

The other series of windows from Saint-Quentin, which must have been in the upper apse of the abbey church, was irremediably ransacked in the sixteenth century, during the siege and shelling of 1557. It seems that, to replace the losses, a large number of figures of apostles and prophets, which had been made at the end of the thirteenth century for the eastern transept and the areas between the transepts, were placed in the upper choir. The earliest of them (the only ones of concern in this chapter) are found in the first window to the south of the axis. Saint Marcellus, Saint Piatus and Saint Eugene are represented, the last almost

31 Saint-Quentin (Aisne), former collegiate church of Saint Quentin, chevet clerestory, bay 202, left light, upper registers: Saint Marcellus; between 1225 and 1230.

entirely modern. Despite considerable restoration to the figure of Saint Marcellus, from the sixteenth century to the present day, the silhouette has the same elegance and the same type of hair and face as those seen in the Lady Chapel. The color of the figure, however, is different: large areas of quite a violent red intrude in the halo and mantle, and the tracing of the folds is somewhat modified and seems to belong to a later date (1230–1235?). The vestiges of such high-quality work that survive at Saint-Quentin are a strong testament to the perfection of the art of stained glass in this area of France—one which has, unfortunately, suffered from a succession of wars, massive destruction and the failure of archeologists to appreciate it.

The Champagne Region: Orbais and Troyes

A miraculously preserved and largely unknown work of this same time and "school" is the glass in the chapel of the castle at Baye.

The village of Baye, to the south of Epernay in the Marne region of France, belonged to the diocese of Soissons until the nineteenth century. A very ancient castellany was maintained there throughout the Ancien Régime; the castle still belonged to the heirs of the lords of Baye until recent times. The castle's chapel is a lone survivor of the Gothic period, built in all likelihood at the beginning of the thirteenth century, perhaps between 1215 and 1218. Its windows, though seriously damaged over the centuries, were carefully restored about fifteen years ago. The amount of original glass is considerable and includes both a Christological and a hagiographical program. Three windows are dedicated to the Son of God: a Tree of Jesse, a Childhood and a Passion, the last set in the axial window. Two windows illustrate the Lives of Saint John the Evangelist and of Mary Magdalene; the latter cycle includes a sequence on the Resurrection of Lazarus, while other windows apparently completed the series.

The Jesse Tree window, with numerous figures of kings as well as the Virgin and Christ, 32 has apparently been moved from its original location. The quality of drawing is so close to that in the windows at Saint-Quentin that an attempt has been made to attribute them to the same glazier's workshop. At both Saint-Quentin and Baye, formal refinement goes beyond the example of Laon and Soissons, as if a kind of mannerism had taken hold of the style, so strong and "classical" at the start. The Saint John the Evangelist window, though less well preserved, shows the same qualities, as does the Childhood window. Like the windows at Saint-Quentin, those at Baye represent a stylistic stage that could be considered a late evolution were it not for the pictorial treatment, clearly derived from that of northeastern France, which occurs again, during the first third of the thirteenth century, in Champagne, in the Ile-de-France and even in Normandy.

Also worthy of mention is the little Crucifixion set in a small window in the south transept of the former abbey church at Orbais; unfortunately, it is very corroded. This building will be 33 discussed again later.

The windows in the ambulatory and radiating chapels of the cathedral at Troyes can also be legitimately linked to this widespread northern French movement. With a few exceptions, these windows must date between 1215 and 1230. The construction of the cathedral began in 1206, or perhaps earlier, but the building sustained serious damage in the upper regions in 1227. The ambulatory and its decoration clearly predate this disaster. (The upper regions were rebuilt from after 1227 until around 1240,[8] and will be discussed later.)

The legendary windows in the ambulatory have undergone numerous changes as well as abusive restoration. Most of this occurred in the nineteenth century, when an excessive and abitrary desire to complete the windows brought about changes in the original placement, the elimination of numerous panels and the substitution of modern ones, often so well done that they have mislead scholars. The present iconographic program is virtually incomprehensible: that is, its arrangement is clearly not authentic. The central chapel is dedicated to the Virgin Mary and to the Christ Child, but one of its principal components—the Tree of Jesse—has been moved to another chapel farther to the north. The axial bay of this chapel now contains a Childhood of Christ surmounted by a Death of the Virgin, dubiously 34 arranged with modern ornamentation. It is framed by two almost entirely modern windows depicting the Childhood of the Virgin and a second Childhood of Christ, the latter with

32 Baye (Marne), chapel of the castle, bay 1: Tree of Jesse (detail), The Virgin Mary; ca. 1210-1220. Cf. cat. 17.

33 Orbais l'Abbaye (Marne), church of Saint Pierre, south transept, bay 22: Crucifixion; ca. 1210–1220.

34 Troyes, cathedral of Saint Pierre, ambulatory, axial chapel, bay 0: The Life of the Virgin Mary (detail), Presentation of Christ in the Temple; ca. 1210 (tracing by Lisch, ca. 1850). Cf. cat. 91.

35 Troyes, cathedral of Saint Pierre, ambulatory, 3rd north radiating chapel, bay 33: border with plant motifs; ca. 1200.

▷ ▷

36 London, Victoria and Albert Museum: The Prophet Daniel, panel from the Jesse Tree window in the cathedral of Troyes (?); 1210–1215. Cf. cat. 93.

typological scenes. The second windows from the axis, on each side, contain representations of the Public Life of Christ. The one to the north is coherent and very interesting; the corresponding window to the south, however, is in disorder and has been considerably modernized. In the first radiating chapel to the north are windows dedicated to Saint Andrew and, perhaps, to Saint Nicholas. The first radiating chapel to the south has two windows that are partly ancient, both pertaining to Saint Peter. None of these windows is very satisfying; only a few iconographic details, the Temptation of Christ and the Story of Simon the Magician are of interest to the specialist.

It is the stylistic quality of these works at Troyes that is the most important. There was undoubtedly a strong and well-established local tradition in southern Champagne that was fostered by the exceptional prosperity of that city, renowned for its great fairs and for the power of the counts of Champagne, who chose to be buried in Troyes Cathedral. A series of twelfth-century windows, probably from the Romanesque cathedral, displays extraordinary stylistic quality and testifies to contacts with workshops in the Meuse valley.[9] These works, made in the last quarter of the twelfth century, were reused in the Gothic cathedral; some remained *in situ* until the nineteenth century. Among the thirteenth-century windows in the last radiating chapel to the north in the ambulatory are two borders of unequal size, with large motifs of exceptional richness that belong to this twelfth-century tradition. Furthermore, some figural panels from the ambulatory chapels at Troyes retain certain characteristics of this pre-Gothic period. The symmetrical, rigorous compositions are comparable to historiated compartments at Saint-Denis or Chartres or to the Life of Saint Matthew at Notre Dame in Paris, as well as to certain works at Canterbury and Sens from about 1200. Until an

35

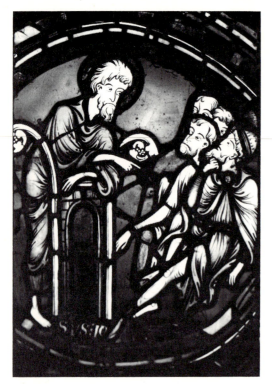

37 Rouen, cathedral of Notre Dame, nave, north aisle, 3rd chapel, bay 43, 4th light, 3rd register: Saint John the Baptist Preaching; ca. 1205–1210.

38 Champs-sur-Marne, castle, storage depot of the Monuments Historiques: Head of a Sleeper, fragment from the Legend of the Seven Sleepers of Ephesus window in the cathedral of Rouen; ca. 1205–1210. Cf. cat. 70.

▷
39 Worcester (Mass.), Worcester Art Museum: Messengers before the Emperor Theodosius, panel from the Legend of the Seven Sleepers of Ephesus window in the cathedral of Rouen; ca. 1205–1210. Cf. cat. 70.

in-depth study of this ensemble can be undertaken, the style can only be generally associated with several tendencies, one of which is allied to Soissons and Laon stained glass. The artist responsible for the Tree of Jesse seems to have joined to elements from northern France the traditions of Troyes. In the figures of the two kings, in the Virgin and in the Christ Child with softly draped clothing and small massed folds, this great master uses a delicate treatment of faces, devoid of exaggeration, and he was a good colorist. The same hand or a closely related one can be seen in three other works in the Lady Chapel—the central Childhood window and the two windows relating the Public Life of Christ.

It is clear, however, that not all the windows in the radiating chapels were produced by the same workshop, or even in the same style. The scenes from the Life of Saint Peter are particularly beautiful because of their strong colors, which are not restricted to the "simplified" Chartrain formula and include frequent use of green and yellow tones. Noteworthy too are the compressed compositions, shortened figural proportions and stiffening of the drapery, all of which point to the fact that other workshops contemporary with the Tree of Jesse workshop collaborated in the decoration of the Troyes ambulatory during the first third of the thirteenth century. These workshops are less interesting, since their works are neither the most beautiful nor the most successful. This ensemble at Troyes stands completely apart from the monumentalized world of Chartrain stained glass and the first evidence of mannerism in the Ile-de-France.

An origin in Champagne or even at Troyes has already been suggested for ten stylistically similar, superb prophets from a Tree of Jesse in the Victoria and Albert Museum, London.[10] This seems plausible, though it cannot be confirmed that they are the lost prophets from the Tree of Jesse at Troyes. The beauty of the figures lies in their noble proportions and bearing and in the elegance of their faces, but also in the masterful execution of pictorial details, whether in hair, hands or in the sinuous folds standing out in large panels as if lifted by the wind. The plant ornamentation and the border of superimposed leaves accompanying the prophets can also be found at the cathedral of Troyes, although it is not certain that these elements are typical of the Champagne region.

Rouen: The "Master of the Seven Sleepers of Ephesus"

The earliest works in stained glass at Rouen are also part of the mainstream of northern French tendencies outlined above. The construction of the present building began at the west end (subsequently entirely redone in the fifteenth century), around 1200 or earlier, on the site of the previous cathedral. There was a consecration in 1225, but it is not known what stage had been reached in the building, since work continued in the transept until the last quarter of the thirteenth century and in the Lady Chapel into the fourteenth.[11] Despite enormous losses subsequently, Rouen Cathedral presents examples of stained glass for the entire thirteenth century and the beginning of the fourteenth, often of great importance. Consequently, it will be discussed here frequently.

Of interest in the present context is the glass from the windows in the nave aisles. They were taken down in the fourteenth century so that the walls could be opened for the side chapels, but they were not completely destroyed. Some were reused in the third and fourth chapels on the north side of the nave, where they have been known since the Middle Ages as the *Belles-Verrières* (literally, "beautiful windows"). Several panels unquestionably date to the beginning of the thirteenth century (about 1210–1220), notably the remains of the John the Baptist and the Childhood cycles and, the most famous recently, the Legend of the Seven Sleepers of Ephesus.[12]

The Childhood scenes are poorly preserved, and the series is incomplete. Despite the strong line, already Gothic in style, the original compositions are uncertain, and the overall composition of the original window still cannot be reconstructed. The Story of John the Baptist and the Legend of the Seven Sleepers were produced by the same workshop, which can be linked beyond all question to northern France during the first quarter of the century. Even better than in the panels remaining in Rouen, these stylistic traits can be seen in the panels now in American museum collections, notably in the Worcester Art Museum, Massachusetts, and the Pitcairn Collection (The Glencairn Museum) in Bryn Athyn, Pennsylvania. Certain aspects can be compared to the windows at Laon or even to those of Canter-

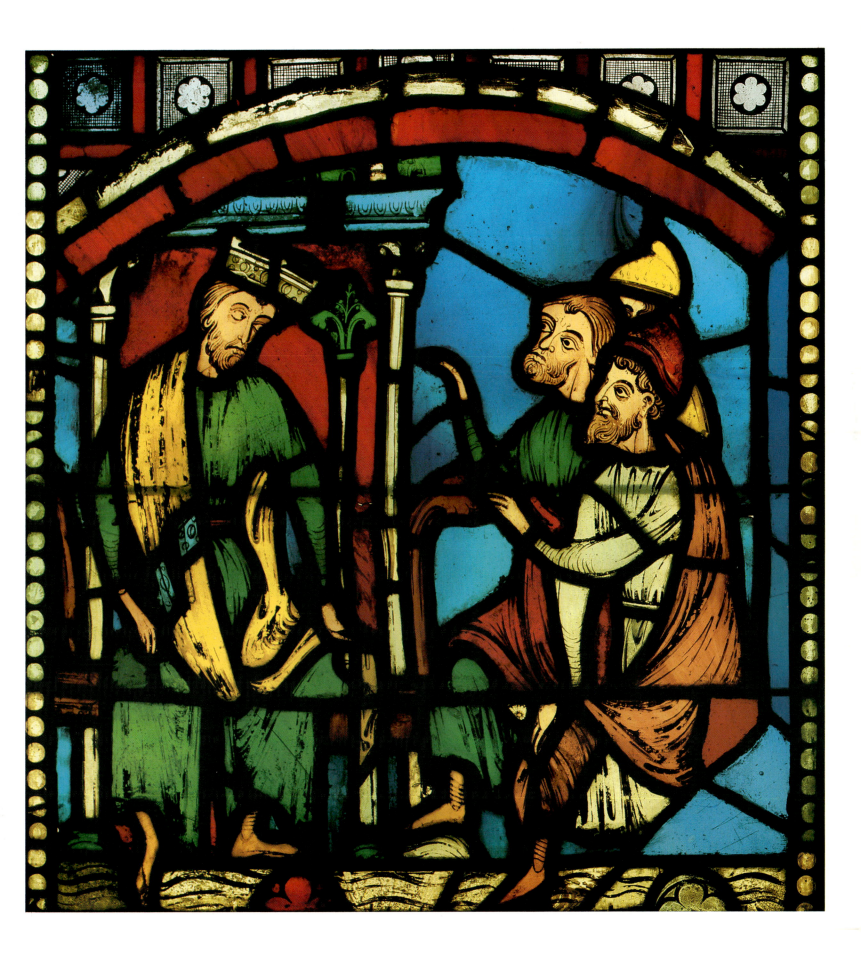

bury: the freedom of the gestures, the softness of the drapery, and the intense and almost "classical" expressions on the faces. The colors are saturated: several blues, strong purples, greens and reds, all of which are enhanced by white in the frames or in the details of the scenes. This was undoubtedly the work of a great master, whose style cannot be seen anywhere else, neither at Laon, Paris, Sens nor Chartres. Since Norman art before 1200 is still not known well enough, the local origin of the Rouen artist cannot be determined.

The decoration, of which few vestiges remain, consists of a pale blue rectilinear mosaic with red fillets, the equivalent, more or less, of Chartrain models from the first two decades of the thirteenth century. These masterpieces—virtually unknown until quite recently—influenced glazing inside the cathedral, resulting in the admirable development of Norman stained glass in the last third of the thirteenth century and in the fourteenth. The series on Saint Severus and Saint Catherine in the *Belles-Verrières* panels can be linked in some respects to the work of the first Rouen workshop (1210–1220). The much better-known series in the ambulatory and in the chapel of Saint Jean jouxte les fonts will be discussed later.

Paris and the Ile-de-France

The Ile-de-France region was more closely linked to the style of Soissons and Laon during the first quarter of the thirteenth century. There, all Gothic architecture at the end of the twelfth century and at the beginning of the thirteenth often followed northern French examples. Monumental sculpture at this time was in large part the result of the Laon innovations, as was manuscript illumination, for the character of painting in Paris cannot yet

40 Paris, cathedral of Notre Dame, west rose: The Virgin in Glory Surrounded by Prophets, the Signs of the Zodiac, the Labors of the Months, the Virtues and Vices (detail), Kindness; ca. 1220. Cf. cat. 53.

▷
41 Paris, cathedral of Notre Dame, west rose: The Virgin in Glory Surrounded by Prophets, the Signs of the Zodiac, the Labors of the Months, the Virtues and Vices (detail), Cowardice; ca. 1220. Cf. cat. 53.

52

be distinguished from that of the northern milieu. In stained glass, an important but poorly preserved work survives—the west rose of Notre Dame in Paris. The program included the Virgin Mary at the center, surrounded by twelve prophets, the Signs of the Zodiac, the Labors of the Months, and, in the upper periphery, the Virtues and Vices. Does this ambitious program to some extent represent a condensation of earlier iconographic schemes such as those in the two rose windows of the cathedral at Laon? We do not know. Only a dozen thirteenth-century panels survive. The lower part of the rose was redone shortly after 1500; and the remainder, including the figure of the Virgin Mary, is modern.

The original medallions are strongly monumental in both dimension and scale of execution. The figures are reminiscent of those in the north rose at Laon, but this is a more self-conscious art, and the position of the figures is more elegant and studied. In facial types and in the lines of the drapery, there are still some links to the 1200 Style of northern France, but they have lessened: Parisian art seems to be tending more toward the strictly Gothic in certain formal simplifications that suggest volume and movement. Some of the representations of Virtues and Vices or of the Labors of the Months are distinguished by their energetic lines and modeling, contrary to the mannerism visible at Saint-Quentin or at Baye. Though it has not been well studied and its original sections are hard to read, the west rose of Notre Dame in Paris provides major evidence of a stage in the formation of the Gothic style—an art of the capital—in Paris.

A second rose from this same period (about 1220?) is that in the collegiate church at Mantes. The building was strongly influenced by Notre Dame in Paris. Likewise, the Last Judgment window from the west facade betrays the northern characteristics we just discussed, though the archaizing character is not so strong nor the compositions so balanced. It may have been the theme of the Last Judgment that incited the artist to render the silhouettes in a more agitated way and to fill the medallions with more figures. Despite numerous restorations, the overall effect is very impressive, thanks to the relatively strong palette, closer to that employed in the second quarter of the thirteenth century than to that used at the turn of the century.[13]

In Paris and its surroundings, few vestiges of glass from this period remain. Most are of little importance and, on the whole, very restored. At Bussy-Saint-Martin (Seine-et-Marne), there are several medallions pertaining to Saint Martin. At Villers-Saint-Paul (Oise), there is an interesting Virgin and Child. In the Aisne region, fragments of a Life of Saint Pantaleon are divided between two bays in the former cathedral at Noyon. At Fossoy (Aisne), there is a medallion showing the Incredulity of Saint Thomas.[14]

Chartres: The "Master of Saint Eustace"

It was not until after 1225 that ensembles of high-quality stained glass appeared in this region. Their style, though no longer derived from northern examples, is echoed in works of high quality from 1215 or earlier at the cathedrals of Chartres and Bourges. At Chartres, the recognizable work of the "Master of Saint Eustace" is so close to the glazing in the Lady Chapel at Saint-Quentin as to suggest that the master was a member of that workshop. In every respect this glass differs from the rest on the north side of the nave. The tonality is cool, dominated by the juxtaposition of blues and greens. The armature is similar to that at Saint-Quentin: canted squares flanked by medallions provided with curved armatures. The ornament is simultaneously archaic—the border derives from the Romanesque Crucifixion in the cathedral of Poitiers—and very modern, because the background between the medallions is filled with acanthus scrolls. This decorative refinement has sometimes been compared to that found at Canterbury. The figural style combines the mastery of balanced and sometimes symmetrical compositions with the ease of movement of the figures within the frame. The figures are elongated and elegant, their drapery sinuous and soft as at Laon and Soissons; the noble and beautiful heads evoke irresistibly the mannerism mentioned at Saint-Quentin and Baye.

Did this master produce other windows at Chartres? Previously, we have suggested that his workshop was responsible for the Last Judgment in the west rose (around 1215) and for several upper windows in the nave.[15] Nothing has yet confirmed this hypothesis; however, a precise stylistic study of the windows at Chartres still remains to be done.

42 Bourges, cathedral of Saint Etienne, chevet, ambulatory, central bay, no. 4: Last Judgment (detail), The Damned Being Driven toward Leviathan; ca. 1210–1215. Cf. cat. 19.

Bourges: The "Master of the New Alliance and the Last Judgment"

A workshop very close to the "Master of Saint Eustace" and related to the style of Laon and Soissons has been confirmed at Bourges Cathedral; it produced two of the most beautiful windows of the early thirteenth century—the New Alliance and the Last Judgment windows 43,

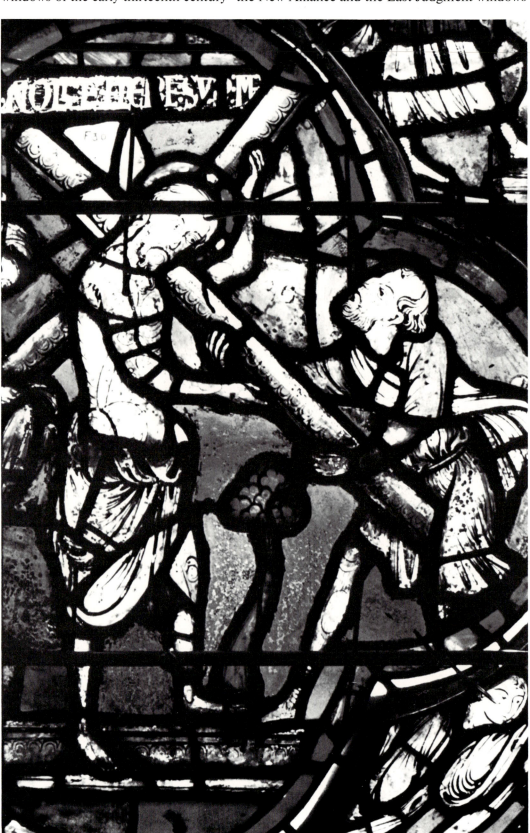

43   Bourges, cathedral of Saint Etienne, ambulatory, central bay, no. 3: The New Alliance (detail), Christ Carrying His Cross; ca. 1210–1215. Cf. cat. 18.

in the central bay of the ambulatory. These are important works for Christian iconography of this period, and they have already been studied in a major volume by Cahier and Martin.[16] The profound and complex iconography of the New Alliance window is perhaps the apex of Christian speculation and biblical typology, reduced to its essential moments here: the Carrying of the Cross, the Crucifixion and the Resurrection. The meaning of several scenes in the Last Judgment window remains a mystery. These glass paintings from the early thirteenth century are of great importance, for it is certain that the ambulatory and its chapels were in use for religious services before 1214.[17]

The archaizing style of northern France is manifested in the ease of composition in the Carrying of the Cross, in Moses Striking the Rock or in the angels in the Last Judgment carrying the instruments of the Passion. The style of northern France can likewise be seen in the fluid elegance of the long drapery folds with their narrow lines, in the classical beauty of the heads and in the almost antique faces that recall the finest panels at Soissons. The mixture of the northern style with other styles from south of the Loire can perhaps be seen in the general composition of the windows, in the ornamentation and in some details of execution. While the question has not been sufficiently studied, it seems that the "Master of the New Alliance" also participated in the decoration of the upper choir. Its extraordinary figures of Saint Peter, John the Baptist, Saint Stephen and the Blessed Virgin, though simplified, have their stylistic base in northern France, with centers at Laon and Soissons.

The Formation of Gothic Style

Parallel to this vast current, allied so perfectly to the 1200 Style, with its archaizing and Byzantinizing characteristics as well as with others more typically its own, there evolved, south of the Seine, a strong and varied art of stained glass based on twelfth-century traditions. The most famous examples of this trend are the windows in Chartres Cathedral. Many art historians, as we mentioned earlier, consider Chartres the major, or even the sole, creative center for all stained glass of the early thirteenth century. The decoration of the cathedral went step in step with the very rapid reconstruction of the building after the fire of 1193/1194, and by about 1210 the wonderful ensemble of stained glass that we still admire today was already in place in the nave. The choir windows were probably mounted around 1225, and those in the transept about ten years later. Almost all the windows at Chartres have been preserved in their original location, a situation that is unique in France. The one hundred sixty-four windows, almost all dating from the thirteenth century, form the largest surviving medieval ensemble in the realm of glass painting. Consequently, it is natural that Chartrain glass has been widely discussed, though until now its stylistic origins have not been the major focus of research. Moreover, the enormous size of the ensemble has discouraged art historians from undertaking a careful study of these windows, terribly corroded over the past few decades, and thus rather illegible now.

In fact, the windows at Chartres cannot be dissociated from a wider series of attempts at glazing, the importance of which is still not well understood, though windows were numerous in this region in the twelfth century. At Chartres itself, the three windows in the west facade (circa 1145–1155) survived the fire of 1193/1194. Furthermore, in the lower Loire region, in Maine and in Poitou, considerable glazing was undertaken during the twelfth century at Le Mans, Angers and Poitiers. Thus, in western France, a truly Romanesque style of glass painting evolved—sometimes close to the style of wall painting, sometimes to that of manuscript illumination. Foreign influences from northern France had been almost completely overcome, except at Chartres where the three windows in the west facade were clearly inspired by Saint Denis.

This style, which was still Romanesque, continued in stained glass until the very end of the twelfth century and even extended into the first years of the thirteenth. Examples are the remains of lives of Saint Peter and Saint Paul at Le Mans, the easternmost lateral windows in the choir at Poitiers and the Virgin in Majesty at Angers.[18] It is logical, therefore, to begin by studying these proto-Gothic works, still somewhat Romanesque, whose echo can be seen in certain windows at Chartres and Bourges.

44 New York, The Metropolitan Museum of Art,
The Cloisters Collection: God Closing the Door to
Noah's Ark, from the Noah window of the cathedral
of Saint Pierre at Poitiers; 1190–1200.

Poitiers

The stylistic continuity between Romanesque stained glass and that of the beginning of the thirteenth century is clearly evidenced in the cathedral at Poitiers, where a fine workshop produced the three windows in the chevet—at the center, the Crucifixion; framed on the right by a Life of Saint Peter and, on the left, by the Legend of Saint Lawrence.[19] Unfortunately, the earliest windows from the thirteenth century or the very end of the twelfth were lost in part during the siege and pillage of the city by the Huguenots in 1562. Only some panels of the Story of Noah from the first north window closest to the eastern end (dedicated to Genesis) are preserved in American collections;[20] however, others are known thanks to early photographs taken between 1882 and 1884. The principal traits of the three Romanesque windows in the chevet are recognizable and hardly diluted: restless figures, schematized folds and hard, synthetic modeling in the faces. The second double window on the same side of the choir survives in a somewhat restored state, completed by modern pieces at the bottom. It represents the story of Abraham and Lot, notably the episode of the incestuous relationship between Lot and his daughters. This work is curiously composed: the scenes are linked by very wide framing fillets that give continuity to the composition. The same principle, with certain variations, can be seen in all the other thirteenth-century windows on this side of the church.

In the second north window in the nave is a Story of Isaac; it retains all the Romanesque stylistic references of the fragments of the Noah window mentioned above. In the north transept arm are two other windows with the Story of the Patriarch Joseph, which are fairly well preserved but done in a more relaxed style. These windows were probably made after 1210, since this part of the building belongs to the second building campaign that continued through a good part of the thirteenth century; the lower parts of the west facade were not built until the 1250s.

The location of the Joseph windows indicates that the north side of the building must have been reserved for the Old Testament. Later rearrangements are apparent, of course.

45 Poitiers, cathedral of Saint Pierre, choir clerestory, north side, bay 105: Story of Lot and Abraham (details, right), King Abimelech Gives Abraham back his Wife; (left), Sarah Returns to Abraham; ca. 1210–1215.

For example, the hagiographic panels like the Saint Blaise, from another window of the transept, have been moved and often reconstructed by adding fragments. The south side of the building suffered even more. It was undoubtedly reserved for the New Testament as is proven by the remains of a Childhood and a Passion of Christ, which can be seen in the bays of the choir. In the south transept arm, the remains of windows illustrating the Parable of the Prodigal Son, Dives and Lazarus, and vestiges of a Public Life of Christ have been identified with some difficulty. Thus, the glazing ensemble at Poitiers, as it was conceived and realized between the beginning of the thirteenth century and the 1230s, offered a remarkable and very homogeneous iconographic cycle.

45   It is also likely that local traditions of both technique and pictorial execution (which can be seen best in the windows depicting Abraham, Lot and Isaac) remained strong for an extended period. Straight-bar armatures are used throughout. The fairly elementary arrangement of scenes is based on superimposed medallions, except in the Isaac window and one of the Patriarch Joseph windows. The colors are relatively light in the best-preserved areas but rather dark in those with heavy restoration. Another local peculiarity already seen in the twelfth century is placing the glass so it reads top to bottom, contrary to the usual pattern in northern France and even at Chartres. Certain details of ornamentation would be repeated at Angers, such as backgrounds decorated with foliated scrolls or rather with curved stems ending in a flower-shaped ornament. The figural style of the windows in the transept remains archaic, repeating certain Romanesque compositional patterns but overloading them. The drawing of the choppy and schematized folds and the rendering of the rather stout and expressive faces with large, globular eyes remains close to twelfth-century stained glass. It seems as if faithfulness to the local glazing traditions of Poitou was part of provincial resistance to northern art, which continued until the middle of the thirteenth century in the architecture and sculpture of Poitou. However, this did not impede the spreading of this local style beyond the region: a great "master" of Bourges was connected with Poitou, as will be discussed later. Given the extraordinary political and religious importance that Poitiers enjoyed, this is not surprising.

Angers

During the twelfth century, fairly intensive glazing activity also developed in and around Angers, important elements of which survive, principally at Angers Cathedral.[21] In the last quarter of the twelfth century, when the vaulting of the Romanesque nave was transformed, a series of windows was undoubtedly made to complete those produced during the third quarter of the century. Three of these windows have been satisfactorily preserved: those depicting Saint Vincent, Saint Catherine and the story of the Dormition and Glorification of the Virgin Mary. For some unknown reason, they have all been placed in the north nave windows. They are closely related to the windows at Poitiers and Le Mans in style, ornamentation and certain technical peculiarities like the subdivision of the windows with straight bars. The stylistic originality of this series has already been discussed in *Le Vitrail roman*; certain juxtapositions of scenes in the Saint Vincent window and in the Funeral of the Blessed Virgin prefigure complex Gothic compositions, as Emile Mâle has observed. The first works from the thirteenth century in the cathedral at Angers are the majestic Virgin and Child (probably from the transept), being adored by two bishops of the Beaumont family; the Life of Saint Martin, formerly in the west facade and now divided between two bays of the choir, and elements now installed in windows of the south transept that were very much restored in the eighteenth century.[22] The style of this group is not homogeneous but remains firmly within the Romanesque tradition of the region. In the windows depicting the Life of Saint Martin—which are the best preserved—the thickness of the outlines, the heaviness of the lines, and the summary and somewhat schematized folds clearly indicate the dependence of the Angevine workshop, at the beginning of the thirteenth century, on the work of the preceding century. Parallels with earlier stained glass can even be seen in the palette, notably in the limpid blues used in frames and backgrounds.

  The entire series could be considered as a transition toward the windows in the choir. Here the problems are more complex, first of all because of rearrangements that cannot all be traced, because of iconographic disorder and, finally, because of uncertain chronology. It has often been said that the choir at Angers was not built until after 1274; however, this

◁ 46   Poitiers, cathedral of Saint Pierre, bay 107: Story of Isaac: The Sacrifice of Isaac (detail), An Angel Prevents Abraham from Killing his Son; ca. 1210-1215. Cf. cat. 63.

47   Angers, cathedral of Saint Maurice, chevet clerestory, bay 102, left light: Legend of Saint Maurillus (5th register, left compartment, detail), Shepherd Cured by Saint Maurillus (?); ca. 1230-1235.

48   Angers, cathedral of Saint Maurice, chevet clerestory, bay 101: Life of Saint Julian of Le Mans
(detail), Saint Julian Cures a Woman Possessed by
the Devil; ca. 1240.

hypothesis does not stand up to archeological analysis. It is likely that the entire choir was completed around the years 1245 or 1250.[23].

As for the windows in the choir, none (except for sixteenth-century additions) can be later than these dates. Two windows depicting Thomas Becket and Saint Julian of Le Mans are more recent than the others and may be dated to the first half of the century; they will be discussed later. Eight other works from the first quarter of the thirteenth century form a homogeneous ensemble in a rather rough and heavy style, perhaps because of the dimensions of the compartments, which were meant to be viewed from a distance: a Tree of Jesse window, two Christological windows (a Childhood and a Passion) and a number of hagiographic windows illustrating the lives of Saint Peter, Saint John the Baptist, Saint Lawrence, Saint Eligius (or Eloy) and Saint Maurillus. This ensemble is largely devoid of Chartrain influence and follows the traditional style seen in the Life of Saint Martin, although the compositions are perhaps more crowded and the figures stand out more clearly from the background. The folds are drawn quite softly, and facial expressions have become less stereotyped. The ornamentation (also archaic) encroaches on the figural areas because of the width of the borders and the framing fillets. Despite all the damage sustained by these windows, the general effect was certainly very beautiful before more recent damage from corrosion.

It is interesting to consider the role that this very traditional glass painting played in the general evolution of Gothic stained glass in France and to wonder what the relationship may be between this style and the art of the second quarter of the thirteenth century seen at Chartres and Bourges. A partial answer is provided by the two more recent windows depicting Thomas Becket and Saint Julian of Le Mans; they have borders with the arms of the Beaumont family, many members of which occupied the episcopal see of Angers until 1240. These works are not by the same hand, nor are they from the same workshop. The Saint

▷
49   Angers, cathedral of Saint Maurice, choir clerestory, bay 108, left light: Life of Saint Thomas Becket
(lower registers), Pursuit of Thomas Becket by Knights
on Horseback and then in a Boat (?); 1235–1240. Cf.
cat. 14.

Thomas Becket window uses the abundant Angevine ornament without much modification; the Saint Julian window, covering two lights, uses a small-scale mosaic background and narrow borders of a very modern type, though the division of the window into half-medallions is also an innovation in this milieu. The Thomas Becket window is related iconographically and stylistically to Chartrain glass with the same subject in the chevet. The Saint Julian one, much more delicate and elegant in execution, is more modern and more like the work of the "Master of Saint Chéron" at Chartres.[24] Consequently, we can say that it was through external influences that Angevine stained glass was transformed and modernized around 1235–1240. The greatest contribution of this center to the formation of Gothic art is work from around the years 1200, an echo of which can be seen even at Chartres.

Le Mans

The third principal center of Romanesque glass painting in western France does not seem to have been very active around 1200 and during the first quarter of the thirteenth century. The construction of the new choir at the cathedral of Le Mans did not begin until around 1218 or 1220, and the enormous amount of work that was involved in building the understructure of the chevet must have continued over a number of years.[25] The first truly Gothic windows (now in two radiating chapels) date from the years 1235–1240. However, among the windows set in the nave aisles and in the first chapel south of the choir during the nineteenth century, there are a number of elements of uncertain date that seem to be from the beginning of the thirteenth century. These panels are as interesting as the windows at Angers and Poitiers. The tradition of Romanesque stained glass at Le Mans, where evolution was so interesting in the twelfth century, left its mark on these remains, some of which are dedicated to Saint Vitalis and to Saint Valeria of Milan (parents of the first patrons of the cathedral, Saint Gervase and Saint Protase) and others to Saint Peter and Saint Paul. Analogies with the glazing at Angers can be seen in the ornamentation (the framing borders or the backgrounds with coiling plants ending in flower-shaped ornaments). The style of the scenes is less rigorous than at Poitiers, while the panels depicting Saint Vitalis and Saint Valeria are characterized by the same heaviness of design, forced facial expressions and lack of flexibility as in the figures at Poitiers. The elements from the lives of Saint Peter and Saint Paul are somewhat different: more elegant but at the same time very close to those of the Legend of Saint Ambrose, now installed in the western bay of the south nave aisle and datable to the 1190s.[26]

These windows from the first quarter of the century (so important at Angers and Poitiers and so mediocre in the cathedral of Le Mans because of their present condition) should be compared with panels that belonged to the same intermediary period between the twelfth and thirteenth century and which are dispersed among various buildings in the Loire area: at Les Essards,[27] Charentilly[28] and Montreuil-sur-le-Loir (for the most part now in the St. Louis Art Museum)[29] and finally the windows in the church at Civray-de-Touraine, which are particularly problematic because of their exceedingly dark coloring, which may result from a very advanced state of corrosion.[30]

Chartres

In many respects, Chartres is the apogee and the apotheosis of the art of stained glass. In no other edifice is the original effect as "authentic," allowing us to imagine the spirit of the men who made these windows and that of the men for whom they were made. Even if the quality of the windows were mediocre—which it is not—the splendor of the hundreds of supernatural figures and the thousands of multicolored scenes would be sufficient to overwhelm us with awe.

Few historians have succeeded in breaking away from this enchantment, which makes any attempt at analysis or criticism very difficult. While the iconography and history of the windows at Chartres are well known, the study of their style has only just begun.[31]

The construction of the Gothic cathedral (started in 1194) was sufficiently advanced in 1210 for altars to be set up within the church. The chapter of canons did not take possession of the large choir until January 1, 1221, undoubtedly the moment of its completion. The windows in the choir that carry "signatures" of identifiable donors and, consequently, can be dated, are from between about 1215 and 1235 for the most recent. The windows in the eastern face of the north transept arm, which are clearly more recent, could not have been completed until between 1225 and 1235. The rose window and the upper lights in the south transept arm, donated by the Dreux family, were glazed between 1217 and 1225. The north rose was executed at the expense of the French royal family after 1223. The first windows must have been those in the nave—the oldest part of the church, which probably served as a temporary choir before 1221—these should be dated between 1200 and 1210/1215. Thus, only thirty-five years were needed to finish this colossal enterprise.

The monumental program of stained glass at Chartres is very coherent and may be considered as an examplar. The lower windows are filled with very numerous small scenes, for the bays are more than 8 meters high and subdivided into compartments of various shapes set against rinceaux or mosaic grounds. The windows are subdivided either by irons forged into the shape of the curvilinear compartments or medallions, or by straight bars. The upper windows generally contain a single figure per bay. In the transept, where the openings are larger, two figures are set within each light. In the very high, narrow light in the apse, the figures are superimposed in tiers of two or three. This compositional system is found again in some bays in the choir and the transept. Three rose windows (west, north and south) complete the ensemble, each set above tall lights and conceived with an admirable sense of scale and monumentality.

The iconographic program, on the other hand, is relatively loose and seems to be the product of several ideas. In the upper regions, four large cycles are developed at the farthest points of the cathedral. In the apse, five large lights are devoted to the Blessed Virgin—her life, the prophecies concerning her and her triumph among the angels. The same theme of the Glorification of the Virgin reappears in the north transept arm; here, however, Mary is represented as Ecclesia, Queen of Heaven, surrounded by doves symbolic of the Gifts of the Holy Spirit, by precursor-kings and Old Testament high priests. In the south transept arm is the Glorification of Christ, who is surrounded by Evangelist symbols, angels and the elders of the Apocalypse. Below it, the concordance between the Old and the New Testaments is developed: four prophets supporting Evangelists on their shoulders. Finally, in the west, the Last Judgment is set in the rose window.

Between these immense cycles, however, figures of saints and scenes whose distribution is not logical have been installed. Sometimes the placement of a single window can be justified, for instance those dedicated to the Blessed Virgin near the northeast column of the transept crossing above an altar dedicated to Mary. Sometimes a coherent cycle was begun but interrupted, for example the apostles in the north transept arm. As a general rule, the special devotions of the donors—kings, princes, nobles, canons of the chapter, craftsmen or merchant guilds—seem to have determined the choices of subjects.

The same was true of the lower windows. It may be that, when the work began, there was a program that called for representations of the Old Testament on the north side of the nave, beginning with the History of Noah (46 or LXIV)—a window that was completed—and on the south side a cycle devoted to the New Testament, including the Life of Saint John the Evangelist (48 or IV), which was also completed. However, this program was rapidly abandoned.[32] Nevertheless, some windows were installed for discernible reasons: in the last nave bay, where the principal altars must have been set up until 1221, there is a "typological" Passion window (37 or LIX) and one dedicated to Our Lady of Chartres (38 or IX). Only in the nave and the transept does one finds stories from the Old Testament (Noah and Joseph) and from the Parables (the Good Samaritan and the Prodigal Son). In the choir, the decoration of apostles in the axial chapel is coherent, while the lives of the saints are somewhat random. Compared to the iconographic programs at Bourges, or perhaps at Troyes, the one at Chartres seems disorganized, as if it had been affected by contradictory ideas deriving from fervent devotion to Our Lady of Chartres and to specific saints.

All this disorder is probably a symptom of pious impatience to see the sanctuary of the Virgin Mary completed as soon as possible, as well as the result of a number of generous and almost simultaneous gifts. The task was immense. Several glaziers were undoubtedly called upon to work at Chartres at the same time, which may explain the diversity of the earliest nave windows. In the series of lower windows alone, it is possible to distinguish the works of six different artists and workshops. Despite recent studies, it is still unclear whether these windows are the work of distinct workshops or whether they resulted from more

50 Chartres, cathedral of Notre Dame, nave, north aisle, bay 45: Life of Saint Leobinus (2nd register, left border), Wine Merchant Donating a Cup; ca. 1200–1210.

65

collaboration within a single workshop. At this stage, however, it is possible to suggest classifications and regroupings, even though they may be provisional.

One of the first jobs undertaken was the repair of the three western windows that had been damaged by the fire in 1193/1194. This was the work of one artist, undoubtedly trained elsewhere, and who was strongly affected by the Byzantinizing art of 1200.[33] If not the same hand, at least a similar tendency can be seen in the nave window with the Death and Funeral of the Blessed Virgin (42 or VII).

Delaporte has already isolated a homogeneous group of three other windows—those depicting Saint Leobinus (45 or LXIII), Saint Nicholas (39 or LX) and Noah (47 or LXIV).[34] The style is rather heavy but energetic, with an admirable decorative effect, especially in the fourteen scenes of the Flood. A relationship has been proposed between this "Master of Saint Leobinus" and the "Master of the Good Samaritan" at Bourges Cathedral.[35] The Bourges windows, however, are of better quality and also seem earlier. The work of both artists still shows traces of the "Romanesque" art of western France in style; they probably came from Angers, Poitiers or Le Mans. However, at Chartres the master quickly assimilated new ideas under the influence of the varied milieu where he was called upon to work, and consequently he abandoned the "Romanesque" characteristics that remained in use at Bourges. Was this master responsible, in a later stage of his career, for the Good Samaritan window (44 or VI) and the Saint John the Evangelist window (48 or IV)? While this has been suggested,[36] it does not seem to us to be the case, despite certain superficial analogies that seem to link these windows. The energetic gestures, the restless folds, the forced expressions on the faces and the "skeletal" anatomy of the bodies may evoke the art of western France somewhat; here, however, forms are elongated, stretched, broken and freely distributed on the ground of the medallions. In a sense it is in works such as this that a certain expressive, taut, abrupt mode of Gothic painting was formed.

A third workshop responsible for windows in the nave at Chartres was already mentioned above in relation to the restoration of three western windows around 1200. This workshop produced the windows depicting the Death of the Virgin (42 or VII), Saint Mary Magdalene (46 or V) and perhaps the original parts of the typological Passion (37 or LXI). It could be termed the "classical" workshop given its desire for harmony and for formal balance of groups, its search for a certain linear continuity in the rendering of drapery folds or in the flow of the figures. Details of the execution are similar to other works such as the Good Samaritan window, as if the glaziers worked under the direction of a number of "cartoon makers". The same difficulties plague the analysis of the sculpture in the transept at Chartres.[37] In any case, the "workshop" of the Death of the Virgin was very important for the formation of Chartrain style.

In addition to the works of the three principal "workshops" in the nave, there are windows in a completely different, even foreign, style. Such is the famous Saint Eustace window (43 or LXII), which was discussed at the beginning of this chapter.[38] A second hand appears in the Prodigal Son window (35 or LVIII); its derivation remains mysterious, but it may be related to the energetic and harmonious style seen in a group of windows in the cathedral at Sens: the Good Samaritan and Prodigal Son windows. The Joseph window (41 or LXI) has, again, a different derivation. Its incisive, caricature-like style distinguishes it from the other windows; it derives neither from western nor from northern France, and there are no apparent links to other styles around 1200.

To establish the relationships between these windows and the development of Chartrain sculpture, on the one hand, and miniature painting of the early thirteenth century such as the Pontifical of Chartres (Orléans, Bibl. Mun., ms. 144)[39] on the other, these questions must be examined sequentially. The compositions in the Pontifical are very close to those in Chartrain windows and suggest connections with a number of the workshops active in the nave of Chartres Cathedral.

The analysis of the upper nave windows is difficult, because they are fairly illegible from the ground. It is probable that they were done by the same workshops as the lower windows, but the evidence is not completely clear. In any case, there are two different styles. One is strongly archaizing: elongated figures with very small heads, shown frontally, and drapery with long folds forming stereotyped fan-shaped pleats at the bottom. Typical of this pattern are the Saint Laudomarus (142 or LXVI), the Saint Mary of Egypt (142 or LXV) and the Virgin and Child (138 or LXXI) windows, whose lack of volume is very far from the Gothic style. There may be a connection, in the delicate lines and elegant figures, between the

51 Chartres, cathedral of Notre Dame, nave, south aisle, bay 48: Life of Saint John the Evangelist (4th register, left compartment), The Exiled Saint John Leaves by Boat for Patmos (detail), Head of the Saint; ca. 1205.

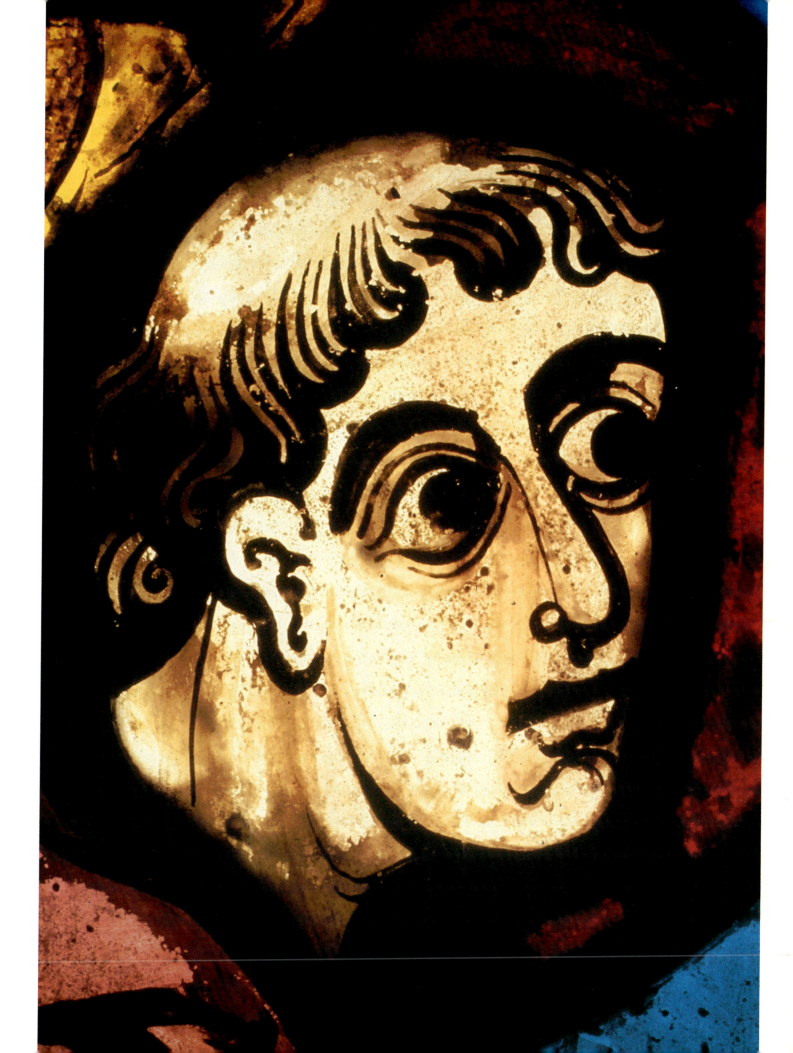

52 Chartres, cathedral of Notre Dame, nave, south
aisle, bay 42: Death, Assumption and Coronation of
the Virgin Mary (middle registers), The Vigil of the
Apostles at the Virgin Mary's Deathbed; Christ and
His Angels Welcome His Mother's Soul; Mary's Body
Is Laid in the Tomb by the Apostles; ca. 1200–1210.

53 Chartres, cathedral of Notre Dame, nave, north aisle, bay 44: Parable of the Good Samaritan; ca. 1205–1210. Cf. cat. 28.

technique employed in these windows and the work by the "Master of Saint Eustace". The second "workshop," in the windows of Saint James the Greater (40 or CXVIII), Saint Peter (140 or CXIX), the Unknown Apostle (135 or CLXIV) and others, is different from the first. According to F. Meyer, this workshop came from Champagne;[40] this is likely, since there are clear relationships to Saint Remi at Reims in the strong, almost fierce expressions of the figures, in the monumental Gothic poses and amply treated folds "in relief". This style can clearly be seen best in the upper windows on the north side. There are many possible links to other glazing centers, as suggested by the window with the three superimposed prophets (141 or CLXXIII), where analogies with the windows in Trinity Chapel at Canterbury can be seen in the ornament and in the drawing of figures.[41] It is likely that better viewing and photographic documentation will provide the means for a new analysis.

The atmosphere in the transept and the choir differs from that in the nave. These windows are no longer disconnected first attempts but mature works of a much more homogeneous nature. Differences of "hand" or workshop have little effect on the general definition of the style, while differences of quality are perhaps more distinct. The ornamentation, composed of unpainted pieces of glass, occasionally becomes banal or even summary. In the Apostles windows in the north transept arm (117 and 119 or CXXXIX, CXL, CXLII, CXLIII), the cartoons are repeated.

Nevertheless, the most elaborate works in the cathedral are found in the choir and in the transept. Among the twenty-five lower windows in the ambulatory and its chapels, the most important are those by a large workshop that often collaborated with others and is defined by two famous windows depicting Charlemagne (7 or XXXVIII) and Saint James (5 or XXXVII). Set next to each other, these windows serve as the basis for a large series of

54 Chartres, cathedral of Notre Dame, ambulatory, bay 7: The Story of Charlemagne (lower registers), Voyage of Charlemagne to Constantinople; ca. 1220–1225. Cf. cat. 24.

55 Chartres, cathedral of Notre Dame, ambulatory, bay 7: The Story of Charlemagne (detail), Building a Church in the Presence of Charlemagne; ca. 1220-1225. Cf. cat. 24.

stained glass. Related to the Charlemagne window are those of the Apostle Thomas (23 or XLVI), Saint Stephen (13 or XLI), part of a window with Saint Savinian and Saint Potentianus (17 or XLIII) and others. Related to the Saint James window are the beautiful Saint Julian window (21 or XLV), the Story of Saint Anthony window (30 or XIII), and others we shall enumerate.

The Charlemagne window, an absolutely epic illustration of the *Chanson de Roland*, is exceedingly well known; there are few renditions as evocative as the scene of the Miracle of the Spears at Pamplona or the Agony of Roland at Roncesvalles. It is one of the most typical windows of the Chartrain style—calm, rather precious in the delicate handling of modeling, rather limp in the treatment of drapery, a little severe in the way the figures are cut off; balanced, without being picturesque; precise and harmonious. Of course, the brilliance of the glass and the contrasts in color (though somewhat mitigated by the clear radiance of the blues) counteract to some extent the rather monotonous regularity, as do the originality and variety of composition and ornament.

If one had to define the style of Gothic painting based on such examples (which, by the way, are rather like a certain type of Chartrain sculpture), the accent would not be on formal tension or the dynamism of lines and expressions but on the calm, full volumes, the sovereign legibility of the figures and the lack of ornamental or expressive stylization, although this definition would not be applicable to all of Gothic painting—or even to all of Chartrain art.

This very great master was not an innovator; he was part of a line of artists at the beginning of the thirteenth century who practiced the balanced style of the "Master of the

Death of the Virgin". The Saint James and Saint Julian windows are similar in style, but their masters put more stress on softness of drapery and refinement of technique. The elongated faces of their figures, with long noses and hair falling around the necks, are stamped with a strange expression of kindness—almost of melancholy. In the ambulatory, there are several variations of the style of this principal "workshop". Some seem to be earlier, such as the Life of the Virgin window (42 or XVI), with its beautiful colors and overloaded design with multiple lines. The formal spirit of this window—and of those less successful ones deriving from it in the chapel of the Apostles—can be compared to that of the left portal in the north facade at Chartres.

It is not possible to enumerate here all the other "workshops," which can hardly be qualified as secondary. For example, another recently analyzed master was responsible for the extensions to the *Belle-Verrière*.[42] The panels, representing episodes from the Public Life of Christ, are of exceptional quality, and the master who made them was probably trained 56 outside Chartres. His work is characterized by its energy, emphasis, ease and harmony; it is rather like certain contemporary works in the cathedral at Sens by the "Master of the Parables". This masterpiece is dated around 1215; it is certain that this artist exerted a strong influence on the "Master of Saint Chéron" workshop, one of the most remarkable at Chartres.

Canon Delaporte was the first to recognize that "workshop," to which he attributed a number of legendary windows: the windows dedicated to Saint Chéron (15 or XLII), Saint 58 Remigius (12 or XXVIII), Saint Jude and Saint Simon (1 or XXXV), Saint Pantaleon (11 or XL), and so forth. Delaporte also felt that the handling of these windows was mediocre, more schematic and harder than that in other windows at Chartres. The work of this master can be dated to 1220-1230 thanks to "signatures" of the donors, who were canons of the chapter and local nobles.

In a more general overview of French stained glass in the thirteenth century, the work of this artist and his workshop becomes very important. The hardening of his style corresponds to a phase of development in Gothic sculpture in Amiens and Paris after the portal of the Coronation of the Virgin at Notre Dame in Paris. Unlike the 1200 Style with its ease almost reminiscent of the Antique, the "Master of Saint Chéron" monumentalized form by emphasizing volume with broken folds and schematized formal lines. The Gothic values of his work can best be seen in the upper windows of the south transept at Chartres. The large figures in the eastern face of this part of the building, with that extraordinary masterpiece, the window of Saint Denis and Clément du Mez (116 or CII), lead toward the exceptional 59 rose at Dreux and the five bays acting as its base. These windows represent one of the most evocative programs of Christian iconography, comprising parallels between the Old and the New Testaments, with the Evangelists set on the shoulders of four prophets who surround 10 the figure of Ecclesia. These windows were donated by Pierre de Mauclerc, count of Dreux (and duke of Brittany through his marriage), one of the principal adversaries of Blanche of Castile and her son, King Louis IX of France. In all likelihood, the donation took place between 1217 and about 1225. The expressive force of the images and their monumental authority surpass all proto-Gothic works of the first quarter of the thirteenth century. This is one of the first manifestations in glass painting of a truly Gothic style that would prevail for a large part of the thirteenth century.

Returning to the small scenes in the ambulatory windows, the Saint Chéron window shows a precise relationship with contemporary cathedral architecture: it is composed in registers set under pointed and trefoil arcades. Another essential comparison is that between the figure of Clément du Mez and the statues representing Saint Theodore (?) and Saint 60 George, added to the south porch of the transept around 1225; these are innovative works of Gothic sculpture. The workshop of the "Master of Saint Chéron" continued its work (much more mediocre) in the north transept, notably in the rose of France, which was undoubtedly offered by Blanche of Castile and her son between 1230 and 1235. Later, the influence of this workshop will be seen at the cathedral of Le Mans.

The work of this master, though one of the finest working at Chartres after 1220, did not eclipse that done by other masters in the upper windows of the choir. In the bays of the 4 hemicycle is quite a strange collection of work executed by a number of very great glass painters. The central window with the Life and Glorification of the Virgin might appear archaic in composition and style, but in the adjoining window to the north is an extraordinary, oversized archangel by an entirely different "hand," which is impressive in its stylistic

56 Chartres, cathedral of Notre Dame, choir, south side, bay 30: Our Lady of the *Belle-Verrière* (additions from the early 13th century, lower register), Temptation of Christ on the Mountaintop; 1210-1215. Cf. cat. 26.

57 Chartres, cathedral of Notre Dame, south transept arm, east wall, bay 118: Saint Cosmas and Saint Damian (in the lower register), Father Geoffroy, the Donor, Praying in Front of an Altar; 1225–1230.

▷
58 Chartres, cathedral of Notre Dame, ambulatory, 1st north radiating chapel, bay 15: Legend of Saint Chéron (in the lower register), The Donors at Work; (left), Workers Verifying That the Building is Plumb; (in the other compartments), Sculptors at Work; (2nd register, left), Saint Chéron Taken to School by his Parents; (right), He Recites a Lesson; (3rd register), Saint Chéron Refuses to Marry; (4th register), Having Become a Priest, the Saint Goes to Italy and Exorcises a Young Woman Possessed by the Devil; ca. 1220–1225. Cf. cat. 25.

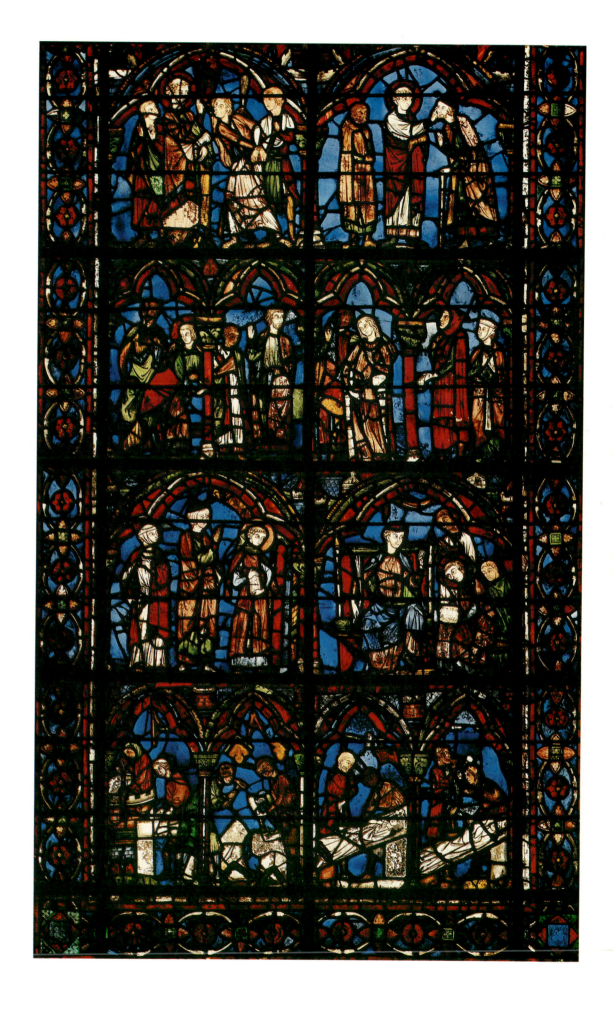

59 Chartres, cathedral of Notre Dame, south transept arm, east wall, bay 116, right light: Saint Dionysius (Denis) Hands the Banner of the Abbey of Saint Denis to Jean Clément du Mez; 1228-1231. Cf. cat. 29.

60 Chartres, cathedral of Notre Dame, south porch, left portal, left splay; Soldier-Saint (Theodore?); ca. 1230.

▷

61 Dreux, Musée municipal d'Art et d'Histoire: Herod Receives the Magi, fragment from a Childhood of Christ window in the church of Saint Pierre at Dreux (?); ca. 1220-1225. Cf. cat. 35.

authority and strength of coloring (101 or CXXI). To the south, the window adjoining the axis shows an immense, asymmetrical figure of Moses, with an expression that is practically unique in Chartrain glass (102 or CXIX). With the figures in the south transept, these are the most imposing examples of monumental Gothic painting created during the first quarter of the thirteenth century. They were never surpassed by later works better adapted to Rayonnant Gothic architecture.

The style of a number of workshops from the ambulatory can be recognized in the lateral windows of the upper choir: isolated figures like the large, traditional Virgin and Child (113 or CXXXIV) or compositions with large superimposed scenes such as the Pilgrims from Saint James at Santiago de Compostela (114 or CVI and CXXXIII). Other windows have "evolved" even further and are later in date: the middle part of the "legendary" window with Saint Savinian and Saint Potentianus (17 or XLIII) in a rather awkward, exaggerated and

62 Vendôme (Loir-et-Cher), church of La Trinité, north transept arm, east wall, bay 23: Virgin in Glory (detail), Head; ca. 1215. Cf. cat. 97.

mannerist style and the Saint Thomas Becket window (18 or XXV) with its emaciated, asymmetrical figures whose style already suggests Parisian influences of 1235. It seems as if Chartrain production declined and disintegrated after 1230 as its teams of sculptors had done a few years before.

The panels preserved in the museum at Dreux, from what must have been a considerable ensemble in Saint Pierre at Dreux,[43] are in the Chartrain tradition of the first quarter of the thirteenth century, as is a beautiful head of the Virgin, now installed in the north transept in La Trinité at Vendôme. The work of *Clemens vitrearius carnotensis* at Rouen Cathedral, however, cannot be discussed here since it is much later in date.[44]

61
62

63 Bourges, cathedral of Saint Etienne, ambulatory, central bay, no. 3: The New Alliance (detail), Moses and the Brazen Serpent; ca. 1210–1215. Cf. cat. 18.

64 Bourges, cathedral of Saint Etienne, chevet clerestory, bay 200, left light: Virgin and Child (detail), Heads; ca. 1220–1225.

65 Bourges, cathedral of Saint Etienne, ambulatory, bay 3: Parable of the Good Samaritan (8th register, central medallion), The Traveler Attacked by Robbers; ca. 1210–1215.

Bourges

The workshops at Bourges have always been—mistakenly—connected to those of Chartres. Bourges Cathedral is more or less contemporary with Chartres and was probably begun at the end of the twelfth century in accordance with a more archaic formula. An inspection of Bourges Cathedral in 1214, known from textual sources, proves that the main part of the ambulatory was serving as a place of worship,[45] and it can be deduced that the windows in this part of the building were in place. The ambulatory bays were much smaller than those at Chartres, particularly in the tiny radiating chapels that were added during construction.

The ambulatory windows are complex assemblies with armatures forged into the shapes of the compartments; in the radiating chapels straight irons enclosed tiny rectilinear panels. The ornamentation combines a number of ideas, one growing out of the work done by the workshops of western France (Angers and Poitiers) and characterized by schematized rinceaux ending in daisies, and the other with small-scale painted mosaics as at Chartres.

The borders—very rich in conception—can also be compared to those at Chartres; others derive from Poitevine models. The framing fillets around the historiated compartments often have double beading and are linked together by bosses *(fermaillets)* or brooches, following a formula that would soon be abandoned in the thirteenth century.

43
63

Three very different styles can be distinguished in the lower windows of the figural sections. That of the "Master of the New Alliance and the Last Judgment" has already been discussed. He undoubtedly also worked on the poorly preserved windows in the first north radiating chapel, which are modern in parts: the Saint Dionysius (Denis) window, the Saint Peter and Saint Paul window and the Saint Martin window.

The iconography of the Bourges windows is a perfect example of coherence imposed by a scholarly theological program. It is even possible that it was devised by Saint William, archbishop of Bourges from 1200 to 1209. In the axial chapel, there was probably a series with a Childhood of Christ and a Jesse Tree (windows lost since the sixteenth century). Around these were theological comparisons between the Old and the New Testaments and

66 Bourges, cathedral of Saint Etienne, ambulatory, bay 16: Life of Saint Thomas (5th register, left medallion), Saint Thomas Preaching the Gospel and Distributing Alms; ca. 1210–1215.

67 Bourges, cathedral of Saint Etienne, ambulatory, bay 14: The Apocalypse (7th register, right medallion), Ecclesia Nourishing and Crowning the Two Testaments (?); ca. 1210–1215.

between moral lessons drawn from the lives of prophets and saints and the parables of Christ. The New Alliance, one of the most profound typological lessons of the Middle Ages, corresponds to the Last Judgment; the Passion scenes correspond to the visions of the Apocalypse; the Parable of the Prodigal Son parallels the moral lesson of the Relics of Saint Stephen. The Parable of the Good Samaritan corresponds to the story of Dives and Lazarus; the life of the Apostle Thomas parallels the story of the Patriarch Joseph, both considered lessons in salvation. The windows in the radiating chapels were dedicated to the lives of saints venerated at the time: Saint Stephen, Saint Nicholas, Saint Peter and Saint Paul, Saint Dionysius, Saint Martin, Saint James, Saint John the Baptist, Saint John the Evangelist, Saint Mary Magdalene and Saint Mary of Egypt.

There has been much speculation on possible thematic connections among these works.[46] The iconographic program of the upper windows is a veritable statement of the relations among the figures of the Old and the New Testaments, with the Prophets up to Saint John the Baptist set in the north, and the Evangelists and Apostles in the south, flanking the majestic figure of Ecclesia, who is accompanied by Saint Stephen, patron of the cathedral, carrying a representation of the cathedral itself. Later, in the upper ambulatory windows, figures of the canonized archbishops of Bourges would surround a Virgin and Child and 64 Christ the Judge. This series is unfortunately incomplete, some of the figures to the south

68 Bourges, cathedral of Saint Etienne, ambulatory, bay 15: History of the Relics of Saint Stephen (lower medallion), Saint Stephen's Tomb Is Opened in the Presence of the Patriarch of Jerusalem; ca. 1210–1215.

▷
69 Bourges, cathedral of Saint Etienne, ambulatory, bay 5: Parable of the Prodigal Son (detail), The Prodigal Son Leaving his Father's House; ca. 1210–1215. Cf. cat. 20.

70   Châteauroux (Indre), former church of the Grey Friars (now a cultural center), bay 0: Last Judgment (detail), Christ the Judge; ca. 1230–1240. Cf. cat. 32.

having been lost. Saint William, responsible for building the cathedral, is shown with a halo, proving that this ensemble must date after his canonization in 1218.

A second master, known as the "Master of the Good Samaritan" was responsible for the Good Samaritan window, the Passion and the Apocalypse windows in the ambulatory and for the Saint Nicholas, Saint Mary Magdalene, Saint Mary of Egypt and the Martyrdom of Saint Stephen windows in the radiating chapels. Only a few authentic panels from the last window survive.[47] The style of this painter was vehement; some of the scenes from the Passion, the Good Samaritan and the lives of the saints are animated by exceptional energy, conveyed through gesture, the fall of folds and the fierce expressions of wild eyes and of violently drawn locks of hair. The coloring in these panels is lively and different from most of the palettes used at Chartres. The colors employed are pure white, yellow and green (except in the Apocalypse window, which was heavily reworked in the nineteenth century), while in the Chartrain palette blue and red predominate.

Although there are some "modern" aspects in the composition of the Good Samaritan and Apocalypse windows, this very great master remains faithful to the late Romanesque esthetic of western France, seen at Angers and Poitiers.[48] The ornamentation used by his workshop confirms this hypothesis: the master must have come from western France. His forceful artistic personality had an impact on the region, seen in the church of Saint George at Poizieux[49] and even in Burgundy, where it can be recognized in two windows in the chevet of the church at Semur-en-Auxois.[50] However, this rather traditional tendency is not found in the upper windows of the cathedral, more particularly not in the choir, as if the master and his workshop had left Bourges around 1215.

The third and principal master has been named the "Master of the Relics of Saint Stephen". His virtuosity can be seen in the general distribution of the compositions, the ornamentation and the variety of figural style. His masterpiece—the Relics of Saint Stephen window—though fairly extensively restored in the nineteenth century, uses a very daring method of dividing the figural compartments: quarter circles are set on their points yet perfectly filled by the figures. The Tempest at Sea during the translation of the relics of Saint Stephen is a masterpiece of ingenuity in the play of axes and levels in the composition. The Dives and Lazarus window is striking in the vigor of its blue and red mosaic grounds, against which are set the quatrefoils and half-circles of the historiated scenes, with their great expressive vivacity and perfect legibility. The same workshop "master" was responsible for the Prodigal Son window, which is also curiously arranged in panels set against mosaic grounds. Its picturesque account of this parable is charming, but the outlines of the figures are difficult to characterize because of their great variety. Only the heads, too large for the thin bodies, with their sad expressions due to the large eyes, the long noses and the receding chins can be distinguished from the style of the other two artists who worked in the ambulatory.

Clearly this style, which has some analogies with that of certain workshops in the nave at Chartres (i.e., that of the "Saint Leobinus Master"), did not lead directly to the development of Gothic style. It remained halfway between Romanesque traditions, which it no longer followed but of which it shows traces, and works of much greater power such as those produced by other workshops at Bourges and Chartres during the first quarter of the century. Nevertheless, it is likely that this workshop—probably local in origin—continued to work on the upper windows and on those in the inner ambulatory and transformed its style as the general trend changed. The large figures of prophets and apostles in the right part of the choir can probably be traced to this workshop, always behind the obviously later style of the intermediate level that contains Christ the Judge and the canonized archbishops.

Other churches in the area reflect the various stages of evolution seen at Bourges: from the first years of the century, the beautiful Virgin and Child at Orçay (Loir-et-Cher);[51] from the final period, the intermediary windows at Bourges and the windows in the Grey Friars' Church at Châteauroux, especially the large Last Judgment, which is very archaic in composition but close to Bourges workshops in style.

Thus, it is possible that the influence of Bourges was not very widespread and was rapidly countered, in the area around the Loire, by northern influences from Chartres and Paris. Nevertheless, the exceptional quality of the windows in the ambulatory and the radiating chapels at Bourges and the monumental development in the upper windows must be counted among the greatest achievements in stained glass in the first third of the thirteenth century.

▷
71   Bourges, cathedral of Saint Etienne, ambulatory, bay 6: Passion of Christ: The Last Supper (detail), Head of Christ; ca. 1210–1215. Cf. cat. 21.

72 Sens, cathedral of Saint Etienne, ambulatory, bay 13: Parable of the Prodigal Son (4th register, left compartment), The Eldest Son, Returning Home, Interrogates Two Servants; 1210–1215.

73 Chartres, cathedral of Notre Dame, north transept arm, Job portal, voussoir: Mordecai and One of Esther's Servants; ca. 1220.

Sens

It is very difficult to place the windows in the cathedral at Sens in the general evolution of French glazing in the thirteenth century. Sens was an important religious and artistic center for the Ile-de-France, for Burgundy and Champagne, and perhaps even an international center because of its relationship with England. The major part of the present cathedral was built in the twelfth century between about 1130 and 1140; the facade and the towers were built at the beginning of the thirteenth century. However, the building was seriously damaged by fire in 1184, necessitating significant repair. The upper parts of the nave and choir date from the second quarter of the thirteenth century, as do the windows in this part of the building. On the north side of the ambulatory, however, are four bays from the twelfth-century construction, with windows representing the parables of the Good Samaritan and the Prodigal Son and illustrating the lives of Saint Eustace and Saint Thomas Becket. The date of these four windows has been variously set: before the fire of 1184,[52] which does not seem possible or, alternatively, at the beginning of the thirteenth century, which seems likely but is only based on formal comparisons.

Two very distinct styles can be seen. The Saint Eustace and Saint Thomas Becket windows have a clear relationship to the windows at Canterbury, not only in composition but also in ornamentation and pictorial execution.[53] The other style, perhaps earlier, is the series of the two parables. In a sense, these compositions are simpler, but at the same time they are highly original. The narrative cycle of the Prodigal Son is treated in a series of medallions shaped like quatrefoils overlaying a canted square that rests on floral frames independent of

72

74 Sens, cathedral of Saint Etienne, ambulatory, bay 15: Parable of the Good Samaritan (lower and middle quatrefoils, from top to bottom), the Traveler Is Attacked on the Road to Jericho; the Samaritan Takes Him on his Horse to the Innkeeper; (lateral medallions, middle), scenes from the Exodus from Egypt; (below), scenes from the Passion; ca. 1210–1215. Cf. cat. 80.

PREDICAT[O] S[AN]C[T]OME AD P[O]PVLVM

75 Sens, cathedral of Saint Etienne, ambulatory, bay
19: Life of Saint Thomas Becket (detail), Thomas
Becket Preaching to the People; ca. 1210–1220 (?). Cf.
cat. 81.

the border. While this system might seem archaic, it has some correspondence with contemporary monumental sculpture from Sens or Paris. The style of the scenes is likewise very 73 forceful, thanks to the juxtaposition of the figural elements rather than to the relationships of the figures (clearly legible against their blue grounds) to one another. The nobility of certain figures could be compared with the Laon-Soissons style were it not for the additional bluntness and stylization seen in the poses and faces. These same characteristics can be seen in the Good Samaritan window, though it was conceived in a more complex manner, with 74 compartments of canted squares and large side foils. The standard symbolism of this parable is particularly clear here: corresponding to the three principal scenes of the attack and rescue of the merchant are twelve scenes from Genesis, Exodus and the Passion. While some figures may seem heavy because of the insistence on line and modeling, they are close to contemporary efforts at Bourges and, above all, at Chartres (the Public Life of Christ at the bottom of the *Belle-Verrière*).

Is this style indigenous to the Ile-de-France or to Paris, or is it at least a local product, whose sources can be sought in manuscript illumination or in sculpture, since hardly anything is known about glazing in the area around Paris before 1220–1225? In any case, these works are among the masterpieces of the first quarter of the century.

The two hagiographic windows are similar only in composition and ornamentation. There are wonderful plant scrolls, comparable to those at Canterbury[54] here and there in the ornamentation; the framing borders with Kufic characters are very rich. In the Saint Thomas Becket window, the scenes set in grouped indented medallions are extraordinarily symmetrical and stable, because of the "bridges" constantly used in the lower part of the scenes. 75

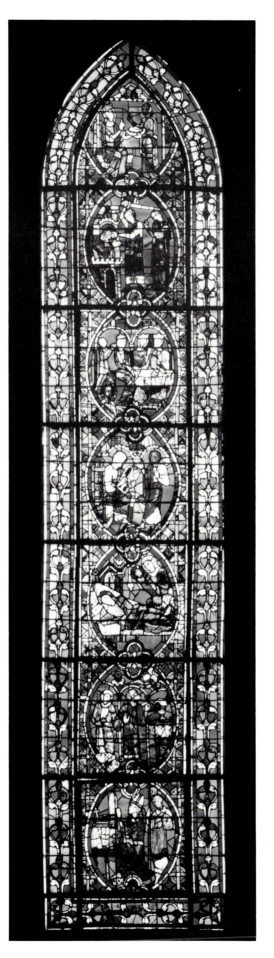

76 Lyons, cathedral of Saint Jean, chevet, bay 0: The Redemption; 1215–1220. Cf. cat. 46.

77 Lyons, cathedral of Saint Jean, chevet, bay 1: Life of Saint John the Baptist; after 1225. Cf. cat. 47.

This work lacks the forceful lines found in the Good Samaritan window; nevertheless, the execution and iconographic invention are exceptional, as has occasionally been noted. The composition of the Saint Eustace window is unexpected: large spindle-shaped medallions set around canted squares. The backgrounds have a number of superimposed ornamental schemes composed of carefully worked acanthus scrolls and mosaics. The elongated compartments, often reserved for accounts of maritime expeditions or river crossings, give rise to unusual compositions, in which the "bridges" are replaced by waves or hillocks. The figures are long and thin, with small heads, and represent a style intermediary between that of Canterbury and that of northern France. Theories about the English origin of Sens glazing or the Sens origin of the Canterbury windows cannot be accepted without caution, since the close analogies are balanced by equally clear differences. The windows are of very high quality, far from those in the axial chapel and upper windows, too recent for discussion in this chapter.

Lyons

A final ensemble in the cathedral at Lyons is even more complex in origin and in relation to the evolution of stained glass at this time in France. Its originality was already noted by Emile Mâle, who stressed the Byzantinizing character of the glass, contrary to Chartrain art.[55] The present cathedral of Lyons, the primatial church of the Gauls, was rebuilt after 1170, beginning at the eastern end. It was not until around 1215 or 1220 that the chapter decided to glaze the seven windows in the lower level of the apse. These windows survive today. The iconographic program reflects the religious and political preoccupations of this institution. The principal window, in the axis, is dedicated to the theme of the Redemption; [76] this is flanked by small compartments in the border with typological subjects. Another window treats the Childhood of Christ; its border is also animated with small medallions containing figures of Virtues and Vices, according to an iconographic formula resembling the one used in the voussoirs of the left portal in the western facade at Laon. The other windows are hagiographic, illustrating the lives of Saint John the Baptist, patron of the [77] cathedral; Saint John the Evangelist, on whom the Church of Lyons based its apostolic heritage; Saint Stephen, Saint Lazarus, chosen for Autun (the suffragan bishopric of Lyons) and Saint Cyprian of Carthage, whose relics had been given to Lyons by Charlemagne.[56]

The works are extensively restored. While they present a unity of conception that is still Romanesque—with one medallion per register, framed by wide borders—the figural areas vary in style from one window to the other. Four follow Byzantinizing conventions: the Redemption, the Saint Lazarus, the Saint John the Evangelist and the Saint Cyprian windows. This is not surprising in a region where this tradition had been popular since the beginning of the twelfth century. Romanesque survivals in stained glass also follow this tendency,[57] which was revived, at the beginning of the thirteenth century,[58] by new Byzantine influences coming from Italy and perhaps even from the Holy Roman Empire.

The three other windows were executed by different workshops, which followed formulae imported from northern France, from the Ile-de-France and even from Burgundy;[59] consequently, they are related to the evolution of "French" stained glass. The ornament too conforms to the northern and French tradition of mosaic grounds based on models from Chartres and Bourges for six of the windows, and for the seventh (the Lazarus window), on simple foliated scrolls. This mixture of patterns from various sources should not be surprising. Around 1225, at the time of the creation of the most recent of the works, Gothic style was becoming fully defined, pushing back Romanesque and Byzantinizing traditions, and Lyons is the perfect example of this trend.

The Second Quarter of the Thirteenth Century in France: Rayonnant Style III

At the beginning of the second quarter of the thirteenth century, important changes took place in the western world, not only in political and philosophical realms but also in art. The brilliant reign of Frederick II (1220–1250) notwithstanding, the decline of the Holy Roman Empire had already begun. The rise of the Capetian dynasty was underway, and with it came a rapid growth in Parisian theological thought, led by such masters as Saint Thomas Aquinas and Saint Albert the Great, often known as Albertus Magnus.

In some ways, the new trend in architecture corresponded to these changes. Rayonnant art appeared about 1225–1230 in the Ile-de-France and in the Champagne; it embraced subtlety in its forms, elegance in its lines, and a rationalization in structure and decoration. We can see in these traits, simultaneously, the ascendancy of scholasticism and of the new religious and secular sensibility focused on reality and emotions. It was only then, in our opinion, that a truly Gothic figural style emerged, that is, conforming to a Gothic stylistic mode that had conventional methods of working and arbitrary distortions, and yet a concern for reality. Examples are the last western portal of Notre Dame in Paris with the Coronation of the Virgin, the early sculpture at Amiens and the last Chartrain sculptures in the north facade and on the rood screen. Manuscript painting did not really follow this movement, remaining faithful (until about 1235) to the old *Muldenfaltenstil* with undulating folds so characteristic of the 1200 Style.

In France, the firmest reaction against this past was in the art of stained glass. Examples that come to mind are the work of the "Parable Master" at the cathedral of Sens and, especially, that of the "Master of Saint Chéron" at Chartres.[1] Just as Parisian and Amiens sculpture of 1220–1230 may seem to lack charm in comparison to works from the beginning of the century, so too the work of the "Master of Saint Chéron"—with its severity, its broken folds and its simplified modeling—may seem to lack quality, as some writers have maintained. Yet this is precisely the token of the stylistic renewal that affected a large part of the thirteenth century. This not to imply that this artist was an innovative genius—he certainly was not—for similar reactions occurred simultaneously elsewhere, in both sculpture and painting, though it has not been possible as yet to date and localize them. The interesting figures in the upper choir of the collegiate church at Saint-Quentin have already been discussed in the previous chapter; there certain characteristics of this style occur without any possible reference to Chartrain art. The same is true of a series of panels of unknown date at Rouen Cathedral, set in the *Belles-Verrières*. Finally, it is difficult to demonstrate that the art of the "Master of Saint Chéron" was the source of Parisian creations in the 1230s.

Paris and the Surrounding Region

The Vicinity of Paris

Thus, there were parallel developments, the most effective undoubtedly in Paris; however, little is known of activity in the capital from 1220 to 1230. The west rose in Notre Dame and the one at Mantes already belong to the past. No traces of glass painting remain from the new building campaign at Notre Dame in Paris, during which the upper windows were remade, and the side chapels in the nave were progressively opened after 1225. It may be that they only installed colorless grisaille windows.

Surviving elements of painted glass from this period must be sought in the small churches in the region around Paris. The best-known series is from the church at Gercy (now preserved in the Musée de Cluny).[2] Two well-known panels from a Tree of Jesse survive.[3] The very traditional iconographic formula acts as a support for a style already hardened in comparison to works in the 1200 Style. Thus, the softness of the folds contrasts to a certain degree with the more rigid stylization of the faces, especially those of the Virgin and of Christ. The exact date of this glass from a small window in the Romanesque church is not known. The history of the building in the nineteenth century is complicated and ultimately led to its purchase by the State in 1884. The two panels were probably made in the stylistically unsettled period between 1220 and 1230. A Christological series from the same church survives: an Annunciation to the Shepherds, angelic musicians and a figure of Synagoga. Ornamental elements from the same window, inserted between bars forged into the shape of the historiated compartments, can be dated to about 1230 or shortly thereafter. The figural style is characterized by a marked hardening of faces and the abandonment of the pictorial preciousness of the first quarter of the century.

It is in the third, fragmentary and very restored series from Gercy of the Life of Saint 79 Martin that the decisive qualities of the stylistic renewal of the second quarter of the thirteenth century can be seen: bold colors, asymmetrical compositions, rigid figures and a preference for line instead of modeling, similar to the style of the "Master of Saint Chéron" at Chartres. Thus, these disparate examples enable us to ascertain certain lines of evolution in the Paris region.

The windows at Saint-Germain-lès-Corbeil, like those in numerous churches in the vicinity of Paris (Brie-Comte-Robert and Donnemarie-en-Montois)[4] belong to a group that has not 78

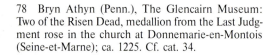

78   Bryn Athyn (Penn.), The Glencairn Museum: Two of the Risen Dead, medallion from the Last Judgment rose in the church at Donnemarie-en-Montois (Seine-et-Marne); ca. 1225. Cf. cat. 34.

▷
79   Paris, Musée de Cluny, deposited with the Service des Monuments Historiques: The Miracle of the Pine Tree, panel from the Life of Saint Martin window in the abbey of Gercy (Essonne, now destroyed); ca. 1220. Cf. cat. 39.

80 Saint-Germain-lès-Corbeil (Essonne), church of Saint Vincent, chevet, bay 100, rose: The Paschal Lamb, encircled by scenes from the lives of six saints; ca. 1225.

been well-defined stylistically. They can be dated between 1220 and 1230, and in certain respects, they are evidence of the "transition" in this very active area. In comparison with the rose window at Mantes or the western rose of Notre Dame in Paris, innovations are evident. The scale is less monumental (perhaps because of the smaller size of the buildings themselves), and outlines are progressively emphasized, at the expense of the detailed treatment of figures by the use of thicker colors. Ornament is reduced or subordinated to the figural panels. The color is harsher than in windows in the 1200 Style from northern France.

The quality of these windows is very uneven. At Saint-Germain-lès-Corbeil, very fine artists created three lights in the chevet, representing a Passion of Christ, a Tree of Jesse to 81 the north and a Life of Saint Germanus to the south. In the oculus over the three bays is the Lamb, surrounded by six scenes depicting the martyrdom or pious deeds of saints particu- 80 larly venerated in the diocese of Paris. The execution of the ensemble is not homogeneous and is certainly the work of more than one painter. The very beautiful central window could strictly be compared to certain innovative tendencies of the first quarter of the century in the "nervousness" of the poses, the facial features and the anatomy. The oculus scenes, which have more authority along with a certain heaviness, are characteristic of the "modernism" of the years 1225 to 1235 and completely reject the 1200 Style, clear traces of which can still be seen in the Tree of Jesse at Gercy. In comparison to those at Gercy, the windows at Donnemarie-en-Montois and Brie-Comte-Robert seem awkward, provincial and, perhaps, later in date. In any event, it was not from this style that Parisian art as seen in Saint Germain des Prés emerged around 1235. However, the art of glass painting at Saint-Germain-lès-Corbeil, and at Chartres too, must be considered in this genesis.

▷
81 Saint-Germain-lès-Corbeil (Essonne), church of Saint Vincent, chevet, bay 0: Passion and Ascension of Christ (detail), Head of an Apostle Witnessing the Ascension; ca. 1220–1225. Cf. cat. 73.

94

82 Paris, church of Saint Germain des Prés, 1st south radiating chapel, bay 4: The Marriage of the Virgin (detail), panel from the Life of the Virgin window in the Lady Chapel (destroyed) of the former abbey of Saint Germain des Prés in Paris; 1240–1245. Cf. cat. 54.

▷
83 New York, The Metropolitan Museum of Art: Saint Vincent and Archbishop Valerius in Chains, panel from a Life of Saint Vincent window in the Lady Chapel (destroyed) or the refectory (destroyed) of the former abbey of Saint Germain des Prés in Paris; 1240–1245. Cf. cat. 55.

Saint Germain des Prés

In Paris itself, before or at the same time as the Sainte Chapelle, two other once-famous buildings were added to the north of the abbey church of Saint Germain des Prés: the refectory and the Lady Chapel. The work of the architect Pierre de Montreuil, they can be dated between 1234 or 1235 and 1243 or 1244.[5] Both were destroyed during the French Revolution and their windows widely dispersed. Only a few panels survive in Saint Germain des Prés, in a radiating chapel of the choir; others are now in a composite window in the former abbey church of Saint Denis. The majority, however, are now in museums outside France: in the Victoria and Albert Museum, London; the Germanisches Nationalmuseum, Nuremberg; The Metropolitan Museum of Art, New York and the Walters Art Gallery, Baltimore.[6] Occasionally panels from the same ensemble appear on the art market, but they quickly disappear into private collections. | 82

   The greatest archeological problem concerning these windows is where they were originally placed in the thirteenth-century buildings. Early descriptions, especially that of Sauval from the beginning of the eighteenth century, seem to indicate that only the choir in the Lady Chapel was decorated with full-color glass, the side windows being glazed in colorless grisaille. References to the refectory are lacking. When it became a library in the seventeenth century, its windows would surely have been removed. P. Verdier and other authors attribute many of the surviving series to the refectory, and others to the Lady Chapel;[7] and, in fact, there are considerable differences in both style and iconography among the surviving works from Saint Germain des Prés. A series with the Life of the Virgin, or perhaps her Child- | 86 hood—at Saint Germain des Prés, in London and at Nuremberg—is in a style that would be termed coarse were it not so expressive.[8] The ornamentation of the panels is characterized by great preciosity, with painted mosaics joined by pearling. Clearly this series must have been in the chapel's chevet. The strong, saturated color of these panels conforms to the tendencies of the mid-thirteenth century and represents a real departure from the past.

   A second series, from which many more panels survive, is clearly the work of another workshop doted with many talents. One of the windows that can be fairly well reconstructed

84 New York, The Metropolitan Museum of Art: Saint Vincent and Archbishop Valerius in Chains (detail), Head of Saint Vincent, panel from a Life of Saint Vincent window in the Lady Chapel (destroyed) or the refectory (destroyed) of the former abbey of Saint Germain des Prés in Paris; 1240–1245. Cf. cat. 55.

85 London, Victoria and Albert Museum: Seated King and a Soldier, panel from a window in the Lady Chapel (destroyed) or the refectory (destroyed) of the former abbey of Saint Germain des Prés in Paris; 1240–1245. Cf. cat. 56.

▷
86 London, Victoria and Albert Museum: Saint Ann Waiting for Joachim, panel from a Life of the Virgin window in the Lady Chapel (destroyed) of the former abbey of Saint Germain des Prés in Paris; 1240–1245. Cf. cat. 54.

depicted the Passion and Martyrdom of Saint Vincent; most of its panels are in New York or Baltimore.[9] The inclusion of this saint in the sanctuary of Saint Germain des Prés is easily explained—the abbey, founded in the sixth century, was named for Saint Vincent. According to tradition, important relics of the martyr were brought to the Parisian abbey by the Frankish King Childebert I. The style of this second series is quite distinct from the first. A checked pattern set with rosettes, executed with minimal care, encloses the narrative scenes economically and harmoniously. The figures stand out clearly; the hardness of the outlines is often repeated in both drapery and faces. This is truly the "hardened" Gothic style of the second quarter of the century that we mentioned in relation to the "Master of Saint Chéron". Several panels of uncertain iconography (in New York, London and at Saint-Denis) belong with this very beautiful window, which has such an easily understood message; in all probability they represent the Translation (by large royal cavalcades) of the Relics from Saragossa to Paris, the Foundation of the Parisian Monastery by Noblewomen or Noblemen and Miracles Performed by the Relics of the Saint, but these identifications cannot be proven.[10] It may seem unusual to have such hagiographic richness in the Lady Chapel when the number of panels with the Virgin or with Christ is so few. Be that as it may, these inadequately identified scenes display the admirable clearness characteristic of the

83,

85

Martyrdom of Saint Vincent panels; sometimes the pictorial quality even approaches that in the Sainte Chapelle, though the artists are not the same. The simplified but vividly colored oblique-lattice design of the ornament in the panels is characteristic of the mid-thirteenth-century esthetic. The narrow borders are well-suited to the double or quadruple lights of Rayonnant windows, which no longer had room for wide frames.

Some of the scenes from the Martyrdom of Saint Vincent typify Parisian tendencies on the eve of the great royal undertaking in the Sainte Chapelle. The scene with Emperor Dacian Ordering the Arrest of the Saint (now in New York) and the one with Deacon Vincent Preaching (in Baltimore) are rendered with exceptional clarity. The heads are often beautiful, with large eyes and powerful jaws. In the finest panels of this series, the balance between line and modeling is indicative of the resources of Parisian painting between 1235 and 1245. Both trace line and modeling have suffered in many scenes because of flaking, as if the firing had been hasty or, at least, less under control than at the Sainte Chapelle.

The Life of the Virgin series, which in some respects seems more archaic or mediocre, represents another trend of developments in Paris, and it also leads toward the art in the Sainte Chapelle and in the transept roses in Notre Dame.

The Sainte Chapelle

Since the end of the thirteenth century, much has been written on the subject of the chapel in the Palais de Justice, the Sainte Chapelle of King Louis IX, built to house the precious relics of Christ's Passion purchased from Emperor Baldwin II of Byzantium.[11] Two records of its dedication in 1246 and 1248 are preserved, the latter dictated by the departure of the king on a crusade; the documents mention the windows and the duties of glass painters responsible for their conservation.

The date that work began on the windows has often been the subject of discussion. The relics were purchased in 1239 and brought to the palace in Paris. It is not known whether work on the chapel meant to contain them began in 1240 or only in 1242, but study of what survives today in this stupendous edifice suggests that, as soon as the architectural plans were drawn up, work on the glass began. In certain windows—notably in the Joshua cycle—finished panels had to be adapted to a change in the ironwork that held the window mullions in position. Thus, it can be established that this immense glazing program was painted, assembled and installed within six years, between about 1242 and 1248. To achieve this, numerous glaziers must have been employed (between twenty to thirty), divided in various workshops but working on a single formal and iconographic program.[12]

The glass has not survived intact. The western rose was redone in a totally new style at the end of the fifteenth century, and in the seventeenth, floods and damage destroyed all the windows in the lower chapel. Then, in the eighteenth century, many windows on the north side were damaged during the construction of the new Palais de Justice. In 1806, the installation of the judicial archives provoked the removal of nearly two hundred panels, some of which are now in private collections in France and abroad. Finally, in 1837, King Louis Philippe decided to restore the Sainte Chapelle to its original state. After long and serious study, restoration of the glass began in 1848 and was completed in 1855; therefore, there are additions and replacements in the glass visible today. The Genesis window is almost entirely modern; others, especially on the south side, are relatively well-preserved. In any case, it is thanks to the restorers of the Romantic era that this monument of Saint Louis's era was renovated with such success.

The idea behind the complex iconography was grand, and doubtless inspired by a great theologian (perhaps Mathieu de Vendôme). To glorify the Relics of the Passion, and especially the Crown of Thorns preserved in this sanctuary, a theological program showing the history of the universe from Genesis to the End of Time was erected round the central Passion window. In the chevet, the Passion of Christ was accompanied by a Childhood window, a Tree of Jesse window and windows with the two Saint Johns. These were linked to the biblical cycle by windows showing the great prophets. On the north side of the church between the Creation and the Book of Judges, scenes from Exodus, a commentary on Deuteronomy, the Campaigns of Joshua and the Story of Gideon and Samson are developed with a prolixity never before achieved. On the south, after the windows with the prophets Ezekiel and Daniel, there is an immense window dedicated to Judith and Job, then the

87 Paris, Sainte Chapelle in the Palais de Justice, Upper Chapel, bay 14 or A: History of the Relics of the Passion (detail), Displaying the Crown of Thorns; between 1242 and 1248. Cf. cat. 62.

Esther window and the one devoted to the First Book of Kings. The cycle then stops abruptly to allow for the History of the Relics of the Cross and of their Translation from Constantinople to Paris. The west rose window (now of the fifteenth century) originally represented the End of Time, i.e. the Apocalypse. This ambitious program is further sustained by numerous allusions to the royalty of Israel, of Christ and, finally, of the king of France, whose arms appear in many of the windows and who is represented in the Relics window.

Stylistic questions about the glazing have in large part been resolved. It was long held that the principal masters and craftsmen came from Chartres and, in fact, in the complex compositions defined by forged bars, there are a number of schemas that derive from the choir, and especially from the nave, at Chartres. Likewise many of the borders with superimposed half-bouquets of leaves can be related to Chartrain works. But the ensemble at the Sainte Chapelle surpasses the Chartrain model both in figural style and technique.

Some compositions are archaic (the Genesis, Judith and Job windows) with medallions simply superimposed. Others (the Esther window) are clearly much more modern in approach, with the systematic juxtaposition of half-medallions. The ornament was renewed by the abundant use of heraldic motifs or even, in certain cases, simplified in the extreme, e.g. in the Passion window. In the figural areas, three principal workshops have been distinguished, which in turn can be divided into a number of "secondary" groups. The principal workshop was responsible not only for the central Passion window but also for all the north windows and all those in the apse except for the Ezekiel panels. The presence of different workshops did not, however, affect the overall stylistic unity. The repetitions from the same cartoons, the figures copied from one another and the insufficient firing, which has led to paint loss in some pieces, have often been criticized. It is true that the glazing as a whole shows signs of a certain amount of haste, easily understandable when one considers the time necessary for a window's execution at that period. Nonetheless, the great variety of the overall compositions, the deliberate choice of ornament and the pictorial quality of the scenes cannot be denied.

The windows in the Sainte Chapelle cannot be judged in comparison to the extremely careful work done at Sens or Bourges. Here, the new Parisian style, which is lively and free with a rapid graphic character, as described in Saint Germain des Prés, is realized fully. The elongated, slightly fragile figures, often stand in a hip-shot or curved stance. The elegant poses, narrow limbs and small heads are in keeping with the rapid drawing that emphasizes the axes of a shape more than its modeling, and the silhouette more than the volume it encloses. This is the refined, almost mannerist Parisian reaction against the great monumental style of the first third of the century.

The overall effect was homogeneous, as we have said, and the conception of the entire glazing program must be attributed to a single "master-overseer," although three distinct workshops can be distinguished. Their characteristics are outlined briefly below.

The first, and the most important by virtue of the number of windows executed and its subsequent influence, is also fairly complex. A number of "hands" can easily be recognized by certain specific traits of figure drawing among the collaborators whose idiosyncrasies blended together in the common activity. The compositions of this "workshop" are harmoniously distributed and fill the frame of the compartments: figures overlap each other in groups; the embryonic architecture is reduced to the barest indications—an arcade, a tower or a tent; landscape elements are stereotyped, especially the trees (always the same) with green, red or yellow leaves in unified clumps resembling artichokes. The figures are always fairly large in relation to the frame, their gestures measured and their poses calm. Even in the midst of battle, gestures and poses are not agitated. Perhaps this calm and harmony derive from the configurations of the folds, whether of mantlets flung over coats of mail or worn over long tunics, or of the short robes of messengers and executioners. The pleats are always soft but straight, and hardly indicate the movements of the body; there are no breaks or complicated folds. As we pointed out, the execution is rapid and simple, and a few lines are sufficient to indicate the drapery, a few strokes of grisaille to model the faces. There are analogies between the style of this workshop and of those working in Saint Germain des Prés (especially in the narrative series, vestiges of which are preserved at Saint-Denis and in the Victoria and Albert Museum in London).

The differences among various "hands" within this workshop are palpable. The best, most representative works are those of a master glazier we have named for the central window, the

88 Paris, Sainte Chapelle in the Palais de Justice, Upper Chapel, bay 10 or C: Book of Esther (detail), Esther and Ahasuerus at the Feast; between 1242 and 1248. Cf. cat. 61.

89 Paris, Sainte Chapelle in the Palais de Justice,
Upper Chapel, bay 0 or H: Passion of Christ (detail),
The Crowning with Thorns; between 1242 and 1248.
Cf. cat. 58.

90 Paris, Sainte Chapelle in the Palais de Justice,
Upper Chapel, bay 5 or K: Book of Judges (1st light to
the right, 11th register), Marriage of Samson; between
1242 and 1248.

"Passion Master". His style is characterized by elongated figures, heads with regular, rather inexpressive features and drapery with simple yet soft folds.

The work of a very distinguished collaborator can be seen in the left light of the second bay north of the axis, appropriately dedicated to the prophet Isaiah. The figures are shorter and stouter, with heavy jaws in the strongly modeled faces and heavier paint in the drapery. Panels by this "Isaiah Master" can be seen in windows on the north side—in the Exodus, Numbers, Deuteronomy and Joshua windows.

A third artist, who was not so talented as the others, worked on the Jesse light. His drapery is simplified to the point of losing all relation to the body it covers; his heads are often strange and ugly, with long noses and heavy beards and mustaches. A more extensive analysis would allow these differences to be more precisely outlined and to discover others, especially in the rendering of folds: sometimes graphic and dry, and sometimes modeled with a great deal of grisaille and forming deep "scooped" folds, as in the Numbers window. The deeply scooped folds, already discussed in relation to the "Master of Saint Chéron" at Chartres, can be seen elsewhere in the Sainte Chapelle, especially in the Judges window.

The "Ezekiel workshop" is clearly distinct—no craftsmen from the principal workshop seem to have worked there. The compositions are often symmetrical, and architecture plays an important role; the figures are fewer, elongated and have small heads. The drapery folds are often stiff and even angular as they fall. The facial type is characteristic: long, thin noses and almond-shaped eyes. The technique is finer and more precise but also less solid in the application of paint. It is a much more expressive art, which might be considered quite evolved if there were any indication of its subsequent influence, but there

91 Paris, Sainte Chapelle in the Palais de Justice, Upper Chapel, bay 11 or N: The Exodus from Egypt (2nd light from the right, 11th register), The Feast of the Tabernacles; between 1242 and 1248.

92 Paris, Sainte Chapelle in the Palais de Justice,
Upper Chapel, bay 4 or F: Book of Ezekiel (detail),
Vision of the Four Beasts and the Four Wheels; be-
tween 1242 and 1248. Cf. cat. 59.

▷
93 Philadelphia, The Philadelphia Museum of Art:
The Army of Holofernes Crossing the Euphrates,
panel from a window dedicated to Judith and Job in
the Sainte Chapelle, Paris; between 1242 and 1248. Cf.
cat. 60.

94 Paris, Bibliothèque Nationale: ms. nouv. acq. lat. 2294, Maciejowski Bible: fol. 3 (detail), Paris, ca. 1245.

is none. In any case, the best-preserved panels from the Ezekiel and Kings windows—though rare—are among the most beautiful in the Sainte Chapelle.

The third "workshop", which was responsible for the Judith and Job and for the Esther 93, windows, is no less interesting. All the characteristics of its style seem to separate this glass from the other windows in the building: the faces are expressive and drawn with small lines; the men's hair is curly, while the women's hair styles are complicated (they sometimes wear hairnets, for example). The poses are varied and demonstrative, the compositions clear and open, the folds simplified and often drawn with broken lines. Some details are typical of this workshop—trees with multifoil leaves, the clothing and fabrics (tablecloths, for instance) decorated with small designs drawn with a pointed tool in a layer of paint.

Parallels with this style can be drawn to miniature painting of the mid-thirteenth century, not, as so often suggested, to such works as the great *Moralized Bibles* of Paris—Oxford and London (the original version of which is in the cathedral of Toledo), but to the Maciejowski 94 Bible in the Pierpont Morgan Library (M. 638), New York, two leaves of which are in the Bibliothèque Nationale in Paris (nouv. acq. lat. ms. 2294) and to another bible from the Ludwig Collection (formerly in Aachen),[13] now in the J. Paul Getty Museum in Malibu, California. Other comparable manuscripts are the "Dominican group" defined by Robert Branner.[14]

The extraordinary quality of the windows in the Sainte Chapelle cannot be overemphasized. The quality of the material is obvious, since these thirteenth-century windows are almost intact and do not show the corrosion usual in glass of this period, despite centuries of exposure to the pollution of Paris. The quality of firing and of manufacture are also remarkable, for the loss of paint—which was rapidly and lightly applied—is not so marked as in other windows from the same period, notably those in Saint Germain des Prés. The quality of invention is also notable, despite the repetition of numerous cartoons and the almost industrialized execution of the background mosaics. The compositions of windows by the "Master of Judith and Job" is often moving in its artistic effect. The fragile nude figure of Judith purifying herself in the water the night before Holofernes's murder is a case in point, as is the strange scene, farther up in the same window, where Job is having his head shorn 95 after all the trials God imposed on him. There is a purity of arrangement and a sharp sense of the event in this scene, which is surely one of the masterpieces of thirteenth-century painting. A third example of composition is the Ezekiel window, where the Prophet Ezekiel 92 forms an extraordinary image, without precedent or subsequent influence: he is depicted skeleton-like, wearing an overly large gown, and his pointed, bird-like head is looking at the sins of Israel. Other examples are the carefully rendered groups of warriors or people before Moses or Joshua, evenly distributed, carefully dawn and fitting into the compartments with ease: the event is clearly expressed in both form and significance. While other glazing programs may provide equally exceptional examples, nowhere are they as numerous as at the Sainte Chapelle. In the final analysis, this royal enterprise dominated production in the region and, in our opinion, surpassed all its contemporaries.

95 Paris, Sainte Chapelle in the Palais de Justice, Upper Chapel, bay 8 or D: Story of Judith and Job (detail), Job Has His Head Shaved; between 1242 and 1248. Cf. cat. 60.

Workshops Deriving from the Sainte Chapelle

Workshops from the Sainte Chapelle were without question active in the nave at Soissons, which was still under construction. In the aisles, they created a huge cycle illustrating the books of the Old Testament—Exodus, Leviticus and the Book of Judith. Only a few panels 96 remain, regrouped in the axial chapel of the ambulatory, where they were transferred, probably during the eighteenth century.[15] The windows' ornamentation is close to that in the Sainte Chapelle, with heraldic mosaics composed of fleurs-de-lis and castles of Castile. The general conception of the scenes and the figural style represent the same stage of formal development as Parisian glass, but with less elegance than at the Sainte Chapelle.

The former collegiate church at Saint-Julien-du-Sault in Burgundy (built in the mid-thirteenth century) is a second, less clear example of probable Parisian intervention.[16] The subjects of these windows, if they were properly restored in the nineteenth century, are the Childhood and the Passion of Christ, the Life of the Virgin and the lives of Saint Margaret, Saint Nicholas, Saint Blaise, Saint Peter and Saint Paul and the two Saint Johns. The ornament clearly follows the examples in the Sainte Chapelle: half-borders and heraldic background mosaics. The style is more difficult to discern, since it is not homo-

96 Soissons, cathedral of Saint Gervais et Saint Protais, chevet, axial chapel, bay 1: Life of Moses (5th and 6th registers, from left to right and from bottom to top), Jethro Giving his Daughter to Moses; The Hebrews Marking the Lintels of their Doors with the Blood of a Lamb; Moses Climbing the Mountain; Pharaoh's Daughter Finding Moses; ca. 1250. Cf. cat. 82.

geneous, despite the unifying efforts of nineteenth-century restorers. Parisian tendencies are undeniable, and one of them seems to have come from the Sainte Chapelle. A scholar has recently attributed a number of the windows to the "Isaiah Master" from the principal workshop at the Sainte Chapelle.[17] Other windows in a more relaxed style are more closely related to the workshops of Saint Germain des Prés. Unfortunately, there is no complete monograph on these windows and, above all, no comprehensive attempt to determine the authenticity of this glass, which was so altered during nineteenth-century restorations.

In Paris itself, it is not surprising to find the glass painters of the Sainte Chapelle working on the two rose windows in the transept of Notre Dame. The north rose was probably constructed and glazed first, during alterations to the nave and the enlargement of the transept, undertaken around 1225 and not completed in the choir until the beginning of the fourteenth century. The principal theme of the rose (finished before 1255) is the Glorification of the Virgin, sitting majestically in the center and surrounded by eighty Old Testament figures: patriarchs, prophets, kings, high priests, ancestors of Christ and angels praising the Mother of God. The rose fits in well with sculpture on the north transept portal and the *porte rouge* ("Red Door"), both of which are dedicated to Our Lady, patron of the cathedral, who is represented as the Queen of Heaven, as Ecclesia or as the Mother of Christ. The manifold figures in this window correspond to an enlargement of the bay (which now measures almost 13 meters in diameter); each of the sixteen main divisions is subdivided into two and then four sections. The two scenes in the spandrels beneath the rose are difficult to explain but seem to be related to the Antichrist and the End of the World.

Despite numerous restorations and some reuse of earlier panels, the style can be easily related to that of the Sainte Chapelle workshops, even to the point of recognizing some of the same hands. At Notre Dame one can see the same elegance, the same subtlety of drawing and painting and the same energy in the outlines of pieces and in the rendering of drapery. This style, seen in and around the Ile-de-France until about 1260, changed quickly.

98

97 Paris, cathedral of Notre Dame, north transept arm, rose: Glorification of the Virgin (detail), Moses the Judge; ca. 1250–1255. Cf. cat. 52.

98 Geneva, Musée d'Art et d'Histoire: Censing Angel, medallion from a spandrel below the north transept rose in the cathedral of Notre Dame, Paris (?); ca. 1250–1255.

The south rose in Notre Dame, like the entire facade of the south transept, was built after the completion of the north rose. A text inscribed under the foundation of this facade gives the date the work began: February 12, 1258. In dimensions and general shape, the south rose takes its inspiration from the one in the north transept but with some technical improvements in the lower spandrels. However, it underwent considerable restoration in the eighteenth century, and its composition was modified at the time of Viollet-le-Duc's work. The general subject has been partially altered by the reuse of Romanesque medallions pertaining to the Life of Saint Matthew.[18] In the main, however, the subject is the Glorification of Christ amid apostles, saints and martyrs, as well as Christian "knights" and cohorts of angels. The theme of the Wise and Foolish Virgins (which may seen unusual in this context) is not in actual fact unusual, since it pertains to a kind of Last Judgment: Christ appears in the heavens among all those who testified for Him; angels carry the instruments of the Passion, and the Parable of the Wise and Foolish Virgins, a theme corresponding to the separation of the elect from the damned, fit in well.

The style is representative of Parisian art in the mid-thirteenth century, which grew out of the work of the Sainte Chapelle workshops; however, despite the very high quality of the original glass in the south rose, the style has begun to evolve toward less elongated forms, sometimes drier in execution and less at ease in their formal invention. This kind of change is comparable to that seen in the clerestory in Le Mans Cathedral (created between 1250 and 1270). It is most unfortunate that none of the upper thirteenth-century windows in the Parisian cathedral's choir survived destruction in the eighteenth century.

It was long believed that work deriving from the Sainte Chapelle style established itself throughout France, especially in the cathedrals of Le Mans, Tours and Clermont-Ferrand.[19] While glass in all these buildings belongs to parallel tendencies, it is, nevertheless, characterized by profound modifications of the Parisian style.

Normandy: Rouen and Coutances

Although the direct influence of a master, like the "Master of Saint Chéron" at Chartres, cannot be seen at Rouen, it does seem that formal hardening at Rouen, which we shall attempt to analyze, was the equivalent of this tendency as it was of the Parisian ones.

The windows in Rouen Cathedral have always been thought to derive from the workshops at Chartres, and the signature of *Clemens vitrearius carnotensis* on a panel in the lower register of the second Joseph window has been cited as absolute proof. What do we note when looking more closely at the Rouen cycles? In the previous chapter, we saw that in the first decades of the century a fine workshop there (the Seven Sleepers of Ephesus) took its inspiration from the northern style of glass painting and that several, somewhat less successful hagiographic series (now reset in the *Belles-Verrières* in the nave) also derived from the northern style. A local tradition was thus certainly established, which, in some respects, modified Chartrain influences after 1220–1225.

In this category are several windows from the second quarter and the mid-thirteenth century: six complete windows, still in their original place in the ambulatory and in a radiating chapel (the latter, dedicated to Saint Peter and Saint Paul, is poorly preserved and will not be discussed), and an incomplete window (now in the north transept) representing the Martyrdom of Saint Vincent. The five ambulatory windows depict the Legend of Saint Julian the Hospitaller, the Story of the Patriarch Joseph (in two windows), the Parable of the Good Samaritan and a Passion accompanied by typological figures. The overall program can no longer be determined; what survives is rather incoherent and fairly unusual iconographically. The fifty-five compartments dedicated to Joseph are surprising and divided in two, and the typological program is particularly protracted: thirty compartments, only eight of which pertain to the Old Testament. In the Good Samaritan window too, which is completely lacking in any symbolic commentary of the parable, there are an excessive number of narrative panels.

As Ritter has already noted,[20] these traits are characteristic of the second quarter and the mid-thirteenth century. The *Bible Moralisée* (conceived around 1225) illustrated the Bible in more than 5,000 scenes: occasionally, this meant illustrating a single sentence with three or four scenes. These iconographic traits point to a rather late date for the glass, even if the style indicates otherwise.

The style is not homogeneous; the Passion window and the scenes from the Martyrdom of Saint Vincent are characterized by clean lines and sharp modeling. The painting would be termed heavy or excessive if it were not for the admirable expressiveness of both the composition and the figures. The Joseph, the Good Samaritan and the Saint Julian windows, on the other hand, are softer in style—the lines are less incisive, the modeling lighter and often more obliterated. The quality of this group of windows varies: there is occasional awkwardness when placing the figures or fitting them into the compartments.

99 Rouen, cathedral of Notre Dame, ambulatory, bay 12: Passion of Christ (11th register), Symbolic Crucifixion; ca. 1235.

Neither of these two workshops worked at Chartres, despite the signature of *Clemens* at the bottom of one of the Joseph windows and despite the great number of artists who were active there. It is the general composition of Rouen windows that is reminiscent of Chartres, the subdivision by straight bars as in some windows in the choir at Chartres and the border ornament, a more careful study of which would show rather numerous Chartrain influences. In the backgrounds, the relationship is less well established. The general palette, in which blue and red dominate, conforms to the development of French stained glass from about 1230 to 1245, when these windows were made. Rouen will be discussed again in the context of the remarkable evolution of glass in this region during the last third of the century.

The second cathedral in Normandy that has preserved much of its glass from the second quarter and the middle of the thirteenth century is Coutances Cathedral. In the north transept arm are three tall lights representing the Story of Saint Thomas Becket and the Legends of Saint George and Saint Blaise. This part of the cathedral was built after 1225; the glazing must be dated between 1230 and 1240, even if it is characterized by great conservatism. There are large medallions or superimposed diamond-shaped or oval compartments in the lights, which are meant to be seen from a distance. The same principle was used in the clerestory of the choir at Chartres but in shorter openings. The ornament is fairly archaic, especially the wide border of the Saint George window, which is perhaps explained by the dimensions of the bay. The overall color is lively, a characteristic of the middle of the century, the major contrast being between red and blue. The handling is difficult to judge because of the extent of restoration. The scale is monumental, and the execution somewhat summary. The compositions betray the general tendency after 1230 toward simplified ornament and pictorial compositions and toward a rapid monumental style, as can be seen better a little later in the upper choir at Troyes Cathedral.

At Coutances, two new series of glass are found in the clerestory windows on the north side and in the hemicycle of the choir. The first series, poorly preserved, was thought to have come from the south transept and to have been placed in the choir in the fifteenth century; this hypothesis seems to have little basis in fact. The subjects are probably the two Saint Johns and the Public Life of Christ (the Resurrection of Lazarus?). The clerestory windows in the hemicycle are a little clearer. The composition in large medallions is repeated, somewhat modified by the narrowness of the lights; in particular, the borders have been eliminated for the most part. The scale of the mosaics has increased, and the relaxed style of figuration has a very provincial character that is only distantly related to the main tendencies of Gothic painting. One window is so poorly preserved that it is no longer legible. Two of the others are dedicated to the Childhood of Christ, followed by two dedicated to the Glorification of the Virgin and two devoted to saints of the diocese with archangels overhead.

The windows in the radiating chapels of the ambulatory are, in some instances, better preserved and of higher quality. The compositions, always arranged with straight bars, sometimes thrust the figured half-medallions toward the sides of the light so that the mosaics fill the space in the center of the window, following a pattern that is not new and was already used in Bourges from 1215; the frames are reduced to half-borders. The style of the finest panels in these windows is similar to that already seen at Rouen Cathedral, which will appear again at Le Mans. The iconography is most interesting; it portrays the unusual legends of Norman saints, Saint Marculphus and Saint Laudus, the latter a legendary bishop of Coutances.

Northern France: Beauvais and Amiens

Parallel to the evolution of glass we have seen in Paris is the development in the great buildings in the Beauvais region and in Picardy. The cathedral of Beauvais was rebuilt after the fire of 1225; its ambulatory and chapels were finished around 1235, or 1240 at the latest.[21] It was about this time—and not later as some have suggested—that the windows of the axial Lady Chapel were made, the only glazing of the first half of the thirteenth century to survive in the cathedral. Three double windows, each surmounted by a rose, show a Tree of Jesse and a Childhood of Christ in the axial window; in the two lights to the south are the Miracle of Theophilus, while to the north is a heavily restored window with scenes from a

100 Beauvais, cathedral of Saint Pierre, Lady Chapel, bay 2: Legend of Theophilus (right light, 5th register from the bottom), Theophilus Prostrate before a Statue of the Blessed Virgin, Seeking her Help; ca. 1240.

10

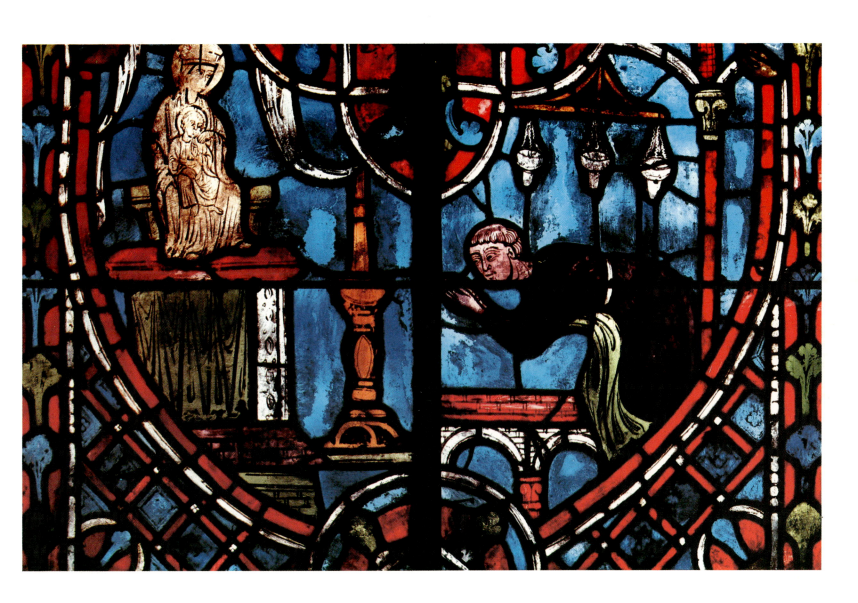

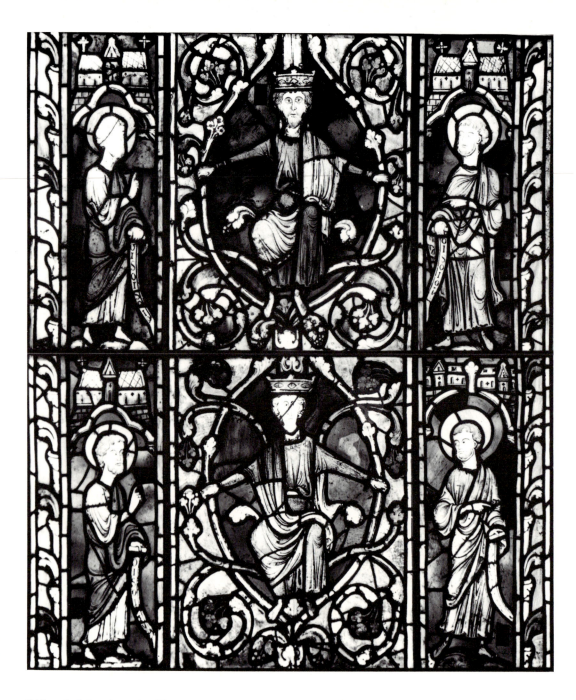

101 Beauvais, cathedral of Saint Pierre, Lady Chapel, bay 0: Tree of Jesse (left light, 4th and 5th registers), Kings and Prophets; 1240–1245.

101

Life of Saint Martin (?) among other subjects. It is very likely that these hagiographic windows were intended for a different location.

The compositions are subdivided by straight bars and consist of numerous scenes, each set in a quarter circle, arranged in groups of four in a large oval medallion. Only the Jesse Tree differs, with its traditional arrangement in rectangular panels. The borders are quite narrow, the background vividly colored and carefully painted. There is nothing revolutionary about this glass, which follows the traditions of the first quarter of the century. The ornamental fillets are extremely simple; the scenes they enclose show the "modern tendency" of the Beauvais style. As in the work of the "Master of Saint Chéron," the small-headed figures with their elegant yet brisk gestures are well separated from each other. The drawing and poses remain rigid, however. Representations of architecture, furnishings and vegetation (e.g. the branches of the Jesse Tree) are very carefully rendered, as are the fairly differentiated faces with their expressive eyes. The statue of the Virgin in the Miracle of Theophilus window is a delicately executed miniature statuette.

These forms can scarcely be compared to the more rapid, virtuoso style of Parisian art at the Sainte Chapelle. It has been thought that this style may have been inspired by the Laon

▷
102 Champs-sur-Marne, castle, storage depot of the Monuments Historiques: King, panel from a Jesse Tree window in the cathedral of Notre Dame at Amiens; ca. 1245. Cf. cat. 13.

114

103 Champs-sur-Marne, castle, storage depot of the Monuments Historiques: Saint Giles in the Forest, panel from a Saint Giles window in the cathedral of Notre Dame at Amiens; ca. 1245.

tradition of the beginning of the century, but the chronological interval is too great and the inspiration too remote for this to be the case. It is possible that in northern France around 1230 a truly Gothic tendency asserted itself everywhere, as the architecture of Amiens around 1230 indicates. Beauvais will be discussed again later, for the clerestory in its choir is an important work of the last third of the century.

Amiens presents different, even more difficult problems because of the great extent of the destruction of its thirteenth-century glass. This Picardy cathedral, begun around 1218 or 1220, has lost all the glazing in its nave, the oldest part of the building (completed around 1236 or even earlier). The choir, with its much more modern architecture, was built between 1236 and 1269.[22] It is already an advanced masterpiece of Rayonnant architecture, with a pierced triforium and numerous narrow lights in the upper bays. The Lady Chapel built around 1242 (?) was, in some respects, a model for the Sainte Chapelle in Paris.

Unfortunately, however, the windows from this part of the church and from the transept were largely destroyed by all sorts of accidents, artillery fire and systematic destruction: by canons in the eighteenth century, by members of the French Revolution and, finally, by negligent restorers in the nineteenth century, who removed some glass and mixed together original cycles that are now incomplete. Then, in 1921, there was another disaster—a fire in the studio of the glass painter Socard, which destroyed much of the glass from the radiating chapels that had been taken there for restoration. The distribution of the original glass in these chapels is now incoherent. Remains of a Jesse Tree and a Life of the Virgin are located 102 in the bays of the side chapels in the choir, which was certainly not their original location. Many other panels from the Jesse Tree were among the debris from the 1921 fire. Since the nineteenth century, the incomplete series of original glass have been completed with new archeological panels, often well-made, by Alfred Gérente, Louis Steinheil and Nicolas Coffetier.[23] In other windows are series (incomplete, of course) depicting the Passion of Christ mixed with a Childhood, a Life of the Virgin and a (much damaged) Life of Saint Leonard, and scattered remnants of a Genesis cycle. Some of the windows that were damaged by the fire in 1921 are being restored by J.J. Gruber's studio: in addition to the Jesse panels, there are a number of panels from the Saint Giles and the Saint James 103 windows. Several panels from a Life of Saint Eligius are now in an American museum. In addition to the Tree of Jesse, scenes from the Life of the Virgin, the Childhood and the Public Life of Christ and His Passion were also, no doubt, placed in the Lady Chapel. However, the riddle of this glazing program has not been solved—the surviving elements are not homogeneous either in iconography or style. In the numerous tall lights in the other chapels around the choir, there must have been fully developed cycles both from Genesis and from the lives of the saints. In one bay of the north transept are fragments of the lives of two English kings, Saint Edmund and Saint Edward the Confessor, which are perhaps still in their original openings.

As for ornamentation, most of the mosaics have trellis leading, notably the central window in the second radiating chapel to the south. The borders are very interesting: some have leaves, others fleurs-de-lis and castles of Castile. A third type of border, with langued leopards or affronted and superimposed birds, is very important in the history of Gothic ornament and quite frequent at the beginning of the fourteenth century, especially in Normandy. Stylistic analysis of these panels is difficult because of their poor condition; however, not all are of the same date. The archaism of some suggests that they come from the nave and date before 1236; the mannerism of others (such as the Jesse Tree) recalls works dating after 1250. Parallels to windows in the Sainte Chapelle are numerous but lacking in precision. Most of the series—the scenes from the Life of Christ and of the Virgin, large parts of the Jesse Tree—are in a very hard style that evokes the period of the Life of Saint Vincent windows in Saint Germain des Prés and the "principal" workshop of the Sainte Chapelle. On the other hand, some figures from the Tree of Jesse, and especially the hagiographic scenes such as the panels with the Life of Saint Giles, are characterized by a certain softening of paint and line, notably in the faces, similar to works dating after 1250.

A better understanding of this large ensemble is important. It may be that the geographic distance from the capital produced a certain remoteness from strictly Parisian tendencies, as was the case with manuscript painting in this area after 1250 or 1260. Let us hope that a close study of the panels still in place, those being restored and those dispersed in public and private collections, will further our knowledge on this point.

Champagne: Reims, Châlons, Orbais, Troyes

The windows in the cathedral of Reims, which should be not only an important landmark but also an essential point of comparison, are, unfortunately, little more than wreckage carefully put back together after the First World War. The building was begun in 1212, or even earlier.[24] Work progressed rapidly over twenty years in both the transept and the precincts of the choir. Problems beginning in 1232–1234 were followed by a complete work stoppage. When work began again, about 1236–1238, the initial project for the overall elevation was modified, and the upper windows were lengthened by raising the vault of the upper choir. The choir must have been completed in 1241; the nave and facade, planned and started at the beginning of the century, did not acquire their final shape until after 1245. There is proof that the upper parts of the facade were still under construction in the fourteenth century.

Apparently, the initial glazing program was conceived before 1235. In the west side of the south transept arm, a double window survives. It represents, on the one hand, Saint John the Baptist and Archbishop Henri de Braisne (1227–1240) and, on the other, a majestic Virgin and Child above a beautiful architectural rendering, designated as the Church of Reims. The glass is obviously no longer in its original window and was enlarged for use in the two lights that it has probably occupied since the thirteenth century.[25] In relatively good condition, this window can serve as a point of departure for the study of the original glazing in the upper choir at Reims, which in all probability dates after 1241. Unfortunately, all that remains after the bombardment of the cathedral in September 1914 are conscientiously restored windows; the extensively damaged remains were taken down over a period of years after the disaster.

The present program corresponds well to that of the Gothic church: it is a glorification of the metropolitan cathedral of Reims with a Virgin in Majesty and a Crucifixion in the double central window of the apse and, above them, Archbishop Henri de Braisne and an architectural representation of the Church of Reims. The other ten windows in the choir contain images of the apostles surmounting aediculae that represent the churches of the diocese of the province or effigies of suffragan bishops of Reims. In some ways, the glazing program repeats that in the choir of Saint Remi at Reims (built at the end of the twelfth century), in which all the archbishops of Reims up to the time of Henri de France were represented around the church's patron saint and the Virgin Mary.[26]

The originality of the cathedral's glazing, however, lies in the representations of the church facades, pierced by rose windows and flanked by towers, with angels at their summits. The carefully studied images betray a blend of reality, convention and architectural fantasy rendered in manifold sparkling colors.[27] Naturally, because of the heavy damage in 1914, it is difficult to analyze the style of these windows. The work of four successive workshops has been posited. It would seem, rather, that the Reims workshops collaborated, for they certainly decorated the lower windows and those in the transept in a single "campaign".

Several major stylistic tendencies can be observed. The style in the Henri de Braisne transept window, mentioned above, can also be seen in some of the choir windows: elongated figures with wide, massive faces; soft folds that are still fluid and distinct from the "archaic" style of Reims sculpture and more like the well-established Champagne tradition already found in Saint Remi at Reims, at Soissons and at Baye. This style can be seen in the apse window and in the Saint Thomas and Bishop of Châlons window. The other tendency is much more innovative and related to the expressive style of the second quarter of the century. Faces are often distorted and presented sideways, proportions exaggerated, postures more varied. The drawing of the folds has "hardened"; sometimes they are broken or have projecting beaks and deep "scoops", i.e. strongly modeled troughs in the drapery. Characteristic of this style are the Saint Barnabas window, the window with the Bishop of Thérouanne and the figure of Saint Paul.[28] The overall palette is relatively homogeneous, with blue and red dominating, but the use of yellow and green is more important than in the Ile-de-France or Normandy. In these windows the ornament has been cut in large scale; most of the background motifs are circular and unpainted. The borders are typical of the thirteenth century for the most part, but wider than is usual this late in order to fill the cathedral's immense bays.

The glass saved from the bombardments in 1914 has been regrouped and reset in the four east windows of the nave clerestory. There are four figures of French kings, only one of

104   Reims, cathedral of Notre Dame, choir clerestory, bay 103: The Church at Châlons Upholding the Apostle Philip: 1240–1250. Cf. cat. 66.

whom is identified by an inscription: KAROLUS, (Charlemagne?). Each king is set above an image of an archbishop of Reims. In three double windows on the south side, the archbishops are identified by inscriptions: Donatian, Viventius, Baruch, etc.—the first prelates of Reims. The ornamentation was in large part redone following early documents during the restoration that began around 1920. It corresponds to the standard type of the first half of the century: wide leafy borders and numerous framing fillets. While it is difficult to appreciate the style of these large figures, it seems that much of the upper-nave decoration was done by the same artists who worked on the later parts of the choir that date shortly after 1240.

The rose in the north transept now contains an incomplete series of Genesis panels in disarray.[29] Like many other windows in the cathedral, the rose was heavily restored as early as the seventeenth century; in all the historiated medallions, there are only two original heads. These can be dated about 1250, which is rather surprising, since this transept arm was built fifteen years before. At the extreme western end of the cathedral is the beautiful large rose window surmounting a glazed triforium. The figures in the triforium evidently allude to a royal coronation, perhaps to that of Clovis. The Dormition, Glorification and Heavenly Triumph of the Virgin are represented in the rose window. The date of the glass must correspond to the very controversial date of the construction and decoration of the facade and its reverse, which can only have been accomplished in the second half of the century, even if the work on the upper story lasted even longer.

The importance of Reims sculpture in this part of the cathedral for the evolution of art after 1260 will be discussed later. It perpetuated the "mannerism of Reims" and simultaneously brought about a new figural style, expressive and powerful.

Beyond Reims, towards central Champagne and its capital at Troyes, is the cathedral of Châlons-sur-Marne and the former abbey church at Orbais, both of which have interesting collections of stained glass.

The chevet of Châlons Cathedral, newly constructed and glazed before 1240, retains three windows:[30] a Crucifixion placed between the Virgin Mary and Saint John, a Christ in Glory 105 and a Virgin and Child surrounded by local saints and holy bishops such as Elaphe, Donatian, Memmius and Alpinus, as well as by the apostles Paul, John, etc. Despite their very traditional style these windows are not without interest, and their palette is original. White is used for the backgrounds, and strong colors like red and blue are used only for accents. The ornament is weak and schematized. The drawing of figures and folds would be reminiscent of some of the cathedral's twelfth-century glass if the tendency toward a hardening of forms did not correspond to the general evolution in art from 1230 to 1250. At Châlons, there is no hint of Parisian mannerism and no reference to the Chartrain models mentioned earlier. This beautiful, little-studied glass is a testament to the variety rather than to the unity of work produced by workshops in Champagne between Reims and Troyes.

The former abbey church at Orbais near Epernay was glazed from the end of the twelfth century[31] into the thirteenth; only a few poorly preserved fragments remain. In the central window of the apse clerestory are some awkwardly finished panels representing a Christ and a Virgin. The head of a saint decorates a window on the south. The very beautiful grisailles in the choir will be discussed later, for they are among the oldest and most significant works of this type, from the beginning of the thirteenth century.

As noted above, local and northern traditions were very strong in Troyes itself until about 1230. A large new glazing program was completed there about 1230 in the triforium bays and in the clerestory of the choir. After the collapse of the upper parts of the church during construction in 1227, they were rapidly rebuilt according to a new architectural model, thereby perhaps inaugurating the Rayonnant, or "Saint Louis," style.[32]

The overall effect of the choir clerestory at Troyes is striking because of the strong palette used and the expanse of the windows. Divided into numerous lights like those in the Sainte Chapelle, the windows at Troyes form a continuous screen of multicolored glass. The glass is fairly well-preserved, with almost all the early pieces still in their original position, except for the triforium glass, some of which has clearly been cut down and rearranged. The style of the whole ensemble is homogeneous enough so that there is no strong contrast in scale or color. The restorations in the nineteenth century, though extensive, have not altered the overall effect of the glazing. The iconographic program is interesting and original, except for

105 Châlons-sur-Marne, cathedral of Saint Etienne, chevet clerestory, bay 100, lower registers: (left), Calvary; (right), Saint Memmius, Bishop of Châlons; ca. 1240–1250.

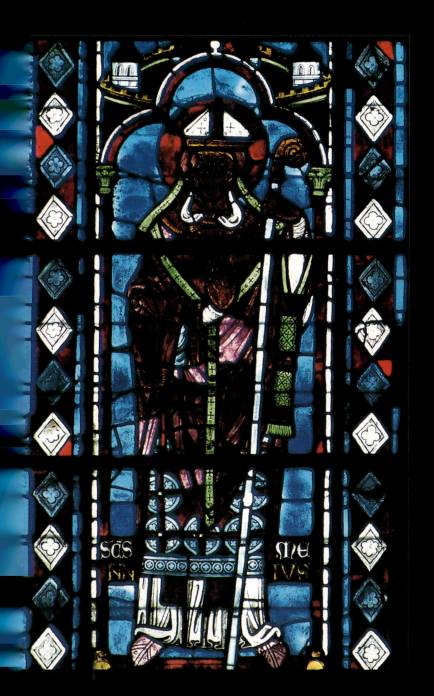
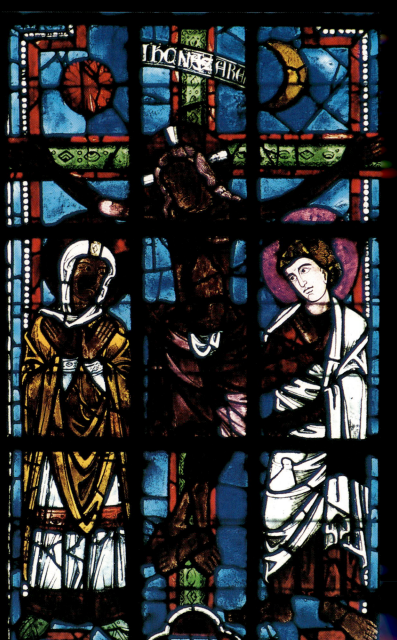

106 Troyes, cathedral of Saint Pierre, chevet clerestory, bay 202: Life of Saint John the Evangelist: (left,
from bottom to top), Saint John Writing; Saint John
Drinking from the Poisoned Chalice; Saint John in
the Cauldron of Boiling Oil; (right), Emperor Domi-
tian Who Tortured and Exiled the Evangelist; Miracle
of the Reeds Turned into Gold Rods; Death of Saint
John; ca. 1245.

the triforium with its jumble of figures, which include prophets, a Synagoga, an Ecclesia, a Judith and the Prophetess Anna. It is possible that the now-mutilated original program on this level presented a Crucifixion placed between Ecclesia and Synagoga, flanked by a fairly comprehensive group of Old Testament prophets and prophetesses.

The upper windows, on the other hand, are at least explicable if not logical. Around the central Passion of Christ window are windows with the Childhood, the Life of the Virgin and of various saints like Saint John the Evangelist, Saint Peter and Saint Paul, etc. In addition, there are singular works depicting a kind of secular and ecclesiastical hierarchy with popes, kings, princes and bishops, the Parable of the Wise and Foolish Virgins, the Miracle of Theophilus and the Translation of Relics to Troyes after the sack of Constantinople in 1204. Thus, the program included many subtle ideas—the glorification of the Church of Troyes and of its relics and patrons as well as a series of moral lessons like the Miracle of Theophilus or the parable. The whole ensemble was no doubt produced by a single group of glass painters working together under the direction of one man. The scale of execution is the same throughout: the figures (two or three registers high) are surrounded by wide borders, necessitated by the dimensions of the lights. All this ornament—representing the arms of France in the Theophilus window—is standard and summarily executed. The scenes generally fill the surface between the two borders. There are no true backgrounds (except in the Saint Peter window), but, instead, broad ornamental bosses divide the scenes.

The subtle ornament of the mid-thirteenth century has been replaced here with a more restrained expeditious art. The figures belong to the "hard" Gothic style, with rigid silhouettes, a system of broken folds and even modeling in which the faces and hair are often harsh. Let us not exaggerate: some figures have lively and engaging expressions, for instance in the window depicting the Wise and Foolish Virgins or in the Childhood of Christ. The variety in the cast of features is remarkable, and sometimes a great sensitivity is evident when denoting character. It stands to reason that this glass is entirely separate from the Parisian style of the 1240s as seen at the Sainte Chapelle. Like the upper glazing in Reims Cathedral, the glass at Troyes may represent a monumental reaction in principle to the ornamental splendor of glass painting in the first quarter of the thirteenth century, notably at Chartres. The figural style at Troyes can, of course, be compared to work by the last Chartrain workshops, but the relationships are only superficial; Troyes glass adopts little of the strength and monumentality of the figures at Chartres. The next monument of stained glass in Champagne would be the extraordinary masterpiece of Saint Urbain at Troyes, dating after 1265.

The Burgundian Workshops

The Burgundian monument richest in thirteenth-century stained glass is undeniably the cathedral at Auxerre. (Sens, not a Burgundian monument, was discussed above.) Original in concept, the cathedral at Auxerre cannot easily be set into the evolution of the French Gothic style. Probably begun about 1215, it does not seem to have been used before 1235, although a bishop was buried in the choir in 1233.[33] The age and shape of the windows pose difficult problems that have yet to be resolved;[34] there is no question that the windows in the choir clerestory have traditionally been dated too late. The iconographic program was seriously impaired by the destructiveness of the Huguenots in the sixteenth century and then during successive restorations in the nineteenth century. In the beautiful Lady Chapel, the partly original glass of a Jesse Tree and a Miracle of Theophilus cycle have been reset in the side lights of the chevet. (The central window is modern.) The thirty bays of the ambulatory contained a very complete cycle extending from Genesis to the Stories of Samson and David from the Old Testament, and a second cycle with the best-known Christian saints and the most venerated saints in the diocese such as Saint Germanus of Auxerre, Saint Priscus and Saint Mammas, along with the Parable of the Prodigal Son. None of these windows is complete. The scenes have often been reset out of order to fill up the windows, making the study of the workshops responsible for the glass—so jumbled today—very difficult. Some windows, such as the two depicting Saint Nicholas or the one with Saint Martin, follow the standard Chartrain formula of ornamental abundance dating from the beginning of the century: scenes joined in large circular quadrants or in stars and

107 Auxerre, cathedral of Saint Etienne, ambulatory, bay 20: Legends of Abraham, Noah and Lot (3rd and 4th registers, from left to right), The Sacrifice of Abraham; Abraham Offers Food to the Angels; Angels Announcing the Destruction of Sodom; the Intercession of Abraham; Lot Greets the Angels; Lot's Wife Welcomes the Angels; ca. 1230–1235. Cf. cat. 16.

108 Auxerre, cathedral of Saint Etienne, ambulatory, bay 8: St. Martin's Miracle of the Pine Tree (2nd register, right panel); ca. 1250.

▷
109 Auxerre, cathedral of Saint Etienne, ambulatory, bay 13: Life of Saint Andrew (lower register, left medallion), An Old Man Named Nicholas Comes to Ask for Saint Andrew's Help (detail), Head of the old man; 1235–1240.

set against heavily painted mosaic grounds with rich borders and numerous framing fillets. The figural style cannot be linked to any of the Chartres workshops, however, despite a certain stiffness reminiscent of tendencies inaugurated by the "Master of Saint Chéron" workshop between 1220 and 1235.

Another group of legendary windows at Auxerre has a quite different general concept: the scenes are contained in hexagonal compartments, while the ornament on the ground is composed of richly handled rinceaux (though simple by comparison with Sens or Canterbury) or of delicately painted rectilinear leading. Included in this group are the Genesis, Patriarchs, Samson, Saint Andrew and Saint Margaret windows. The quality is uneven, as if collaborators of varying talent were employed in this important and prosperous workshop. The works in which stylistic qualities are most evident betray a great freedom of composition, successful expressive invention, great pictorial care and a general stiffening of silhouettes, characteristic of the time but not dependent on Parisian or Ile-de-France models.[35]

A third series, perhaps slightly later, composed of the Saint Peter and Saint Paul window and of some parts of the Saint Martin window, is clearly derived from art in the Sainte Chapelle. The dependence on Paris is particularly evident in both the figural style and the painting technique; it does not extend, however, to the ornament or to the general composition of the windows.[36] The last workshop hardly stands out from the overall tendency for the lower windows at the Auxerre work site and seems to have been active between 1235 and 1250.

Despite serious restoration, the clerestory windows are also highly original in iconographic and formal terms. All the lower panels of the windows are modern. The present arrangement, which is not entirely logical, is probably not original. The bays in the first eastern aisle nearest the transept are filled with figures of saints and with two images of Christ in Glory. As at Reims Cathedral, these images have probably been moved from their original location; however, they are not much earlier than the rest of the glass. In the axis of the apse, a beautiful Crucifixion and a Christ in Majesty are grouped under a Christological rose window. The workmanship of the rose is very refined, in contrast to the more brutal conception and treatment of the clerestory lancets. The present arrangement of the figures is

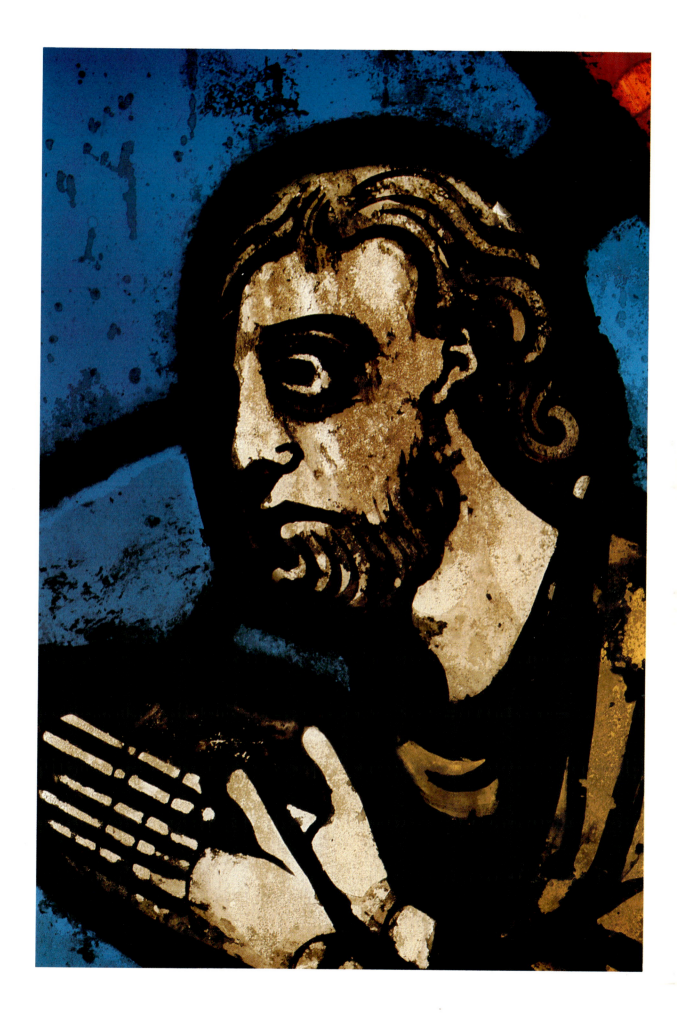

110 Auxerre, cathedral of Saint Etienne, ambulatory, bay 12: The Apocalypse (detail), The White Horseman; 1230–1235. Cf. cat. 15.

illogical. Near the central window are Saint Stephen, patron of the cathedral, and Saint Germanus, the great bishop of Auxerre, as well as Saint Lawrence and Saint Amator. The roses over these two windows have a very rare and significant iconography: on one side, the Liberal Arts; on the other, the Vices and Virtues. Prophets and apostles follow in disarray; the poor quality of these figures has already been noted, due perhaps to early and to modern restorations. Some heads are primitive, even quite ugly, and summarily modeled. Two tendencies can be seen in the poses. The first respects the verticality of the figures and has neatly separated drapery folds; the other is coarser and more vehement, using strongly molded, bulky folds thrown across the body.

It is difficult to find antecedents for this style; it does not seem to come from either the great tradition of Chartres or of Champagne at Reims and Troyes. Among the most obvious peculiarities are the wide borders of grisaille with colored fillets and ornamental bosses. The introduction of very lightly painted grisaille around the middle of the century, and especially in its second half, is crucial to the evolution of stained glass (at least in France) and will be discussed in another chapter. It is important to note that, in the Lady Chapel, two "donors" windows, with the Virgin and Saint Stephen, also have wide colorless panels with colored fillets corresponding to the unusually broad grisaille grounds in the upper windows.

Two other groups of windows are important for Burgundy: those in the former collegiate church at Saint-Julien-du-Sault and in Notre Dame at Dijon, as well as the remains of the glazing from the church at Saint-Fargeau. The majority of the very damaged glass at Saint-Julien-du-Sault has already been discussed in the context of the direct influence of the Sainte Chapelle. Notre Dame at Dijon, however, does not follow that tendency at all. The building at Dijon, built near the castle of the dukes of Burgundy, is of exceptional quality; however, only a few pieces of thirteenth-century glass remain in the north transept. The church was begun about 1220 and was probably completed around 1250. Therefore, the glazing in the five lights of the gallery below the rose window can, no doubt, be assigned to the end of the first half of the thirteenth century.

The compositions are very simple: wide lozenges, medallions or pointed quatrefoils subdivided in the center by a vertical bar. The decoration on the rinceaux ground is very rich, and the framing fillets are wide and heavily ornamented. The borders, on the other hand, are very narrow. The figural style is difficult to judge because of extensive restoration, but it does not seem to be related to that of any known workshop in Burgundy or the

▷
111 Geneva, Musée d'Art et d'Histoire: The Kiss of Judas, panel from a Passion of Christ window in the church of Saint Ferréol at Saint-Fargeau (Yonne); 1250–1255. Cf. cat. 72.

112 Livry (Nièvre), church of Notre Dame, bay 1: Virgin and Child; 3rd quarter of the thirteenth century. Cf. cat. 45.

113 Champs-sur-Marne, castle, storage depot of the Monuments Historiques: Saint Peter Awakened by an Angel, quatrefoil from a Saint Peter window in the church at Semur-en-Auxois (Côte-d'Or); after 1240 (?). Cf. cat. 79.

▷
114 Lausanne, cathedral of Notre Dame, south transept arm, rose: Image of the World; ca. 1235. Cf. cat. 109.

Ile-de-France. While the scenes are fairly open, the figures are squat and heavy—reminiscent of the first quarter of the century. The glass painting was undoubtedly very beautiful and very carefully executed, but ninteenth-century restorers also had a hand in it.

An isolated work whose true importance can no longer be evaluated, the stained glass in Notre Dame at Dijon, nevertheless, stands as a Burgundian example of a style that was not derived from the Ile-de-France and that is probably related to the evolution of glass painting at Lyons.[37]

The remnants of the glazing at Saint-Fargeau are no longer in place. Some years ago, Jean Lafond identified Gothic glass from this church in the Musée Ariana in Geneva;[38] it had been removed from Saint-Fargeau in 1876 or 1877 by Didron the Younger and subsequently acquired by the founder of the Geneva museum. While considerably altered in the nineteenth century, the windows have a rather heavy style similar to the work done by some of the workshops at Auxerre. The ornament is fairly traditional, yet certain expressive figures testify to the quality of the workshops.

In the Nièvre area, the Virgin and Child in the church at Livry relates more to central France, Berry and the Loire, than to Burgundy, both in representation and handling. The Saint Peter cycle in Notre Dame at Semur-en-Auxois is also worthy of note; its nervous line-work is not related to the painting style at Saint-Germain-lès-Corbeil as has been recently asserted.

111

112

113

Lyons and Lausanne

The low windows in the apse at Lyons, which date before the first third of the thirteenth century, have already been mentioned. The large figures of prophets in the clerestory of the straight bays in the choir can be dated to the years 1235–1240.[39] There is a certain similarity to the majestic prophets at Bourges and to the figures in the upper choir at Auxerre. Thanks to important nineteenth-century documentation, the extent to which these figures have been restored can be determined.[40] One of the heads of the prophets is very famous; it was removed from the building in the nineteenth century and turned over to the State, which has exhibited it frequently since 1953.[41]

The large rose window in Lausanne Cathedral is one of the masterpieces of western Gothic art in both its form and its meaning. Very good studies have largely resolved the main historical, stylistic and iconographic questions about this monument, which is related to the cathedral at Lyons in many ways.[42] The north transept can probably be dated to the 1230s; the execution of the rose by a certain Pierre d'Arras was no doubt finished before 1235.

Is the Lausanne rose related to the developments in northern France during the first quarter of the century? It is clearly later than the ensembles at Laon, Soissons and Saint-Quentin and made after the west rose of Notre Dame in Paris. However, it is the general concept and iconography that are arresting at Lausanne. The general format of the rose is quite distinct from Chartrain or Parisian formulae, in which figures or scenes radiate around a central oculus. At Lausanne, a square interrupted by foils, with a smaller square set in the center, is placed within a circular rose window. This is an Image of the World developed in space and time and a symbol of knowledge. In the central square (now replaced) were figures of *Annus* (the Year), the Sun, the Moon, Day and Night. In the inner foils were the Four Seasons and the Twelve Months; in the outer ones, the Four Elements—Fire, Earth, Water and Air—surrounded by the Signs of the Zodiac and representations of the Sciences of Divination. In the angles of the large square were the Rivers of Paradise and eight representations of monsters of the earth such as satyrs.

A complete reading of this theological and universalist rose required substantial scholarship and ingenuity. Even the form of juxtaposed squares and circles had profound meaning, suggesting the roundness of the sky and the quadrature of the earth. It is unquestionably the most sophisticated example of thirteenth-century stained glass. The stylistic problems it presents are difficult, though numerous original sections remain in the present rose. Relationships with France are clear—even with the west rose in Notre Dame in Paris—but the style has hardened and become almost schematized. The medium scale of the figures (although they were meant to be seen at a fairly great distance) forced the artist to virtuosity in the rendering of plants, objects and attributes. The paint is abundant and even heavy; the folds often stiff and straight, almost metallic.

Thus, the formal evolution of the Lausanne rose fits into the great movement of the second quarter of the century, although it has absolutely no relation to Parisian or Chartrain work of the same time. Burgundy, it should be remembered, followed its own course, prompted by a force we could term "international," not only in architecture and sculpture but also in glass painting.

Bourges and Chartres: The Last Glazing Campaigns

It is necessary here to return to Bourges Cathedral, where building and decoration continued after 1225–1230. The nave windows are problematic, since large, lightly painted grisaille windows, original or modern, now invariably fill them, the formal type corresponding to the mid century. However, a large number of roses in the windows on the upper level of the aisle and of clerestory windows contain figures and scenes. This is all the more surprising since the roses in the choir and the chevet are decorated with plant motifs or geometric mosaics.

The iconography of the nave roses is quite inconsistent. On the upper level of the aisle on the north side are seated and crowned talking figures (ancestors of Christ or Kings of the Apocalypse?). On the south side of the aisle is a very confused mixture among which elders of the Apocalypse, crowned saints and an Annunciation can be recognized. In the clerestory windows the arrangement is not any more logical. There are fewer elements on the north side than on the south, among them a few paired saints. On the south side are two Marian scenes: an Annunciation and a Coronation of the Virgin as well as paired saints. Thus, the 116 panels do not constitute a program but rather testify to the numerous changes that the original glass underwent. In the westernmost bay in the choir, the figures of prophets on the north side are in a much rougher style than those in the eastern bays. Corresponding to them in the southern windows are two figures of saints and an unidentified bishop, also in a fairly hard style, characterized by broken folds, and of mediocre quality.

It is difficult to imagine the original appearance of the nave at Bourges based on these elements. In the roses, there are a number of large medallions that provide important evidence for the introduction of the "hard" style, though they do not seem to be derived from Chartrain or Parisian examples: for instance, the Annunciation in the clerestory and a number of royal figures. Another important factor intervenes here: many of the figures of saints and kings on the intermediate or upper levels are very "mannerist" in form, with hollow cheeks, prominent foreheads and disquieting, unbalanced expressions that contrast with the harmony proper to the first part of the century. The poses themselves are exaggerated, since we are forced to view the limbs aslant, covered with heavily painted drapery that does not fall straight to the ground but follows diagonal patterns that are sometimes illogical. These same traits will recur at the cathedral of Le Mans, and even at Chartres, and indicate an overall evolution in pictorial style.

The windows in the north transept and some of the windows in the ambulatory at Chartres still need to be discussed. As noted above, the workshop of the "Master of Saint Chéron" provided a precocious example (from 1220-1225) of a style with broken folds and schematized painting. This style led to the creation of certain masterpieces such as the glazing in the south transept; it also led to stiff and summary exaggerations, seen after 57 1230-1235 in the upper eastern windows and in the final composition in the north transept arm. The simplifying tendencies of the years 1220-1230 produced an art brutal in both drawing and color in the figures of high priests and prophets that accompany the image of Saint Ann below the north rose at Chartres. In the eastern windows in this transept, there is a series of apostles rendered in a rigid style, dry and stiff, that must be dated to 1230-1240. Furthermore, the mannerist expression alluded to for the window in the nave at Bourges can be seen in some of the windows in the ambulatory (e.g. the Thomas Becket window): small slender figures in dance-like poses, with huge, asymmetrical heads that have no relationship to the calm, almost classical expressions on the faces of the figures in the Sainte Chapelle.

Le Mans

The workshops at Chartres no doubt stopped working about 1245, the period when the workshops at Le Mans were fully active. As noted above, the Gothic choir of this building was constructed slowly because of the enormous foundations it required. Thus, the outer ambulatory and the radiating chapels were not completed until about 1235. There is little that remains of the original decoration on this level: two windows have been reset in a radiating chapel and illustrate the lives of Saint Eligius and of Saint Nicholas.[43] Stylistically, these two windows follow completely different tendencies. The Saint Eligius window developed out of the tradition of western France; Le Mans was one of its great centers around 1200. The Saint Nicholas window, on the other hand, derives from the Chartrain style of the workshop that produced the Charlemagne and Saint James windows.

The windows in the Lady Chapel, very famous for their iconography,[44] are also related to examples from Chartres. This ensemble is now incomplete, having been damaged in the sixteenth century and reconstructed in a highly arbitrary manner in the nineteenth. The Tree of Jesse, the Childhood of the Virgin, the two windows with the Miracles of the Virgin and

117   Le Mans, cathedral of Saint Julien, chevet, Lady Chapel, bay 2: Childhood of Christ (8th register on the right), Flight into Egypt; ca. 1235-1240.

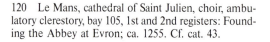

▷ 121 Le Mans, cathedral of Saint Julien, chevet, bay 107, central light: Childhood of Christ (detail), The Nativity; ca. 1250–1255. Cf. cat. 42.

the Passion with typological commentaries are now only partially authentic. Other original panels in the chapel are in the Childhood of Christ window. Christ Among the Gifts of the Holy Spirit, also in a rather conventional style, is depicted in the historiated medallion of a rose window that probably still occupies its original position in the westernmost radiating chapel on the north side.

The choir at Le Mans was built according to the scheme used at Bourges. The upper glazing in the ambulatory is complete. While it has been blackened by corrosion, its authenticity is exceptional for thirteenth-century glass.

On this level there are two completely opposed glazing formulae—the one used in the central window, and the one used in all its surrounding bays on both the north and the south. The central window was the gift of a nobleman, Rotrou V de Montfort, who had himself represented as a kneeling knight presenting his arms (*two leopards passant contournés or*) to the Virgin; these heraldic emblems reappear on his tunic. In the side lights are two imposing, standing figures—Saint Gervase and Saint Protase, patrons of the first cathedral of Le Mans.

The links to Chartres are strong in the monumentality of the images, the stylistic handling and the iconography. The same theme (two allegorical representations of Despair) seen at the bottom of the lights is also found in the windows beneath the north rose at Chartres. The image is strong and powerful because of the ponderousness of the drawing and the plenitude of the color. It stands as one of the masterpieces of Gothic painting in western France in the thirteenth century.

The conception of the other windows at this level is completely different: windows with numerous medallions, often cut into half-medallions and set against ornamental backgrounds, i.e. transposing the formula of the lower "legendary" windows for use in windows further from the ground. To what extent is this formula related to that used on the upper level at the Sainte Chapelle?

The iconography seems to be in disarray: the subjects treated are numerous and often inconsistent within a single bay, which can contain from three to five lights. In some windows, several series of subjects are juxtaposed. There are repeats or reuses of images already found on the lower level, especially in the Lady Chapel. The Glorification and Life of the Virgin recur most frequently, then Christological themes and lives of saints such as Saint Peter (which occurs three times) or Saint Julian (seen twice). This disorder is the

118 Le Mans, cathedral of Saint Julien, choir, ambulatory clerestory, bay 107: Window offered by the vintners (1st light on the left, lower register), The donors; ca. 1255.

119 Le Mans, cathedral of Saint Julien, choir, ambulatory clerestory, bay 107: Window offered by the vintners (2nd light from the left), Life of Saint Julian (4th register), Saint Julian Preaching; ca. 1255.

120 Le Mans, cathedral of Saint Julien, choir, ambulatory clerestory, bay 105, 1st and 2nd registers: Founding the Abbey at Evron; ca. 1255. Cf. cat. 43.

122 Le Mans, cathedral of Saint Julien, choir clerestory, bay 201, right light, middle registers: The Scourging of Saint Gervase; ca. 1254. Cf. cat. 44.

result of numerous and varied donations on the part of abbeys that then belonged to the diocese (Evron and Saint-Calais), by ecclesiastical figures, the nobility and even guilds. For example, the window offered by the vintners establishes the relation between the donation of these works and the consecration of the cathedral's choir in April, 1254—since they arrived late for the ceremony, the vintners had to have a window made as a penalty.

The ornamentation, though varied, is consistent with the trend of the period: the borders are narrow and often reduced to half-borders; the framing fillets are mostly inarticulated; painted detail in the backgrounds is reduced. The ornamental motifs are not really inspired by Parisian examples, and there is, so to speak, no heraldic decoration. In addition to the difference from the central window already noted, the styles of many hands can be distinguished in the scenes; nevertheless, all the windows, with the exception of one, are fairly homogeneous.

The painters working at Le Mans were certainly not from the Sainte Chapelle. While there is some influence of Parisian style, the shapes are more elongated, harder and more agitated than in Paris and form another parallel tendency like those we examined in Champagne and Burgundy. The windows at Le Mans are of exceptional quality and among the finest dating from 1240 to 1255, not only in France but anywhere in western Europe. Their exquisite forms and commanding colors must have been renowned in their day.

On this same level is a window donated by the abbey at Evron that escapes this stylistic definition. Four of its five lights are dedicated to the Childhood of Christ, to the Virgin, to the Legend of Theophilus and to another Marian miracle—the Jewish child of Bourges. The fifth light illustrates the founding of the abbey at Evron. The style is not nearly as evolved as in the main series. The ornament is reduced to narrow borders and half-bosses against an unpainted ground. The uniform compositions are contained in superimposed medallions. The style of the figural panels seems archaic and rustic—doll-like faces with very little modeling, short porportions and conventionally drawn, inelegant folds.

The three windows in the flat chevet of the church at Vivoin (not far from Le Mans) display the same tendencies. Heavily restored in the last century and insensitively completed, these windows show the Childhood of Christ in the central light, the Life of Saint Martin in the left one and the Life of Saint Hippolytus, patron of the church, in the right one.[45] An interesting work painted around 1255, it is nevertheless of very mediocre quality, unlike the exceptional windows at Le Mans.

Let us return to the clerestory of the cathedral at Le Mans. One of the windows on the south side is completely modern. It was made after a hail storm destroyed the previous window. The rest are fairly well-preserved despite some modifications, mostly made in the nineteenth century. The iconographic program is relatively simple. The central window, offered by Bishop Geoffroy de Loudun for the cathedral's consecration in 1254, glorifies the Blessed Virgin and Christ: the Virgin and Child and the Virgin as Intercessor flank Christ on the Cross and Christ the Judge Showing His Wounds. In the lower part of the window, the figure of the donor as a bishop (identified by his shield in the border) is repeated in each of the two lights that form the bay. In the adjoining window to the north are the Martydoms of Saint Gervase and Saint Protase, Saint Stephen and Saint Vincent; the cathedral possessed an important relic of the last.

In the other windows to the north and south are large figures superimposed in pairs within each light. On the north side, prophets are in the lower register and apostles and evangelists in the upper one. On the south side are canonized bishops of Le Mans, all with halos, holding croziers and wearing miters. These are also donated windows, given by bishops or sometimes by the nobility or even guilds, some of which are identified by coats of arms.[46] This extensive series, in which the right windows contain up to six lights that are not easily read from the ground, produces a very majestic effect, although the iconographic and formal presentation are less original.

Stylistically and in terms of palette, the axial window, the left light of the neighboring window to the north and the westernmost window on this same side are distinct from all the other windows on this level. Much lighter in tonality, with a liberal use of white and yellow, these works are expressive to the point of caricature, notably in the Martyrdom of Saint Gervase and Saint Protase. This forceful art seems to have its origins in the lights of the south transept arm at Chartres, with its images of the Evangelists carried on the shoulders of the major prophets—works dating before 1230 that are to be attributed to the "Master of Saint Chéron," the great initiator of the hard style.[47] The westernmost window, with four

123 Le Mans, cathedral of Saint Julien, choir clerestory, bay 223, 2nd light, upper register: Head of an apostle; ca. 1260–1265.

apostles set over major prophets, is clearly of poorer quality than the windows in the chevet and seems to be later; it may represent a late product of the workshop.

123   The second stylistic tendency is seen in windows in which calm, relatively supple forms with powerful expressions dominate. Most are on the north side. Does this style derive from Parisian examples or from precedents in western France?

It has been suggested that a first outline of this formula was tried in Saint Pierre at Chartres; however, the date of the large figures at Saint Pierre has not been satisfactorily established;[48] we are apt to place them after 1260, making the figures at Le Mans clearly earlier.

Are they inspired by models from the Paris region? There is no proof of this, yet it is feasible since the models of Chartres and Bourges are already far away. On the south side, the figures of bishops display a stage of stylistic development that is more advanced toward the mannerism noted repeatedly in this chapter in the rose windows in Paris, the figural roses at Bourges and some Chartrain works. Despite their monotonous frontal postures, the canonized bishops in these windows have bodies with little volume, emaciated faces, hollow cheeks and sunken eyes with a keen, almost uneasy gaze. Seen at close hand, the faces are

135

extraordinarily unreal. Their handling seems very distinct from the traditional art of the mid century with its solid, authoritative modeling.

The dating is at issue here. It seems most unlikely that all the decoration was finished in time for the consecration ceremony in 1254. The axial window may have been in place by this time, but the windows farthest away from the apse were probably not installed before 1260 or 1265.

The latest works in the cathedral at Le Mans date to the last third of the century, during which western France would play a considerable role by turning away from the formula of fully colored glass that is seen in the choir of Le Mans Cathedral. In this respect, the cathedral is exemplary of the tendencies of the mid century, characterized by an almost general hardening of style when compared with the art of the first quarter of the century—an evolution that was not, as has been thought, inspired by the Sainte Chapelle. On the contrary, it took on novel forms according to the region and the workshop. The beginnings of a new esthetic, opposed to that of the first half of the century, were visible in the same period. In the next chapter, on stained glass after 1250–1260, the resistance to and compromises with this new esthetic, which were sometimes surprising and of monumental importance for medieval painting, will be discussed.

The Second Half of the Thirteenth Century in France

A profound change came about in French stained glass, beginning in the period 1255–1260. It spread, to a certain extent, into regions that had not been involved in Gothic innovation up to this point such as the Midi and Lorraine, and it became lighter and then "whiter". The latter phenomena, which had many causes, have been analyzed on numerous occasions.[1] "Full-color" windows—walls of scintillating glass, impressionistic in their effect, of which the Sainte Chapelle is a sort of apotheosis—lost their primacy and were replaced by a new formula in stained glass where translucence and legibility dominated.

The reasons for this change will be discussed later; a study of the monuments shows that it did not happen right away. The renewal of formal and chromatic expression took several decades and a number of attempts (sometimes naive and moving as in the window with the patron saint in Sainte Radegonde at Poitiers) before it became as inventive as the formulae of the preceding centuries. The change underscores the extraordinary possibilities inherent in the technique of glass painting and the talent of the artists who practiced it. As always, the change did not take place in a completely linear fashion: certain provinces, workshops and patrons were not inclined to go along with the innovations and resisted them for a length of time. Consequently, in buildings glazed partly or entirely during the second half of the thirteenth century, one often sees a juxtaposition of earlier traditions in glass painting and of "modern" creations.

Often it is a question of generations. In the cathedral at Clermont-Ferrand, glazing in the radiating chapels remained faithful to the tradition of dark glass in superimposed medallions set against a mosaic ground. The first works were installed around 1260 or 1265, beginning with the axial chapel. In the upper story, decorated in the years 1285–1290, however, the formula chosen makes use of figures set under an architectural canopy and surrounded by grisaille panels. This cathedral in the Auvergne was not an isolated case, and similar examples could easily be cited.[2] But the monument that inaugurated this formula, "*appelée à un grand avenir*" ("destined for a great future")[3] is the cathedral at Tours, where subjects—figures or scenes—are arranged in band-windows and are less important than the light grisaille panels.

Tours Cathedral: A Pivotal Monument

It has often been said that thirteenth-century glass in Tours Cathedral falls within the sphere of influence of the Sainte Chapelle. This is both true and false. Beginning in 1233 or 1234 the cathedral at Tours was rebuilt according to an archaic formula. King Louis IX was interested in this monument and accelerated its construction up to the time of his departure for the crusade in 1248.[4] The earliest windows were those in the radiating chapels, which may have been in place around 1245. A single example of these windows remains: the New Alliance window in the axial bay of the Lady Chapel. The composition, ornamentation and figural style of this very restored work (like the windows in the Lady Chapel of the cathedral at Le Mans) are subordinate to Chartrain traditions descended from the "classical" workshop.

The king's captivity prevented resumption of work at Tours before 1254 or 1255; however, unlike the lower story, the triforium and the upper windows were erected according to resolutely "modern" principles, i.e. derived from Parisian Gothic art. As for the glazing of these two stories, they opened a new stage in the evolution of French Gothic glass, while remaining faithful in many respects to earlier examples.

On the triforium level at Tours, a procession of apostles in the bays of the apse surrounds a Virgin and Child accompanied by two censing angels. The figures are elegant and well placed—at ease inside the light and free within the frame; some are in profile, their feet

124 Tours, cathedral of Saint Gatien, chevet, triforium, bay 103: Apostle; 1255–1260. Cf. cat. 88.

offset. The paint is distributed over large surfaces that model the figures, giving them volume and legibility. Two coats of arms found within the tracery provided M. Lillich with the means of dating this very corroded group of glass to about 1255, which seems plausible.[5] Today the windows in the straight bays contain light grisaille panels. Most of them are modern; however, the few original fragments that survive in the lights on the north side (which can be dated to the second half of the thirteenth century) are sufficient to reconstruct the original concept of this pierced triforium.

There was light glass in the straight bays, blending into the architecture, and full-color glass in the hemicycle, seemingly incrusted behind the arcades, which reproduced in each bay (in a reduced scale) the outline of the upper windows. It was probably here that the new relationship between stained glass and architecture began; in any case, the triforium at Tours is the first evidence of this phenomenon.[6]

The same can be said of the clerestory at Tours, but for different reasons. The earliest windows on this level are contemporary or perhaps slightly later than those in the triforium. Several chronological points of reference enable them to be dated to between 1255 and 1270, notably the "signatures" of donors and events such as the Translation of the Relics of Saint Mauritius in 1267. Thus, the window dedicated to him in the first bay to the north of the axis was probably installed at that time; it was donated by Geoffroy de Freslon, bishop of Le Mans from 1258 to 1269.

The iconographic program is imposing. First of all, there are the full-color windows: a Passion in the axis, as in the Sainte Chapelle, accompanied (on the south) by a Childhood of Christ and a Jesse Tree in the same window. Most of the other windows illustrate lives of saints venerated at the time such as Stephen, Peter, Nicholas, or local saints such as Martin and Julian (formerly identified as Saint Martialis).[7] Royal iconography also plays a role with the depiction of Saint Dionysius or Saint Vincent, a relic of whom had been given to the abbey of Saint Germain des Prés in Paris in 1215 by the future King Louis VIII. A single window treated the Old Testament and illustrated the beginning of the Book of Genesis up to the death of Cain. This choice, as well as a large part of the program, is thought to have been inspired by Archbishop Pierre de Lamballe (1252–1256), a former theologian at the University of Paris, and by his friend, Jacques de Guérande, dean of the chapter. The latter donated the Saint Peter glass in the second window north of the axis when he became bishop of Nantes in 1264.

The formal choice of superimposed medallions is somewhat surprising, but evidence suggests that it derives from the formula glorified by the workshops of the Sainte Chapelle. Nevertheless, there are clear differences from work in the Parisian building, partly due to an adaptation of glass set quite far from the ground, for viewing at this distance. Instead of being divided by armatures forged into the shape of the compartments, the windows have a rectilinear grid. The figural compositions extend over two registers; there are six compositions per light, joined by ornamental bosses, and the decoration has been simplified.

The colors are also distinct from those in Paris. The traditional blue/red harmony has been toned down by the repeated use of yellow and green and by using blue and green together, as they seldom had been up to now, for instance in the Saint Eustace window.[8]

The compartments contain a limited number of figures; consequently, the protagonists in a single scene are sometimes distributed among several medallions, which is an innovation. The figural style, while connected to the Parisian orbit, has developed thinner lines and displays tension that did not exist at the Sainte Chapelle: silhouettes are elongated; they stand on skinny legs; gestures are rapid and sophisticated, and clothing forms angular or prismatic drapery.

It has recently been suggested that these windows were produced in three campaigns between 1255 and 1270, beginning with the windows in the hemicycle, to which the Creation window must be added.[9] According to this idea, they were executed by a single Parisian workshop. In fact, even in the earliest works, the formal qualities of these windows seem close to those of royal manuscripts executed after the return of King Louis IX from captivity such as the Psalter of Saint Louis (Paris, Bibl. Nat., ms. lat. 10525) or the Third Evangelary of the Sainte Chapelle (Paris, Bibl. Nat., ms. lat. 17326).[10] The windows are already far from the Sainte Chapelle style and mark a step towards the mannerism of the 1270s.[11] Given the present corroded and blackened state of this glass, it remains difficult to establish a precise chronology and to evaluate differences among workshops that follow the same formal and stylistic models despite the passage of several years.

125

126

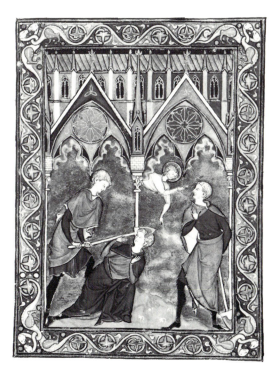

125 Tours, cathedral of Saint Gatien, choir clerestory, bay 207: Genesis (detail), The Fall of Adam and Eve; ca. 1255–1260. Cf. cat. 90.

126 Paris, Bibliothèque Nationale: ms. lat. 10 525, Psalter of Saint Louis, fol. 2: Tobit Dazzled by the Archangel Raphael; after 1255.

28   Two windows do not follow the "full-color" pattern: the Canons of Loches and the Bishops of Tours windows, which face each other across the apse in the first straight bay of the choir. The figures are set under architectural canopies (two per light) and separated by wide bands of light grisaille. This "band-window" type of composition, the earliest preserved examples of which are at Tours, would gain popularity in various forms during the last decades of the thirteenth century.

The formula had already been adopted in the Lady Chapel of Saint Germain des Prés, as both Sauval and J. Lafond attested.[12] It was also unquestionably the choice applied in Saint Denis around 1240–1245 for the clerestory window in the nave, as can be seen from certain extant documents; windows in the apse remained in "full-color".[13] Again, the glazing at Tours seems to derive from Parisian models. Here, however, perhaps because of conservatism (other motives have also been suggested[14]), the master-overseer or the patrons

139

restricted themselves to two windows, which disrupt the unity of the program in both formal and iconographic terms. Are they trial pieces or the result of prior experience? Because the date the windows were executed is not certain, the question is difficult to answer. The Canons of Loches window cannot date before 1259, the year the castle at Loches was integrated into the Capetian domain.

Figural style is essential to understanding the development of glass painting in western France during the last third of the thirteenth century. The presentation of figures is simple, whether frontal (the Bishops of Tours window) or in profile; sometimes the figures are

127   Tours, cathedral of Saint Gatien, ambulatory, 1st south radiating chapel, bay 8: Life of Saint Martin (right light, 3rd register), Mass of Saint Martin; 1270–1280.

▷
128   Tours, cathedral of Saint Gatien, choir clerestory, bay 206: The Canons of Loches, after a color lithograph in BOURRASSÉ and MANCEAU, *Verrières du choeur de l'église métropolitaine de Tours*, Tours, 1849, pl. V; after 1259. Cf. cat. 89.

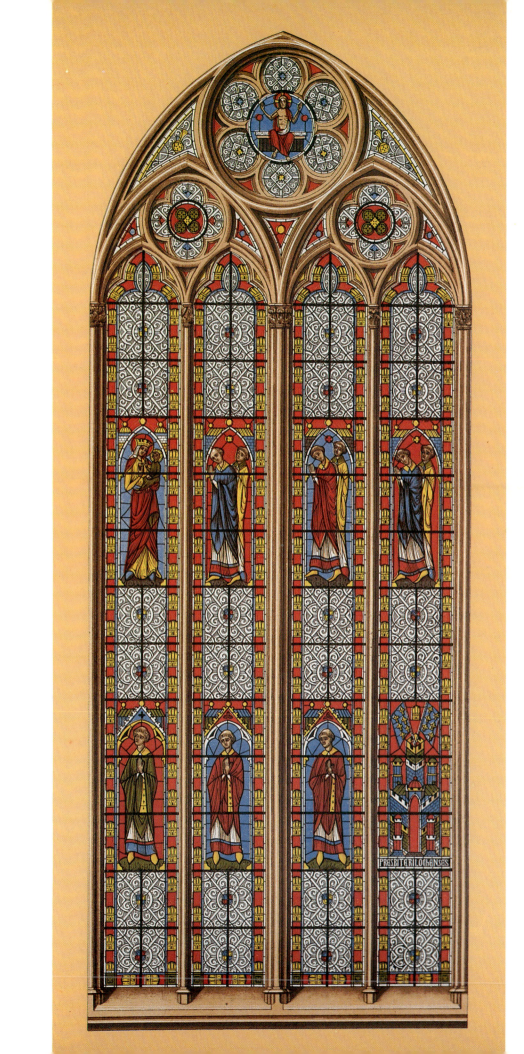

grouped in twos and threes (the Canons of Loches window). The silhouettes show line-work that is still Parisian but already heavier. The pictorial treatment differs from that of the upper "full-color" windows and is closer to the figures in the triforium—the modeling is more brutal, the contour lines more incisive and the details chosen sometimes exaggerated. These new conventions would be echoed by most of the workshops in western France belonging to the "second school" of western France (the first being that of the Romanesque workshops).

After this analysis, the cathedral at Tours, or at least its glazing, seems to be a key monument, a watershed between what would soon be the archaic "full-color" windows and the innovative "band-window", dear to M. Lillich.[15] As for style, the same "mannerism" already seen in the upper windows is present, and the development of specifically French tendencies is evident, notably in the figures of canons and bishops of Tours in the triforium.

A number of windows in the radiating chapels at Tours merit discussion. Most come from the former abbey church of Saint Julien, which explains their poor condition and the obvious modifications. Among them are a Childhood, a Passion, lives of Saint Julian of Brioude and of Saint Ferréol, and several panels from a Creation window, the iconographic sources of which are identical to those in the upper choir.[16] The execution may be contemporary with the first glazing campaign for the clerestory windows but is the product of a workshop with different, more conservative traditions.

This activity continued at least until the end of the century. The Saint Martin window (now divided between two bays in the first radiating chapel to the south, but coming from a window in the transept according to the scholar Boissonnot) is still of very high quality, despite the numerous restorations carried out at the time of the transfer. While the compositions have become less inventive and the treatment is a little more relaxed, the faces display the graphic tension and painterly quality characteristic of western French workshops.

Is the axial window in the church at Saint-Michel-en-Brenne (Indre) to be set within the circle of influence of Tours? Contemporary with the construction of the building in the last third of the thirteenth century, the glass occupies four lights. Figures in scenes mostly taken from the Passion are enclosed in architectural canopies and framed with grisaille panels. The borders retain heraldic decoration consisting of castles of Castile and fleurs-de-lis, and the style follows the angular and already mannerist drawing of scenes found in the clerestory windows at Tours. The connection would be tempting if these formal choices had not become common in the last decades of the thirteenth century.[17]

"Full-Color" Windows: Persistency and Innovation

While the glazing in the cathedral at Tours marks a decisive stage in the evolution of French glass in the years 1255–1260, there are a number of monuments that remained faithful to earlier traditions, confining themselves to windows saturated with color.

Clermont-Ferrand

Because of the extent of its "full-color" Gothic glazing, the cathedral at Clermont-Ferrand is a logical starting point. The colored glass fills all the windows in the radiating chapels with the exception of the axial window in the third chapel to the south, where earlier panels from the Romanesque cathedral are installed.[18] Until very recently, it was thought that the Gothic cathedral at Clermont was begun just before the departure of Bishop Hugues de La Tour for the crusade in 1248.[19] Recent work by M. Davis, however, has allowed the redating of the building campaign to the beginning of the decade.[20] The construction of the radiating chapels must have been slow, because the marriage of the Dauphin in 1262 was not held there; however, the following year a canon asked to be buried *"in novo aedificio"*—"in the new building". Therefore, the construction must have been finished there by that time, and the first windows (in the axial chapel) were probably already, or just about to be, installed. The five radiating chapels, each with three identical bays of two lights surmounted by a tympanum, belong to the first building campaign, which continued in the chapels opening

129 Clermont-Ferrand, cathedral treasury: Last Supper (detail), Three Apostles, fragment from one of the windows depicting Saint Austremonius (?) in the cathedral at Clermont-Ferrand; ca. 1265.

off the straight bays of the choir during another decade, until about 1270. The same time lag can also be observed in the windows.

The glazing program poses certain archeological problems, because the single window in the last radiating chapel to the south opening on the transept contains vestiges of lost windows. One treats the Story of Moses; others the hagiography of the building, of Saint Agricola and Saint Vitalis (the first patrons of the cathedral) and of Saint Artemius, bishop of Clermont in the fourth century. Furthermore, in the composite window, Romanesque panels are installed among others, and one can also see some remains of a Life of Saint Caprasius, bishop of Agen, who was venerated together with Saint Faith (Foy). These elements, which also date to the years 1265–1275, may have come from windows demolished during the construction of the eastern part of the transept. The Lady Chapel deviates from standard iconography: in the center, a Childhood of Christ, flanked by the Miracle of Theophilus to the south and a Life of Saint John the Baptist to the north, where an altar was dedicated to him. The other light illustrates the Parable of the Prodigal Son, which (like the Miracle of Theophilus) provided an example of a repentant sinner. An important Christological cycle containing the Passion and the Resurrection of Jesus and His ties with the Apostles, including an Ascension and a Pentecost, was "thrust aside" into the side windows of the third radiating chapel to the south. The other windows illustrated lives of saints popular in the thirteenth century: Saint George, Saint Mary Magdalene, Saint Margaret and Saint Agatha, or local saints such as Saint Austremonius, "the apostle of the Auvergne," and his disciple Saint Privatus, who evangelized Gevaudan; and Saint Bonitus, bishop of Clermont in the seventh century. In many cases, the chapels were dedicated to these saints.

The legends are illustrated according to the traditional formula in numerous superimposed compartments. Often they extend over the three windows of the same chapel, as in the case of the lives of Saint Austremonius or of Mary Magdalene. The ornamentation derives from models of the first half of the century or from those that became popular after the Sainte Chapelle, e.g. heraldic motifs. Here, however, the resemblance ends. Contrary to what has long been maintained,[21] the workshops responsible for this ensemble were not connected to those in the royal domain and even less to those in the Sainte Chapelle. Although there is a clear hardening of forms, the style is a blend of other traditions that vary depending on the works considered. The survival of Byzantinizing influence can be seen, for example, in the Moses panels; connections with the transept rose in the primatial church at Lyons, or with Burgundian workshops, can be seen in the Childhood window. In the most recent windows such as that of Saint Agatha, the style has evolved toward "mannerist" formulae. The chronology of the ensemble is not certain, and the various workshops have yet to be satisfactorily distinguished. Because of the numerous modifications that these windows have undergone, great caution must be exercised until the material analysis has been completed.[22]

The windows in the clerestory are a dozen years later in date. To the north and the south of the central window with Christ and the Virgin are a procession of apostles followed by prophets. The prophets hold wide scrolls on which one of their predictions concerning the Virgin Mary is written. They are placed beneath architectural canopies in the middle of uncolored grisaille panels, according to the format current at the end of the thirteenth century. The brutal effect has been accented by major restorations of the glass at the end of the last century.[23]

The Ile-de-France between 1260 and 1280

Although full-color glass was outmoded as a formal choice in its compositions and its handling of figures and color, its development did not atrophy. In the Ile-de-France and in Normandy, this formula even led to a new definition of figuration, characterized by a tiny scale of execution and precious, mannerist line-work. This change, which was not confined to stained glass,[24] was linked to the spread of Parisian illumination, the dominant technique—the one that was most imitated—during the last part of the reign of Saint Louis.[25]

In Paris itself, the situation is disconcerting: very little has been preserved from this period, which is known to have been brilliant in architectural and other artistic realms.[26] In the Ile-de-France, the situation is a little better. The church at Saint-Sulpice-de-Favières,

130 Paris, Musée de Cluny: Calvary, Paris (?); ca. 1275–1280.

▷

131 Saint-Sulpice-de-Favières (Essonne), church of Saint Sulpice, south aisle, east wall, bay 6: The Life of the Virgin Mary and the Childhood of Christ; ca. 1255–1260. Cf. cat. 76.

near Etampes, southwest of Paris, and the ancient priory church at Gassicourt, to the northwest of Paris near Mantes, testify to the dynamism and quality of the Parisian workshops and of those associated with them.

The church of Saint Sulpice, the site of an important pilgrimage in honor of the patron saint—Saint Sulpicius, one of the first bishops of Bourges—was rebuilt for the second time beginning in 1245–1250, at the same time as the Sainte Chapelle. The construction of the chevet and the choir demonstrates Parisian virtuosity. They are among the masterpieces of the "Court Style" in the Ile-de-France;[27] the nave, however, was not completed until the fourteenth century. Only three windows of the original glazing survive, two of which are brightly colored.

The first (set in the east bay of the south aisle) is the quintessential Parisian work of the 1260s. Following the historiated type of window, the lights contain a Life of the Virgin. In the multifoil rose in the tracery are a Virgin and Child receiving homage from angels. In the trefoils that top the side lights, Saint Peter and Saint Paul Enthroned participate in the image of glory. The decoration, which is almost completely heraldic, has become lighter, often using a checked pattern of gold fleurs-de-lis and small blue lozenges. The desire for legibility that was often absent at the Sainte Chapelle is in evidence here, enhanced by rapid but precise painterly treatment. Though the scale of execution is small, the compositions are open and limited to two or three people per scene. The plain backgrounds in blue or red occupy a large area, which represents an innovation in comparison with the Sainte Chapelle. The drawing of the slender figures, often standing at ease, manages to suggest movement with just a few lines. It emphasizes attitudes and gestures more than facial expression, following a principle of contemporary Parisian manuscript illumination. The palette, while keeping to the traditional dominance of blue and red, often includes yellow; its use and distribution reinforce the impression of ease and freedom already suggested by other stylistic components.

The second piece of evidence is an incomplete work that has been reused in the axial bay of the chevet with other diverse fragments from lost windows.[28] It consists of two panels from a Life of the Virgin, twenty years later than the one just analyzed: a Nativity and an Adoration of the Magi. The Adoration, which is much better preserved than the Nativity, is of remarkable quality. The composition is organized around two trefoil arcades—one of

131-1

134

132   Saint-Sulpice-de-Favières (Essonne), church of Saint Sulpice, south aisle, bay 6: The Life of the Virgin Mary and the Childhood of Christ (central light, lower register), One of St Ann's Neighbors Is Surprised That She Is Pregnant; 1255–1260. Cf. cat. 76.

▷
133   Saint-Sulpice-de-Favières (Essonne), church of Saint Sulpice, south aisle, east wall, bay 6: The Life of the Virgin Mary and the Childhood of Christ (right light, 2nd register), Presentation in the Temple (detail), The Virgin Mary Holding the Christ Child and Accompanied by a Serving Maid; ca. 1255–1260. Cf. cat. 76.

134 Saint-Sulpice-de-Favières (Essonne), church of Saint Sulpice, chevet, bay 0, right light: The Adoration of the Magi; ca. 1280. Cf. cat. 75.

▷

135, 136 Private Collection (USA): The Visitation and The Nativity, medallions from a Childhood of Christ window in the church at Mantes-Gassicourt (Yvelines); ca. 1270–1280. Cf. cat. 48.

which has unfortunately been mutilated—under which the figures are set. The refined drawing and precise decoration are in keeping with the delicate workmanship. The figure of the Virgin is both natural (even tender in the dreamy look that she gives her Son) and majestic in attitude, close to that of non-monumental Parisian sculpture of the years 1270 to 1280.[29] While the tonality remains dark—a concession to the traditions of the middle of the century—the effect is completely different, renewed by the characteristics discussed.

A similar evolution can be seen in the windows in the former priory church at Gassicourt. The present building dates from the twelfth century, but its eastern sections were redone in the middle of the thirteenth: a flat chevet replaced the circular apse, and the transept was vaulted.[30] Following this building campaign, in the years 1270 to 1280, most of the bays received glazed decoration. The large figures of saints set in pairs under architectural canopies are less interesting than the three historiated windows in the transept and the chevet, for the formal choice in the former is archaic and the iconographic program simple, despite the (rare) presence of Saint Hugh of Semur, who founded the priory in the eleventh century. Moreover, the numerous restorations make an analysis of the style difficult.

The first legendary window contains the martyrdoms of the most popular deacons of the Middle Ages—Saint Stephen, Saint Lawrence and Saint Vincent—in the three lights of the eastern bay in the south transept. The composition is traditional. The shape of the historiated compartments (quatrefoils pierced at the angles by the point of an inscribed square) used since the 1210s, had been revived at the end of the thirteenth century. The type of border had been in use since the middle of the century; however, the small scale of execution and the nervous, fine drawing of the figures are far from that of Parisian workshops

137 Fécamp, church of La Trinité, Lady Chapel, bay 5: Life of Saint Catherine of Alexandria (right light, 3rd register), Saint Catherine Discoursing with Two Philosophers; ca. 1275. Cf. cat. 38.

in the middle of the century and follow more recent conventions from other areas such as Normandy, the Vexin or even Beauvais.

A different workshop was responsible for the Childhood. Only six panels remain *in situ*, regrouped in a window in the north transept; other panels are in an American collection.[31] The compositions, set in oval compartments, are ordered rhythmically by architectural elements. The elegance of the figures is further accented by the preciousness of their gestures and by the straightforward coloring, where white is used for its own sake. Monumentality is sacrificed to refined effects, but the attitudes and gestures retain a certain naturalism nevertheless.

The masterpiece of this ensemble, however, is the axial window in the chevet, illustrating the Passion and the Appearances of Christ between His Resurrection and Pentecost. The narrative prolixity of the work is still great, but the iconographic treatment has been modified: the protagonists are few in number and move without constraint within the oval compartments that are linked by ornamental bosses. In addition to the characteristics analyzed in the preceding works, the style of drawing has become energetic here, (perhaps not exclusively a Parisian trait) and a brilliance of color of a kind previously unknown is attained; it looks forward to art around 1300.

Normandy during the Third Quarter of the Thirteenth Century

When Jean Lafond published the remains of the glass from the chapel of the Commandery of Sainte-Vaubourg near Rouen, which he discovered reused in the abbey church of Saint Denis and in the church at Hautot-sur-Seine (Seine-Maritime), he underscored their gracile, cursive style that was distinct from Parisian art of the middle of the century.[32] The chapel (consecrated in 1264) was originally decorated with grisaille glass on the sides and with legendary windows in the chevet, notably a Childhood and a Passion of Christ. Only a few panels from these windows remain, to which may be added a number of figures of apostles, prophets and knights Templar (mostly fragmentary), many of which have been reinstalled in the Gothic chapel of the Commandery of Elancourt at Saint-Quentin-en-Yvelines, near Versailles. A king from a Jesse Tree that has recently been discovered in an American collection may have belonged to this ensemble.[33] In the best-preserved (although devitrified) panel—the Adoration of the Magi—the composition follows the traditional symmetric pattern, and the colors remain dark. The treatment, while reduced to essentials, is not fully independent of the principles of the middle of the century.

In the legendary series of Saint Catherine and Saint Margaret in the abbey church at Fécamp, figural style in Normandy reaches a stage that will lead to newly invigorated forms. Definite study of these works has not yet been undertaken, and the date of their execution is imprecise. According to Jean Lafond, the series were done in the years 1275–1280.[34] The provenance of these saints' lives is likewise uncertain; their reuse in the straight bays of the Lady Chapel (rebuilt at the end of the fifteenth century on the foundations of the earlier one) is poorly documented.[35] It is not known whether these works belong to the decoration of the first building (constructed in the second half of the thirteenth century) or to that of the chapel of the Virgins situated between the abbot's palace and the prior's dwelling in the monastery, and which was demolished in 1682.[36] As a result of transfer, the cycles are incomplete; they have been reset, and some scenes are not legible.

While retaining the use of "full color," the pictorial and graphic treatment inaugurates a stylistic phase that will be further discussed at the end of this chapter—freedom of composition, figures transformed into figurines with nervous and supple movements accented by precise gestures, often exaggerated by the tapering calligraphic lines of the hands. In drapery, emphasized by the almost abstract shape of the cut pieces, beaked folds are multiplied, and broken folds are accentuated. A few lines suffice to render the energetic expression of the faces and to give movement to the successive ridges of curling hair. The palette was lightened not only by the frequent use of yellow but above all by the introduction of soft color tones such as purplish rose and acid green. These innovations do not stem solely from English and Parisian illumination, as has often been suggested, but also from contemporary illumination in Normandy.[37]

Amiens: Bernard d'Abbeville's Window (1269)

It is necessary to return to the cathedral at Amiens, and specifically, to the axial window in the chevet clerestory. A wide inscription covering the four narrow lights gives the window's date as 1269 and the name of the donor who is offering the window to the Virgin Mary as Bishop Bernard d'Abbeville (1259–1281). The two figures, accompanied in the registers by four angels carrying crowns, are repeated twice. The present disposition is probably not original and results from the combination of several distinct windows. Nevertheless, the date of 1269 has to be retained for the inscription and for one of the series that is close in style, as if it were intended for the middle lights in this bay. The excessively elongated figures are tightly framed within the narrow lights. The body of the Virgin extends over more than three of the four registers in which her silhouette is placed. Her very small head retains a lively expression of benevolent tenderness for her Son. A tendency towards enlarged proportions was already nascent in certain windows of the middle of the century such as the Saint James windows, the remains of which are now stored at Champs-sur-Marne, or in the extensively restored figures in the triforium. Here the tendency attains a monumental expression that is absolutely exceptional. This is also one of the first times that pictorial treatment becomes linear—reduced to trace lines that are more or less wide, and more or less emphatic. The palette is also considerably lighter because of the repeated use of large areas of white and light blue. Finally, figures are presented under canopies, fictitious architectural elements that will attain ever more importance in stained glass from the 1270s.

Lorraine

Besides Alsace, which will be discussed in the next chapter, Lorraine retains windows in "full color," datable to the middle of the century and the decades that followed. Until then, Lorraine had not been a *terre à vitraux* ("a center of glass painting"): from the Romanesque period, there is only one survival, a small Crucifixion of Saint Segolina at Metz.[38] From the beginning of the thirteenth century, there are the few stray vestiges of a Life of Saint Paul from the church of Saint Paul au Cloître at Metz, reused in a window in the south transept of the cathedral. The scenes are set against a rinceaux ground, a popular motif in the Romanesque period in France and in the Holy Roman Empire.[39] The heavy treatment follows certain conventions of stained glass in Champagne in the years around 1200.[40]

Gothic architecture arrived late in Lorraine, as did stained glass. The earliest examples date only from the 1240s, notably at Toul, an important center where French and German traditions met. At the cathedral, two poorly conserved windows from this period remain. Since 1836 they have been installed in the chapels oriented to open on the transept. They come from the bays in the chevet, which were rebuilt from 1220 or 1221 and glazed several decades later, thanks to the generosity of Bishop Roger de Mercy (1230–1253).[41] The glass is very mutilated and includes numerous scenes (such as the one on the left) that cannot be deciphered. In the scene on the right are elements from a Life of the Virgin, now in disorder. Under the circumstances, it is difficult to judge the style. The treatment remains awkward, even naive, and far from the virtuosity of "French" workshops; it is more receptive to German taste.

The windows that interest us in the former collegiate church of Saint Gengoult at Toul are much better preserved than those in the cathedral. The church was founded in the tenth century; rebuilding began in the middle of the thirteenth century and continued during the fourteenth and fifteenth centuries. A different workshop was associated with each building campaign, as Abbé J. Choux has recently observed.[42] The earliest window, datable to the years 1260–1270, is in the axis of the chevet; it is composed of two long, narrow lights surmounted by a rose and depicts, on the right, a Life of Christ and, on the left, the Life of Saint Gangolfus, patron of the church, a virtuous knight whose wife had him murdered. The arrangement remains simple: fourteen superimposed medallions, one per register, flanked by wide vegetal borders that seem precious. The often symmetrical compositions are not very inventive. The stocky proportions of the figures are made even heavier by labored modeling. The decoration follows the conventions of German *Spätromanisch* style: framing the compartments with a number of wide fillets, some of which are richly decorated.[43] On

138 Amiens, cathedral of Notre Dame, chevet clerestory, bay 200, right lights, 3rd to 6th registers: Bishop Bernard d'Abbeville Offering a Window to the Virgin Mary; 1269.

139 Toul (Meurthe-et-Moselle), church of Saint Gengoult, chevet, bay 0: Life of Saint Gangolfus (left light, 7th register), The Adulterous Behavior of Gangolfus's Wife Ganea; 1260–1270. Cf. cat. 87.

140 Avioth (Meuse), church of Notre Dame, nave clerestory, bay 111: Life of Christ (2nd light from the left, 6th register), Adoration of the Magi; after 1300.

the other hand, the dark coloring uses the blue/red harmony preferred by French workshops until the middle of the century.

The "full-color" formula was retained in Lorraine during the last quarter of the thirteenth century and the beginning of the fourteenth. In the church of Saint Gengoult this can be seen in a number of windows, for example the Saint Agatha window. The ornament has become more "French": mosaics with flaccid lead lines, heraldic motifs such as fleurs-de-lis for the backgrounds or castles of Castile for the borders. This last tendency also dominates other works, for instance the window in the church at Choloy-Ménillot near Toul,[44] and the remains of two windows dedicated to Saint Deodatus, the cathedral's patron saint, in the cathedral of Saint Dié.[45] On the other hand, German tradition predominates in several isolated medallions illustrating the martyrdoms of numerous apostles in the cathedral at Metz.[46] Dating from around 1300 or slightly thereafter is a Life of Christ in Notre Dame at Avioth (Meuse), fifteen medallions of which survive. In these, the scale has become thinner and the style of drawing, while still somewhat awkward, has become supple, in imitation of French models. Some scenes are set against damascene grounds—one of the decorative innovations of German stained glass dating to the end of the thirteenth century.

Let us return to the church of Saint Gengoult. The glazing in the eastern parts of the church was conceived according to a formal program (now partly destroyed) that would become widespread during the last third of the thirteenth century. Polychrome windows were set into the axis of the building to capture a certain brilliance, and light grisaille windows were set around them in the straight bays of the choir. Sometimes such grisaille windows were used in conjunction with one figure (as here); at other times with several, or even with scenes. Use of this formula extended rapidly, varying with architectural conditions and workshops. It totally changed the conditions underlying glass painting.

Predominately Colorless Grisaille Windows and Mixed Windows

Typology of Grisaille Windows in the Thirteenth Century

The predominately colorless grisaille window was probably born at the same time as stained glass. Romanesque grisaille, discussed in *Le Vitrail roman*,[47] will not be treated here, nor will the conditions of its development during the thirteenth century, which were outlined in the first chapter of this book. We only need reiterate that this type of window seems to have been more widely used from the twelfth century than preserved elements would suggest, for these works were more vulnerable to damage than those in full color containing iconography. Moreover, the quality of this glass was surely one of the major reasons for its disappearance—it became corroded and opaque, thus necessitating change. This was also the case in the first half of the thirteenth century, but the number of windows being made at that time was so great that numerous examples remain, notably in Champagne (Essômes, Troyes, Sens, Orbais, Reims) and in cathedrals (Chartres and Bourges).

The tradition of unpainted grisaille (blank glazing) with "Cistercian" decoration (principally strapwork), persisted throughtout the thirteenth century in buildings as different as Saint Jean at Sens (around 1240), Saint Jean aux Bois (1220–1230), the abbey church at Saint-Martin-aux-Bois (1260–1270) and the cathedral at Châlons (1250). Paradoxically, none of these was built by the order of Bernard of Clairvaux;[48] Cistercian influence does not seem to have been a determining factor in the continuing use of grisaille. Other arguments have been advanced to justify this choice, for example the distance from the ground of the clerestory windows of the choir in the cathedral at Beauvais (1260–1270).[49]

Most of the grisaille windows were painted, i.e. enlivened with plant motifs, usually espaliered with flower-shaped ornaments and leaflets which, until the middle of the century, remained confined within the leading and enclosed in geometric figures. The latter—circles, ovals and lozenges—are set axially to the window and connected by fillets forming a network that became increasingly flaccid. Beginning around 1200, the geometric figures were set against a ground with fine cross hatching known as *cages à mouches* (literally, "fly screens"), which altered the light further and brought floral elements into prominence. The use of color, reduced to a few accents at first, gained ground after 1240 and began to be used in the fillets in which compositions were set, or was transformed into big brooches as in Saint

141 Saint-Jean-aux-Bois (Oise), church of Saint Jean, bay 4, 3rd and 4th registers: Grisaille with plant motifs connected by fillets; ca. 1230.

Urbain at Troyes (around 1270–1280). In the last decades of the century, the plant constructions became continuous, lengthened to form narrow rinceaux and freed themselves from the constraints of the cut glass. Their motifs crossed the leading and were set in counterpoint to it, like branches spreading freely along a trellis. The hatched ground disappeared at this point.

The decorative repertory, with its generally summary but heavy style of drawing, was not modeled (except in some borders) on the full-color windows and followed its own evolution. In the earliest examples, the drawing of the leaves is broadly rendered but undifferentiated. After 1220–1230, they became slightly more delicate and were decorated with small berries arranged in clusters, as in a window in the cathedral at Chartres.[50] Not until around 1250–1260 did some recognizable individual elements appear, mixed with the preceding ones, as in Saint Urbain at Troyes. This vocabulary would become naturalistic, taking as its model the ivy leaf, the strawberry plant, or even clover, as in the cathedral at Sées (around 1280) in the last decades of the thirteenth century.

Some windows did not follow these currents, notably in Champagne during the first quarter of the thirteenth century. Among the numerous, often incomplete examples of grisaille that decorate the former Benedictine abbey church at Orbais, near Epernay, several have juxtaposed circular motifs, abundantly trimmed with painted leaves and enlivened with touches of color. Their arrangement and the density of the decoration connect them with German grisailles—a sort of carpet from which the German windows take their name *(Teppichfenster)*—and are characteristic of late Romanesque art in the Holy Roman Empire.

In the earliest examples, probably datable to the end of the twelfth century, plant motifs are confined within a frame that is richly decorated. Then, in later examples from around 1210–1220, the floral montage becomes relaxed, and the frame is lightened and standardized into a smooth narrow fillet that links the compositions together, as is usual in this type of window. A number of buildings in northern France have glass that follows this formula. In Saint Remi at Reims, some of today's modern examples were done after plates in Cahier and Martin's book. Other windows are at Essômes (Aisne) and in Saint Jean aux Bois, where, in one instance, the background has a *cage à mouches* (fine hatching), probably indicating a later date of execution, around 1225.[51]

The choir of that former abbey church has a historiated window with a Passion of Christ in the axial bay; it is contemporary with the series of light windows that surrounds it. One of the grisaille windows seems to be isolated from the rest by its luxurious composition, which is close to that of windows in the abbey church at Heiligenkreuz. While the connections may be fortuitous, it is more likely that they were the result of the use of pattern-books such as the *Reuner Musterbuch* (Vienna, Österreichische Nationalbibliothek, cod. 507), of which the means of diffusion are still unknown.[52]

The chromatic effect of grisaille glass from the beginning of the thirteenth century and of the same glass from the end of the century is completely different. The earlier grisaille is composed of thick glass often greenish or pinkish in tone; translucence varies with each piece. The later glass, however, is almost milky white and has a previously unknown, regular transparency.

The quality of the glass had changed as its manufacture became less empirical. This was due to improvements in the method of purifying sand from its metallic oxides and to a steadier means of fusing the glass paste. Methods of glass-blowing were also perfected, resulting in larger and thinner sheets of glass, generally produced in this period in France by using the crown process. These discoveries were also helpful in producing tinted glass, which became more transparent, smoother and less loaded with coloring matter. The means of executing glass also improved in part; cutting became easier, and larger scale pieces could be used, which followed and emphasized the lines (sometimes sinuous) of the painted shapes. Leading became lighter; painters began to use different artists' tools such as the brush to animate the modeling. Before or around 1300, engraved glass (originally intended for meticulous work on coats of arms) and silver stain, which "added a second tint to the natural color of the glass,"[53] would complete these major changes. They will be discussed later in the chapter.

The relationship of stained glass to architecture changed around 1260; these modifications probably resulted from the formal requirements of the new stained glass. In any case,

142 Bryn Athyn (Penn.), The Glencairn Museum: Grisaille with columbine-leaf decoration, panel from a window in the cathedral at Sées (Orne); ca. 1280. Cf. cat. 78.

143 Orbais l'Abbaye (Marne), church of Saint Pierre, choir clerestory, bay 104, right part of the 2nd register: Circular grisaille motifs decorated with leaves; after 1200.

144 Saint-Jean-aux-Bois (Oise), church of Saint Jean, bay 0: Passion and Resurrection of Christ (upper register, right compartment), Censing Angel; ca. 1225–1230 (?).

"mixed" glass, which combines broad surfaces of grisaille panels (now white) with a restricted number of colored panels reserved for iconography, immediately profited by these changes.[54]

The Success of "Mixed" Windows after 1260

The formula of the mixed window that we discussed in the Bishops of Tours or the Canons of Loches windows at Tours reached formal maturity only after several decades. Various attempts, beginning at the end of the twelfth century in Champagne and Burgundy, preceded those windows and were discussed in earlier chapters.[55]

The earliest evidence in western France is the Virgin in Majesty in the cathedral at Angers. The association of light and colored panels was not exactly an innovation around

1260–1270. On the other hand, its almost immediate general use is a remarkable fact, all the more so since the windows offer several types of composition. Apart from the band-window arrangement, other solutions were tried: alternating colorless and brightly colored lights, the latter incorporating two superimposed figures in Saint Pierre at Chartres (around 1260)[56] and placing historiated bands at different levels in the window, generally in the middle as in the upper choir of La Trinité at Vendôme (around 1300).[57] An extreme example is provided by scenes set directly against a colorless ground, as in the Saint Radegunda window (around 1280) in the church dedicated to her at Poitiers.[58]

The closer one gets to 1300, the more the grisaille surfaces are developed to the detriment of the historiated or figural sections, which seem to be suspended in a colorless window. To remain legible, these compartments became lighter and were surrounded by architectural frames—niches or tabernacles—giving them their own autonomy. This formula also influenced the style of the scenes: compositions had to be refined and drawing of figures more distinct; these became clearly different, even opposed to one another, depending on the workshop or the region.

In France from 1260, the implantation of this type of window was rapid in buildings as different and distant from one another as the Lady Chapel at Saint-Germer-de-Fly, the cathedral at Beauvais, Saint Urbain at Troyes and, a little later, the cathedral at Sées. Once again, little of this formula has been preserved in Paris or the Ile-de-France; noteworthy are the very restored figures of apostles at Linas (Essonne).[59] Nevertheless, this formula must have been employed at numerous work sites, perhaps in Paris at Notre Dame, after the work in the ambulatory, or in the cathedral at Meaux, where several chapels were glazed between 1280 and 1300. On the other hand, new provinces, where stained glass had not previously penetrated, began to produce it: the edges of Brittany and the Midi, where Gothic architecture enjoyed an intense development.

An inventory points to areas of dense concentration: western France with an original figural style that was often "Expressionist" in its pictorial brutality; Normandy which, on the contrary, evolved towards a non-monumental and subtle character that would lead to mannerism. Champagne was in the vanguard though, because of Saint Urbain at Troyes, a "revolutionary" monument in terms of architecture and stained glass.

To understand the compositions and effects of Parisian glass in the last decades of the thirteenth century, one has to turn to the Valois and the Vexin to the north of Paris. The former abbey church at Saint-Germer-de-Fly, on the outskirts of the French Vexin, was built around 1180 in accordance with the principles of the "first" Gothic architecture and completed under the abbacy of Pierre de Wesoncourt (1259–1272); it contained a Lady Chapel imitating Parisian models of the middle of the thirteenth century.[60]

Where the glass retains its original presentation, it follows the formal principles of the second half of the thirteenth century: predominately colorless grisaille in the side bays, full-color windows in the two bays on either side of the axis and figures in bands for the center window. Because of their poor condition, it is now difficult to judge the full-color windows. In the two lights in the north, in addition to eleven Romanesque panels from a window in the abbey church,[61] there are ten medallions with a Life of Saint Geremarus and the famous panel with Abbot Wesoncourt directing the building of the chapel, a panel that was contemporary with the construction. In the south window is a Life of Christ, of which the coherence is questionable; it was also executed by the same workshop. The scale has been reduced; yet the method of drawing maintains the rigidity already seen in the series at Amiens from the middle of the century. The coloring is likewise relatively dark.

The same style can be seen in the axial window, in the figures superimposed in pairs in each light: at the left, Christ the Creator; at the right, a Calvary, under which are placed two effigies of the patron saint of the abbey. These compartments, covering four brightly colored registers, are set between unevenly arranged grisailles. The circular motifs, linked by a network punctuated with colored flowerets that accent the symmetry and verticality, are related to those in a grisaille window preserved in the museum at Arras and dated to the 1260s.[62] At Saint-Germer, the background retains the cross-hatched 'fly-screen' ground. In both cases, the ivy leaf has started to become part of the plant decoration.

In the north of the Valois is a former abbey church at Saint-Martin-aux-Bois, an Augustinian foundation that is surprising in its verticality. The building, begun around 1245, falls more or less into the circle of Amiens. The apse is no more than a screen of glass divided into seven immense bays that are separated in the middle by a mural band, and each divided

145 Saint-Martin-aux-Bois (Oise), church, chevet: overall view; 1260 (?).

146   Beauvais, cathedral of Saint Pierre, chevet clerestory, bay 302: Saint John the Evangelist (?) and Saint Paul; around 1270.

147 Beauvais, cathedral of Saint Pierre, chapel of Saint Vincent, bay 14, 3rd to 8th registers: (left light), The Calling of Saint Peter and Saint Andrew; (right light), Crucifixion of Saint Peter; (under each scene), The Donor, Raoul de Senlis; 1290–1295.

into three lights. The glass is light, producing an almost diaphonous effect, with the exception of a single full-color, figural panel inserted into the central light of the bay and next to the north axial window. This compartment (no longer in its original place) shows the donor, Jean de Rouvilliers, who lived around 1260; thus the glass in this ensemble has generally been assigned to that date. Nevertheless, the style of the figure remains difficult to ascertain. The coloring and the handling make it similar to windows in the Lady Chapel of the cathedral at Beauvais (around 1235–1240); the cutting and the arrangement of the medallions are similar to those at Sainte-Vaubourg (around 1265).[63] The decoration of the grisaille varies from window to window. It has been relatively extensively restored on the one hand and, on the other, is not specific enough in its drawing or decorative motifs to allow precise dating. In any case, the formal principles—magnified here by the architecture, in which grisailles are used to the maximum in the bays and color panels are restricted to a few "vignettes"—must have been frequently employed from 1260: they appear again in the cathedral at Rouen.

The vaults of the straight bays of the choir in the cathedral at Beauvais collapsed in 1284, causing grave damage.[64] Nevertheless, the glass in the hemicycle did not break and was preserved. It had been reinstalled a dozen years earlier, between 1268 and 1272, in accordance with the band-window formula.[65] The figures—Christ Crucified at the center, and the Virgin Mary Surrounded by the College of Apostles—form a continuous band in the middle 146 of the immense bays in the choir clerestory. Because of their soft tones, they harmonize with the blank-glazed panels, most of which have very densely interlaced designs. Solidly set under gables that are not very developed, they diverge from the schematized and rigid Amiens style seen in the (contemporary) Bernard d'Abbeville window and are closer in cutting, drapery system and the way the clothing is worn to several apostles (such as Saint Simon in the choir clerestory at Saint-Quentin), probably executed in the preceding decade.

Rebuilding continued at Beauvais until 1324, but the windows in the straight bays were not installed until later, in the last years of the episcopacy of Jean de Marigny (1313–1347), who is represented as a donor in two windows.[66] The iconographic program lost some of its formal coherence; sometimes it brought together isolated figures of saints and sometimes groups illustrating hagiographic episodes like the Stoning of Saint Stephen.

On the lower level in the second south radiating chapel dedicated to Saint Vincent, the two side windows (offered by Canon Raoul de Senlis, who died in 1293 or 1294) anticipate 147 the refined formula of the beginning of the fourteenth century. The scenes, restricted to two per window, are presented under architectural canopies adorned with numerous gables and pinnacles. These ensembles are surrounded by grisailles with motifs that had become current by the 1280s. In another innovation, the image of the donor, repeated four times, is independent and placed in panels under the scenes depicting Saint Vincent (to whom the chapel was dedicated) and Saint Peter, patron of the cathedral. M. Cothren has shown that the figural style is close to manuscripts painted in Picardy around the 1280s—the Psalter and the Book of Hours belonging to Yolande of Soissons, executed at Amiens (New York, Pierpont Morgan Library, M. 729).[67]

In the realm of this association of uncolored grisaille glass with brightly colored areas disposed in bands or lights, Normandy seems to have played an important role with the cathedrals at Sées and Evreux, and also with the cathedral and the castle's chapel at Rouen, some elements of which are now in the Musée de Cluny in Paris. Several of these series will be discussed later.

In the cathedral at Rouen, in the chapel of Saint Jean jouxte les fonts, which opens on the north transept arm, are windows that are unfortunately almost entirely modern in the grisaille areas; they replace the grisaille destroyed during the bombings of 1944. Clearly all this decoration was redone during the second half of the thirteenth century, perhaps because of a private donation by the Le Tort family, who founded a chaplaincy here in 1266. 148 Members of the family were represented in the central window at the foot of the Virgin and Child. Other windows in this chapel treat the subject of the Baptism of Christ, and a seated Virgin and Child in the tracery are contemporary with this work. The style here is quite distant from that of the traditional workshops of Rouen, which were active in the nave and the ambulatory. The colors are attenuated, and the pictorial style is thin and refined, though there does not seem to be a relationship between this glass and Parisian art. There is, nevertheless, a general tendency accepted in Normandy as in Champagne during this period of the evolution of Gothic painting. It is also important to underscore the distance between this Rouen style and the "style of western France," which extends from Saint Pierre at Chartres to La Trinité at Vendôme and on to Evron.

The other contemporary Rouen series is also extremely important and is well known thanks to the work of J. Lafond.[68] It consists of four apostles, now in the Musée de Cluny. They probably come from the castle King Philip Augustus originally had constructed at Rouen, however, from the chapel, which was not built until the end of the reign of Louis IX. Although they are band-windows, the figures and the grisaille panels are badly juxtaposed, which probably means they have been reworked. The grisaille motifs seem to depend on models from the 1260s; the same date has been advanced for the figures but is perhaps a little too early. Various saints—Peter, Paul, John the Evangelist and James the Greater—are 149

148 Rouen, cathedral of Notre Dame, transept, chapel of Saint Jean jouxte les fonts: Azon le Tort and Members of his Family Offering Windows to the Virgin Mary; ca. 1266. Cf. cat. 69.

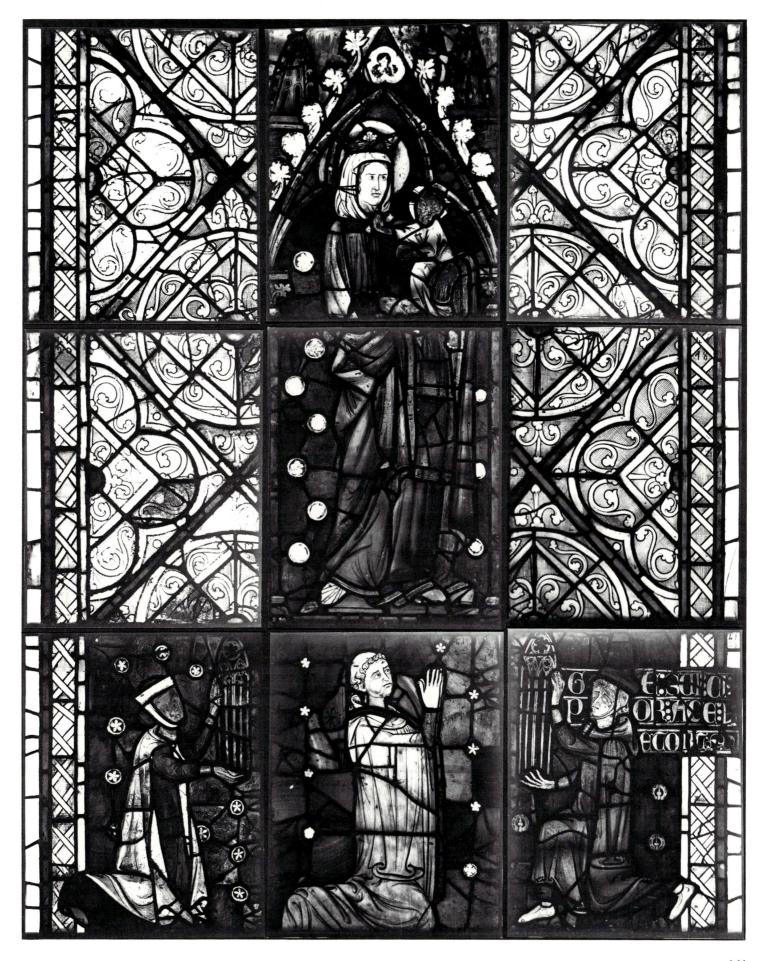

149 Paris, Musée de Cluny: Saint Peter, panel from one of the chapels of the royal castle at Rouen (?); ca. 1260–1270. Cf. cat. 71.

150 Evreux, cathedral of Notre Dame, nave, south aisle, bay 34: Massacre of the Innocents (detail), Herod and a Soldier; ca. 1270.

▷
151 Bryn Athyn (Penn.), The Glencairn Museum: Canons Listening to Saint Augustine Explain his Rule, panel from a window in the cathedral at Sées (Orne); 1270–1280. Cf. cat. 77.

seated on thrones with uprights ending in animal-head terminals. Their poses are free: Peter, for example, is set on the diagonal. The silhouettes, drawn energetically, show a vitality that is unusual, especially in the expression of the faces with "cuneiform" eyebrows that contrast with the supple treatment of hair and beards in the Fécamp series depicting Saint Catherine and Saint Margaret, which are given a later date. The coloring also breaks away from the traditions of the middle of the century with its extensive use of green.

Compared to masterpieces of the fourteenth century like the Virgin and Child donated by Raoul de Ferrières, the works of the second half of the thirteenth century in the cathedral at Evreux seem less important, especially since their study is not easy. The transformations in the nave were accompanied by the installation of windows, remains of which can be found in the clerestory of the western bays. The elements are dated to the years between 1260 and 1270. Several panels have been reinstalled in the flamboyant windows in the south aisles of the nave. The adaptation to these bays involved changes and modifications that are at times difficult to evaluate. The subjects, sometimes repeated, are set in several distinct series and come from different parts of the building. Consequently, the workmanship is not homogeneous, yet it follows tendencies introduced in Normandy around 1260–1270, characterized by thinner silhouettes, more legible compositions and lighter palettes. The place of Evreux in this new stylistic context remains a delicate question. Was it a center with its own stylistic dynamism or a junction between Paris and Rouen?[69]

The cathedral at Sées in Basse-Normandie was probably built between 1250 and 1260 and glazed from about 1270 to 1285, as the "donors' signatures" indicate. The glass has suffered considerable damage: many panels were removed in the nineteenth century and are now in collections outside France.[70] Despite the work of J. Lafond, this glazing ensemble has not been given the prominence it deserves in the evolution of French stained glass at the end of the thirteenth century. First, several windows used iconographic formulae that would be widely developed in the fourteenth century (especially in the cathedral at Rouen) such as standing figures under architectural canopies tracing the history of the building in the windows of the Lady Chapel, which formerly had been reserved for Christological and Marian iconography. A surprisingly hard trace line, which appears almost as if incised in metal, is found in the authentic parts. In the drapery, the folds are indicated by heavy lines that run counter to each other and intersect. This "violent" quality can also be found in the historiated panels accompanied by grisailles in the Saint Nicholas Chapel and in the Saint

Augustine Chapel. (One scene from the Saint Augustine window has been replaced by a copy; the original is now in the Pitcairn Collection.) The delicate and well-defined leaves of the grisaille contrast with the still strongly colored subjects. The episode of Jesus in the House of Simon in the Saint Mary Magdalene Chapel, though unfortunately extensively restored, surpasses them in this respect. The faces have acquired the unnatural expressiveness characteristic of the "school" of western France. In the band-windows in the clerestory of the choir, this extreme style of drawing, reinforced by strong colors, was retained for several apostles. Others, on the contrary, are more "classical" in effect, similar to the figures in the Saint Latuinus Chapel, which opens onto the north transept arm. One window represents Bishop Jean de Bernières (1278–1284), who finished the building of the cathedral. The unity of the glazing is exceptional but disguised by numerous restorations. As J. Lafond has written, the glazing campaign must have been completed in fifteen years by a workshop composed of three painters. Their origin—or more precisely their formation—though unknown, was perhaps Rouen or Paris as Lafond has suggested. Another possibility is Le Mans, where the Geoffroy de Loudun window, though several decades earlier, already contained the early beginnings of this new calligraphic rendering, in which case that glass would be a possible source of this "school" of western France to which Sées also belongs. [151]

The "School" of Western France

Chartres: Saint Pierre

M. Lillich has demonstrated the importance of the Gothic glass in Saint Pierre at Chartres to this "school" of western France. It is significant first of all for its extent: the glass covers all the clerestory windows and some of the bays in the pierced triforium. There are full-color windows in the hemicycle and mixed ones in the very developed choir, where historiated windows alternate with large figures surrounded by colorless grisaille. (In the windows nearest the choir, however, the figures are set against a mosaic ground.) The abbey church was rebuilt in two main campaigns. The first, which lasted about a decade (from 1151 to 1165), involved the building of the ambulatory and the radiating chapels. The second campaign, begun before the end of the twelfth century, lasted until 1250–1260 and was followed by the enlargement of the upper parts of the choir. Thus the church was not finished until the 1270s, or more likely 1280. The glazing was realized in numerous stages too. According to M. Lillich, the earliest windows are in the straight bays of the choir, except for two windows datable to the 1270s in the eighth bay. The rest of the glass is said to have been executed beginning in 1240–1250 and was intended for the clerestory windows in the nave. To confirm this, stylistic arguments focus above all on an analysis of the grisailles.[71] The composition of this glass is unusual for the years 1240 to 1250; colored lights with large [10] figures alternate with Old Testament patriarchs superimposed in pairs under small canopies. Two of them are not shown frontally but in profile, as in the triforium in the cathedral at Tours or in Saint Urbain at Troyes. A study of the figures' relatively heavy proportions, the drapery and the treatment points to similarities with the Tours series, datable to the 1260s: the drapery does indeed fall in angular, rigid folds. The brilliant colors may derive from those characterized by large areas of white and yellow, used by the workshop that made the Geoffroy de Loudun window in the cathedral at Le Mans. The two windows of the 1270s with two female figures (sibyls perhaps) clearly resemble figures from Le Mans. A date between 1260 and 1270 would consequently seem appropriate for these patriarchs, regardless of whether or not they were originally intended for their present location. Relationships to the other monuments in western France can already be seen, underscoring the fact that the origins of this "school" go back to the years 1255–1260.

The six (originally seven[72]) windows in the hemicycle form a homogeneous series. The presence of Saint Louis (canonized in 1297) in the axial bay is important and provides a *terminus ante quem*. M. Lillich, however, believes that this figure was added to the original program.[73] The brilliantly colored windows show figures on two levels set under inhabited niches, and there are narrative scenes in the tracery tympana. In the axial bay, in addition to Saint Louis, Saint Gilduin, benefactor of the abbey, is depicted and, in the lower registers,

152 Chartres, church of Saint Pierre, nave clerestory, bay 218: Life of the Virgin Mary (right light, 4th register), Meeting at the Golden Gate; ca. 1305–1315.

▷
153 Chartres, church of Saint Pierre, nave clerestory, bay 222: Life of Saint Dionysius (Denis) (right light, 3rd register), Saint Dionysius Preaching to the People of Paris (detail), Head of a clergyman; ca. 1305–1315. Cf. cat. 31.

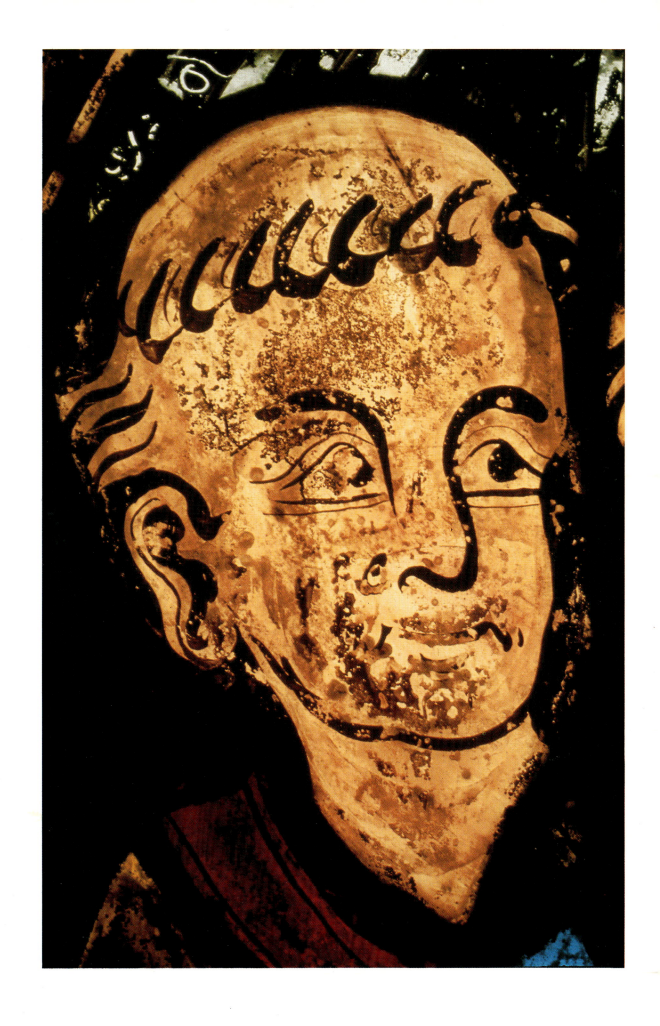

the familiar program of a Calvary and a Virgin and Child. They are surrounded by a procession of apostles, martyrs and saints. The quality of execution of the niches contrasts with the figures, rendered in a simplified but heavy manner. The repeated use of the same cartoons, though cleverly varied, almost gives the impression that the glass was hurriedly produced. The glass in the nave is in the same stylistic vein but more marked in manner. In 152 the numerous registers of the historiated windows, the vitality of the compositions and accented colors compensate for narrative simplification and summary treatment. Similarly, in the figurative windows, the elegance of presentation counteracts the somewhat abrupt style of drawing. The presence of several donors allows this ensemble to be dated between 1305 and 1315, i.e. shortly after the hemicycle. The apostles occupy the north side of the nave where the historiated windows are dedicated to the Passion and the lives of Saint John the Baptist, Saint Peter and Saint Dionysius. On the south side are the Virgin Mary, then 153 figures of Ecclesia and the abbots of Saint Pierre who alternate with a Virgin window, probably donated by Beatrix de Montfort l'Amaury, and Saint Catherine and Saint Agnes windows, among others.

Stylistic conditions have changed, as at Sées, no matter what the series of glass (choir, hemicycle or nave). None is derived from Parisian models but rather from stylistic currents in opposition to that tradition. Most take their characteristics from the former Plantagenet realm, where Romanesque references still survived, e.g. the window from the abbey at Evron in Le Mans Cathedral. Others derive from the "hard" Chartrain style (the Geoffroy de Loudun window also at Le Mans). This reaction, which cannot date before the 1260s, provoked the birth of a new type of formal expression to which Saint Pierre at Chartres belongs.

Vendôme: La Trinité

Several windows in the clerestory of the choir in the church of La Trinité at Vendôme fall within this problematical new expression. A Cluniac foundation of Geoffroy Martel, Count of Vendôme, dating from 1032, the abbey was the goal of frequent pilgrimages because it

154   Vendôme (Loir-et-Cher), church of La Trinité, chevet clerestory, bay 202: Pierre d'Alençon Giving the Holy Tear to the Abbot of La Trinité; ca. 1280. Cf. cat. 98.

possessed a remarkable relic—a Holy Tear—one of the tears that Christ is thought to have shed at the death of Lazarus. The abbey church, consecrated in 1040, was renovated a number of times before the end of the thirteenth century. Around 1280, it was "modernized": the triforium levels and the upper windows in the chevet and choir were redone. As soon as the bulk of the work was finished (around 1280–1290), the new bays were glazed.[74] Despite numerous repairs, notably in the sixteenth century, the ensemble remains coherent. The renovation of the glazing was not limited to the upper levels, however; it extended to the bays in the radiating chapels, which contain decorative grisailles from the end of the thirteenth century in the light heads and the tympana of the windows. The same is true of the triforium level, where the grisailles are better preserved. The program of the seven upper windows, decorated with mixed glass, is original in comparison with other ensembles from the second half of the thirteenth century. The scene in the axial bay relates to the church's dedication and shows a Trinity with the Man of Sorrows, surrounded by Evangelist symbols, which echoes a Romanesque iconographic scheme. In the adjoining bay to the south, Pierre d'Alençon (1258–1284), Count of Vendôme, with his coat of arms stamped on his tunic, is represented offering a new casket to the abbot of La Trinité to hold the famous relic; behind him several clergymen are standing.[75] The presentation, which extends over the three lights of the bay, is analogous to that of isolated figures under architectural canopies with delicately worked cords of foliage. The borders repeat the usual heraldic motifs: fleurs-de-lis and castles of Castile. The apostles and saints, arranged in bands, fill the middle registers of the adjoining windows.

The two windows at the entrance to the choir are interesting. To the north, next to the figure of Saint Benedict, are the arms of Jeanne de Châtillon, who died in 1292. She was the wife of Pierre d'Alençon and the donor of the ensemble according to M. Lillich. To the south are Saint Barnabas, Saint Philip and Saint Eutropius, depicted as he was being martyred, and Saint Louis with a halo, thus dating after 1297, the year of the king's canonization. Stylistic analysis confirms this historical reading.

The five windows in the apse have formal elegance and sharp drawing attenuated by more energetic handling, in which the characteristics of the manneristic art that probably derives from Tours can be recognized. The two windows at the entrance to the choir have figures that produce the opposite effect—voluminous, flaccid and set heavily beneath architectural niches. Although the line is insistent, it lacks vigor and almost dissolves into these massive forms. This stylistic change might indicate a lag of several years between the two series. The first may have been executed before the death of Pierre d'Alençon; the second later (around 1290) but before the death of his wife in 1292.

Evron

The windows in the choir clerestory of the former abbey church at Evron (Mayenne), once part of the diocese of Le Mans, belong to the "school" of western France. Like La Trinité at Vendôme and Saint Pierre at Chartres, this church was partially rebuilt at the end of the thirteenth century and during the first quarter of the fourteenth.[76] The nave, which dates to the beginning of the eleventh century, was extended by two bays, and the building was given a wide transept and an imposing choir. During and after this work, the choir clerestory was decorated with glass, the original arrangement of which was probably transformed at the end of the nineteenth century. Most of the figures are now presented under highly developed architectural niches that probably replace grisaille panels.[77] The ensemble has been seriously altered and suffered losses over the centuries.[78] Today the program is incomplete. A Trinity with the Man of Sorrows, accompanied by the Virgin and Saint John in the axial bay (as at Vendôme) is flanked by two windows dedicated to local legend—the founding of the abbey—which was previously represented in the cathedral at Le Mans.[79] In three other windows are a very restored Adoration of the Magi, figures of saints (to the north) and of apostles (to the south). In addition, four figures of bishops are preserved in American museums.[80]

The ensemble retains strong coloring; however, the handling of the figures reveals a formal evolution. The earliest ones (the apostles) are heavy figures, shown frontally or in three-quarter view, and relate to Saint Louis, Saint Barnabas and Saint Philip at Vendôme,

154

155, 156 Bryn Athyn (Penn.), The Glencairn Museum: Two Bishops, panels from a window in the choir clerestory at the church of Notre Dame de l'Epine at Evron (Mayenne); after 1320. Cf. cat. 36.

▷

157 Dol-de-Bretagne (Ille-et-Vilaine), former cathedral of Saint Samson, bay 100: Passion of Christ (4th light from the left, 3rd register), Washing the Disciples' Feet (detail), Head of Saint Peter; after 1280. Cf. cat. 33.

who have already been studied. As at Vendôme, this workshop does not succeed in suggesting volume and tries to replace it with an insistent line: a date around 1300 seems plausible. The bays in the hemicycle belong to a later glazing campaign, certainly begun after 1310, thanks to gifts from the Châtillon family. Proportions are less thick-set, and facial features are reinforced.

The most original series, however, is that of the bishops, now in American museums. Their original placement is still unknown but may have been the first south bay in the choir after the transept crossing.[81] The bishops are seen from the side, in more or less marked hip-shot stances, under carefully worked architectural niches that contrast with their voluminous outlines, summarily painted with large lines. To make up for it, careful attention is given to the very large hands and, above all, to the faces that follow the curve of the trefoil niche that contains them. A few strong, angular lines are sufficient to give them an astonishing vitality; details are almost entirely eliminated in favor of a brutal effect that is far from the delicate style of the first quarter of the fourteenth century in Normandy and the Ile-de-France. Touches of silver stain, restricted to the clothing and the hair, suggest that the series does not date earlier than 1320.[82]

155

Dol-de-Bretagne

The construction of the Gothic cathedral at Dol-de-Bretagne, north of Rennes, began with the west facade after 1220 and continued in numerous building campaigns until 1265.[83] The earliest remains of the glazing date from these years and consist of three figures of bishops, shown frontally beneath architectural canopies. Now installed in the upper windows of the transept, the bishops were probably originally set in the nave clerestory. Despite numerous restorations, it is possible to link them to the work of one of the workshops active in the upper stories of the choir of the cathedral at Le Mans—the one responsible, among other things, for the window donated by Jean de Fresnay.

The same vigor can be seen in the main window that illuminates the Anglo-Norman-style flat chevet. This large, eight-light window, surmounted by a tympanum, consists of a vast program linked to the traditions of this church. It follows the principles of legendary windows: superimposed medallions and pierced quatrefoils set against a mosaic ground. The tracery contains a Last Judgment, as in Sainte Radegonde at Poitiers; a Childhood and Passion of Christ, a Legend of Abraham, as well as the lives of Saint Margaret and Saint Catherine are depicted in the lights. The final two treat local traditions connected with the history of this venerable institution: a Story of Saint Samson, founder of the building, and figures of the first bishops of Dol surrounded by their suffragans. The formal and coloristic choices are archaic, still close to the formulae of the middle of the century: the mosaic ground, for example, is still worked and decorated with crossettes. The figures are archaic too, and a number of hands can be distinguished. The compositions are crowded, the figures stocky, the faces doll-like and rather expressionless. Some elements of grisaille remain in several windows in the triforium and the choir clerestory; the motifs are close to those in the windows at Sées (about 1280). These fragments, which were more numerous in the nineteenth century, may date to the episcopacy of Thibaud de Pouancé (1280–1301), who was actively interested in work on his cathedral.[84]

Fragments now in the churches at Saint-Méen-le-Grand (Ille-et-Vilaine) and Léhon (Côtes-du-Nord) are connected with Dol.[85] In the principal window at Saint-Alban (Côtes-du-Nord), on the contrary, in the window dedicated to the Passion of Christ, the colors have become softer; hesitant touches of silver stain are joined to the traditional mixture of blue and red to make it lighter. The drawing inaugurates a more elegant, freer style. The border decoration (the arms of Brittany and Castile) allows the glass to be dated to the reign of Duke John III and his wife Isabelle, i.e. between 1312 and 1328.[86]

Poitiers: Sainte Radegonde

Does the widely published window of Saint Radegunda in the church dedicated to her at Poitiers belong to this "school" of western France? A royal foundation and the site of pilgrimages, the building was partially rebuilt during the second half of the thirteenth century.[87] The nave was rebuilt in two successive campaigns beginning in the east; the two eastern bays date from the middle of the century, while the other two only date from the third quarter of the century. The windows were installed as the work progressed. Some were donated by Alphonse, Count of Poitiers, brother of Louis IX, who died in 1271. The program was originally much more extensive than it now appears. As was common in this transitional period, it included full-color windows, mixed ones like that of Saint Radegunda and predominately colorless grisaille windows. However, the windows suffered serious damage as a result of the Huguenot bombardment in 1562. Modern restorations, notably that done by Henri Carot at the end of the nineteenth century and that by Francis Chigot after 1950, have given the glass a false unity by joining panels of diverse origins in the same windows. Among others, vestiges of a Childhood, a Public Life (?) and a Passion of Christ are all grouped in the lights under the Last Judgment rose donated by Alphonse of Poitiers, who is represented in the window in the second north bay of the nave.[88] The situation is all the more regretable since the windows belong to different stylistic trends.

The two mixed windows that have been preserved use formulae that are very different, almost the opposite in their effect. The incomplete Childhood cycle is sophisticated: multi-foil historiated compartments arranged in the middle of fields of grisaille that replace the mosaic ground of the legendary windows and, in the borders, superimposed bouquets. The

158 Dol-de-Bretagne (Ille-et-Vilaine), former cathedral of Saint Samson, bay 100: Life of Saint Samson (6th light, 4th register), Samson Cures the Daughter of Prince Privatus; after 1280. Cf. cat. 33.

159 Poitiers, church of Sainte Radegonde, nave clerestory, bay 111: Life of Saint Radegunda (lower register), Saint Radegunda Washing the Feet of the Poor (detail), The Poor; ca. 1270. Cf. cat. 64.

▷

160 Bryn Athyn (Penn.), The Glencairn Museum: The Visitation, panel from the Childhood of Christ window in the church of Sainte Radegonde at Poitiers; 1270–1280. Cf. cat. 65.

161 Reims, cathedral of Notre Dame, back of the west facade, left side, lower register: Man in Armor Receiving Communion; ca. 1255.

162 Troyes, church of Saint Urbain, chevet, glazed triforium, bay 5: The Passion of Christ (right light), Washing of the Disciples' Feet; ca. 1270. Cf. cat. 95.

▷

163 Troyes, church of Saint Urbain, choir clerestory, bay 103, left light: The Prophet Zachariah; ca. 1270. Cf. cat. 96.

grisaille motifs arranged in ogee arches enclose the carefully executed scenes symmetrically. The figures have balanced proportions, similar to those in the Childhood window (around 1260) in Saint Julien at Tours, now in the cathedral there. The palette remains traditional; the faces, however, are executed in white glass as at Gassicourt. Thus, this Poitevine cycle does not belong to the "school" of western France but has affinities with the Court Style around 1260.

The figures in the Saint Radegunda window, on the contrary, are set against the grisaille field. The short, restless forms are not enclosed in compositions but freely disposed in bands. The faces, with forced, even grimacing expressions are emphasized by trace lines. On the other hand, the folds and drapery are schematically rendered with a few thick lines. Modeling has been replaced by a nervous style of drawing, already seen in the window from the abbey at Evron in the cathedral at Le Mans (1255-1260). Like the windows at Le Mans, there is a faithfulness here to Romanesque patterns, but it is at odds with the new principles that the workshops clearly had difficulty in adopting, provoking a reaction that J.J. Gruber has called "the absence of style".

In this same stylistic current are the Last Judgment rose, donated in 1269 by Alphonse of Poitiers , the sixteen medallions from a Passion set beneath it and the remains of the Saint Blaise and Saint Lawrence windows in the first north bay of the nave. The colors, though often obliterated by Carot's work, are surprising in their brillance. The frames for the scenes remain very wide and are sometimes linked by continuous wide fillets, reviving a pattern seen in the cathedral at Poitiers at the beginning of the century. The figures appear to be weightless, like marionettes in more or less rigid poses. A number of hands can be recognized in these windows, which must be dated close to the rose donated by Alphonse of Poitiers, i.e. around 1270-1275.

The characteristics of the "school" of western France are a simplified style of drawing, heavy proportions, faces with forced, often "Expressionist" features and a palette that has difficulty becoming lighter. Far from being monolithic, this style varies according to the center and the workshop. Its sources are difficult to determine. There is a faithfulness to Romanesque patterns and difficulty in copying "Parisian" models or, more accurately, an inability to combine the two styles.

In this group, the window from the abbey at Evron in the upper ambulatory at Le Mans (around 1250-1260) has often been cited as a starting point of this style, along with the Canons of Loches window and the Bishops of Tours window in Tours Cathedral (around 1260). The works by the "Master of Geoffroy de Loudun" in the cathedral at Le Mans (around 1254) might be added to this list. Nevertheless, it is difficult to determine the role that these works had in the elaboration of this "style," which produced works of true originality between 1260 and 1320/1325, for example the historiated windows in the nave clerestory in Saint Pierre at Chartres.

Opposed to this tendency are several works such as the Childhood cycle in Sainte Radegonde at Poitiers (around 1270) and the Pierre d'Alençon window in La Trinité at Vendôme, which develop the formulae that grew out of the art of the Court Style in the 1260s, probably through Tours.

Saint Urbain at Troyes: A Revolutionary Building

With Saint Urbain at Troyes, Champagne gained an exceptional place in the evolution of Gothic stained glass that could not have been anticipated when considering provincial works such as the north rose in the cathedral at Reims (around 1250).[89] The events following the foundation of the church by Pope Urban IV on the site of his birth are well known. The building was erected rapidly; the choir and the transept were undoubtedly finished for the consecration in 1266. Despite a fire the same year, services were held in the church in 1277, and a large number of windows were probably installed by that time. Subsequently work slowed and came to a halt at the end of the fifteenth century before the completion of the nave, which was not finished until the beginning of the twentieth century.[90] The building, with its restrained dimensions in both plan and elevation, inaugurates a new concep-

164 Mussy-sur-Seine (Aube), church of Saint Pierre lès Liens, chevet clerestory, bay 200, central light: Calvary (detail), Christ on the Cross; after 1300. Cf. cat. 50.

tion of the Gothic sanctuary, characterized by purer luminosity and greater spatial unity. Saint Urbain is the most accomplished example of formal change because of its subtle volumes, the precision of its linear composition and the sparse colors of its windows, which are, however, warmed up by figured bands, ornamental bosses and colored fillets set against the almost colorless grisailles. Such overall harmony suggests that the glazing was in large part completed at the same time as the building. The five windows on the upper level in the apse are decorated with wide borders containing the arms of Pope Urban IV (1261-1264), those of the chapter of Saint Urbain and of Thibaud V of Champagne, king of Navarre.

9

The glazing, however, has undergone repairs and losses over the centuries.[91] Today it decorates two stories—corresponding to the triforium and the clerestory—in the choir and the apse; the eastern bays in the transept and the oriented chapels likewise contain many original pieces so that the original intention has been preserved. On the upper level of the choir and the apse, the three-light windows are decorated with almost colorless grisaille; the colored figures under architectural canopies are arranged in bands and fill the upper part of the bays. These elements are unified by borders, most of which have wide heraldic motifs. In the tympana are colored and historiated medallions at the center of the roses, animating the grisailles in the tracery.

The program, however, is in disarray and has become difficult to interpret. The axial window contains a Calvary scene (with a modern Christ at the center), surrounded by figures of patriarchs and prophets, who can be identified by scrolls bearing their names. Repetitions, and losses indicate that the ensemble has undergone alteration and that it probably once extended to the transept windows. In the same way, the historiated medallions in the tracery often have no iconographic relationship to the figures below them.

Ancestors and prophets are freely disposed under architectural canopies with gables and pinnacles that are sometimes inhabited by birds and little monsters. The figures are shown walking, in profile or in three-quarter view, but rarely frontally; their gestures are vehement and expressive, like the two statues of prophets (?) preserved in the Musée des Beaux-Arts at Troyes (around 1270).[92] The angular line of the folds and the deep, brusque fold-marks of the drapery are similar to contemporary or slightly earlier sculpture in Champagne, especially to the figures on the reverse of the west facade of Reims Cathedral, as L. Grodecki has already noted.[93] The light and rich palette, despite being weakened by corrosion, contributes to the powerful impression given by the ensemble.

163

161

Different tendencies can be observed in the historiated quatrefoils in the triforium. These panels, dedicated to the Passion, seem to be inlaid into the grisaille panels. The many colored fillets keep them from being lost in the vast areas of white. The handling is as exceptional as on the upper level, for example in the background with natural foliage rinceaux on a very small scale, which imitates the decoration of both German glass and that in Parisian manuscripts of the 1270s. Despite the differences in style—precise and nervous in the axial bay, and more balanced in the others—a strong sense of the art of modeling animates the compositions. The figures generally have short and wide proportions, round heads with curly hair, precise and rapid gestures—characteristics already visible in many of the medallions in the tympana. This formal quality anticipates the art of the years around 1300 in the reduction of scale, the autonomy of individual compositions and the subtle coloring; thus, these panels have been compared to royal manuscripts such as the Breviary of Philip the Fair (Paris, Bibl. Nat., ms. Lat. 1023).

162

The decorative grisaille are of exceptional quality too, first of all because of their almost colorless glass, which provides purer and more unified lighting. On the upper level, seven cartoons were utilized for nine windows. Most can be linked to the tradition of Champagne in the first half of the century. They are combined with colored fillets, which are more numerous in the triforium, to give warmth to the neutral effect of the blank glazing. The grisailles in the Lady Chapel, original elements of which are grouped in the two south windows, show a formal advance over contemporary models. The motifs are usually composed of quatrefoils set over lozenges. At the center of each is a small medallion decorated with a human head, often a monster or a grotesque. Painted on red, purple or green glass, these motifs are so refined in execution that their date cannot be earlier than 1290-1300. At that time, this principle can also be observed in Alsatian glass; it would be taken up again with zest in Normandy from the early fourteenth century.

To the southeast of Troyes there is a church at Mussy-sur-Seine, built at the very end of the thirteenth century, with an apse derived from the architecture of Saint Urbain.[94] The windows, which were heavily reworked in the nineteenth century, are the result of two glazing campaigns. The grisailles in the triforium, which are not painted, may date to the end of the thirteenth century. The decoration of the backgrounds is related to Burgundian grisailles, known through the works of Amé in the last century.[95] The mixed windows on the upper level, with their heraldic borders, use clover-leaf decoration in the grisaille panels. The Calvary in the axial bay, the Virgin Mary with two donors at the left, and Saint Peter between an abbot and a bishop at the right are set under architectural canopies and deviate from Troyes formulae. The cut of the pieces of glass, accenting the dense modeling, is traditional in its mass and contrasts with the brilliant colors. J. J. Gruber has already emphasized the originality of this ensemble, situated at the junction of a number of stylistic currents, most of which are Burgundian.

Southeastern France and the Midi

In southeastern France, in Saint Jean at Lyons, the construction of the Gothic cathedral was accompanied by the installation of stained glass. A very restored series of prophets (completed in the nineteenth century), belonging in the straight bays of the choir, was finished around 1240. The transept roses were done before 1250, while the bays in the hemicycle of the choir were decorated in the 1260s with rudely worked figures of apostles set against grisailles similar to those in the cathedral at Auxerre. The Coronation of the Virgin in the axial window dates from the very end of the century. Already rendered with the lighter palette, it is one of the earliest surviving examples in French stained glass of a subject that had been widely developed in sculpture for over a century.

In the Midi, the development of stained glass was concurrent with that of Gothic architecture. Many buildings lost a good part or all of their original glazing during the following centuries. In the cathedral at Limoges, for example, only a few very restored figures survive in the clerestory, along with grisailles (also repaired in the nineteenth century) and a few fragments in the tympana of the radiating chapels.[96] The earliest vestiges of windows are those in the cathedral at Béziers, which have been reinstalled in a composite window mounted during the second half of the eighteenth century. They may predate the works by the great workshops at Saint-Nazaire (begun in 1269) and in the cathedral at Narbonne (begun in 1273).[97]

The connections between the glass painters of southern France and those of northern France are not well known. The southern workshops apparently had their own dynamism that was adapted to the specific requirements of a local architecture that was often quite different from northern formulae, for instance in the conception of volume. Stained glass may have been used to complement wall painting, which remained popular in the south through the Middle Ages. Thus, without being behind the times, brightly colored legendary glass with superimposed medallions continued to be created until the middle of the fourteenth century, notably in Languedoc.

The windows in Saint Nazaire et Saint Celse at Carcassonne, a building with an exceptional Gothic chevet, were executed during the episcopacies of Pierre de Rochefort (1300–1322) and Pierre de Rodier (1323–1329).[98] The program has been considerably altered through subsequent repairs such as the installation of sixteenth-century glass around the axial window in the chevet. Following work by Viollet-le-Duc, the glass was excessively restored by Alfred Gérente. Some panels were removed and replaced by copies; others were obliterated or badly reworked.[99] The axial window in the chevet, dedicated to the Life of Christ, is considered the earliest because of the dull colors. Other windows in the choir depict the lives of Saint Peter and Saint Paul and of the patrons of the church, Saint Nazarius and Saint Celsus of Milan. These are related in large medallions of complex shapes set against backgrounds with curved or diagonal leading. The compositions are elegant, and the handling is refined. The arrangement of figures under trefoil arches in the Jesse Tree window is traditional; yet the draughtsmanship is supple and precise. The most important work is the Tree of Life, which was inspired by Franciscan spirituality and probably copied from a manuscript. The grisailles that decorate several of the chapels were probably redone after older examples.

165 Carcassonne, church of Saint Nazaire et Saint Celse, transept, chapel of the Holy Cross, bay 10: The Tree of Life (middle registers), Christ on the Cross; ca. 1310. Cf. cat. 23.

The glazing in the former cathedral at Narbonne is more varied and later in date. In addition to brightly colored legendary cycles and decorative grisaille windows, it includes a series of figures under high architectural canopies framed by grisaille panels, which imitate northern examples. Early and frequent reworkings, which completely obliterated some sections, have made the study of this glass difficult. Also from the first quarter of the fourteenth century are the grisailles in the cathedral at Toulouse, a few panels preserved in Bordeaux Cathedral and in the church at Saint-Emilion, the motifs of which suggest later models.

The First Use of Silver Stain

The introduction of silver stain, already mentioned in this chapter, provided stained glass painters with the means to complete the change of formal and chromatic patterns that had begun thirty years before.[100] This remarkable technical accomplishment freed the glazier from the constraints of leading: silver oxide allowed a piece of white glass to be colored with yellow without any cutting, and it modified the tonality of glass so that two shades could be set together without the addition of a lead. The oxide, usually placed on the outside of the glass, fused into the glass during firing; when used on the inside of the glass, it was handled like paint. Stained glass was consequently renewed, enriched and even made simpler by this process.

The recipe had been used since the sixth century in Egypt for the decoration of vases. It reached the West at the end of the thirteenth century through a work written between 1276 and 1279 by Alfonso X the Wise, king of Castile—*El Lapidario*.[101] A copy must have reached the court of France shortly thereafter, and the preparation of silver stain, included in the book, was rapidly exploited thanks to the diligence of the members of the royal family, perhaps Marie of Brabant, second wife of Philip the Bold who may have appreciated its usefulness.[102] This hypothesis is very appealing, since it would provide proof of the use of silver stain in France before 1300. It is possible, since J.J. Gruber claims to have noticed a blue glass highlighted with silver stain to give a local green tone in a clerestory window in the cathedral at Sées that is datable to about 1280–1290. However, the first securely dated example of the use of silver stain in France is in a small window of the rural church at Mesnil-Villeman (Manche) and only dates to 1313.[103]

The adoption of this process corresponded to the formal preciousness and chromatic refinement that was popular then: a few touches of silver stain were sufficient to animate a line, to strip away its hardness and to give it a surprising brilliance. This agreement between style and technique, while still difficult to explain, responded to real need—within a quarter of a century, a large number of workshops in France and in Europe were using silver stain with more or less success.

Normandy and the Ile-de-France around 1300: The Triumph of "Mannerism"

The windows in the choir and apse of Saint Urbain at Troyes inaugurated a formal style that was simultaneously expressive and refined. This pictorial expression—with regional variations—would spread through France during the first third of the fourteenth century, producing virtuoso, almost immaterial works. The chromatic effects were modulated and pale; delicately colored figures and scenes were surmounted by architectural niches inspired by the patterns of contemporary Gothic architecture, brightening the grisaille surrounding them. Line, drawing and detail aimed for legibility despite a reduction in scale; this resulted in a new spatial quality and a renewal of icongraphy in its conception rather than its forms. Paris probably played an essential role in the elaboration of this new formal choice. No work has survived there, however.

Only Normandy has preserved works that testify to the stylistic changes that the art of stained glass underwent during the first third of the fourteenth century. The earliest evidence, unfortunately, is poorly preserved. The windows in the apse of the Lady Chapel in La Trinité at Fécamp are filled with remains of three hagiographic windows that have original subjects: the Life of Saint Edward the Confessor, Anglo-Saxon king in the eleventh century and benefactor of the Norman abbey where he spent his youth; the Life of Saint Louis, the earliest to survive; the Lives of the Hermit Saints, a legend referring to the origins of Egyptian monasticism. The three series are thought to come from the original Lady Chapel that was demolished at the end of the fifteenth century. They are consequently incomplete, and their original arrangement is unknown, though they may have been set in bands.

Each scene is surmounted by an architectural canopy the same height as the scene itself. The canopies have little towers and pinnacles connected by flying buttresses; birds are set at the tops of these finely worked niches. The compositions are arranged on a number of levels in an effort to create new spatial depth. The style of drawing breaks with traditional formulae in its suppleness and precision. Modeling is reduced in favor of refined and rapid line-work. Differences can be observed in the handling of the elongated figures in the Saint Edward panels and the squatter ones in the Saint Louis glass. The colors must have been extremely bright but are now darkened by corrosion. The date given to this ensemble by J. Lafond—the 1310s—underscores the rapidity with which the glass painters assimilated the new ideas that probably developed out of contemporary Parisian (and perhaps English) manuscript illumination.[104]

Beginning in the first decades of the fourteenth century, workshops produced great masterpieces in this new technique of translucent painting in the Ile-de-France and in Normandy. The first was in the Navarre Chapel, probably constructed between 1310 and 1320, on the south flank of the choir in the collegiate church at Mantes.[105] Unfortunately, however, this annex is poorly dated. Of the original glazing, only a few panels dedicated to the Passion of Christ and preserved at Champs-sur-Marne survive, along with a few painted architectural fragments still *in situ* in the tympana of the bays and some panels from the armorial borders.

The ensemble, though heavily reworked in the nineteenth century, testifies to the stylistic renewal that occurred at the beginning of the fourteenth century. The small-scale compositions are set against damascene grounds with foliage in rinceaux and are enclosed by cusps

166 Fécamp, church of La Trinité, Lady Chapel, bay 1, left light, 2nd register: Edward the Confessor and his Wife Edith Take Vows of Chastity; after 1308. Cf. cat. 37.

shaped like spandrels. The forms, with their nervous and precise outlines, are painted on white glass that contrasts with the lively colors of the drapery and the grounds. Light touches of silver stain are used to highlight certain medallions. Despite numerous restorations, the scenes are strikingly legible, and their preciousness is accompanied by expressive vigor, which is an innovation.

The second monument is the Lady Chapel in Rouen Cathedral; glazing must have started around 1310 (?) and would have been completed before the end of the first quarter of the fourteenth century. The new style is admirably employed: the sixteen figures of the canonized bishops of Rouen, in full color, are set beneath architectural canopies surmounted by gables and framed by grisaille panels enhanced with colored fillets that are enriched with delicate foliage in which silver stain plays its luminous and precise role. The borders are full of fantasy, abandoning earlier patterns: parrots, wild men and angelic musicians have been added to the decoration. The overall palette—dominated by light blue, purple, yellows and greens—also contrasts with the principles of monumental stained glass in the thirteenth century. The decoration of the choir at Saint-Ouen would begin, in the same spirit, a few years later; it would produce an even more grandiose realization of this style than the forms invented for this chapel.

167   Rouen, cathedral of Notre Dame, Lady Chapel, bay 7, 1st light on the right: Saint Ouen; 1310–1320. Cf. cat. 67.

▷

168   Champs-sur-Marne, castle, storage depot of the Monuments Historiques: Pilate Washing his Hands (?), medallion from the Navarre Chapel (?) of the former collegiate church at Mantes (?); 1st quarter of the 14th century.

169   Champs-sur-Marne, castle, storage depot of the Monuments Historiques: Christ Outstretched on His Tomb, panel from the decoration in the Navarre Chapel of the former collegiate church at Mantes (?); 1st quarter of the 14th century.

Europe in the Thirteenth Century V

At the end of *Le Vitrail roman*, to which this volume is a sequel, Louis Grodecki emphasized how complex the elimination of Romanesque formulae was.[1] In France, the survival of Romanesque trends—for example in western France and in the Lyons area—inhibited the arrival of Gothic innovations before the second third of the thirteenth century, while Chartres, with the "Master of Saint Chéron," already put forward a "hard style" in the same period.[2] In other European regions, formal change was not better synchronized: political, religious and economic conditions accelerated or retarded the change.

The transition from Romanesque to Gothic took varied forms. In the Holy Roman Empire, the late Romanesque style continued to be popular beyond 1250, and the *Zackenstil*, with its "broken folds," employed Gothic schemas that were already mannerist in its ultimate phase.[3] England, on the contrary, followed a movement that was parallel to stained glass in France, and from 1260 welcomed a precious, non-monumental style close to manuscript illumination. Furthermore, the dynamism of architecture ensured an important place for stained glass until the 1280s. The medium even reached the Mediterranean world, which had refused or been disinclined to adopt it earlier.[4]

The prestige of French stained glass, above all during the reign of Saint Louis, thanks to the Sainte Chapelle, attracted admiration and potential donors—kings, princes, chapters, even cities—which sought to imitate it. The itinerant nature of the workshops, which can sometimes be reconstructed,[5] and the circulation of model-books, which must have been very extensive, facilitated copies of cartoons or, more precisely, the integration of formal principles and new decorative motifs that blended with regional repertories and sometimes even eliminated them. These changes often led to original creations that surpassed French models, for instance the architectural canopies that changed into fairy-tale tabernacles in the Holy Roman Empire from the 1260s.[6] Each region reacted differently; moreover, preserved works are often widely separated from one another, making comparisons difficult. From the beginning of the fourteenth century, technical innovations such as silver stain and engraved glass resulted in the elaboration of a common formal vocabulary, reinforced by iconographic transformations that followed the same pattern, under the influence of a renewal of Franciscan spirituality.[7]

England

The history of stained glass in England in the thirteenth century is difficult to reconstruct. Little of what was executed has survived, because of extensive destruction, principally in the sixteenth century. The losses are even more regretable given the high formal quality of the glass that has survived. Many surviving works are no longer in their original location, for instance the fragments from the cathedral at Salisbury; others are no more than *membra disjecta*—often obliterated—such as the vestiges of the stained glass from the cathedral at Lincoln, recently studied by Nigel Morgan.[8]

Canterbury and Lincoln: Two Glazing Campaigns of the Early Thirteenth Century

Paradoxically, as the thirteenth century began, the glazing campaign at Canterbury (extensively discussed in *Le Vitrail roman*) was already very advanced. A large number of windows were in place, the earliest dating from 1175–1180, the result of an ambitious glazing program.[9]

170 Canterbury, cathedral, north choir aisle, 2nd window: The Parable of the Sower; ca. 1200 (?).

▷
171 Lincoln, cathedral, south transept arm, gallery below the rose, 2nd light from the left, 2nd register: Banquet Celebrating the Return of the Prodigal Son (detail), Musician and Guest; ca. 1210–1220. Cf. cat. 101.

They are the product of a number of artists whose style often follows archaizing formulae, like the "Master of the Parable of the Sower". Work was stopped before completion, however, between 1207–1213, during the exile of the archbishop and the chapter at Saint-Omer in France. When they returned, before the translation of the relics of Thomas Becket to Trinity Chapel in 1220, they had a new series of windows made, most of which honor the saintly archbishop and relate the miracles worked through his intercession.[10]

Much of this work must have been done by painters who were brought to France during the years of exile and who worked on the Continent, elaborating the cartoons and programs. Sens has long been suggested as one of their training centers.[11] Chartres, especially the Joseph window,[12] has also been suggested by Madeline Caviness. Many questions remain, however.[13] At Canterbury, as a matter of fact, the work was done by different painters; one such as the "Master of Petronella" (named for a nun cured at Thomas Becket's tomb) is traditional in his treatment and arrangement of compositions. Another, the "Master of Fitz-Eisulf" (named for another miraculously healed person), used a more refined style of drawing and emphasized contour to the detriment of modeling, while remaining close to the earliest artistic formulae of this exceptional ensemble—one of the most important examples of the 1200 Style in Europe.[14]

Nevertheless, the panels most affected by innovations are the figures of ancestor-kings such as Hezekiah, today in an upper window on the north side of Trinity Chapel, dated to the 1220s or shortly after.[15] The spatial transformations and formal modifications show a

flexibility and ease that is opposed to the hard line of the "Master of Saint Chéron"; however, these figures are close to the seated figures of David and Ezekiel that decorate a north bay in the clerestory of the chevet at Chartres Cathedral (1220–1225?).[16]

A similar evolution can be seen in most of the panels of stained glass from the cathedral at Lincoln, despite the obliterated and disorderly state of the glass. Its execution dates to the first third of the thirteenth century, with the exception of a series of apostles that can be dated to the middle of the century.[17] The single medallion from a window with the Parable of the Prodigal Son shows analogies to the later windows at Canterbury that illustrate the miracles performed at the tomb of Thomas Becket. Despite the work of J. Lafond and N. Morgan, this ensemble—originally comparable in quality to Canterbury—remains difficult to analyze because of the extent to which it has been changed.

There were a minimum of fifteen windows, some hagiographic (with John the Evangelist, Matthew, Nicholas, Dionysius, etc.), some Marian (with the Life and Miracles of the Virgin) and some typological; in short, the program was analogous to those in French cathedrals from the first half of the thirteenth century.[18] Only the rose in the north transept, dedicated to the Last Judgment, has remained in its original location and undergone little modification.

BERNIVS·

172   Dorchester (Oxfordshire), abbey church of Saint Peter and Saint Paul, bay 3, 2nd register: Saint Birinus Receiving his Archepiscopal Cross; middle of the thirteenth century. Cf. cat. 100.

The treatment of the theme follows the English tradition, but comparisons can be established with contemporary French roses at Chartres and at Mantes that illustrate the same subject. N. Morgan dates the Lincoln rose to around 1220.[19] The means of dividing certain medallions, the energetic handling of several figures (the angels carrying the instruments of the Passion) and the treatment of decoration suggest a similar date. The ensemble at Lincoln was certainly the product of a number of workshops such as that responsible for the Legend of Theophilus, whose figures with elongated proportions display an elegance and graphic suppleness rarely seen in France at this time.

From the middle of the century, a series of eight standing figures survives—Isaiah and seven apostles—which Nigel Morgan has compared to a group of Apocalypse manuscripts, whose style is related to illuminations by Matthew Paris and his workshop.[20] Some figures such as Saint Paul, the best preserved of the group, were certainly of very elegant design and workmanship. Comparisons are, however, difficult to find, since the windows from the second third of the thirteenth century preserved in England are so few, so widely dispersed and often in bad condition[21]—an astonishing fact when compared to the profusion of French glass from this period. Neither the vestiges of the Jesse Tree at Salisbury (about 1230)[22] nor the few panels at Petham in Kent, now in the crypt at Canterbury, nor those from the county of Oxford recently studied by Peter Newton,[23] can serve as a comparison; the lacunae are simply too great to allow pertinent comparisons among these elements.

English Grisaille

From the beginning, the figures in the cathedral at Lincoln may have been associated with almost colorless grisaille panels. If so, they would be the earliest examples of mixed glazing preserved in England, and their development would be contemporary with mixed glazing in France.[24]

173 York, cathedral, north transept arm, north wall: Five Sisters window; ca. 1260.

174　Salisbury, cathedral: Tree of Jesse (detail); ca. 1230.

Windows in uncolored grisaille seem to have been in current use in England from the twelfth century.[25] The examples in England from the first half of the thirteenth century, like those in France, are not uniquely preserved in Cistercian buildings: most are in cathedrals (Canterbury, Lincoln and Salisbury). It seems that, on the English side of the Channel, this type of glazing enjoyed a particularly wide popularity. The famous Five Sisters window at York, from around 1260,[26] has no equivalent on the Continent in terms of the breadth of its surface and overall effect, unless it is the chevet in the former abbey church at Saint-Martin-aux-Bois. In the cathedral at York, however, the relationship between architecture and stained glass is not the same as in the Picardy abbey church, where the walls were almost completely hollowed out for the windows.

Moreover, the composition and the drawing of motifs (difficult to read today) are complex in their organization and style of drawing, and distant from contemporary examples preserved in France and in the Holy Roman Empire.

These formal discrepancies seem to have endured for a few more decades, at least among certain workshops, for instance at the chapterhouse of Salisbury Cathedral (1280–1290)[27] and in the church at Stanton Harcourt near Oxford.[28] The leaves used are still palmettes, distributed in symmetrical rinceaux and enclosed in medallions emphasized by a colored fillet. In France at this time, nature was readily copied: branches were arranged freely and without restraint. Only in the windows of Merton College at Oxford do oak, strawberry and holly leaves appear; the college's windows will be discussed later.

The Second Half of the Thirteenth Century: Court Art

The building of Westminster Abbey, undertaken in 1245 by King Henry III, Saint Louis's brother-in-law, marks the beginning of the penetration of Parisian art into England and the commencement of a brilliant period in English painting, above all in manuscript illumina-

175   London, Westminster Abbey, Jerusalem Chamber: Stoning of Saint Stephen; ca. 1250.

176   London, Westminster Abbey, Jerusalem Chamber: Ascension of Christ; after 1250 (condition in 1880–1885, after WESTLAKE, vol. I, 1881–1884, p. 118).

177 Oxford, Merton College, chapel, choir: Saint Stephen; between 1289 and 1311. Cf. cat. 102.

tion. However, very little remains of the windows that were executed at that time—only six historiated medallions, now exhibited in the "Jerusalem Chamber," part of the former hostelry at the western entrance to the abbey.[29] Their handling and colors are close to contemporary French products such as the ensemble in the Sainte Chapelle.

Beginning in the 1270s, the band-window began to compel recognition in England. The transformations of the Decorated Style in architecture—buildings with grand dimensions, pierced with multiple lancet windows surmounted by tympana with complicated tracery—required more translucent windows, especially since the ornamental molding was becoming increasingly angular.[30]

The spread of the Court Style and the development of the "school" of East Anglia influenced the evolution of stained glass: as in the Ile-de-France and Normandy, it lost its monumental character to graphic and chromatic preciousness, which was underscored by the transparency of the glass.[31] Using the delicate forms of the tracery and copying grotesques from manuscripts, the painters set their figures beneath stepped baldachins, with uprights composed of miniaturized architectural elements. They reduced the scale of execution and transposed the art of the illuminator into glass, framing the panels with grisaille decorated with naturalistic foliage, as in the windows in the choir of the Merton College Chapel at Oxford.

The college was founded in 1264, by the bishop of Rochester, Walter de Merton, but the chapel is later. The choir windows, which associate grisailles decorated with specific foliage with full-color bands containing figures under canopies, are characteristic of the change in English stained glass at the end of the thirteenth century. The miniaturesque quality is reinforced by a carefully worked execution, an elaborate palette for the full-color areas and plant decoration that copies nature. Furthermore, the donor, Henry de Mamesfeld, had himself represented (one of the first representations of a donor preserved in England) at least twenty times, kneeling and holding a scroll that unfurls in bands, reading: MAGISTER HENRICUS DE MAMESFEL[D] M[E] FECIT.[32] A member of Merton College and then chancellor of the University of Oxford between 1298 and 1311, this bishop wanted to have himself represented like the apostles whom he was honoring; consequently, he is depicted on the same scale as saints, which is both surprising and rare in this period. Usually the habit in England was to have one's coat of arms represented, as in the west window of the church at Selling in Kent, where (around 1300) the figures in bright colors, among which are a Virgin and Child in the center of a five-light bay, rest on large coats of arms that act as pedestals.[33] Also at this time, in the first decade of the fourteenth century, silver stain was used—timidly at first and then becoming current, as in the Saint Catherine window at Deerhurst in Gloucestershire or in the choir of Exeter Cathedral between 1310 and 1320.[34]

In the following decades, English stained glass would continue along these lines, i.e. it adopted the innovations such as the enlargement of the canopies over figures and scenes, which appeared simultaneously almost everywhere. It evolved towards a type of "mannerism" which, though perhaps less expressive than mannerism in France or in the Holy Roman Empire, was often surprising in its subtlety of line and colors.

Spain

León: Spread of the French Style

French influence was strong in Spain in the thirteenth century, above all in the Christian realms of Aragón and Castile. Historical conditions favored the spread of this influence well before the victory at Navas de Tolosa in 1212. Gothic architecture had penetrated into Spain at the end of the twelfth century,[35] but stained glass remained a marginal art form, even after the reconquest of the peninsula in the battle of Seville in 1248. Islamic tradition left its imprint even on Christian buildings for a long time. It is no accident that the cathedral at León is the only church to have such an extensive series of glass from the thirteenth century.

The building, on which construction was begun by Bishop Martin Fernández in 1254/1255, just after his election, follows in the French tradition. Its plan is Reimsian, and its "Rayonnant" elevation naturally includes a pierced triforium. The architect, Henrique, was probably

178 Deerhurst (Gloucestershire), priory, church, south aisle, western bay: Saint Catherine of Alexandria; early 14th century.

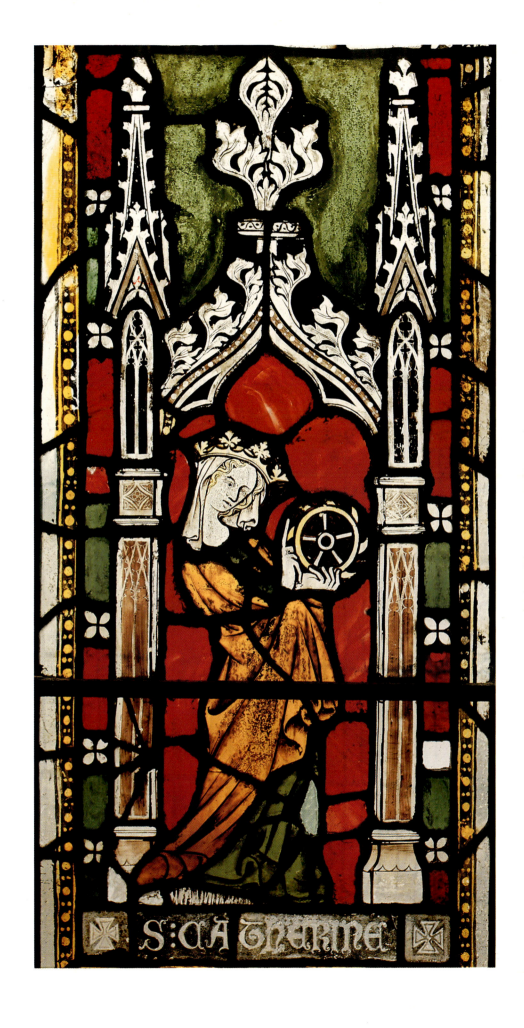

179 León, cathedral, nave clerestory, north side, bay 225: The Hunt window; 3rd quarter of the 13th century. Cf. cat. 11.

acquainted with Parisian workshops from the middle of the century,[36] and stained glass, consequently, was a logical, essential part of the decoration. The earliest windows (probably datable to the last four decades of the thirteenth century) have survived in poor condition. Many of them have been mutilated, some have been rearranged, and a number are no longer in their original locations.[37]

One series is composed of legendary windows that occupy the bays in three of the five radiating chapels and depict the Life of Christ and the lives of a number of saints such as Martin and Clement. These windows often include panels from other periods, and they were drastically restored in the nineteenth century.[38] The composition, the palette and the scale of execution of the authentic scenes, which are set against two-color mosaics decorated with small motifs, are comparable to those in lower French windows from the years 1240 to 1250. The drawing is heavy, and the execution is awkward. Only in the Legend of Saint Froilanus is a more "modern" composition adopted: the more broadly treated scenes are set under architectural canopies (three per panel), as in some of the windows in the cathedral at Clermont-Ferrand (around 1260).

A second series of stained glass fills several upper windows in the chevet and on the north side of the nave. For the most part, these are standing figures (superimposed in pairs) of patriarchs, Old Testament kings and prophets, sometimes accompanied by donors. The ensemble has been so heavily reworked that it is difficult to reconstruct the original program. It is highly probable that there were royal allusions, as in Saint Remi at Reims, given the personality of King Alfonso X, the Wise (1252–1284). Prophets and patriarchs, some of whom can be identified by inscriptions, are set under relatively well-developed architectural canopies with trefoil arcades inside. This detail points to a date late in the thirteenth century. The style is, nonetheless, unpolished and had long been abandoned north of the Pyrenees.[39] The cramped figures seem to be constricted by the drapery that is decorated with large colored lozenges. Another, perhaps later group has gaunter features inspired by French works from the middle of the thirteenth century. The glazing ensemble is characterized by saturated color, with red and blue dominant.

The Hunt window is not, however, characterized by this rather monotonous style. Three 179 of its lights illustrate a royal cavalcade, from which the window takes its name. The two other lights have a more up-to-date subject of musical angels and representations of the Liberal Arts. The Hunt sequence is said to have originally been set in a window in the royal palace of Alfonso X and to have been used in the cathedral at León in the fourteenth century. The subject, which is unique in European glass of the thirteenth century, is the best indication of the glass's original provenance. The scene is divided into three lights depicting superimposed horsemen accompanied by archers and surrounded by animals running under the horses' hooves. The figures are of different sizes, lively and animated. Their anecdotal treatment seems to derive in part from the style of Alfonso X's *Las Cantigas* illuminations, especially the manuscript preserved in the Escorial Library (ms. T. I. I).[40]

It was this same wise, humanist king who included in one of his works, *El Lapidario*, the recipe for silver stain that would revolutionize the technique of stained glass in France and England around 1300. The work was translated from Arab into Castilian before 1250 and was recopied between 1275 and 1279, thanks to the initiative of Alfonso X. A copy apparently reached the court of France, where it met with rapid enthusiasm, as we explained.[41] Did Alfonso X recognize the possible application of silver stain to the art of stained glass? Does the Hunt window come from his palace? If the answers are affirmative, the glaziers at León were either ignorant of the recipe or did not take advantage of it, since their style and technique are so dependent on archaizing principles that had become outmoded in the Ile-de-France from the third quarter of the thirteenth century.[42]

The Holy Roman Empire (1250–1330/1340)

Stained glass in the Holy Roman Empire, whatever the center or the workshop, did not follow the same stylistic trends as in France.[43] It is difficult to define the boundaries between the late Romanesque style, which survived until the middle of the thirteenth century, and the Gothic style, which quickly became "mannerist". In the Rhineland, for example, the

▷

180 Andernach (Rhineland-Palatinate), Namedy, former Cistercian abbey church, bay 0, 4th register; Calvary; 3rd quarter of the 13th century.

style of the windows in Sankt Kunibert at Cologne (1215–1226/1230) is still Romanesque and in the same tradition as the Landskron family window at Heimersheim an der Ahr from the middle of the century.[44] At the same period, two panels from a Life of the Virgin, preserved in the Schnütgen-Museum at Cologne, are characterized by more rigid drawing.[45] In both cases, however, outlines are preferred to modeling, yet the effect remains distinct.

Reticence to follow the French example lasted longer in painting than in architecture. Thus, in the cathedral at Cologne (begun after 1248 on French principles), the first glaziers remained faithful to the iconographic and formal traditions of late Romanesque stained glass; the architects were practicing *opus francigenum* before the master glaziers.[46] Furthermore, the relationship between architecture and stained glass was different in the Holy Roman Empire than in France and England at the same period: stained glass never attained the degree of colored saturation that is seen in French buildings such as the Sainte Chapelle or in the choir clerestory in Le Mans Cathedral. Light tints were always more numerous, notably greens and yellows, which remained dominant for a long time, and white backgrounds were never abandoned.[47] Colorless grisaille, often with big motifs, was occasionally used instead, for instance in the former Cistercian abbey church at Namedy (Andernach township) near Bonn.[48]

The phenomenon of "whitening," which characterized the evolution of glazing in France and England after 1260–1270, did not occur in the Holy Roman Empire except in rare instances. Grisaille and colored historiated or figural areas were used together, but the combinations were different. On the one hand, motifs were often rendered on a larger scale than in France and arranged like the motifs on a carpet; on the other hand, the naturalistic vocabulary was taken from different botanical examples: oak leaves were very popular. Color continued to be used over large areas, as in Saint Thomas at Strasbourg or in the Dominican church at Colmar.[49] Decorative panels were used as bases or above the figures. The figures were generally crowned by architectural canopies, which became one of the essential aspects of stained glass in the Upper Rhine region.[50] Beginning in the years 1320–1325, Italian perspective began to be employed in these baldachins, notably at Königsfelden in Switzerland. The successive stages of this stylistic change, which resulted in the adoption of Gothic formulae in German glass, will be analyzed. The nature of the changes varied with the region and the workshop.

181 Heimersheim an der Ahr (Rhineland-Palatinate), parish church, apse, bay 0: Saint Maurice; middle of the 13th century.

182 Marburg, church of Sankt Elisabeth, apse, central window: Synagoga; ca. 1240.

▷
183 Mönchengladbach, St-Vitus-Münster, apse, bay 0: Typological window (right light, 5th register), Adoration of the Magi; ca. 1275. Cf. cat. 5.

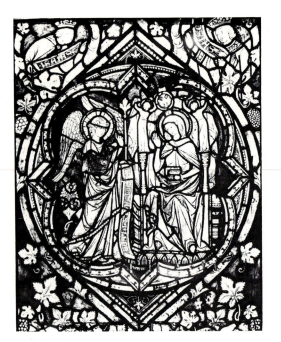

184   Cologne, cathedral, Saint Stephen Chapel, bay 16: The Annunciation, panel from a typological window in the church of the Dominicans (now destroyed) in Cologne; ca. 1280. Cf. cat. 2.

The End of the *Zackenstil* and the First Manifestations of Gothic Style

In the middle of the thirteenth century, the evolution of glass painting in the Holy Roman Empire almost always emanated from the forms and figural concepts of the *Zackenstil*, or "broken-fold style".[51] Major works, already discussed in *Le Vitrail roman*, were created at Frankfurt, Naumburg and Strasbourg, testifying to the vitality of this stylistic phase that was characterized by a vehement style of drawing, rigid and angular forms, and a range of violent colors. Some of these components may seem contradictory, such as plasticity with Romanesque excesses already weeded out or ornament that remained, on the contrary, as abundant as in the twelfth century. Until now, Thuringo-Saxon illumination has always been considered the principal source of this style.[52] By adding sculpture as another source, Peter Kurmann has provided formal dimensions that had been lacking.[53]   182

In stained glass, the mature *Zackenstil* dates to the 1250s, or perhaps from 1240 in the historiated roses in the south aisle of the cathedral at Strasbourg.[54] This date, suggested by Victor Beyer, has not been unanimously accepted.[55] This style, with its energetic, sometimes almost abstract forms, already "mannerist" in effect, would compel recognition from several German workshops. They would, however, be rapidly subjected to other influences —local on the one hand, Byzantinizing on the other—which would continue until the end of the thirteenth century, for example in the series of prophets and angels from the choir in the abbey church at Heiligenkreuz in Austria (1295–1297).[56]   208

The arrangement of the glass often stayed set within multifoil frames until the first third of the fourteenth century, even after the adoption of a method of drawing and treatment that were more Gothic, for instance the typological medallions in the cloister of the Augustinian abbey at Klosterneuburg, most of which have been reset in the neighboring Saint Leopold Chapel (around 1330).[57] These frames contained verses from the Bible that explained the scene represented, creating a close relationship between text and image, as in the altar by Nicholas of Verdun (now an altarpiece, 1180–1181).   212

The *Zackenstil* evolved differently according to the region and the workshop. Almost without exception, the goal was to suggest new emotional relationships between the protagonists of a single scene, and the attempts were often successful. A comparison among the three principal typological windows *(Bibelfenster)* from between 1250 and 1280 preserved in the Rhineland makes it easier to understand these transformations. The *Bibelfenster* was one of the essential iconographic orientations of German glass in the thirteenth century.[58]

The earliest *Bibelfenster*, in the axial bay of the Three Kings Chapel in the cathedral at Cologne, is still Romanesque in its use of space—crowded compositions, heavy treatment and ornament still in keeping with earlier traditions.[59] Herbert Rode dates its execution to the 1260s.

The second *Bibelfenster* decorates the choir in the abbey church of Saint Vitus at Mönchengladbach, finished around 1275; the typological window in the axis of the chevet dates from that period.[60] Following the usual custom, the left light is reserved for the Old Testament and the right for the New. Each contains the same number of historiated compartments, but the shapes differ in each light; the decoration also varies. At Mönchengladbach, ornament remains abundant and colors lively, but the drawing is softer and the scenes less dense—the figures are no longer crowded together as in the preceding window, and their relationships have become "humanized". The execution is distinguished by softer modeling, tints that are "blended" better, and by more cursive contours.[61]   183

The third work is from the Dominican church at Cologne, now reset in a bay of the Saint Stephen Chapel in Cologne Cathedral. A different formal stage has been reached, and the decoration hardly depends on Romanesque traditions any longer. Both the shape of the compartments and the scale of execution are innovative in comparison with the preceding examples. The style of drawing has become calmer for the figures, which show much more feeling—one of the essential characteristics of European Gothic painting around 1300.   184

Regensburg: Romanesque Survivals

▷
185   Regensburg, cathedral, chevet clerestory, bay 302: Acts of Mercy and the Passion of Christ (detail), Pentecost; ca. 1310.

Not all centers accepted these changes so easily. The cathedral at Regensburg was partially rebuilt after a fire, beginning in 1273, in a manner that was different from contemporary German constructions and probably done in opposition to French Gothic taste.[62] The choir   185

was glazed under Bishop Nicholas von Ybbs (1313–1340), with the aid of numerous donors. The glazing program was ambitious and composed of legendary windows, except in the axial bay of the choir clerestory. It mixed traditional Christological and hagiographic subjects with new themes such as the "Acts of Mercy" (Matthew 25:34–46), dear to Franciscan spirituality. In this series, there are numerous Romanesque survivals in both the conception and distribution of decoration in the windows; the same is true of their composition. The figure style is already more refined, underscoring the fact that it changed more quickly than the other components, which were more resistant to change. This situation can be seen in several examples in Swabia and in Austria.[63] Gothic conventions seem to have been more readily accepted for compositions and figures, and more slowly for the arrangement of the windows.

Strasbourg:
Workshops Responsible for Glazing the Nave of the Cathedral

Work at the Alsatian cathedral was one of the essential links to Parisian art in the Rhenish region during the second half of the thirteenth century.[64] French workshops had already exerted an influence on sculpture there, notably on the Column of Angels in the south transept arm (1225–1230).[65] This influence was much more timid in the realm of stained glass, which displayed a mixture of other earlier and specifically local traditions, for example the two figures of Solomon and the Queen of Sheba, now on the facade of the north transept (1220–1230).[66] The assimilation of French forms took place gradually during the second half of the century. However, the nave (built between 1254 and 1275) was a Parisian work, and the rood screen (built around 1260?) was executed by a Reims workshop.

The case of the glazing in this part of the building is entirely different: most of the glass painters who worked in Strasbourg belonged to the Rhenish milieu, but there were occasional mutual influences among the workshops.

The glazing program was simple, but the reuse of figures of emperors from the Romanesque nave in the north aisle and other, later transformations make the study of this glass difficult. On the triforium level, there was a Genealogy of Christ, of which only a few authentic elements remain, for instance the head of Melchi, preserved at the Musée de l'Œuvre Notre-Dame. The clerestory windows contained a series of saints: on the north are figures of men including popes, warriors, the martyrs of the Theban Legion, Fathers of the Church and early bishops of Strasbourg; on the south are women saints grouped with a Virgin and Child in the first eastern window. In the western bays are more recent works: on the south, a Judgment of Solomon (1340–1345) and an Adoration of the Magi, which is partially nineteenth-century; on the north, Virtues Overcoming Vices (1340–1350?).

The north aisle follows the German imperial tradition, reusing certain royal figures from the clerestory windows of the Romanesque nave and adding others to it. However, this sequence was reduced when the addition of the Saint Lawrence Chapel necessitated the removal of the two easternmost bays in the nave. On the south, only the historiated roses studied by Victor Beyer remain from the original glazing.[67] They decorate the tympana of the five broad, short bays that contain a narrative cycle devoted to Christ and the Virgin Mary (executed between 1325 and 1340–1345).

It is much more difficult to follow the stylistic "stages" of this ensemble. In a recent monograph, Roger Lehni, following the hypothesis of Christiane Wild-Block, identified no fewer than five workshops active in the cathedral between 1250 and 1280, the date of the completion of the nave.[68] Most of them remained faithful to German art of the Rhine region, while often using more flexible and plastic formulae that coincided with the tendencies of contemporary Gothic art. In fact, from 1250, the glaziers who practiced the *Zackenstil* were infected by French conventions in both iconography and style. V. Beyer and L. Grodecki have already drawn attention to this phenomenon in the series of historiated medallions in the south aisle. The most conclusive example is the Virgin and Child in the second bay from the east (1240–1250).[69] This workshop was responsible for other works in the cathedral—on the north side, in the triforium level and in the upper windows.[70]

The same stylistic tendency can be seen in works executed for other churches in the city such as the Dominican church, begun in 1254 and consecrated in 1260, for the general chapter of the Dominican order held that year. Only some disfigured panels of the glazing

186 Strasbourg, Musée de l'Œuvre Notre-Dame: Solomon and the Queen of Sheba, medallion from a lateral window in the apse of the church of Saint Thomas; ca. 1270. Cf. cat. 86.

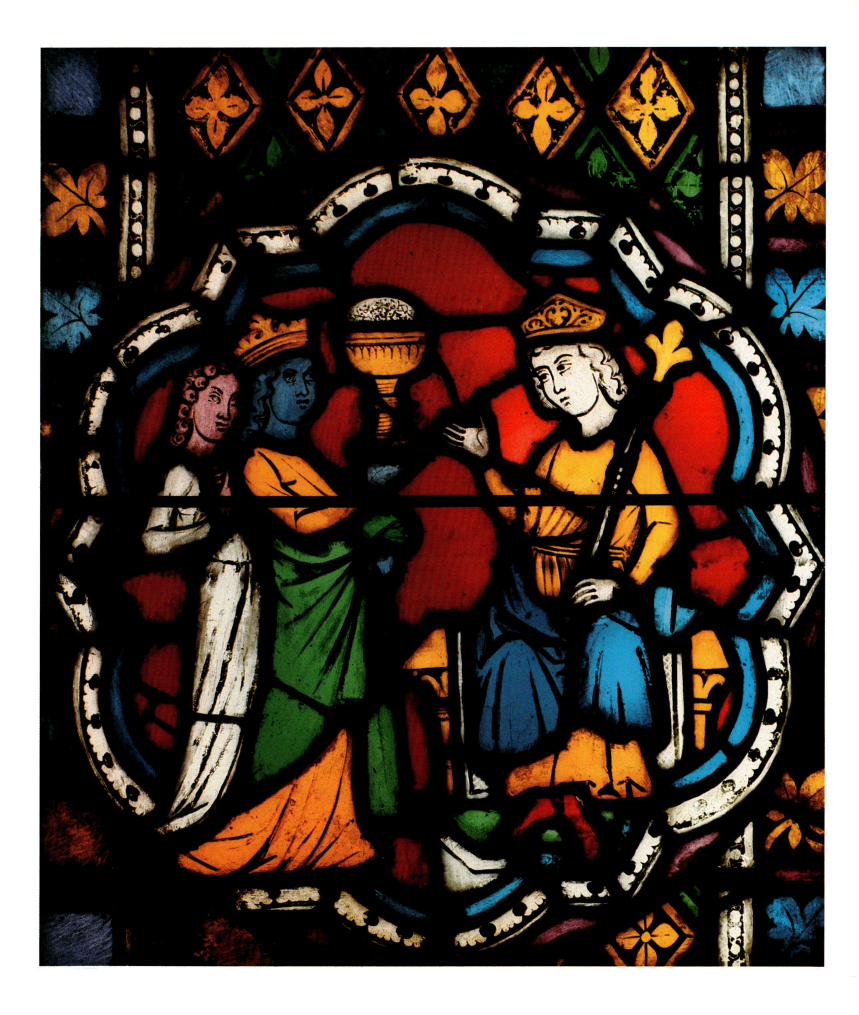

from these years survive, remounted at the end of the nineteenth century in a number of bays in the Saint Lawrence Chapel at the cathedral. The preserved scenes have a wide variety of subjects: episodes from the Old Testament, scenes from the Life of Christ and the lives of the saints and remains of a Jesse Tree.[71] These panels, which come from several distinct series, have formal and decorative analogies with series from Swabia that are datable to the last decades of the thirteenth century or even to the beginning of the fourteenth. Elements from a Life of Saint Bartholomew, patron of the church, which have also been reused in a bay of this chapel, show a style that is softer and calmer.

The few medallions preserved from the historiated windows in the chevet of Saint Thomas at Strasbourg, now exhibited (with one exception) at the Musée de l'Œuvre Notre-Dame, come from the same milieu. The building was rebuilt after 1269–1270, beginning with the choir, and the panels probably date from the years following this reconstruction. Most of them show Old Testament scenes. They retain complex framing with alternating foils and cusps. The scale of execution has lost the monumental character it had in the historiated roses in the south aisle of the cathedral. Compositions have become relaxed, and the drawing and treatment are softer. This arrangement is even clearer in the only authentic fragment—a Life of Saint Thomas—a half-medallion originally in the axial bay. The simple form of this panel, the frame composed of two smooth fillets and the mosaic ground against which it is set make the panel almost completely devoid of the conventions seen in the works previously studied.[72] The originality of the Strasbourg milieu, which may have had one or more workshops, was dissipated in favor of an overall simplification that was characteristic of Parisian art after 1250.

The other bays in the triforium and the clerestory of the cathedral were done by different workshops. To simplify the discussion, let us say that these groups of glaziers worked from east to west, undoubtedly following the rhythm of construction. Even in the earliest sections (the upper windows in the second bay on the south side and the third on the north side), the effect is different from that created by monumental figures following *Zackenstil* tendencies; e.g. Bishop Biulfe, which was reused in the transept.[73] In the upper nave, the figures are superimposed in pairs in each of the four lights in the bays. The saints in the south window are presented frontally—crowned, and with halos—holding the palm of martyrdom in one hand and an illuminated lamp in the other, like the Wise Virgins. The drawing is elegant and soft, seeking to define the volume of the body. The execution is refined, and the decoration of the drapery simplified. The still saturated palette uses the blue and red grounds that became increasingly important in Alsatian and Swabian windows around 1300. The architectural crown set over each figure, animated with birds, is no longer a simple canopy but already a tabernacle.[74] A notable evolution can be seen in the subsequent windows in the third and fourth bays. The treatment becomes drier and more rapid, while maintaining the "mannerist" style of drawing. Ornament also becomes sparer.

In the westernmost bays of the nave, on the south, is a Judgment of Solomon with one protagonist in each light. Its formal elegance and the daring of the architectural tabernacles set over the figures anticipate the apostles in the Saint Catherine Chapel (1340), which postdate it by about twenty years.[75] The choice of that scene underscores the persistence of Solomon iconography at the cathedral since the twelfth century, especially in stained glass.[76] In the first bay on the north, next to the west block, is a window with Virtues Overcoming Vices, in a calligraphic style datable to the 1340s. It is thought to have been set originally in an aisle window.[77]

On the triforium level, there is more modern than authentic glass; nevertheless, the stylistic evolution shows that this level was glazed on the north from east to west. Each figure is represented standing, with his name accompanied by the words QUI FUIT, set around his head in the amortizement of the light, like Saint John the Baptist in the first eastern arcade. The lower part of that figure has been redone, but the head is original. Despite its poor state at present, characterized by loss of paint, the formal characteristics seen in the figure of Saint Biulfe are evident, continuing the tendencies of the *Zackenstil*.

After this piece, stylistic expression changed and seems to be related to certain heads of apostles from the destroyed rood screen that are preserved in the Musée de l'Œuvre Notre-Dame. Such is the case of the head of Melchi, with its firm, cursive style of drawing and its short, wavy hair. Consequently, the products of this workshop can be dated to the 1260s.

◁

187 Strasbourg, Musée de l'Œuvre Notre-Dame: Melchi, panel from a Genealogy of Christ window on the triforium level of the cathedral of Notre Dame in Strasbourg; ca. 1260 (?). Cf. cat. 85.

188 Freiburg im Breisgau, Augustinermuseum: Virgin and Child, panel from the axial bay in the choir of the church of the Dominicans at Freiburg im Breisgau; ca. 1290.

199

The few authentic faces in the westernmost bays on the north are reminiscent of portal statues in the west facade and are later—between 1280 and 1290. The historiated windows in the south aisle of Strasbourg Cathedral will be discussed later.

Workshops in Alsace and the Upper Rhine Region

The originality of the stained glass windows in the nave of Strasbourg Cathedral lies in the enlargement of the architectural canopies over the figures rather than in the figural style. R. Becksmann has demonstrated the essential role of the Strasbourg workshops in the development of this formal and decorative principle in the regions of the Upper Rhine—in Alsace, Swabia and the Lake of Constance area.[78] This "architecture in glass" changed the composition of stained glass windows in these regions and became an autonomous form regulated by its own typology. The ultimate product would be the Saint Catherine Chapel (around 1340) in the cathedral at Strasbourg: in the eight registers of each light, only two are reserved for figures, the others being filled by tabernacles composed of fairy-tale scaffolding.

The vitality of the Strasbourg workshops, along with those of the Upper Rhine, enabled the art of stained glass to take great strides from the years 1260–1270. The building undertaken at that time by the orders of mendicant friars favored this dynamism. Their churches, built according to architectural principles that resulted in a renewal of volume in buildings, were generally pierced by numerous large bays with relatively small tympana. Glass painting found a privileged terrain in this kind of building, favorable to new formal conjectures even before the abandonment of the ideals of poverty and simplicity that these orders had professed at their beginnings. Notable examples exist at Strasbourg, Colmar, Freiburg im Breisgau and Esslingen. The building activity extended to rural churches such as Saint Martin at Westhoffen near Saverne,[79] to collegiate churches such as Sankt Florentius at Niederhaslach, southwest of Strasbourg,[80] and to abbey churches, many of which are Cistercian, for instance at Kappel am Albis, southwest of Zurich,[81] and at Heiligkreuztal in Swabia.[82] In these last monasteries, principles of decoration and color have been neglected in favor of vividly colored figures and stories.

Other techniques, for instance the drawing of architecture, frequently practiced in this region, probably helped the master glaziers to build the formal vocabulary of these tabernacles. R. Becksmann has compared them to architects' working drawings, even suggesting that the painters took their inspiration directly from master masons.[83] Certain motifs in these baldachins seem to copy elements from projects that architects drew beginning around 1275 for the west facade of the cathedral at Strasbourg, many of which have been preserved in the Musée de l'Œuvre Notre-Dame.[84] This situation is different—even contrary—to that in France and England, where architectural canopies always remained fictitious architecture that did not depend on actual models. In the Upper Rhine regions, these architectural motifs underwent modification, especially in their arrangement. The glass painters rendered the realistic character of the architecture void by using blue or red quarries in the grounds against which figures and architecture stand out, as in the Crucifixion window from the destroyed church at Mutzig west of Strasbourg, in the Musée de l'Œuvre Notre-Dame.

Because of its architectonic composition on several levels, this window marks a new formal stage.[85] Executed by a Strasbourg workshop, its arrangement is balanced: in the lower registers, underneath niches surmounted by tabernacles, are figures of the Virgin and Child (replacing Saint Paul), Saint Maurice on horseback (patron of the building) and Saint Peter. They are isolated from one another like statuettes in a triptych, the upper part of which has been reserved for a Calvary; its three figures are arranged in niches—Christ in the center, the Virgin and Saint John in the side lights—and integrated into the vast painted architecture. The tabernacles give this representation a formal unity that is reinforced by the way the glass is cut into rectangular quarries. The coloration accentuates this coherence: glass in light tones for the architecture to make it more linear, saturated colors for the decorated backgrounds of small lozenges and vivid colors for the figures. The figure style has certain analogies with the style of drawing and the handling of the Klingenberg window from the cathedral at Constance, now preserved in the cathedral at Freiburg im Breisgau.[86] This work, which is somewhat later than the Mutzig Crucifixion of 1310, is datable to the years 1315–1317.

188

192

189

190

189 Strasbourg, Musée de l'Œuvre Notre-Dame: drawing for the elevation of the west facade of the cathedral at Strasbourg (project B, not carried out); ca. 1270.

▷

190 Strasbourg, Musée de l'Œuvre Notre-Dame: Crucifixion, window from the axial bay in the church of Sankt Mauritius at Mutzig (Bas-Rhin, now destroyed); ca. 1310. Cf. cat. 51.

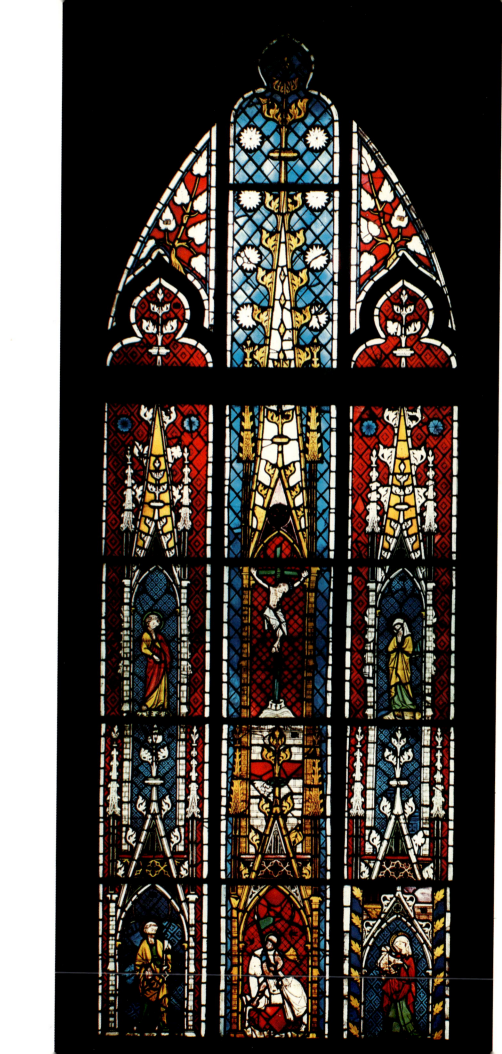

191 Wettingen (Aargau), former Cistercian abbey church, cloister, north side, 3rd bay, tympanum, central hexafoil: Cistercian Monk Kneeling at the Feet of a Virgin and Child; ca. 1280.

192 Kappel am Albis, Cistercian abbey church, nave, bay 0: Crucifixion (right light, 2nd register), Saint John the Evangelist; ca. 1310.

Such similarity is not limited to just these two works but extends to an entire ensemble of stained glass in this region, underscoring the cross influences among the workshops in Alsace, the Constance region, Swabia and the area around Baden. Most of them use the tabernacle, which did not immediately become stereotyped. On the contrary, it evolved according to various tendencies that often left room for invention. The important place given to architecture renewed the entire conception of the stained glass window, while the place given to figures or narrative events was considerably reduced—all over Europe in fact.[87]

In the Upper Rhine region, this phenomenon was linked to the enlargement of the bay and gave rise to particular types of mixed windows. Panels of grisaille could be placed inside painted architecture, as in the abbey of Lichtental at Baden-Baden (around 1310),[88] or grisaille panels could develop above the architecture, filling the rest of the bay, as in Saint Thomas at Strasbourg (around 1325).[89]

Beginning in the final quarter of the thirteenth century, Strasbourg glass painters went beyond the borders of Alsace and formed a vast community with those beyond the Rhine, taking in regions as far away as Swabia. This situation gave rise to emulation among the Upper Rhenish workshops that extended their activities as far as the monasteries around Zurich, for instance the Cistercian abbey at Wettingen (Aargau).[90] Until about 1280, however, these painters had difficulty in breaking away from the conventions of the *Zackenstil*, as evidenced by the typological series at Wimpfen im Tal (1270–1280), preserved in the Hessisches Landesmuseum at Darmstadt.

Important changes occurred in the last decade of the century, renewing the orientation of the glass painters who adopted a more refined but mannerist style, in keeping with the evolution of Gothic forms before 1300. This movement was not limited to the medium of stained glass; it was also important in manuscript illumination, often the work of monastic ateliers. Such production was often of a very high quality and determined the evolution of painting in this region, as can be seen in the Gradual of the Dominican nuns at Sankt Katharinental (Thurgau), datable to the 1310s.[91] Relationships can be seen between the style of this manuscript and that of the historiated window in the Cistercian convent at Heilig-kreuztal in Swabia (around 1312). The delicate and incisive style of drawing in figures of saints set under tabernacles is related to work in the Constance region, another active area for glazing at the beginning of the fourteenth century. Important examples are the Klingen-berg window (1313–1317) from the cathedral at Constance, preserved in the cathedral at Freiburg im Breisgau, panels from a Life of Christ from the choir of the Dominican church at Constance (around 1320), reset in the castle at Heiligenberg, northeast of Constance, and the Crucifixion window at Frauenfeld-Oberkirch (1320–1330), southwest of the same city. Their execution shows analogies with the Crucifixion from Mutzig in Alsace, underscoring the use of analogous sources.

The Ensembles in Swabia

There are many glazing programs in Swabia that have clear connections with Alsatian stained glass, as Hans Wentzel has established.[92] From the last decades of the thirteenth century, monuments at Stetten, Urach and Lauffen on the Neckar[93] testify to the development of glass painting in Swabia. The most important series is the one that decorated the choir in the *Ritterstiftskirche* in the church of Sankt Peter at Wimpfen im Tal, near Stuttgart, the remains of which are now in the Hessisches Landesmuseum at Darmstadt. Datable to the years 1270–1280, these typological medallions retain a heavy and insistent draughtsman-ship that still derives from the conventions of the *Zackenstil*.

This development continued during the first quarter of the fourteenth century, and the city of Esslingen, southeast of Stuttgart on the Neckar, was its center. Building by the orders of mendicant friars, who were firmly entrenched in this region, favored the activity of the glass painters. At Esslingen, itself, a number of churches received stained glass windows during the first quarter of the fourteenth century, for example Sankt Dionysius, the Frauen-kirche and the Franciscan church of Sankt Georg. These windows were sometimes strictly ornamental, sometimes historiated, but most often typological. Several Christological cycles have an original iconography that integrates scenes from the Apocryphal Childhood of Christ such as the Virgin Taking Her Son to School in the Frauenkirche at Esslingen.[94]

193 Darmstadt, Hessisches Landesmuseum: Lioness Reviving her Cubs, medallion from a typological window in the *Ritterstiftskirche* at the church of Sankt Peter at Wimpfen im Tal (Baden-Württemberg); 1275–1280.

194 Esslingen, Frauenkirche, chevet, bay 3: Life of ▷ the Virgin Mary and Childhood of Christ (detail), The Blessed Virgin Taking Jesus to School; ca. 1320. Cf. cat. 4.

195 Esslingen, Franciscan church of St. Georg, apse, ▷▷ bay 0: Typological window (detail), The Flagellation of Christ; 1310–1320. Cf. cat. 3.

In the earliest windows, those in Sankt Dionysius at Esslingen (end of the thirteenth century), the compositions remain archaic, with multifoil compartments joined together by fillets. The handling remains heavy and busy, contrasting with the desired effect of delicacy and mannerism. An entirely different quality can be seen in the windows executed for the Frauenkirche and for the Franciscan church during the first quarter of the fourteenth century, where the treatment responds to the demands of a soft, fine style of drawing that employs the refined conventions of Gothic painting around 1300. Various tendencies can be observed, however. The choir in the Franciscan church at Esslingen was glazed between 1310 and 1320, according to an original system reconstructed by H. Wentzel.

At the center was a typological window with three lights, surrounded by four windows with two lights each, which are completely ornamental, a blend of white plant motifs and brightly colored frames, in keeping with the traditions of German stained glass.[95] In the axial window (where only eighteen of the original forty-five panels remain), the central light is

dedicated to the Life of Christ, while the side ones treat Old Testament events: to the left, 195
events that occurred before the Law of Moses *(Ante Legem)*, i.e. having to do with the first
books of the Bible; to the right, later events announcing the coming of Christ *(Sub Lege)*.
The fifteen scenes in each light were presented in trefoil compartments, the form of which
repeated—on a small scale—that of the heads of contemporary lancets. The compositions
have extraordinary formal authority, for the protagonists are placed on several levels. The
drawing is energetic and rapid, abandoning superfluous details and retaining only essential
lines. Despite abundant modeling, the execution is refined. This is one of the first German
windows where silver stain is used with mastery.

At the Frauenkirche, the Childhood window (about 1320) is more interesting than the 194
typological window that repeats the pattern used in the Franciscan church of Sankt Georg.
The handling of this glass has evolved toward an even more refined style: the elegant
silhouettes move with courtly gestures and observe each other with tender gazes. Each light
in the Childhood of Christ is a succession of long spindles, framed by a wide fillet decorated
with leaves. Fine architectural motifs accentuate the inside and outside of the curves like the
medallions in the Navarre Chapel at Mantes. The scenes are set against a ground decorated
with small ivy leaves that emphasizes the overall preciousness. The scale of execution has
been reduced. The figures are "sketched in" with a few lines. Gestures, on the other hand,
are marked to make the relationships between the protagonists more precise, in imitation of
contemporary illumination.

These conflicting orientations indicate the presence of a number of workshops at
Esslingen, perhaps coming from Speyer at the beginning of the fourteenth century.[96] These
painters worked not only for urban churches but also for monasteries in the area such as the
Dominican monastery at Wimpfen am Berg. Only twenty panels from the axial window in its
chevet survive; they were reused in the nineteenth century in several windows in a hall of a
castle. Originally the window contained three lights with thirteen scenes each. As in the
Franciscan church at Esslingen, the central light was devoted to Christ and the one on the
left to the Old Testament; however, the one on the right dealt with Saint Dominic, whose life 196
was used as a parallel to that of the Saviour.[97] The formal invention of the compositions is
surprising; for example in the scene of the Burning Bush, where God and Moses are set
off-center from the axis of the medallion, the kneeling Moses seems almost like the trunk of
a tree in which the half-length figure of God appears. While the style of drawing is cursive, it
possesses strong authority. The frame inside the compartment evokes the other windows at
Esslingen. Analogies with Alsatian glazing, particularly with the Dominican church at Colmar,
can be seen in the decoration.

These Swabian panels have been dated between 1299 and 1310, because of the arms of
the family of Conrad of Weinsberg, founder of the building, which are still in place in the
perforations of the tympanum. Light touches of silver stain have been employed. With its
formal maturity, this series testifies to the quality of glass painting in Swabia and to its links
with other centers of the art in the Upper Rhine region. Likewise, it points to certain
subsequent orientations towards increasingly marked preciousness.

Alsace at the Dawn of the Fourteenth Century

The last decades of the thirteenth century and the beginning of the fourteenth were a time
of intense activity for stained glass workshops in Alsace: in Strasbourg itself and its surroundings, in the choir of the Dominican church at Colmar (1283–1291), in Sankt Florentius at
Niederhaslach, whose choir was decorated beginning in 1287, in the church at Westhoffen
(1280–1300) or in the one in the cemetery at Ostwald (1290–1300).

A fire in Strasbourg Cathedral in 1298 necessitated new work there. The ensemble of five
windows in the south aisle was not begun until 1325. These four-light windows illustrate the
lives of the Virgin and of Christ in a narrative, even familiar, fashion in the spirit of the *Biblia
Pauperum*. The first window furthest to the east treats the Virgin and the Childhood of
Christ; the second, the Public Life of Christ; the third, His Passion; the fourth, His Supernatural Life and Posthumous Appearances and the final one, the Last Judgment. The initial
sense of unity, suggested by the fact that there are four registers in each window and that the
dimensions of the scenes are the same, does not stand up to close examination. Each

196 Stuttgart, Württembergisches Landesmuseum:
Moses and the Burning Bush, panel from a typological window in the church of the Dominicans at
Wimpfen am Berg (Baden-Württemberg); between
1299 and 1310. Cf. cat. 7.

197 Königsfelden, former Franciscan abbey, church: view of the chevet; 1325–1330. Cf. cat. 106.

window has a particular arrangement that reflects the stylistic changes in this ensemble, executed between 1325 and 1340. The series shows the evolution in the glaziers' work.

In the earliest window, they used schema and decoration deriving from "French Gothic" art such as pointed canopies over the scenes; subsequently, they distanced themselves from these formulae and finally returned to more German patterns, derived from the principles of typological windows *(Bibelfenster)*, where rinceaux crown the compartments and shelter the prophets, as in the Public Life of Christ window. In the third window the rinceaux appear in continuous bands above the scenes. In the last windows, the compositions free themselves from these frames, and the scale of execution increases. Similar modifications can be seen in the figural style. In the first bays, it is refined, but the style of drawing becomes more summary in the later ones—a single cartoon is used repeatedly, especially to represent the Elect in the Last Judgment window. The handling becomes less and less heavy; likewise in the palette, the tones become ever less saturated and increasingly pale; white and yellow are used over large areas.

Three workshops were probably responsible for this cycle. The earliest was responsible for the Life of the Virgin and the Childhood of Christ around 1325–1330. The next two windows must have been done by two other painters from the same workshop, between 1330 and 1335, and the last windows by a third workshop around 1340, when the Saint Catherine Chapel was being constructed at the eastern end of the nave, which necessitated the removal of the earliest windows.[98]

In Strasbourg at the beginning of the fourteenth century, other workshops were active in the churches in that city such as Saint Guillaume (before 1310)[99] and above all in Saint Thomas, where two medallions (illustrating the Coronation of the Virgin, around 1310) in the north transept arm fill the entire width of the bay and give a formal autonomy to each of the scenes. This principle—very important for the evolution of stained glass in the Holy Roman Empire—would be taken up again often during the fifteenth century. In the nave, the tabernacles are the only elements of the glazing to survive; they count among the most extraordinary and attractive examples in this period (around 1325).

Königsfelden

The vitality of the Upper Rhenish workshops was exceptional between 1250 and 1350. It is no accident, then, that it was in this region that the foremost work of the period was produced—the choir ensemble in the former Franciscan abbey church at Königsfelden, 197 southwest of Zurich, then on the borders of the dioceses of Basel and Zurich.

The convent was built on the site where the Hapsburg Emperor Albert I was assassinated by his nephew, Duke John of Swabia, on May 1, 1308. The convent was Franciscan and had been founded there by the Hapsburgs, whose political power was recent. Queen Agnes of Hungary (1280–1364), widowed in 1301, had the monastery built in memory of her father, and its church became the mausoleum of the family. The church was constructed in two campaigns: first the nave, then the choir between 1325 and 1330. The eleven windows that decorate the choir were installed gradually as the building was constructed, beginning in the east. The glazing program was settled at the beginning of the construction. It emphasizes Franciscan spirituality, while integrating the particular devotions of the Hapsburgs who donated the windows, in which they are frequently represented.

The bays in the chevet are reserved for Christ, with a Passion at the center, a Childhood in the south bay and the Appearances of the Risen Christ in the north one. The following windows depict saints who were usually venerated at the time, either as standing images or in a particular episode from their lives. Included are the Virgin Mary, the apostles, Saint John the Baptist, Saint Catherine and Saint Nicholas.

The two other windows are dedicated to the founders of the Franciscan order—Saint 198 Francis and Saint Clare—and the last one to Saint Ann, devotion to whom was greatly increasing at this period.

The ensemble has surprising formal and chromatic unity. The windows, however, do not have the same arrangement: some are historiated, others figurative, but all have the same quarry grounds, which reinforce their coherence. Each series takes up again the formal and decorative principles traditional in Upper Rhenish stained glass since the years 1250–1260.

▷
198 Königsfelden, former Franciscan abbey, church, choir, bay 8: Life of Saint Francis of Assisi (detail), Saint Francis Preaches to the Birds; 1325–1330. Cf. cat. 108.

▷▷
199 Königsfelden, former Franciscan abbey, church, choir, bay 2: The Childhood of Christ: Adoration of the Magi (detail), King Gaspard; 1325–1330. Cf. cat. 107.

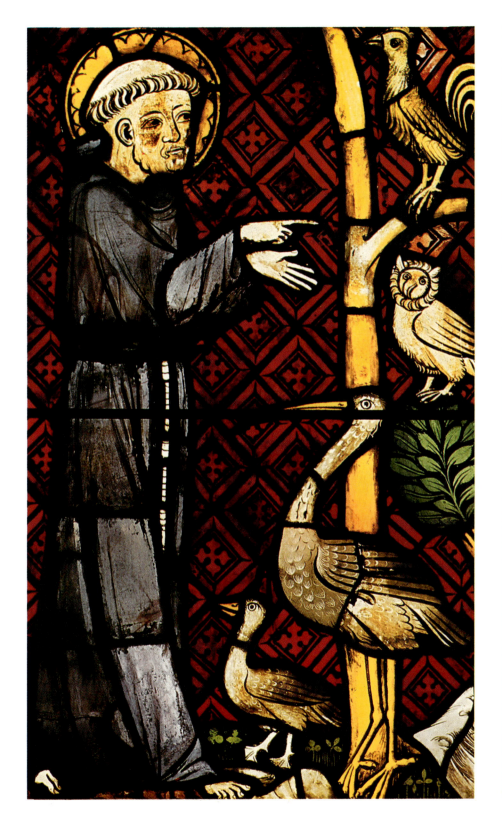

200 Königsfelden, former Franciscan abbey, church, choir, bay 6: The Apostles Judas, Matthew and Simon; 1325-1330.

The historiated windows, such as the Passion in the axial bay, are composed of several large medallions that fill the entire width of the bay, as was already the case in the two medallions with the Coronation of the Virgin in Saint Thomas at Strasbourg (around 1310). In a number of windows, the medallions are replaced by pierced quatrefoils, a form that was revived in the 1270s. The scenes continue through the three lights of the window without regard to the mullions. The compartments (four per window) are supported by atlantes, which are either animals, half-length figures of angels or grotesques that resemble those in manuscripts but on a monumental scale—an original choice. This type of grotesque had already been used by certain workshops in the region, notably by the one that decorated a Cistercian breviary (around 1300) that is now in the library at Lucerne.[100]

The ornament copies formulae that were used in Upper Rhenish stained glass, but the formal exploitation of them is new. The leaves and flowers are enlarged and combined with coats of arms. The backgrounds between the medallions are often covered with architectural motifs animated with heraldic lions, like the Throne of Solomon window in the Dominican church at Colmar (around 1320).[101] Other historiated windows adopt the tabernacle form, for instance the Childhood and the Appearances of the Risen Christ windows 199 that frame the axial bay.

The figures are placed either singly or in small groups in one of the three lights, following a principle that had already appeared in the Crucifixion window at Mutzig (around 1310) and that became a general pattern around 1320 in this region. The figures in the Apostles 200 windows at the entrance to the choir are superimposed in pairs in free and supple poses. The tabernacles crowning them have streamlined proportions; some of them have even become larger than the figures they shelter. For the first time in the art of stained glass, the bases on which several figures of saints stand are represented with perspective; the same is true of some of the tabernacles.

The treatment of scenes and the figural style at Königsfelden also surpass numerous contemporary creations from this region. In the historiated windows with large medallions, the scenes are conceived like paintings and have their own formal autonomy. The landscape and architecture seem to derive from Italian works. Perspective is used in a rather unorthodox way in the earliest window (the Passion); for example, in the scene with the Entombment, the uprights of the tomb on which the body of Christ lies recede in opposite directions, nullifying the intended effect. A few years later, around 1330, perspective is more successfully employed in the Saint Ann window. Nevertheless, the calligraphic style of drawing in this glass derives from Upper Rhenish works, above all from manuscripts of the Lake Constance region. The slender silhouettes with their elegant movements and poses, their calm and expressive faces and their naturally treated hair and beards, give the figures a formal ease that is rarely attained in this period. The arrangement of folds and drapery shows an awareness of schemes that were not native to this region. The ornament, on the other hand, remains traditional: for instance backgrounds with decorated bull's eyes against which the scenes stand out, or very wide framing fillets stamped with very jagged leaves, like those in the Childhood window in the Frauenkirche at Esslingen. The blend of colors is 194 bright, and its range varied and delicate—highlights of silver stain are used in some of the architectural motifs. The ensemble was created between 1325 and 1330, and the donors, usually represented at the base of the windows, often enable each of the works to be dated.

The slight development visible within this series has given rise to a number of suggestions. It is possible, as Emil Maurer has theorized, that Queen Agnes brought together highly experienced artists, probably from Strasbourg, who were aware of pictorial innovations such as Italian perspective.[102] They were responsible for a work that has as much importance in the history of glass painting as the work of Jean Pucelle has in manuscript illumination—their creations herald the International Gothic Style.

The Rhineland: Cologne and Altenberg

Cologne was a city where Gothic formulae penetrated rapidly, at least in the realm of architecture. Its cathedral (begun in 1248) was modeled after the one at Amiens. In painting, however, the adoption of Gothic formulae was not as rapid. Romanesque traditions survived over many decades, not only in Cologne but also in the Rhineland generally. Only some Gothic ideas had been accepted; others had been rejected. Gothic spatiality and form appear

201 Cologne, church of Sankt Gereon, sacristy, 2nd north bay, tympanum, central rose: Christ in Majesty Surrounded by Evangelist Symbols; ca. 1320–1330.

around 1300 in the medallions with the Life of Saint Stephen preserved in various museums.[103] The shape of the medallions is somewhat simplified, despite their foils and cusps. The pieces are cut rather geometrically, and the draughtsmanship is summary. The beards and hair in corkscrews or curls are some of the few decorative elements in these panels, whose exact provenance is unknown.

The windows in the sacristy in Sankt Gereon derive from a different formal milieu, close to the art of the court. The building was constructed around 1310 according to standards for decorated architecture: the bays, emphasized by slender colonnettes, are divided into narrow lights and crowned by tympana pierced by multifoil roses and multiple spandrels. The stained glass was installed in the following years (around 1320–1330) and arranged in band-windows, which were popular then in France and England.

Saints venerated at the time such as Saint John the Baptist, John the Evangelist and, above all, local saints like Gereon (patron of the church) and the Three Magi, holding an attribute or a palm of martyrdom, stand in niches with architectural crownings that are only slightly developed. Among others in the openings of the tympanum are a Christ in Majesty, and a Crucifixion in the oculi of the roses. In the spandrels are angels forming a celestial court, their attitudes adapted to the curves of the tracery. The ivy-leaf grisailles are arranged in rinceaux and cut by light blue fillets, imitating contemporary French and English models. The execution is precious and uses silver stain as highlights in drapery and architecture. The thin figures are shown in hip-shot stances, the drapery and folds emphasizing their gestures and the movement of their bodies. The light tones accent the similarities to court art. The influence of manuscript illumination by Johannes von Valkenburg at the end of the thirteenth century is tangible, but references to English illumination are even stronger.

202 Darmstadt, Hessisches Landesmuseum: Grisaille decorated with leaves and grape vines, panel from the former Cistercian abbey church at Altenberg; ca. 1260.

▷
203 Esslingen, church of Sankt Dionysius, bay 4, 1st light, 4th register: Ornamental grisaille decorated with stars, from a window in the apse of the Franciscan church at Esslingen; 1300–1310.

On the other hand, the series of Old Testament kings at the cathedral owes much of its effect to "French" models from around 1320. The quarry grounds against which the figures stand out were taken up by the majority of German workshops beginning around 1320 and recall the tendencies of contemporary Upper Rhenish stained glass. A religious and artistic center, Cologne facilitated the implantation of Gothic forms in the workshops of the neighboring cities and regions, which adopted them with varying success.

Among the Cistercian abbeys of the thirteenth century, the one at Altenberg in the Rhineland is a rare example that preserved the greater part of its original decoration and remained faithful to the precepts of the Cistercian order, set forth at the beginning of the twelfth century.[104] A number of ensembles testify to the fact that the Cistercians had accepted images from the middle of the thirteenth century, for example Namedy (Andernach township), near Bonn, Coisdorf not far from Wiesbaden and even Neukloster near Rostock.[105] 18

The church at Altenberg, begun in 1255, remains a simple structure, while following the model of Amiens, as did Cologne Cathedral. Its glazing was accomplished in several campaigns beginning in the 1260s.[106] Unlike contemporary French grisailles, motifs are always large in scale; leaves are generally represented frontally, and rarely in profile. They 20

204 Brandenburg an der Havel, Dom St. Peter und Paul, choir: Virgin and Child; ca. 1295. Cf. cat. 1.

were arranged symmetrically, while during the same period in France and in England, plant elements were freely arranged within geometric frames.

This obedience to Cistercian rules is even more remarkable since, during the thirteenth century, light grisaille windows (where, paradoxically, color played an important role) were being created in the Holy Roman Empire. The relationship between architecture and stained glass was not the same as in France and England; motifs were often arranged like those on carpets *(Grauteppich)*, which was rarely the case in France, except at Orbais. Around 1300, German ornamental windows became saturated with colors, for instance in Alsace, Swabia and the area around Baden; alternatively, they were enlivened with animals such as parrots and lions, for example in the church of the Hermits of Saint Augustine at Erfurt.[107]

Northern Germany and Saxony

The art of stained glass in the northern regions of the Holy Roman Empire did not enjoy the same development; works are less numerous. Soest, which was an active center in the twelfth century, has few remains from the thirteenth. The completion of work on Strasbourg Cathedral facilitated the penetration of Gothic traditions, which the painters exported into these regions and even further. An excellent example is the Virgin and Child in the cathedral at Brandenburg near Potsdam. Datable to the years around 1295, the drawing in this figure is more "French" than the Strasbourg models to which it is habitually compared.

In Lower Saxony, the amortizements of the windows in the cloister of the Cistercian abbey at Wienhausen were decorated with a Passion cycle, figures of apostles and floral motifs. The style of drawing in this glass is complicated, indeed mannered. The freedom of the palette and the simplification of the handling underscore an awareness of modes in keeping with Gothic art around 1300. U.D. Korn has emphasized the relations between these small panels and panel paintings such as the Isenhagen altarpiece, now in Hannover.[108] The artists who created these works resided either in Lübeck or in Lüneburg. From there they spread out as far as Scandinavia, working, for example, in the church at Lye in Gotland around 1320.[109] In Saxony, the workshops remained faithful to *Zackenstil* principles, in which works of rare quality were produced, e.g. the cathedral at Merseburg (around 1250) or the one at Meissen, which is a little later in date[110] and was already discussed in *Le Vitrail roman*.

Then there occurred a distinctive phenomenon, which J.J. Gruber has termed the "absence of style". The workshops did not succeed in overcoming the confines of their training so they could adopt new schemae; this is exactly what happened in the Lady Chapel of the cathedral at Halberstadt (around 1330)[111] and to a lesser degree in the vestiges of a Virgin cycle in the Franciscan church at Erfurt (first quarter of the fourteenth century) where, only a century before, true masterpieces had been created.[112]

The Eastern Borders

Further to the east, in present-day Austria, the earliest examples from this period date to the third quarter of the thirteenth century. Of these, the series with Wise and Foolish Virgins in the church of Sankt Bartolomäus at Friesach in Carinthia (around 1260–1270) has stylistic links with contemporary Salzburg manuscript illumination. This is easily explained by the fact that Friesach was one of the possessions of the archbishops of Salzburg on the road between Vienna and Venice. The figures follow the particular tendencies developed by the *Zackenstil* in this region. The forms are cut into somewhat "jagged" shapes, emphasized by the arrangement of their robes and mantles; the poses are contorted; the faces, framed by long hair, are still strongly modeled and number among the most expressive examples of this stylistic tendency in the Holy Roman Empire.

Many of the important works in Austria during this period decorate cloisters, where bays sometimes received stained glass. Few examples have been preserved, some in Germany, others in Austria.[113] Heiligenkreuz and Klosterneuburg, two powerful Cistercian abbeys near Vienna, have preserved extensive elements of their glazing. Both establishments were founded by Margrave Leopold III of Babenberg, a member of the family that "ran" this region between the end of the tenth century and the middle of the thirteenth. While the

203

204

205

206

▷
205 Wienhausen (Lower Saxony), Cistercian abbey, cloister, south side, bay 4, tympanum: Christ's Entry into Jerusalem; 1330–1340. Cf. cat. 6.

206 Friesach (Carinthia), church of Sankt Bartolomäus, choir, north side: Wise Virgin (detail); 1260–1270.

▷
207 Heiligenkreuz, Cistercian abbey, cloister, wash house, bay 6: Babenberg Window (detail), Margrave Leopold III; ca. 1280. Cf. cat. 8.

earliest panels (around 1220) in the cloister at Heiligenkreuz are still grisailles with plant decoration in keeping with the Cistercian principle of chromatic rigor, the same is not true of the second series (about 1280) that employs both human figures and color. These windows light the admirable wash house at Heiligenkreuz built during the thirteenth century.

Of the eight windows in it, one was originally dedicated to the house of Babenberg, 207 portraits of whose members, though largely redone in the nineteenth century, are now visible in two of the windows. Despite the modifications, the effect is still prodigious. Members of the family, wearing brightly colored court clothing and carrying symbols of their rank, are placed on grounds covered with small rinceaux encircled by multifoil frames. Two compartments are filled with schematic representations of the largest abbeys the family founded—Heiligenkreuz and Klosterneuburg. The handling remains precious and is accentuated by the polychromy of the costumes; however, the treatment of folds and the angular fall of the drapery prefigure the ensemble of prophets and angels that decorate several 208 windows in the chevet of the abbey church (around 1295).

Like the figures of the Babenberg family, those in the chevet are depicted in multifoil frames—one of the essential characteristics of Austrian stained glass at the end of the thirteenth century and in the first half of the fourteenth.[114] They also stand out against "worked" backgrounds similar to those in the preceding series. Between the figures, which

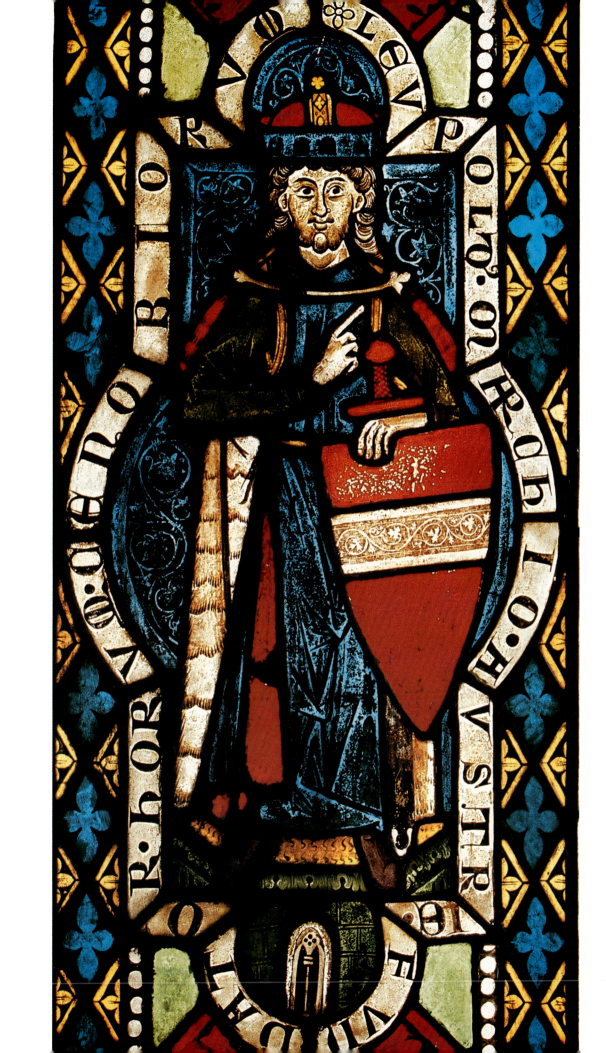

208 Heiligenkreuz, Cistercian abbey, abbey church, choir, bay 1, central light, 11th and 12th registers: The Prophet Habakuk; 1290–1295.

209 Saint Walpurgis (near Saint Michael, Styria), chapel of ease, chevet, bay 3: Wise Virgin; 1295–1297. Cf. cat. 10.

are superimposed by twos or threes within the same light, are "carpets" and borders with multicolored geometric motifs. The superabundant ornament holds in check the formal authority that the rigid style of drawing and monumental treatment confer on these figures; Byzantine influence, though weakened, is present and can be ascertained in certain iconographic details such as the representation of angels in half-length figures.

210 Graz, Steiermärkisches Landesmuseum, Johanneum: Christ Giving a Blessing, medallion from the former Franciscan church at Bruck an der Mur (Styria); end of the 13th century.

211 Nuremberg, Germanisches Nationalmuseum:
Virgin and Child panel from the cathedral at Wiener
Neustadt (Lower Austria); 1300–1310.

212 Klosterneuburg, Cistercian abbey, Saint Leopold Chapel: Christ Healing the Man Born Blind, panel from the cloister; ca. 1330. Cf. cat. 9.

In the chapel at Saint Walpurgis near Saint Michael in Styria, a large number of the characteristics of presentation and decoration already outlined can be seen in the series of saints and Wise and Foolish Virgins. Changes have taken place, however, in the figural style—the poses have become freer and less constrained by the frame; the silhouettes have become thinner, and some of the figures stand in a slightly hip-shot stance. Modeling has been toned down in favor of angular contour lines, this multiplicity of angles creating an almost mannerist impression. The work has been dated to the years 1295–1297 by a dedicatory inscription set in a scroll held by Saint Walpurgis, the patron of the church and one of the figures preserved from this ensemble, which was originally larger.

This style belongs to the ultimate phase of the *Zackenstil* as it was practiced in the alpine valleys of Austria.[115] Other examples are a bust of Christ from the church at Bruck an der Mur, now in the Johanneum at Graz, which can also be dated to the same years.

At the beginning of the fourteenth century, Gothic formulae penetrated into these regions, especially the area along the Danube. One of the earliest examples is the Virgin and Child from the cathedral at Wiener Neustadt (Lower Austria), now preserved in the Germanisches Nationalmuseum at Nuremberg and dating from about 1300–1310. This Virgin is in a distinctive style: the figure (the lower part of which has disappeared) is depicted in an architectural frame in a supple pose accentuated by the folds of the robe. The leafy crown the Virgin is wearing is close to that on the Virgin at Brandenburg. The features of her face are strongly marked, especially her mouth, which is characterized by mannerist drawing. The influence of Strasbourg is clear, as it was at Brandenburg.[116]

The typological medallions in the bays on the north and west side of the cloister in the abbey at Klosterneuburg are evidence of an extraordinary mastery in Gothic style during the years 1300–1320. Originally they decorated the lancet heads. In the tracery were "portraits" of the Babenberg family and figures of saints accompanied by abbey officials, notably Prior Stephan von Sierndorf (1317–1335), who provides the date for this group. A number of panels were destroyed in the eighteenth century; those which have survived are exhibited for the most part in the windows of the Saint Leopold Chapel along with other more recent glass.[117]

This typological series was inspired by the program employed for the altar by Nicholas of Verdun. The scenes are enclosed in multifoil frames, which may seem archaic at this period. The frames are inscribed with verses from the Bible explaining the episodes depicted and creating a special relationship between the image and the text as is the case in the altar by Nicholas of Verdun (now changed into an altarpiece), the major work commissioned by the cathedral's chapter around 1180 or 1181.[118] The arrangement of the figures within the compositions and their independence in relationship to one another underscore the mastery of this artist, who perhaps worked in the Capella Spaciosa in the royal palace at Vienna.[119] Like the glass at Königsfelden, this ensemble prefigures the International Gothic style, one of the most active centers of which was Vienna.

Italy

The few stained glass windows from the thirteenth century and the beginning of the fourteenth preserved in Italy make them "incunabula". Consequently, they have been very well studied. Furthermore, most of them decorated two prestigious buildings—the basilica at Assisi and the cathedral at Siena.

Assisi: German Master Glaziers and French Influence

The basilica at Assisi was begun in 1228 on the site where Saint Francis had died two years previously, and from the beginning it was designed on two levels. The building was not consecrated by Pope Innocent IV until 1253, but it was probably nearly finished from the 1240s. It is not necessary to reiterate here the exceptional character of this basilica, which was conceived as one of the high places of not only Franciscan but also Christian spirituality, and whose wall surfaces were particularly well adapted to fresco. Modern scholarship has set the beginning of the painted decoration in the Upper Church around 1280, with a program established to glorify Franciscan doctrine.[120]

213 A portion of the glass that decorated this "monumental reliquary," especially that in the apse, was probably in place before the consecration. The date of its execution has been set between 1240 and 1260. Much has been written about this typological cycle, which deals with the Life of Christ in all its phases from the Childhood through Christ's Appearances After His Resurrection. Despite numerous restorations and replacements, this ensemble is unique in iconographic power in the history of thirteenth-century stained glass. Haseloff was the first to establish the connections between these windows and the German workshops of the middle of the century such as those in the Franciscan Church at Erfurt (1235–1245).[121] More recently, the fundamental study by H. Wentzel has shown that the windows were made by German master glaziers.

The overall effect is different from late Romanesque art, however. The arrangement is more evocative of French art from the middle of the century. The medallions remain complex in format, and the ornament abundant. The rendering of the figures, however, tends towards simplification. The modeling too is abundant, and the style of drawing rigid, comparable to that of the glazing at Erfurt and Merseburg datable to the second third of the thirteenth century, which has been habitually linked to the Umbrian cycle. Even in the colors, differences with German works can be seen: the tones are purer and flatter, like those in French Gothic painting.

R. Haussherr has recently prepared a long iconographic study of this ensemble, outlining the depth of exegetical comparisons. (The meaning of some scenes, however, has yet to be resolved). Instead of a single typological window as was common in the Holy Roman Empire, this program extends over three windows, suggesting a profound knowledge of the Old and New Testaments, the relationships between them and, above all, the images used to depict them. The composition follows that used for this type of window in the Holy Roman Empire: the historiated compartments in each light have a distinct decoration and shape.

Several iconographic traditions mesh here. Some of them are not specifically German but show similarity to works such as the ambo at Klosterneuburg, and especially to cycles such as the typological windows in the choir at Canterbury.[122] There are undeniable links with the anonymous compilation *Pictor in Carmine*, which was composed in England and has been cited by F. Röhrig for Klosterneuburg and by M. Caviness for Canterbury.[123]

With its remarkable spiritual density, this ensemble at Assisi was destined for a privileged place in an edifice toward which the faithful of that time converged. It is interesting to note that even in a country where the vehicle of stained glass remained a marginal art in the thirteenth century, it was nonetheless chosen for the imagery of such a program.

As in the apse, in the nave and the transept there is no clear link between the subjects in the windows and the mural decoration that glorifies the Legend of Saint Francis (1280–1310). Nevertheless, most of these windows are contemporary with the beautiful paintings. G. Marchini has suggested that work on the glazing recommenced after the death of Saint Bonaventura in 1274, who had remained faithful throughout his life to Francis's ideal of poverty.[124] The transept is lit by two four-light windows, each window placed at the end of one of its arms.

The south window in this building, oriented toward the west, illustrates the book of Genesis (in two lights) up to the sorrow of Cain at having killed his brother. The two other lights depict saints seated on thrones under canopies, with their names written on scrolls arranged around them like halos—Agatha, Lucy, Clare, Agnes, etc. On the south is a single historiated window treating the Appearances of Christ and His biblical precursors, with episodes from the Old Testament on the left and from the New Testament on the right. A distinctive development characterizes the episode of the Supper at Emmaus (Luke 24: 28–32), which is treated in a sequence of two scenes. The other window is filled with grisaille of a German type, where color abounds. Five of the eight windows in the nave are reserved for standing figures of apostles, some of whom are accompanied by scenes from their lives. Saint Peter and Saint Paul are missing from this series and perhaps have been replaced by a window that now depicts saints who may have come from the Lower Church. In the first western bay on the north side, Saint Anthony and Saint Francis—considered "new apostles" in Franciscan spirituality—have been added to this ensemble. The window opposite it has an

213 Assisi, Upper Basilica of San Francesco, apse, bay 2: Typological window of the Passion and the Appearances of the Risen Christ (detail), Eliseus and the Sunamitess (?); middle of the thirteenth century. Cf. cat. 103.

unusual theme: the Glorification of Saint Francis by God Incarnate—a frontal figure of Christ holds Saint Francis up before Him as the Blessed Virgin lifts up her Child in the representation in the neighboring light. Above, three angels are superimposed in each light, each holding a *loros* ("staff") in the Byzantine manner and forming a celestial court.[125]

Despite extensive research, certain stylistic problems remain unresolved. The present condition of the glass does not facilitate a solution; in fact, though there are a large number of original panels, many have lost their original paint. According to G. Marchini, the ensemble was the product of two workshops.[126] The first would have been responsible for the windows in the south transept arm and for the first two eastern windows in the nave on the left. In formal terms, they are closely linked to the German world. The presentation of apostles surmounted by ornamental panels recalls Upper Rhenish compositions like those in the Cistercian abbey at Kappel am Albis, even though the crownings are just simple canopies. 192 The association of monumental figures set at the bottom of lights and of legendary medallions superimposed above them might be surprising, if the compartments were not conceived on a large scale. Other details such as the multifoil frames also reveal German influence but tend towards simplification and distribution of colors over large areas. E. Castelnuovo seems correct in thinking that this workshop, like those working in the nave at Strasbourg, derives from traditions in the Holy Roman Empire that were transformed by Gothic influences from France.

A second workshop, named for the "Master of Saint Francis," seems to have been responsible for the rest of the windows. In spite of the present state of these much discussed works, a number of hands are evident, which complicates stylistic problems.[127] In any case, with the exception of the use of multifoil frames, formal links with Rhenish and Austrian glass have almost completely disappeared. The figures have acquired plasticity that is reinforced by strong colors. This association resulted in a renewal of handling (echoes of which will be seen later at Königsfelden)[128] and allowed the construction of a new spatial universe, of which Italy would be the crucible. The work on these windows does not seem to predate the death of Saint Bonaventura; his life-long principles of poverty were rapidly abandoned by Pope Nicholas III Orsini.[129]

Only the glass decorating the single four-light window in the Magdalene Chapel in the Lower Church will be discussed here. The ensemble illustrates the life of the chapel's patron saint. Some elements recall German glass, but these are only small reminiscences such as multifoil frames that differ according to the light. The fillets, having lost their richness, become merely narrow beaded decoration. Pictorial expression is different from that in the preceding series and reveals the influence of Giotto, many of whose students worked on the frescoes decorating the walls in the Lower Church. They were active from 1305, and this hagiographic glass is probably contemporary with their achievements and influenced by work on the frescoes.

Siena: "Painters' Windows"

Art historians have often compared Italian stained glass from the end of the thirteenth century with the nontranslucent painting then popular in Italy, and the issue is particularly interesting for Siena. Since its "discovery," a small Virgin and Child from the Madonna della 214 Grotta Oratory near Siena has been compared to Sienese madonnas of the 1280s, the decade to which the glass is also dated.[130] In her pose, the Blessed Virgin in the oratory is related to Byzantine types of the Virgin Mary, which Sienese painters in particular used as a model until the end of the thirteenth century and in the beginning of the fourteenth. In terms of volume, this Blessed Virgin is actually close to those Virgins. The arrangement of the folds in her mantle, which form a cushion on the left side, accentuates the resemblance to this tradition, which persisted in Siena for a few years. The sad and monotonous expression of the Virgin's face recalls works by Guido da Siena and his circle, despite the loss of paint. She does not, however, possess the plastic balance of the *Madonna* of Crevole, which Duccio must have finished around 1280 (now preserved in the Museo dell'Opera della Metropolitana in Siena).[131] The tender and delicate colors likewise situate this Blessed Virgin in the Sienese pictural milieu, around 1280 or even slightly earlier.

The rose window in the apse of Siena Cathedral is of a completely different quality, and it 215 has even been attributed to Duccio.[132] Everything, or almost everything in it is entirely new,

214 Siena, Pinacoteca: Virgin and Child, panel from the Madonna della Grotta Oratory (?); ca. 1280. Cf. cat. 105.

above all the rectilinear armature supporting the panels instead of stone tracery, which casts shadows on the images. At the center, three square scenes are arranged vertically and illustrate, from bottom to top, the Death, Assumption and Coronation of the Virgin. These compositions appear as independent scenes despite their common theme. Placed horizontally around the central scene, two by two, yet each in a distinct panel, are the saints who protected the city—Bartholomew, Ansanus, Crescentius and Savinus. They are set in multifoil frames reminiscent of German tradition. In the side panels are the four Evangelists with their symbols at their feet, writing at their desks, which are drawn following the laws of perspective. The spatial organization breaks free from earlier Franco-German conventions. The figures are isolated from one another by plain and clear backgrounds; the frames of the compositions have been drastically reduced, giving the ensemble an admirable legibility. The rose is no longer in its original location; it was executed for the former apse of the cathedral in 1287–1288, as proven by a surviving document.[133]

Despite the deterioration of the paint, the style of drawing and forms are related to the plastic art of Duccio and his circle. Was he actually the designer of the cartoon? Such a hypothesis must be considered with a certain amount of reserve today.[134] However, the question of the relationship between painter and master glazier is especially acute here, since the beginnings of glass painting in Siena are still not well known.[135] Collaboration between painter and glazier was rare in France, except in the fifteenth century; it was never as widespread as in Italy at the end of the thirteenth century, where numerous painters "gave" cartoons to be transcribed into stained glass. Did they actually participate in their execution as was the case in the Duomo at Florence in the fourteenth century? What was the situation for the rose window at Siena? Whatever the actual association between painter and glazier may have been, it is certain that the "first modern stained glass" was created at Siena at the end of the thirteenth century.

215　Siena, cathedral of Santa Maria, apse, bay 100, rose: Glorification of the Virgin Mary; 1287–1288. Cf. cat. 104.

Conclusion

At the end of this book, a number of observations come to mind. The first concerns the extraordinary vitality of glass painting during the thirteenth century. Despite widespread destruction over the centuries, many thirteenth-century windows have survived *in situ*, for example at Bourges, Chartres and Strasbourg. The number is so great that not all could be included here, for which we will certainly be criticized. Furthermore, unlike the twelfth century, where often only a single window or a fragment has survived as evidence of a style or a group—for instance the "Gérente head" from Lyons (now in the Musée d'Art et d'Histoire in Geneva)—this is rarely the case in the thirteenth century, where it is almost always possible to link a window to a trend or a stylistic group.

There is no question that the construction sites opened at the beginning of the thirteenth century at Chartres, Laon, Bourges and Paris favored collaboration between workshops and glass painters, who frequently traveled about. The itinerant nature of these artists was important, even if it cannot always be fully reconstructed. It is a point that must be emphasized; although the itinerancy of certain workshops like those of the Laon-Soissons group at the beginning of the thirteenth century and Alsatian glass painters who dispersed after the completion of Strasbourg Cathedral around 1275 is well known. There is much more to be done in this realm. Relationships between workshops and artists need to be further defined. This would provide a better definition of the relationship of a master to his workshop. The first term should be reserved exclusively for truly creative artists, such as the "Master of the New Alliance" window at Bourges or the man who designed the Geoffroy de Loudun window at Le Mans—they were real innovators. There were many artists in the thirteenth century who brought about a renewal of the art of stained glass both in formal and stylistic terms.

Stained glass occupied a central position in the general evolution of thirteenth-century painting. It is likewise in the thirteenth century that stained glass underwent the most important formal and chromatic changes in all its history: "colored mosaics" at the beginning of the century, glass lost its monumental character after 1270 and began to resemble nontranslucent painting. The painterly touch changed as a result, and around the second quarter of the fourteenth century, stained glass accepted formal innovations such as perspective and sought to represent volume, with the result that it became less subject to architecture.

The evolution of glass painting varied, however, with the region or the workshop. Not all areas accepted the revolution that consisted in using silver stain as easily as the Ile-de-France, Normandy or England. The glass painters in the Holy Roman Empire continued the tradition of lively color, but their pictorial line often became mannerist, for the first manifestations of Gothic style in the Holy Roman Empire were late in date—after 1250—but lasted until around 1330 or 1340. Included among them, therefore, are the windows in the choir at Königsfelden (1325–1330) and the typological series in the cloister at Klosterneuburg (around 1330), which herald, a few decades early, the refined character of International Gothic.

The primacy of France in this medium had weakened around 1300. The ensembles at Königsfelden and Klosterneuburg anticipate the evolution of glass painting, renewing it as a medium more rapidly than did contemporary French or English glass. Königsfelden is to the first third of the fourteenth century what the Sainte Chapelle was for the middle of the thirteenth. This geographic displacement in innovation is a precursor of what occurred in the International Gothic style, in which the eastern part of the Holy Roman Empire would play an essential role with such centers as Vienna and Prague.

In both imagery and spiritual significance, stained glass was a privileged reflection of thirteenth-century Gothic art. More than other media, stained glass revealed the self-image of the period: primarily Christian but with reflections of daily life, for instance in images of working or praying donors, scenes of battles, processions or even historic events (the image in the Sainte Chapelle of Saint Louis carrying the Crown of Thorns). At the same time, stained glass undoubtedly caught the viewers' imagination with its distinctive qualities—one can imagine the effect on pilgrims entering Chartres Cathedral. We can only hope that today's viewers will continue to be as amazed by these masterpieces of Gothic art.

Appendixes

List of Bibliographic Abbreviations

Art Bull.: The Art Bulletin

BECKSMANN, 1967: R. BECKSMANN, *Die architektonische Rahmung des hochgotischen Bildfensters: Untersuchungen zur Oberrheinischen Glasmalerei von 1250 bis 1350,* Berlin, 1967.

Bull. Mon.: Bulletin Monumental.

C. Arch.: Congrès Archéologique de France.

CAHIER and MARTIN, 1841–44: C. CAHIER and A. MARTIN, *Monographie de la cathédrale de Bourges,* Part I: *Vitraux du XIIIe siècle,* Paris, 1841–44.

CVMA: Corpus Vitrearum Medii Aevi.

DELAPORTE and HOUVET, 1926: Y. DELAPORTE and E. HOUVET, *Les Vitraux de la cathédrale de Chartres. Histoire et description,* 4 vols, Chartres, 1926.

"L'Europe gothique," Paris, 1968: "L'Europe gothique XIIe-XIVe siècle," exh. cat., Paris: Musée du Louvre, 1968.

FRODL-KRAFT, 1972: E. FRODL-KRAFT, *Die mittelalterlichen Glasgemälde in Niederösterreich 1, CVMA*: Austria, vol. II/1, Vienna, Cologne, Graz, 1972.

GRODECKI, 1959: M. AUBERT, L. GRODECKI, J. LAFOND, J. VERRIER, *Les Vitraux de Notre-Dame et de la Sainte-Chapelle de Paris, CVMA*: France, vol. I, Paris, 1959.

GRODECKI, 1976: L. GRODECKI, *Les Vitraux de Saint-Denis,* Vol. I: *Histoire et restitution, CVMA*: France, "Etudes," vol. I, Paris, 1976.

GRODECKI, 1978: L. GRODECKI, "Les problèmes de l'origine de la peinture gothique de la 'Maître de saint Chéron' de la cathédrale de Chartres," *Revue de l'Art,* nos 40–41 (1978): 43–64.

HAYWARD and GRODECKI, 1966: J. HAYWARD and L. GRODECKI, "Les vitraux de la cathédrale d'Angers," *Bull. Mon.* 124 (1966): 7–67.

LAFOND, 1959: M. AUBERT, L. GRODECKI, J. LAFOND, J. VERRIER, *Les Vitraux de Notre-Dame et de la Sainte-Chapelle de Paris, CVMA*: France, vol. I, Paris, 1959.

LAFOND, 1966: J. LAFOND, *Le Vitrail,* Paris, 1966; 2nd ed., 1978.

LASTEYRIE, 1852–57: F. DE LASTEYRIE, *Histoire de la peinture sur verre en France d'après ses monuments,* 2 vols., Paris, 1852–57.

MÂLE, 1910: E. MÂLE, *L'Art religieux du XIIIe siècle en France,* Paris, 1898; 2nd ed. 1910.

P.L.: Patrologia Latina.

"Radiance and Reflection," New York, 1982: "Radiance and Reflection (Medieval Art from the Raymond Pitcairn Collection)," exh. cat., New York: The Metropolitan Museum of Art: The Cloisters, 1982.

Recensement, I: *Recensement des vitraux anciens de la France,* vol. I (stained glass from Paris, the region around Paris, Picardy and Nord-Pas-de-Calais), *CVMA:* complementary series, Paris, 1978.

Recensement, II: *Recensement des vitraux anciens de la France,* vol. II (stained glass from central France and the Loire valley), *CVMA:* complementary series, Paris, 1981.

RITTER, *Les vitraux de Rouen,* 1926: G. RITTER, *Les vitraux de la cathédrale de Rouen: XIIIe, XIVe, XVe et XVIe siècles, reproductions en héliotypie avec une introduction historique et des notices bibliographiques,* Cognac, 1926.

"The Year 1200," New York, 1970: "The Year 1200: A Centennial Exhibition," exh. cat., New York: The Metropolitan Museum of Art, 1970.

"Vitraux de France," Paris, 1953: "Vitraux de France du XIe au XVIe siècle," exh. cat. by L. GRODECKI, Paris: Musée des Arts décoratifs, 1953.

Vitrail français, 1958: M. AUBERT, A. CHASTEL, L. GRODECKI, J.J. GRUBER, J. LAFOND, F. MATHEY, J. VERRIER, *Le Vitrail français,* Paris, 1958.

Vitrail roman, 1983: L. GRODECKI with C. BRISAC and C. LAUTIER, *Le Vitrail roman,* Fribourg: Office du Livre, 1977; 2nd ed. 1983.

WENTZEL, 1954: H. WENTZEL, *Meisterwerke der Glasmalerei,* 2nd ed., Berlin, 1954.

WESTLAKE, 1881–84: N.H.J. WESTLAKE, *A History of Design in Stained and Painted Glass,* 4 vols., London, 1881–84.

Notes

INTRODUCTION

1 E. MÂLE, "La peinture sur verre en France au XIIIe siècle," in *Histoire générale de l'art (A. Michel)*, vol. II/1, Paris, 1906, pp. 374–92.

2 J. J. GRUBER, "Quelques aspects de l'art et de la technique du vitrail en France; dernier quart du XIIIe siècle, premier quart du XIVe," in *Travaux des étudiants du groupe d'histoire de l'art de la Faculté des lettres de Paris*, Paris, 1928, pp. 71–94.

3 J. LAFOND, "Le vitrail en Normandie de 1250 à 1300," *Bull. Mon.* 111 (1953): 317–58.

4 L. GRODECKI, "De 1200 à 1260," in *Vitrail français*, 1958, pp. 115–58.

5 R. BRANNER, *St. Louis and the Court Style in Gothic Architecture*, London, 1965; J. BONY, *French Gothic Architecture of the 12th and 13th Centuries*, Berkeley, Los Angeles and London, 1983.

6 *Vitrail français*, 1958.

CHAPTER I

1 *Vitrail roman*, 1983, pp. 120–26, cat. nos 41–43, pp. 278–79, ills 98, 104–5.

2 *Ibid.*, pp. 151–57, cat. nos 2–3, pp. 268–69, ills 128–29.

3 L. GRODECKI, "Le chapitre XXVIII de la *Schedula* du Moine Théophile: technique et esthétique du vitrail roman," *Académie des Inscriptions et Belles-Lettres: Comptes Rendus des séances* (Apr.–June, 1976): 345–57; *Vitrail roman*, 1983, pp. 16–17.

4 M. CAVINESS, *The Early Stained Glass of Canterbury Cathedral*, Princeton, N.J., 1977, pp. 107–8.

5 M. T. ENGELS, *Zur Problematik der mittelalterlichen Glasmalerei*, Berlin, 1937; L. GRODECKI, "Le vitrail et l'architecture au XIIe et au XIIIe siècle," *Gazette des Beaux-Arts* 36, no. 2 (1949): 6–21.

6 CAVINESS, *Early Glass of Canterbury Cathedral*, pp. 41–45.

7 M. LILLICH, "The Band-Window: A Theory of Origin and Development," *Gesta* IX, no. 1 (1970): 26–33.

8 GRUBER, "Quelques aspects du vitrail en France," pp. 71–94.

9 L. GRODECKI, "Fonctions spirituelles," in *Vitrail français*, 1958, pp. 40–45.

10 *Ibid.*; see also JEAN DE JANDIN, "Commentaire sur la Sainte-Chapelle de Paris," cited by L. GRODECKI in *La Sainte-Chapelle*, 2nd ed., Paris, 1979, p. 3.

11 P. CLAUDEL, "Préface," in *Vitraux des cathédrales de France*, Paris, 1937, pp. 5–12.

12 *Vitrail roman*, 1983, p. 54, cat. no. 67, p. 286, ills 64–65 (Saint Timothy of Neuwiller).

13 J. BALTRUSAITIS, "Villes sur arcatures," *Urbanisme et architecture* (*Etudes écrites et publiées en l'honneur de P. Lavedan*), Paris, 1954, pp. 31–40.

14 E. FRODL-KRAFT, "Architektur im Abbild: ihre Spiegelung in der Glasmalerei," *Wiener Jahrbuch für Kunstgeschichte* XVII (1956): 7–13.

15 BECKSMANN, 1967.

16 *Vitrail roman*, 1983, pp. 58, 142, 182–83.

17 A. HASELOFF, "La miniature dans les pays cisalpins depuis le commencement du XIIe jusqu'au milieu du XIVe siècle," *Histoire générale de l'art* (*A. Michel*), vol. II/1, Paris, 1906, pp. 297–371; GRODECKI, 1978, pp. 43–51.

18 *Vitrail roman*, 1983, pp. 236–49.

19 R. BRANNER, *Manuscript Painting in Paris during the Reign of Saint Louis: A Study of Styles*, Berkeley, Los Angeles and London, 1977, pp. 61, 65, 124, 129; figs 105, 379.

20 GRODECKI, 1976, p. 144.

21 H. WENTZEL, "Glasmaler und Maler im Mittelalter," *Zeitschrift für Kunstwissenschaft* 3 (1949): 53–62; *Vitrail roman*, 1983, p. 153, ill. 128; L. KALINOWSKI, "Virga Versatur," *Revue de l'Art* 62 (1983): 9–20.

22 M. AUBERT, *Suger*, Saint-Wandrille, 1950, p. 155; see also GRODECKI, 1976, p. 28, especially n. 44.

23 GRODECKI, 1976, p. 29.

24 *Ibid.*, p. 32.

25 See most recently, C. BRISAC, "Le métier de maître verrier au Moyen Age," *L'Histoire*, no. 15 (1979): 54–55.

26 L. GRODECKI, "Le 'Maître du Bon Samaritain' de la cathédrale de Bourges," in *The Year 1200: A Symposium*, New York, 1975, p. 341.

27 On this problem, see most recently, F. PERROT, "Signature des maîtres verriers," *Revue de l'art* 26 (1974): 40–41.

28 DELAPORTE and HOUVET; 1926, pp. 5–8.

29 For the German world, see the recent study by R. BECKSMANN, "Fensterstiftungen und Stifterbilder in der deutschen Glasmalerei des Mittelalters," in *Vitrea dedicata*, Berlin, 1975, pp. 65–85.

30 These elements, however, were often poorly restored or transformed in the nineteenth century, for example, the windows in the upper choir and inner ambulatory in the cathedral at Le Mans, most of which were redone at this time; see C. BRISAC, "Les vitraux du chœur," in *La Cathédrale du Mans*, Paris, 1981, pp. 118–19.

CHAPTER II

1 *Vitrail roman*, 1983, pp. 21–24, figs 7/1–10.

2 F. DEUCHLER, *Der Ingeborgpsalter*, Berlin, 1967.

3 W. SAUERLÄNDER, *La Sculpture gothique en France, 1140–1270*, Paris, 1972, pp. 106, 107, figs 50–52.

4 J. ANCIEN, *Vitraux de la cathédrale de Soissons*, 2 vols., Soissons, 1980 (typewritten).

5 L. GRODECKI, "Les vitraux soissonais, du Louvre, du Musée Marmottan et des collections américaines," *Revue des Arts* X (1960): 163–78.

6 P. VERDIER, "A Stained Glass from the Cathedral of Soissons," *The Corcoran Gallery of Art Bulletin* 10 (1958): 4–20; "The Year 1200," New York, 1970, no. 213, pp. 208–9; for the panel in the Isabella Stewart Gardner Museum, see most recently, M. CAVINESS, E. PASTAN AND M. BEAVEN, "The Gothic Window from Soissons: A Reconsideration," *Fenway Court 1983*, 1984, pp. 6–23.

7 P. HÉLIOT, "Chronologie de la Basilique de Saint-Quentin," *Bull. Mon.* 117 (1959): 7–50.

8 BRANNER, *St. Louis and the Court Style, op. cit.*, pp. 42–45; *idem*, "Les débuts de la cathédrale de Troyes," *Bull. Mon.* 118 (1960): 111–23; N. BONGART, *Die frühen Bauteile der Kathedrale in Troyes*, Stuttgart, 1977.

9 *Vitrail roman*, 1983, pp. 141–47, cat. nos 103–5, pp. 294–95.

10 B. RACKHAM, *A Guide to the Collections of Stained Glass, Victoria and Albert Museum*, London, 1936, p. 32, pl. 4.

11 G. LANFRY, "La cathédrale dans la cité romaine et la Normandie ducale," *Les Cahiers de Notre-Dame de Rouen* 1 (1956): 67–91; *idem*, "La cathédrale depuis le rattachement de la Normandie jusqu'à l'occupation anglaise," *ibid.*, 4 (1960): 5–11, 65–74.

12 J. LAFOND, "La verrière des Sept Dormants d'Ephèse et l'ancienne vitrerie de la cathédrale de Rouen," in *The Year 1200: A Symposium*, New York, 1975, pp. 400–16.

13 For the rose window at Mantes, see A. RHEIN, *Notre-Dame de Mantes*, Paris, 1932, pp. 91–92; *Recensement*, I, p. 130, fig. 74.

14 *Recensement*, I, pp. 90–91 (Bussy-Saint-Martin); p. 161 (Fossoy); pp. 202–3 (Noyon); p. 212 (Villers-Saint-Paul).

15 *Vitrail français*, 1958, pp. 129–30.

16 CAHIER and MARTIN, 1841–44, pp. 2–66, 67–90.

17 R. BRANNER, *La Cathédrale de Bourges et sa place dans l'architecture gothique*, Paris and Bourges, 1962, pp. 61–62.

18 *Vitrail roman*, 1983, pp. 84–85, cat. no. 36, p. 277, ill. 66.

19 *Ibid.*, pp. 70–77, cat. nos 73–74, pp. 286–87, ills 56–59.

20 J. HAYWARD, "The Lost Noah Window from Poitiers," *Gesta* XX, no. 1 [Essays in Honor of Harry Bober] (1981): 129–39.

21 *Vitrail roman*, 1983, pp. 80–86, cat. nos 33–35, pp. 276–77, ills 63–65.

22 HAYWARD and GRODECKI, 1966, pp. 23–32.

23 A. MUSSAT, *Le Style gothique de l'Ouest*, Paris, 1963, pp. 194, 199–201; *idem*, "La cathédrale

Saint-Maurice d'Angers, Recherches récentes," *C. Arch*, 122 (1964): 33–35.

24 GRODECKI, 1978, pp. 50–60.

25 A. MUSSAT, *Cathédrale du Mans*, Paris, 1981, p. 83.

26 *Vitrail roman*, 1983, pp. 68–69, cat. no. 63, p. 284, ill. 55

27 *Recensement*, II, p. 111.

28 *Ibid.*, p. 108.

29 See most recently, J. HAYWARD, "The Redemption Windows of the Loire Valley," *Etudes d'art médiéval offertes à Louis Grodecki*, Paris, 1980, p. 133, fig. 8.

30 *Ibid.*, p. 134, fig. 10; *Recensement*, II, p. 110.

31 DELAPORTE and HOUVET; 1926, pp. 9, 128; (the numbers assigned in this work to the bays in the cathedral at Chartres are given in parentheses); L. GRODECKI, in *Vitrail français*, 1958, pp. 124–34; K.M. SWOBODA, "Zur Frage nach dem Anteil des führenden Meisters am Gesamtwerk der Kathedrale von Chartres," in *Festschrift für H.R. Hahnloser*, Basel, 1961, pp. 37–45; P. FRANKL, "The Chronology of the Stained Glass in Chartres Cathedral," *Art Bull.* XLV (1961): 301–22.

32 P. POPESCO, "La verrière du Bon Samaritain de la cathédrale de Chartres," *Cahiers de la céramique, du verre et des arts du feu* 38 (1966): 136–37.

33 P. POPESCO, *Chefs-d'œuvre du vitrail européen: la cathédrale de Chartres*, 1st ed., Paris, 1970, p. 144.

34 DELAPORTE and HOUVET, 1926, p. 131.

35 GRODECKI, "Le Maître du Bon Samaritain," p. 343.

36 See above, n. 15 of this chapter.

37 SAUERLÄNDER, *La Sculpture gothique*, pp. 22, 110–18.

38 See above, in the first part of this chapter, p. 54 and ill. 14.

39 "The Year 1200," New York, 1970, no. 254, p. 254.

40 Oral communication at the Congrès d'Histoire de l'Art at Berne in 1953; see *Vitrail français*, 1958, n. 24, ch. "1200 à 1260," p. 319.

41 CAVINESS, *Early Glass of Canterbury Cathedral*, p. 100, fig. 212.

42 C. BOUCHON, C. BRISAC, C. LAUTIER, Y. ZALUSKA, "La 'Belle-Verrière' de Chartres," *Revue de l'Art* 46 (1979): 19–22.

43 V. MORÉCHAND, "Les vitraux du XIIIe siècle de l'église Saint-Pierre de Dreux," *L'information d'Histoire de l'Art*, 20th year, (1975): 214–217.

44 See below, chapter III, pp. 111–12 and ill. 18.

45 See above, in the first part of this chapter, pp. 56–7, and n. 16.

46 F. QUIÉVREUX, "Les vitraux du XIIIe siècle de l'abside de la cathédrale de Bourges," *Bull. Mon.* 102 (1942): 253–79; *idem, Les Paraboles*, Paris, 1946, pp. 241–46; GRODECKI, "Le Maître du Bon Samaritain," pp. 339–59.

47 GRODECKI, "Le Maître du Bon Samaritain," especially pp. 343–47.

48 L. GRODECKI, "A Stained Glass *Atelier* of the Thirteenth Century: A Study of the Windows in the Cathedrals of Bourges, Chartres and Poitiers," *Journal of the Warburg and Courtauld Institutes* XI (1948): 100–7.

49 *Recensement*, II, p. 195.

50 L. GRODECKI, in *Vitrail français*, 1958, p. 139; V. CHIEFFO RAGUIN, *Stained Glass in Thirteenth Century Burgundy*, Princeton, 1982, pp. 88–92, figs 136–40.

51 *Recensement*, II, p. 146.

52 See in particular, L. BÉGULE, *La Cathédrale de Sens, son architecture, son décor*, Paris, 1927, pp. 50–55.

53 CAVINESS, *Early Glass of Canterbury Cathedral*, pp. 84–90, 90–93.

54 *Ibid.*, pp. 84–90.

55 MÂLE, "Peinture sur verre au XIIIe siècle," pp. 378–80.

56 C. BRISAC, "Iconographie pseudo-légendaire des fondateurs de l'église de Lyon et reliques carolingiennes," *Actes du colloque international du CNRS, "Les martyrs de Lyon (177),"* Paris, 1978, pp. 299–309.

57 *Vitrail roman*, 1983, pp. 194–98, cat. no. 57, p. 283.

58 C. BRISAC, "Byzantinismes dans la peinture sur verre à Lyon pendant le premier quart du XIIIe siècle," *Actes du XXIVe congrès du Comité international d'Histoire de l'Art*, Vol. II: *Le Proche-Orient et l'Occident dans l'Art du XIIIe siècle*, Bologna, 1982, pp. 203–10.

59 *Idem*, "La peinture sur verre à Lyon au XIIe siècle et au début du XIIIe siècle," *Les Dossiers de l'Archéologie* 26 (1978): 39–43.

CHAPTER III

1 GRODECKI, 1978, pp. 52–60.

2 F. PERROT, "Catalogue des vitraux religieux du Musée de Cluny à Paris," Dijon, 1973, fasc. II, pp. 27–62 [typewritten thesis].

3 *Ibid.*, pp. 38–40.

4 On these works, see most recently, *Recensement*, I, pp. 89–90 (Brie-Comte-Robert, clerestory, eastern rose and windows in the choir: bays 104, 106, 107) and p. 97 (Donnemarie-en-Montois, clerestory, eastern rose).

5 On the dates of construction for these two monuments, see P. VERDIER, "The Window of Saint Vincent from the Refectory of the Abbey of Saint-Germain-des-Prés (1239–1244)," *Journal of the Walters Art Gallery* XXV–XXVI (1962–63): 73–75; BRANNER, *St. Louis and The Court Style*, pp. 68–71.

6 The surviving panels from the thirteenth-century glazing campaign at Saint Germain des Prés have already been the subject of numerous studies, the most important of which are those by VERDIER, "The Window of Saint Vincent," pp. 38–99 and by L. GRODECKI, "Stained Glass Windows of Saint-Germain-des-Prés," *The Connoisseur* (August, 1957): 33–37; (studies or catalogues of specific panels will be cited in the text as they are discussed). The study of these remains has not, however, been completed; the Nuremberg panels have yet to be placed within this ensemble.

7 VERDIER, "The Window of Saint Vincent," pp. 63–93.

8 On these panels in the Victoria and Albert Museum, London, see RACKHAM, *Guide to the Collections*, pp. 30–31; on the panels at Saint Germain des Prés, see most recently, *Recensement* I, p. 46 (bays 2 and 4, 1st south radiating chapel).

9 On the study and reconstruction of this window, see VERDIER, "The Window of Saint Vincent," pp. 39–62, ills 2–24.

10 The iconography of these panels remains difficult to analyze; see GRODECKI, "Stained Glass of Saint-Germain-des-Prés," pp. 34–35, and VER-

DIER, "The Window of Saint Vincent," pp. 89–99; many panels from this series are also in museum collections, notably in The Metropolitan Museum of Art, New York, the reinstalled Saint Vincent window: *Kings on Horseback* (panels 3 and 4), and again in the Victoria and Albert Museum, London: *King Receiving a Soldier* (inv. 5461–1858); see RACKHAM, *Guide to the Collections*, p. 30.

11 On the dates of construction for this building, see most recently, BRANNER, *St. Louis and the Court Style*, pp. 56–65.

12 In the *Corpus Vitrearum Medii Aevi* dedicated to the windows of Notre Dame in Paris and to the Sainte Chapelle, the panels from the Sainte Chapelle now in the Musée de Cluny in Paris, the Musée des Antiquités de la Seine-Maritime in Rouen, the Victoria and Albert Museum in London and the church at Twycross in Leicestershire (GRODECKI, 1959, pp. 337–49, pls 96–101) were analyzed; to these must be added a panel in Canterbury Cathedral, three in the Philadelphia Museum and a fourth in the church at Wilton in Wiltshire (M. CAVINESS and L. GRODECKI, "Les vitraux de la Sainte-Chapelle," *Revue de l'Art*, 1–2 [1968]: 8–14). Recently Jean-Jacques Gruber discovered two cases of glass from the Sainte Chapelle, most of which is modern, but some of which was old pieces sent to the government's storage facility when the restoration workshop closed in 1853 (one of these panels was shown in the exhibition, "Franse Kerkramen—Vitraux de France," Amsterdam: Rijksmuseum [1973–74], exh. cat. by F. PERROT, no. 11, pp. 58–59). Finally four very restored panels were identified by Colette di Matteo in a castle in Burgundy (see L. GRODECKI, "Vitraux de la Sainte-Chapelle récemment découverts," *Bulletin de la Société nationale des Antiquaires de France* [1973]: 112–14).

13 On this manuscript, published in facsimile form by the Roxburgh Club in 1916, see the new edition, S.C. COCKERELL, *Old Testament Miniatures: Medieval Picture Book*, preface by J. PLUMMER, New York, 1975.

14 BRANNER, *Manuscript Painting in Paris*, pp. 118–30. Notable manuscripts in this group are the latin Bible (ms. lat. 16719–16721) and two psalters in the Bibliothèque Nationale (ms. lat. 11760 and 10434).

15 ANCIEN, *Vitraux de Soissons*, pp. 136–56, and more recently, M. CAVINESS and V. CHIEFFO RAGUIN, "Another Dispersed Window from Soissons: A Tree of Jesse in the Sainte-Chapelle Style," *Gesta* XX, no. 1 [Essays in Honor of Harry Bober] (1981): 191–98.

16 G. RHEIMS, "L'église Saint-Julien-du-Sault et ses verrières," *Gazette des Beaux-Arts* 14 (1926/2): 139–62; J. LAFOND, "Les vitraux de l'église de Saint-Julien-du-Sault," *C. Arch.* 116 (1958): 365–69; CHIEFFO RAGUIN, *Stained Glass in Burgundy*, pp. 35–38, 63–66, 67–71, 74–78.

17 V. CHIEFFO RAGUIN, "The Isaiah Master of the Sainte-Chapelle in Burgundy," *Art Bull.* LIX (1977): 483–93.

18 See *Vitrail roman*, 1983, pp. 114, 116, cat. no. 71, p. 286, ill. 95.

19 MÂLE, "Peinture sur verre au XIIIe siècle," pp. 389–94.

20 RITTER, *Les vitraux de Rouen*, 1926, Introduction and pp. 8–9.

21 R. BRANNER, "Le Maître de la cathédrale de Beauvais," in *Art de France*, vol. II, 1962,

pp. 77–92; P. Bonnet-Laborderie, *La Cathédrale Saint-Pierre de Beauvais: Histoire et architecture*, Beauvais, 1978.

22 Branner, *St. Louis and the Court Style*, appendix A, pp. 138–40.

23 On the work of the glass painters in the cathedral at Amiens in the nineteenth century and the changes that they made to the thirteenth-century glazing, see the work of G. Durand, *Monographie de l'église Notre-Dame cathédrale d'Amiens*, Amiens and Paris, vol. II, 1901–1903, pp. 547–76. For the architecture, see the work of A. H. Erlande-Brandenburg, "La façade de la cathédrale d'Amiens," *Bull. Mon.* 135 (1977): 253–93 [VIIᵉ Colloque international de la Société française d'Archéologie Oct. 1-2, 1974].

24 R. Branner, "Historical Aspects of the Reconstruction of Reims Cathedral, 1210–1241," *Speculum* XXXVI (1961): 183–94; H. Reinhardt, *La Cathédrale de Reims*, Paris, 1963, pp. 183–89; F. Salet, "Chronologie de la cathédrale de Reims," *Bull. Mon.* 125 (1967): 347–94.

25 Reinhardt, *Cathédrale de Reims*, p. 184.

26 See *Vitrail roman*, 1983, pp. 138–39, cat. nos 78–80, pp. 287–88, ills 113, 116–17.

27 E. Frodl-Kraft, "Zu den Kirchenschaubildern in den Hochchorfenstern von Reims: Abbildung und Abstraktion," *Wiener Jahrbuch für Kunstgeschichte* XXV (1972): 53–88, ills 31–45.

28 There are analogies between many of the heads of apostles from the upper choir and those representing Saint Paul and the prophet Ezekiel preserved in the Museum of Western and Eastern Art in Kiev. However, these panels, formerly in the Khanenko Collection (formed before 1915), do not come from Reims Cathedral—both their dimensions and iconography bar such an attribution; see X. Muratova, "Deux panneaux inconnus de vitraux français du XIIIᵉ siècle au Musée de Kiev," *Revue de l'Art* 10 (1970): 63–65.

29 On the architecture in this part of Reims Cathedral, see R. Branner, "The North Transept and the First West Facade of Reims Cathedral," *Zeitschrift für Kunstgeschichte* 24 (1961): 197–210. The conclusions of this article were questioned by W. H. Hinkle, "Kunge's Theory of an Earlier Project for the West Facades of the Cathedral at Reims," *Journal of the Society of Architectural Historians* 34 (1975): 208–15, and J. P. Ravaux, "Les campagnes de construction de la cathédrale de Reims," *Bull. Mon.* 137 (1979): 7–66. The glass of this rose has recently been restored by B. Marcq of Reims and is the subject of a study (*mémoire de maîtrise*) by N. Frachon (University of Paris, IV, 1981).

30 The latest studies by J. P. Ravaux fix the completion of the chevet in Châlons Cathedral in the year 1236, see "La cathédrale de Châlons-sur-Marne," *Mémoires de la Société d'Agriculture, Commerce, Sciences et Arts de la Marne* XCI (1976): 176–96, 217.

31 It is the window in the Lady Chapel which should be dated between 1180 and 1190; see *Vitrail roman*, 1983, pp. 129–30 and cat. no. 70, p. 286.

32 On the beginning of this reconstruction, see Branner, *St. Louis and the Court Style*, pp. 42–45.

33 On the building campaigns of this edifice, see Branner, *Burgundian Gothic Architecture*, pp. 38–47 and 105 (cat.).

34 See most recently, Chieffo Raguin, *Stained Glass in Burgundy*.

35 V. Chieffo Raguin, "The Genesis Workshop of the Cathedral of Auxerre and its Parisian Inspiration," *Gesta* XIII, no. 1 (1974): 27–38.

36 Chieffo Raguin, "The Isaiah Master of the Sainte-Chapelle," pp. 483–93.

37 C. J. Thomas, *Les Vitraux de Notre-Dame de Dijon*, Dijon, 1898; E. Fyot, *L'Eglise Notre-Dame de Dijon*, Dijon, 1910, pp. 142–44.

38 J. Lafond, "Les vitraux français du Musée Ariana et l'ancienne vitrerie de Saint-Fargeau (Yonne)," *Genava* XXVI (1948): 114–32; Chieffo Raguin, *Stained Glass in Burgundy*, pp. 58, 64–67.

39 Brisac, *Les vitraux du chœur de Saint-Jean de Lyon*, pp. 64–84.

40 *Ibid.*, pp. 107–10.

41 See most recently, Perrot, "Franse Kerkramen–Vitraux de France," exh. cat., p. 46.

42 J. Bony, "The Resistance to Chartres in Early Thirteenth Century Architecture," *Journal of the British Archaeological Association* XX–XXI (1957-58): 32–52; M. Grandjean, in *La Cathédrale de Lausanne*, Berne, 1975, pp. 72–174.

43 See most recently, Brisac, "Les vitraux du XIIIᵉ siècle," in *Cathédrale du Mans*, pp. 112–13.

44 Mâle, 1910, pp. 282–85, 307–11.

45 This association was first made by Brisac, "Les vitraux du XIIIᵉ siècle," in *Cathédrale du Mans*, pp. 117–18.

46 New identifications for some of these donors were proposed in a chapter of the work by M. Lillich, *Armour of Light*, (in press, to be published in 1985).

47 Grodecki, 1978, p. 61.

48 M. Lillich, *The Stained Glass of Saint-Père de Chartres*, Middletown, Conn., 1978, pp. 10, 22.

CHAPTER IV

1 On this problem, see in particular, Mâle, "Peinture sur verre au XIIIᵉ siècle," p. 393; Gruber, "Quelques aspects du vitrail en France"; J. Lafond, "Le vitrail du XIVᵉ siècle en France," in L. Lefrancois-Pillion, *L'Art du XIVᵉ siècle en France*, Paris, 1954, p. 188; L. Grodecki, "De 1200 à 1260," in *Vitrail français*, 1958, p. 156. Also worthy of note are the papers in the section "Art around 1300" by F. Perrot and A. Prache at the most recent International Congress of the History of Art held in Vienna in 1983.

2 Lillich, "The Band-Window," pp. 26–33.

3 Grodecki, "De 1200 à 1260," p. 156.

4 Branner, *St. Louis and the Court Style*, pp. 37–39, 65–67.

5 M. Lillich, "The Triforium Windows of Tours," *Gesta* XIX, no. 1 (1980): 29–35 and review by F. Salet, *Bull. Mon.* 141 (1982): 239.

6 L. Grodecki, "Le vitrail et l'architecture au XIIᵉ et au XIIIᵉ siècle," p. 156.

7 L. Papanicolaou, "Stained Glass Windows of the Cathedral of Tours," New York: New York University, Institute of Fine Arts, 1979 [typewritten thesis].

8 Gruber, "Quelques aspects du vitrail en France," pp. 75–76.

9 L. Papanicolaou, "The Iconography of the Genesis Window of the Cathedral of Tours," *Gesta* XX, no. 1 (1981): 179–89.

10 Branner, *Manuscript Painting in Paris*, pp. 132–36, 238–39; Grodecki, 1978, p. 61.

11 L. Grodecki, "Saint Louis et le vitrail," *Les Monuments historiques de la France*, no. 4 (1970): 15.

12 Lafond, "Vitrail au XIVᵉ siècle en France," p. 188.

13 M. Lillich, "Monastic Stained Glass: Patronage and Style," in *Monasticism and the Arts*, Syracuse, 1984, pp. 225–33, 241–43.

14 Concerning the problems of light in particular, see Lillich, "The Triforium Windows of Tours," pp. 33–35.

15 *Idem*, "The Band Window."

16 L. Papanicolaou, "Thirteenth-Century Stained Glass from the Abbey Church of Saint Julien at Tours and its Parisian Sources," *Gesta* XVII, no. 1 (1978): 75–76.

17 See most recently, V. Chaussé, "Les vitraux de l'Indre," *Revue de l'Académie du Centre* (1978): 59–63.

18 See *Vitrail roman*, 1983, pp. 190–94, 281–83; C. Brisac, "Les Panneaux romans de la cathédrale de Clermont-Ferrand," *Studies in Medieval Stained Glass, CVMA: USA, Occasional Papers 1*, New York, 1985 (in press).

19 H. du Ranquet, "Les architectes de la cathédrale de Clermont-Ferrand," *Bull. Mon.* 86 (1912): 99; Branner, *St. Louis and the Court Style*, p. 142.

20 M. Davis, "The Choir of the Cathedral of Clermont-Ferrand; the Beginning of the Construction and the Work of Jean Deschamps," *Journal of the Society of Architectural Historians* XL (1981): 181–202.

21 See in particular, H. du Ranquet, *Les Vitraux de la cathédrale de Clermont-Ferrand*, Clermont, 1932.

22 This is currently being prepared by H. Zakin.

23 A. F. Hazzan, "Les Verrières hautes de la cathédrale de Clermont-Ferrand," Paris: University of Paris IV, 1980 [typewritten *mémoire de maîtrise*].

24 A. Haseloff, "La miniature dans les pays cisalpins depuis le commencement du XIIᵉ siècle jusqu'au milieu du XIVᵉ," in *Histoire générale de l'art (André Michel)*, p. 343; G. Vitzhum, *Die Pariser Miniaturmalerei von der Zeit des Hl. Ludwig bis zur Philipp von Valois*, Leipzig, 1907, pp. 4–17; Branner, *Manuscript Painting in Paris*, pp. 237–41; Grodecki, 1978, p. 44.

25 Grodecki, 1978.

26 The surviving panels from this period come from the Sainte Chapelle, where they were used as stopgaps until the restoration of 1848. Most are now in the Musée de Cluny: the Calvary, and medallions with the Life of Saint John the Baptist and the Story of Job (?); see Grodecki, 1959, pp. 337–38, pls 97–98; and Perrot, *Catalogue des vitraux religieux du Musée de Cluny*, fasc. II, pp. 103–7.

27 Branner, *St. Louis and the Court Style*, p. 75; C. Lautier, "Le chevet de Saint-Sulpice-de-Favières," *L'information d'Histoire de l'Art*, no. 1 (1972): 40–45 [17th year].

28 F. Gatouillat, "A Saint-Sulpice de Favières, des vitraux témoins de l'art parisien au temps de saint Louis," *Les Dossiers de l'Archéologie*, no. 26 (Jan.-Feb., 1978): 57–58.

29 See most recently, D. Gaborit-Chopin, *Ivoires du Moyen Age*, Fribourg: Office du Livre, 1978, pp. 137–45.

30 E. LEFÈVRE-PONTALIS, "L'église de Gassicourt," *C. Arch.* 82 (1919): 227–32.

31 For panels in a U.S.A. coll., see the catalogue.

32 J. LAFOND, "Découverte de vitraux à la commanderie de Sainte-Vaubourg à l'abbaye de Saint-Denis," *Bulletin de la Commission des Antiquaires de la Seine inférieure* XIX (1936): 194–96; *idem*, "Le vitrail en Normandie de 1250 à 1300," *Bull. Mon.* 111 (1954): 328–33; and most recently GRODECKI, 1976, p. 49 (n. 31).

33 The Glencairn Museum, Bryn Athyn, Pennsylvania: R. Pitcairn Coll., inv. 03.SG.226. The attribution of this panel to the Gothic glazing, suggested in the exhibition catalogue "Radiance and Reflection," New York, 1982, no. 72, pp. 193–95, does not seem tenable.

34 J. LAFOND, "Les vitraux de l'abbaye bénédictine de Fécamp," in *L'Abbaye bénédictine de Fécamp, ouvrage scientifique du XIIIᵉ centenaire 658-1958*, vol. III, Fécamp, 1961, pp. 99–103.

35 J. VALLERY-RADOT, *L'Eglise de la Trinité de Fécamp*, Paris, 1928, p. 16.

36 *Ibid.*, p. 255, n. 19.

37 See most recently, "Trésors des abbayes normandes," exh. cat., Rouen: Musée départemental des Antiquités de la Seine-Maritime, 1979, pp. 154–57.

38 *Vitrail roman*, 1983, pp. 150–51, 285.

39 *Ibid.*, pp. 17–18.

40 J. CHOUX, "Les vitraux anciens de Lorraine: Richesse et originalité," in *Le Vitrail en Lorraine du XIIᵉ au XXᵉ siècle*, Nancy, 1983, pp. 35–36, 262.

41 *Ibid.*, pp. 36, 252–53.

42 *Ibid.*

43 See most recently, *Vitrail roman*, 1983, pp. 231–40.

44 CHOUX, "Vitraux anciens de Lorraine," pp. 36, 212.

45 M. HÉROLD, in *Le Vitrail en Lorraine du XIIᵉ au XXᵉ siècle*, p. 329.

46 *Ibid.*, p. 264.

47 *Vitrail roman*, 1983, pp. 40–42.

48 *Ibid.*; C. BRISAC, "Grisailles romanes des anciennes abbatiales d'Obazine et de Bonlieu," *Actes du Congrès nationale des Sociétés savantes (Limoges)* (1977): 129–43 [translated into English in *Studies in Cistercian Art and Architecture*, Kalamazoo, 1982, pp. 130–39]; H. ZAKIN, *French Cistercian Glass Grisaille*, New York, 1979, pp. 171–205.

49 M. COTHREN, "The Thirteenth and Fourteenth Century Glazing of the Choir of the Cathedral of Beauvais," New York: Columbia University, 1980, p. 174 [typewritten thesis].

50 M. LILLICH, "A Redating of the Thirteenth-Century Grisaille Windows of Chartres Cathedral," *Gesta* XI, no. 1 (1972): 12.

51 E. FRODL-KRAFT, *Die mittelalterlichen Glasgemälde in Niederösterreich*, Vienna, 1972, *CVMA*: Austria, vol. II/1, p. 101; ZAKIN, *French Cistercian Grisaille*, pp. 137–40.

52 GRUBER, "Technique," in *Vitrail français*, 1958, pp. 66–67.

53 L. GRODECKI, "Vitraux de France," Paris, 1953, p. 28.

54 GRUBER, "Quelques aspects du vitrail en France," pp. 85–89; GRODECKI, "Le vitrail et l'architecture au XIIᵉ et au XIIIᵉ siècle," pp. 18–24.

55 *Vitrail roman*, 1983, pp. 85–86.

56 LILLICH, *Glass of Saint-Père de Chartres*, pp. 25–27.

57 *Idem*, "The Choir Clerestory Windows of La Trinité at Vendôme: Dating and Patronage," *Journal of the Society of Architectural Historians* 34 (1975): 238–39.

58 J. BIDAUT, "Eglise Sainte-Radegonde de Poitiers," *C. Arch.* 109 (1951): 114.

59 *Recensement*, I, p. 82.

60 BRANNER, *St. Louis and the Court Style*, pp. 102–3; L. GRODECKI, *Architecture gothique*, Paris, 1976, pp. 173–74.

61 *Vitrail roman*, 1983, pp. 112–15, 291.

62 *Recensement*, I, p. 251, fig. 136.

63 On this comparison, see also, COTHREN, "Thirteenth and Fourteenth Century Glazing," p. 397.

64 See most recently, S. MURRAY, "The Collapse of 1284 at Beauvais Cathedral," *Acta* III (1976): 17–44.

65 COTHREN, "Thirteenth and Fourteenth Century Glazing," pp. 152–85.

66 *Ibid.*, pp. 209–12.

67 *Ibid.*

68 J. LAFOND, "Vitrail en Normandie de 1250 à 1300," pp. 337–40.

69 *Ibid.*, p. 345.

70 J. LAFOND, "Les vitraux de la cathédrale de Sées," *C. Arch.* 113 (1955): 80; "Radiance and Reflection," New York, 1982, pp. 223–25.

71 LILLICH, *Glass of Saint-Père de Chartres*, pp. 24–39.

72 *Idem*, "Découverte d'un vitrail perdu de Saint-Père de Chartres," *Bulletin de la Société archéologique d'Eure-et-Loir* 13 (1964): 264–68.

73 *Idem, Glass of Saint-Père de Chartres*, pp. 11, 159.

74 *Recensement*, II, pp. 151–52.

75 On this identification, see J. B. DE VAIVRE, "Une représentation de Pierre d'Alençon sur les verrières de la Trinité de Vendôme," *Bull. Mon.* 140 (1981): 305–13.

76 On the reconstruction of this abbey church, see E. LEFÈVRE-PONTALIS, "L'église abbatiale d'Evron (Mayenne)," *Bull. Mon.* 70 (1903): 320–32.

77 Our opinion is supported by the study of the restorations and by the opinion of M. LILLICH, "Bishops from Evron: Three Saints in the Pitcairn Collection and a Fourth in the Philadelphia Museum," *Actes du XIᵉ colloque international du Corpus Vitrearum Medii Aevi, New York, 1982*, New York, Dec., 1984.

78 *Recensement*, II, p. 218, and especially the forthcoming work by M. LILLICH, *Armour of Light*, ch. 8.

79 See above, p. 132, ill. 121.

80 See above, n. 77 and our cat. no. 36.

81 *Ibid.*

82 On the discussion of this dating, see "Radiance and Reflection," New York, 1982, pp. 240–43.

83 R. COUFFON, "La cathédrale de Dol," *C. Arch.* 126 (1968): 37–59.

84 *Gallia christiana*, vol. VI, col. 81.

85 There is no recent study of these remains; see the inventory given in *Arts de l'Ouest*, no. 1, 1977, pp. 85–86, and the introduction by A. MUSSAT to "Le Vitrail en Bretagne," exh. cat., Rennes, 1980, p. 7.

86 MUSSAT, introduction to "Le Vitrail en Bretagne," pp. 7, 18–19.

87 *Idem, Le Style gothique de l'Ouest*, pp. 264–67.

88 R. SANFAÇON, "Un vitrail de l'église de Sainte-Radegonde de Poitiers," Paris: University of Poitiers, 1959 [typewritten *mémoire de maîtrise*].

89 N. FRACHON, "La Rose du bras nord du transept de la cathédrale de Reims," Paris: University of Paris IV, 1981 [typewritten *mémoire de maîtrise*].

90 On this building, see most recently, GRODECKI, *Architecture gothique*, pp. 182–87.

91 The losses that have been identified and published are two panels from a Life of Saint Nicholas (in poor condition), preserved at Portsmouth Abbey, Portsmouth, Rhode Island; see "Medieval and Renaissance Stained Glass from New England Collections," exh. cat. M. CAVINESS (ed.), Harvard University, Cambridge, Mass.: Busch-Reisinger Museum, 1978, p. 38–41, nos 15–16; and a grisaille panel in the Pitcairn Collection at the Glencairn Museum, Bryn Athyn, Penn., published in "Radiance and Reflection," New York, 1982, pp. 215–17, no. 83.

92 SAUERLÄNDER, *La Sculpture gothique*, p. 174, pl. 280.

93 L. GRODECKI, "Les Vitraux de Saint-Urbain de Troyes," *C. Arch.* 113 (1955): 132.

94 F. SALET, "L'église de Mussy-sur-Seine," *C. Arch.* 113 (1955): 320–37.

95 E. AMÉ, *Recherches sur les anciens vitraux incolores du département de l'Yonne*, Paris, 1854.

96 M. AUBERT, "De 1260 à 1380," in *Vitrail français*, 1958, p. 169.

97 J. P. SUAU, "Les débuts du vitrail gothique en Languedoc," *Cahiers de Fanjeaux* 19 (1974): 331–71.

98 M. DURLIAT, "L'ancienne cathédrale Saint-Nazaire de Carcassonne," *C. Arch.* 131 (1973): 564–70.

99 J. P. SUAU, "Alfred Gérente et le vitrail archéologique à Carcassonne au milieu du XIXᵉ siècle," *C. Arch.* 131 (1973): 629–45.

100 J. LAFOND, "Essai historique sur le jaune d'argent," *Pratique de la peinture sur verre à l'usage des curieux*, Rouen, 1942, pp. 39–116; N. HEATON, "The Origin and Use of Silver-Stain," *Journal of the British Society of Master Glass Painters* X, no. 1 (1947–48): 12.

101 ALFONSO EL SABIO, *Lapidario and Libro de las formas et ymagenes*, R. G. DIMAN and L. W. WINGET (eds.), Madison, Wisc., 1980, p. 106.

102 M. LILLICH, "European Stained-Glass around Thirteen Hundred: The Introduction of Silver Stain," *L'Art en Europe vers 1300* (section 6), *25th International Congress of the History of Art*, Vienna, 1983 [abstracts, no page numbers].

103 J. LAFOND, "Un vitrail du Mesnil-Villeman (1313) et les origines du jaune d'argent," *Bulletin de la Société nationale des Antiquaires de France* (meeting of Dec. 8, 1954), pp. 94–95.

104 *Idem*, "Les vitraux de la Trinité de Fécamp," p. 109.

105 J. BONY, "La collégiale de Mantes," *C. Arch.* 104 (1946): 212; for the windows, see most recently, *Recensement*, I, pp. 130–31.

CHAPTER V

1 *Vitrail roman*, 1983, pp. 254–55.

2 See above, p. 67.

3 On the *Zackenstil*, see most recently P. KURMANN, "Skulptur und Zackenstil," *Zeitschrift für schweizerische Archäologie* 40 (1983/2): 109–14.

4 In Italian Romanesque stained glass, the two medallions from Aosta preserved in the treasury of the collegiate church at Saint-Ours are worthy of mention; see G. MARCHINI, *Le Vitrail italien*, Paris, 1955, p. 218, n. 11. In Spain,

the small window illustrating the Martyrdom of Saint Lawrence is the sole surviving work. It is now in the Worcester Art Museum in Worcester, Mass. (inv. 1961-17); see "Medieval and Renaissance Stained Glass from New England Collections," exh. cat., pp. 14-15, no. 4.

5 The issue is very complicated and has an extensive bibliography. See the articles of H. WENTZEL for the Holy Roman Empire and of L. GRODECKI for France, as cited in chapter I, p. 31, n. 21.

6 FRODL-KRAFT, "Architektur im Abbild"; L. GRODECKI, "Architectures peintes dans les vitraux," [Chronical], *Bull. Mon.* 115 (1957): 226-28; BECKSMANN, 1967, pp. 14-15.

7 A. BAILLY, *Saint François d'Assise et la révolution évangelique*, Paris, 1939; for the evolution in the arts, see H. FOCILLON, "Saint François d'Assise et la peinture italienne au XIIIe et au XIVe siècle," in *L'Influence de saint François d'Assise sur la civilisation italienne*, Paris, 1926, pp. 61-82; M.M. GAUTHIER, *Les Routes de la Foi*, Fribourg: Office du Livre, 1983, pp. 138, 154-60.

8 N. MORGAN, *The Medieval Glass of Lincoln Cathedral*, CVMA: Great Britain, *Occasional Papers 3*, London, 1983.

9 CAVINESS, *Early Glass of Canterbury Cathedral*, pp. 25, 47-48.

10 *Ibid.*, pp. 140-46; *idem, The Windows of Christ Church Cathedral Canterbury*, CVMA: Great Britain, vol. II, London, 1981, pp. 192-203.

11 WESTLAKE, 1881-84, pp. 110-13; C. HEATON, "The Origin of the Early Stained Glass in Canterbury Cathedral," *Burlington Magazine* 11 (1907): 172-76; CAVINESS, *Early Glass of Canterbury Cathedral*, pp. 84-93.

12 CAVINESS, *Early Glass of Canterbury Cathedral*, pp. 90-96.

13 L. GRODECKI, "A propos d'une étude sur les anciens vitraux de la cathédrale de Canterbury," *Cahiers de Civilisation médiévale* (1983/1): 59-65 [24th year]; E. FRODL-KRAFT's review of CAVINESS, *Windows of Christ Church Cathedral*, *Kunstchronik* 37 (1984): 229-41.

14 CAVINESS, *Early Glass of Canterbury Cathedral*, pp. 93-94; *idem, Windows of Christ Church Cathedral*, pp. 192-99.

15 *Idem, Early Glass of Canterbury Cathedral*, p. 100, fig. 216.

16 DELAPORTE and HOUVET, 1926, vol. III, pl. CXXX.

17 J. LAFOND, "The Stained Glass Decoration of Lincoln Cathedral in the Thirteenth Century," *The Archaeological Journal* 103 (1946): 128-29, 150; MORGAN, *Medieval Glass of Lincoln*, pp. 33, 45.

18 MORGAN, *Medieval Glass of Lincoln*, pp. 27-32.

19 *Ibid.*, pp. 14-17.

20 *Ibid.*, p. 45.

21 On this problem, see the already outdated work by J.D. LE COUTEUR, *English Medieval Glass*, 1st ed., London, 1926, pp. 140-42.

22 C. WINSTON, "Painted Glass at Salisbury," *Memoirs illustrative of the History and Antiquites of Wiltshire and the City of Salisbury*, London, 1853, pp. 137-59.

23 P. NEWTON with J. KERR, *The County of Oxford: A Catalogue of Medieval Stained Glass*, CVMA: Great Britain, vol. 1, London and Oxford, 1979. [About Dorchester in particular, see also our catalogue; Stanton Hartcourt, pp. 182-83, Stanton Saint John, pp. 189-90].

24 See above, chapter IV, pp. 153-54.

25 There is no general study of this type of window in England; however, see the discussion by MORGAN, *Medieval Glass of Lincoln*, pp. 38-41.

26 J. HASELOCK and D.E. O'CONNOR, "The Stained and Painted Glass," in *A History of York Minster*, Oxford, 1977, p. 370.

27 "Radiance and Reflection," New York, 1982, pp. 229-31, no. 90.

28 NEWTON with KERR, *County of Oxford*, p. 183, pl. 43 f.

29 F.C. EELES, "The Ancient Glass of Westminster Abbey, from a Manuscript Dated 1938," *Journal of the British Society of Master Glass-Painters* 17 (1978/79): 17-30; 18 (1979/80): 47-53.

30 See most recently, A. PRACHE, "Les particularismes: l'Angleterre," in GRODECKI, *Architecture gothique*, p. 192.

31 N. MORGAN, "Art in East Anglia, c. 1300-1360," in *Medieval Art in East Anglia 1300-1500*, London, 1973, pp. 7-22.

32 H.W. GARROD, *Ancient Painted Glass in Merton College, Oxford*, London, 1931.

33 N.E. TOKE, "The Medieval Stained Glass Windows at Upper Hardres," *Archeologia Cantiana* 47 (1935): 170-76.

34 LE COUTEUR, *English Medieval Glass*, p. 95.

35 GRODECKI, *Architecture gothique*, p. 352.

36 BRANNER, *St. Louis and the Court Style*, p. 119.

37 J. FERNANDEZ ARENAS and J.C.F. ESPINO, *Les vidrieras de la catedral de León*, León, 1983.

38 *Ibid.*

39 See above, chapter IV, pp. 175-76.

40 J. GUERRENO LOVILLO, "Las miniaturas," in *Alfonso X el Sabio, Cantigas de santa Maria, édicion facsimil del codice T.I.I. de la Bibliotheca San Lorenzo el Real de el Escorial, Siglo XIII*, Madrid, 1979 [Appendix].

41 *Ibid.*

42 See LILLICH, "European Stained Glass around Thirteen Hundred."

43 See most recently, *Vitrail roman*, 1983, p. 254.

44 WENTZEL, 1954, p. 88.

45 "Rhein und Maas, Kunst und Kultur, 800-1400," exh. cat., Cologne: Kunsthalle, and Brussels: Musées Royaux d'Art et d'Histoire, 1972, p. 343, L 19-20.

46 W. GROSS, "Die Hochgotik im deutschen Kirchenbau," *Marburger Jahrbuch für Kunstwissenschaft* VII (1933): 290-346; R. RECHT, "L'architecture en l'Allemagne et dans l'Empire," in GRODECKI, *Architecture gothique*, p. 264.

47 See, for example, the Saint Maurice preserved in the Germanisches Nationalmuseum in Nuremberg of Rhenish (?) origin; see also WENTZEL, 1954, p. 88; E. FRODL-KRAFT, *Die Glasmalerei*, Vienna and Munich, 1970, pl. III.

48 J. FISCHER, "Einige unveröffentlichte rheinische Glasgemälde," *Zeitschrift für alte und neue Glasmalerei und verwandte Gebiete* III (1914): 104-10.

49 BECKSMANN, 1967, pp. 18-20, 46-58, pls 52-54, 55-57.

50 *Ibid.*, pp. 11-13.

51 *Vitrail roman*, 1983, pp. 249-53.

52 A. HASELOFF, *Eine thüringisch-sächsische Malerschule des 13. Jh.*, Strasbourg, 1897; R. KROOS, *Drei niedersächsische Bildhandschriften des 13. Jh. in Wien*, Göttingen, 1964.

53 KURMANN, "Skulptur und Zackenstil."

54 V. BEYER, "Les roses de réseau des bas-côtés de la cathédrale de Strasbourg et l'œuvre d'un atelier strasbourgeois du XIIIe siècle," *Bulletin de la Société des Amis de la Cathédrale de Strasbourg*, 2nd series, no. 7, 1960, pp. 67-68, fig. 4.

55 In *Vitrail roman*, 1983, the date assigned is 1240-1250; see cat. 102, p. 294. The date was pushed back to 1255 by R. LEHNI, *La Cathédrale de Strasbourg*, Strasbourg, 1978, p. 63.

56 FRODL-KRAFT, 1972, pp. 125-45, col. pl. 4, figs 401 a, b.

57 *Ibid.*, pp. 165-98, figs 564, 581-84.

58 There is no specific study of these iconographic problems; however, see, R. HAUSSHERR: "Der typologische Zyklus des Chorfensters von S. Francesco zu Assisi," in *Kunst als Bedeutungsträger (Gedenkschrift für Günter Bandmann)*, Berlin, 1978, pp. 121-22.

59 H. RODE, *Die mittelalterlichen Glasmalereien des Kölner Domes*, CVMA: Federal Republic of Germany, vol. IV/1, Berlin, 1974, pp. 140-46.

60 See most recently, "Das Gladbacher Bibelfenster: Gefährdung, Restaurierung," exh. cat., Mönchengladbach, Dec. 1976-Jan. 1977.

61 *Ibid.*

62 See most recently, E. SCHURER-VON WITZLEBEN, "Zur Chronologie der mittelalterlichen Farbverglasung des Regensburger Domes," *Zeitschrift für deutschen Verein für Kunstwissenschaft* 36 (1982): 3-21.

63 *Vitrail roman*, 1983, p. 224.

64 For the glazing, see most recently R. BECKSMANN, *Die mittelalterlichen Glasmalereien in Baden und der Pfalz*, CVMA: Federal Republic of Germany, vol. II/1, Berlin, 1979, pp. XXXV-XXXVII.

65 L. GRODECKI and R. RECHT, "Le quatrième Colloque international de la Société française d'Archéologie (Strasbourg, Oct. 16-20, 1968). Le bras sud du transept de la cathédrale: architecture et sculpture," *Bull. Mon.* 129 (1971): 26-37.

66 *Vitrail roman*, 1983, pp. 230, 293-94 (cat. no. 101).

67 BEYER, "Roses de réseau des bas-côtés," pp. 63-73.

68 LEHNI, *Cathédrale de Strasbourg*, pp. 60-68.

69 See above, nn. 54-55.

70 BEYER, "Roses de réseau des bas-côtés," pp. 73-76.

71 *Ibid.*, pp. 76-82.

72 *Ibid.*, p. 85.

73 *Ibid.*, pp. 75-85.

74 BECKSMANN, 1967, pp. 16-17, 109-13.

75 *Ibid.*, pp. 114-17 (Judgment of Solomon window), and pp. 120-23 (windows in the Saint Catherine Chapel): V. BEYER in *La Cathédrale de Strasbourg*, Strasbourg, 1973, pp. 345-49.

76 *Le Vitrail roman*, 1983, p. 230.

77 See most recently, LEHNI, *Cathédrale de Strasbourg*, pp. 68-69.

78 BECKSMANN, 1967, pp. 29-31; *idem, Die mittelalterlichen Glasmalereien*, pp. XXXII-XXXXIV.

78 BECKSMANN, 1967, pp. 144-47; C. WILD-BLOCK, "Les vitraux de Westthoffen," *Bulletin d'Histoire et d'Archéologie de Saverne et Environs* 60 (1967): 4-5.

80 BECKSMANN, 1967, pp. 104-8 (choir windows, around 1287).

81 E.J. BEER, *Die Glasmalereien der Schweiz vom 12. bis zum Beginn des 14. Jahrhunderts*, CVMA: Switzerland, vol. 1, Basel, 1956, p. 97; BECKSMANN, 1967, pp. 86-91 (windows in the north aisle of the nave, around 1310-1315).

82 H. WENTZEL, *Die Glasmalereien in Schwaben von 1200-1350*, CVMA: Federal Republic of

Germany, vol. I, Berlin, 1958, pp. 190–96; BECKSMANN, 1967, pp. 84–86.

83 BECKSMANN, 1967, p. 37.

84 This concerns particularly project B for the west facade of Strasbourg Cathedral; see R. RECHT, "Dessins d'architecture pour la cathédrale de Strasbourg," *L'Œil* 175–76 (1969): 26–33.

85 H. WENTZEL, "Das Mutzigkreuzgangsfenster und verwandte Glasmalerei der 1. Hälfte des 14. Jh. aus dem Elsaß, der Schweiz und Südwestdeutschland," *Zeitschrift für schweizerische Archäologie und Kunstgeschichte* 14 (1953): 159–79; BECKSMANN, 1967, pp. 142–44.

86 BECKSMANN, *Die mittelalterlichen Glasmalereien*, pp. 108, 110–12.

87 GRODECKI, "Architectures peintes dans les vitraux," regarding the article by FRODL-KRAFT, "Architektur im Abbild."

88 BECKSMANN, *Die mittelalterlichen Glasmalereien*, pp. 3–13) (including the panels in museum collections).

89 *Idem*, 1967, pp. 127–29; *idem*, *Die mittelalterlichen Glasmalereien*, p. XXXVI.

90 BEER, *Die Glasmalereien in der Schweiz*, pp. 79–89.

91 "L'Europe gothique," Paris, 1968, pp. 167–68, no. 271.

92 WENTZEL, *Die mittelalterlichen Glasmalereien in Schwaben*, p. 33.

93 *Ibid.*, pp. 197–211 (Stetten); 212–13 (Urach); 227–29 (Lauffen on the Neckar).

94 *Idem*, "Die Madonna mit dem Jesusknaben an der Hand aus Helver," *Westfalen* 34 (1956): 217–33.

95 *Idem*, 1954, pp. 32–33.

96 On the complex problem of the presence of local workshops at Esslingen or workshops coming from Speyer, see BECKSMANN, *Die mittelalterlichen Glasmalereien*, pp. LIV–LVI.

97 WENTZEL, *Die mittelalterlichen Glasmalereien*, pp. 234–43.

98 V. BEYER, "Les vitraux du collatéral sud de la cathédrale de Strasbourg," *Cahiers alsaciens d'archéologie, d'art et d'histoire* 15 (1971): 123–34.

99 BECKSMANN, 1967, pp. 140–42.

100 "L'Europe gothique," PARIS, 1968, pp. 140–42.

101 BECKSMANN, 1967, pp. 57–58.

102 E. MAURER, *Das Kloster Königsfelden* (*Die Kunstdenkmäler des Kantons Aargau*), vol. III, Basel, 1956, p. 346. Maurer uses the term "community of workshops," a theme repeated by BECKSMANN, 1967, p. 93.

103 WENTZEL, 1954, p. 107.

104 ZAKIN, *French Cistercian Grisaille*, pp. 4–7.

105 *Ibid.*, pp. 192–93 (Coisdorf); E. DRACHENBERG, K.J. MAERCKER, C. RICHTER, *Mittelalterliche Glasmalerei in der Deutschen Demokratischen Republik*, Berlin, 1979, pp. 221–23.

106 B. LYMANT, *Die mittelalterlichen Glasmalereien der ehemaligen Zisterzienserkirche Altenberg*, Bergisch Gladbach, 1979; see also R. BECKSMANN's review of this book in *Kunstchronik* 34 (1981): 401–2.

107 See most recently, DRACHENBERG, MAERCKER, RICHTER, *Mittelalterliche Glasmalerei*, pp. 199–200. Research is needed on this bird's appearance as a decorative motif in French and German stained glass at the beginning of the fourteenth century.

108 U.D. Korn, *Kloster Wienhausen, Die Glasmalereien*, n.p., n.d., pp. 40–42.

109 A. ANDERSSON, S.M. CHRISTIE, C.A. NORDMAN, A. ROUSSELL, *Die Glasmalereien des Mittelalters in Skandinavien*, CVMA: Scandinavia, Stockholm, 1964, pp. 196–200, pls 22, 99.

110 See most recently, DRACHENBERG, MAERCKER, RICHTER, *Mittelalterliche Glasmalerei*, pp. 215–16.

111 *Ibid.*, pp. 205–6.

112 See most recently, *Ibid.*, pp. 200–1.

113 J. HAYWARD, "Glazed Cloisters and their Development in the Houses of the Cistercian Order," *Gesta* 12 (1973): 93–109.

114 E. FRODL-KRAFT, "Die 'Figur im Langpass' in der österreichischen Glasmalerei und die Naumburger Westchorverglasung," in *Kunst des Mittelalters in Sachsen: Festschrift Wolf Schubert*, Weimar, 1967, pp. 309–14.

115 E. BÄCHER, *Die mittelalterlichen Glasgemälde in der Steiermark, Graz und Strassengle*, CVMA: Austria, vol. III/1, Vienna, 1979, pp. XXIV–XXVII.

116 FRODL-KRAFT, 1972, p. XXXVI.

117 *Ibid.*

118 *Idem*, "Die Kreuzgangverglasung und der Ambo des Nikolaus von Verdun," *Österreichische Zeitschrift für Kunst und Denkmalpflege* 19 (1965): 28–30.

119 *Idem, Die mittelalterlichen Glasgemälde in Wien*, Vienna, 1962, pp. XV, XVIII; *idem*, 1972, pp. 172–80; *idem*, *Gotische Glasmalereien aus dem Kreuzgang in Klosterneuburg*, Klosterneuburg, 1963, p. 24.

120 See most recently, H. BELTING, *Die Oberkirche von San Francesco in Assisi, ihre Dekoration als Aufgabe und die Genese einer neuen Wandmalerei*, Berlin, 1977, esp. pp. 78–86.

121 A. HASELOFF, "Die Glasmalereien der Kirche zu Breitenfelde und die deutsch-nordischen künstlerischen Beziehungen im 13. Jahrhundert," *Festgabe für Anton Schifferer*, Breslau, 1930, p. 8.

122 HAUSSHERR, "Der typologische Zyklus des Chorfensters der Oberkirche zu Assisi," pp. 115–18.

123 F. RÖHRIG, *Der Verduner Altar*, 1st ed., Vienna and Munich, 1955; CAVINESS, *Early Glass of Canterbury Cathedral*, p. 103.

124 G. MARCHINI, *Le vetrate dell'Umbria*, CVMA: Italy, vol. I, Rome, 1973, p. 88.

125 *Ibid.*, p. 84.

126 *Ibid.*, p. 23.

127 On these problems, see *ibid.*, pp. 69–75.

128 E. FRODL-KRAFT, "Farbendualitäten, Gegenfarben, Grundfarben in der gotischen Malerei," in *Von Farbe und Farben: Albert Knoepfli zum 70. Geburtstag* [published by the Institut für Denkmalpflege of the Eidgenössischen Technischen Hochschule, Zurich], no. 4 (1980): 293–95.

129 See above, n. 124.

130 "L'Art gothique siennois," exh. cat., Avignon: Musée du Petit Palais, June–Oct., 1983, pp. 34–35, no. 1.

131 E. CARLI, *La Peinture siennoise*, Paris, 1955, pp. 35–38.

132 E. CASTELNUOVO, "Vetrate," in *Enciclopedia Universale dell'Arte*, Rome, 1966, col. pl. 755.

133 F. DEUCHLER, *Duccio*, Milan, 1984, p. 216.

134 E. CARLI, *Vetrate duccesca*, 1st ed., Florence, 1946.

135 *Ibid.*

Catalogue

Note

The catalogue is selective; we have included those works that seem the most important today or that are the least well known. The format is as follows:
- The countries are listed below, with the locations within each country listed alphabetically: Germany, entries 1-7; Austria, entries 8-10; Spain, entry 11; France, entries 12-98; England, entries 99-102; Italy, entries 103-105; Switzerland, entries 106-109.
- The works are listed by place of origin, whether or not they have remained there. If they are preserved in a museum, a private collection or are in storage, that is indicated.
- In locations such as Troyes where more than one building is mentioned, the major building (the cathedral) is cited first, followed by the others in alphabetical order.

To facilitate the reader's task, most of the bays—especially in the larger buildings—have been given a number corresponding to the system of France's *Corpus Vitrearum* and used for the additional series, *Recensement des vitraux anciens de la France* (vol. I, 1978; vol. II, 1981; vol. III, 1985 [forthcoming]). The lower register of windows is numbered from 0 to 99, 0 corresponding to the eastern axial bay on the ground level, with odd numbers for those on the north side of it and even numbers for those on the south. On the next higher level, the numbers go from 100 to 199; on the third level, from 200 to 299. Occasionally the numbering employed by the Service des Monuments Historiques or that used in works considered standard references in France (such as the monograph by Delaporte and Houvet on the windows of Chartres, published in Chartres in 1926) has been added in parentheses.

Germany

1 BRANDENBURG AN DER HAVEL, Dom St Peter und Paul: choir
Virgin and Child (Pl. 204)
H. 0.80 m.; W. ca. 0.50 m.
ca. 1295

The Virgin, wearing a purple robe and a red mantle, stands in a hip-shot pose. A white veil held by a crown covers her head, which is surrounded by a large yellow halo. High on her left arm, she holds the Christ Child, who is dressed in a green and white gown and has a red halo. In one hand He holds His mother's veil; in the other, a flower. They stand beneath an architectural canopy.

The treatment of the design is supple; the balance between the modeling, often reduced to shading, and the character of the contours, with subtle line-work, produces a highly elegant effect, similar to small-scale sculpture from the end of the 13th century. The glass bears witness to the influence of Strasbourg workshops, which spread as far as the eastern regions of the Holy Roman Empire.

State of preservation: good.

H. WENTZEL, "Glasmaler und Maler im Mittelalter," *Zeitschrift des deutschen Vereins für Kunstwissenschaft* III (1949): 53-55; *idem*, 1954, pp. 32, 91, ill. 97; D. RENTSCH, *Glasmalerei des frühen vierzehnten Jahrhunderts in Ost-Mitteldeutschland*, Cologne and Graz, 1958, pp. 110-13, ill. 23; E. DRACHENBERG, K.S. MAERCKER and C. RICHTER, *Mittelalterliche Glasmalerei in der Deutschen Demokratischen Republik*, Berlin, 1979, pp. 193-94, ill. 38.

2 COLOGNE, Church of the Dominicans (destroyed): choir, bay 0
Typological window (*Bibelfenster*): *The Annunciation* (Pl. 184)
Each light: H. 13 m; W. 0.93 m.
ca. 1280
Remounted in Cologne Cathedral: ambulatory, chapel of Saint Stephen, bay 16, right light, lower register

The enthroned Virgin, seated at the right, is wearing a yellow gown and a dark red mantle and holding a book in her hand. Above her head, the Holy Spirit is figured as a dove. The two angels standing on the uprights of the throne signal a special iconography: the Virgin as "Queen of the Angels". The angel on the left, with pink wings and a red mantle, holds a white sceptre and a scroll inscribed: AVE MARIA PLENA. Another important iconographic detail is the presence of three roses, in lieu of the usual lily, in the vase next to the angel.

Above the medallion are two prophets among rinceaux (foliated scrolls), typical of German typological windows.

The window comprises two lights with twelve registers, each light having a different composition: the one on the left is devoted to Old Testament scenes; the one on the right to New Testament events.

The treatment is refined. Despite the crowded composition, the legibility of the scene is already Gothic. The lines are firm and follow the shape of the figures exactly. The colors are bright. The figural style prefigures that of illuminations in works like the Gradual of Valkenburg, made in Cologne in 1299 (Cologne, Archepiscopal Library).

The first stone for the new choir in this church of the Dominicans at Cologne was laid in 1271 by Albertus Magnus. The church was destroyed in 1804. In 1891 this window was remounted in the cathedral at Cologne, and five medallions were added.

State of preservation of the medallion: excellent. With the exception of the heads of the two prophets, the panel is modern.

H. RODE, *Die mittelalterlichen Glasmalereien des Kölner Domes, CVMA*: FRG, vol. IV/1, Berlin, 1974, pp. 83-91 [esp. pp. 86-87], pl. 55.

3 ESSLINGEN, Franciscan church of St. Georg: apse, bay 0, 10th register
Typological window (*Bibelfenster*): *The Flagellation of Christ* (Pl. 195)
Dimensions (panel): H. 0.58 m.; W. 0.66 m.
1310-1320
Now preserved in the central light, lower register

The Franciscan church of Sankt Georg at Esslingen contained the most important typological window of the "High Gothic" period in the Holy Roman Empire. Originally the windows consisted of three lights with fifteen superimposed scenes each. The central light was dedicated to the Life of Christ, while the lateral ones contained Old Testament scenes. Only eighteen historiated panels remain at the church, regrouped in the lower registers of the window. Two other panels are preserved in the Altes Rathausmuseum at Esslingen.

The Flagellation panel is cusped: the outer ornamental framing fillet is composed of two "inhabited" rinceaux, each with the bust of a prophet holding an inscription, generally written in German.

There are marked signs of detailing in the handling: this is one of the earliest examples of the use of silver stain (yellow) in the Holy Roman Empire. Flashed glass (*verres plaqués*) are used. The figural style heralds the innovations at Königsfelden, Switzerland. The colors are bright. The glass painting shows a search for new spatial depth, especially as in the scene illustrated here, in the representation of numerous figures from the back.

State of preservation: good.

H. WENTZEL, *Die Glasmalereien in Schwaben von 1250-1350, CVMA*: FRG, vol. I, Berlin, 1958, pp. 138-48 [esp. p. 143, ill. 259].

4 ESSLINGEN, Frauenkirche: chevet, apse, bay 3, left light, 10th register
The Life of the Virgin and the Childhood of Christ: The Blessed Virgin Taking Jesus to School (Pl. 194)
Dimensions (panel): H. 0.75 m.; W. 0.42 m.
ca. 1320

The Blessed Virgin, wearing a green gown and a red mantle with white lining, holds her Son by the hand. He is wearing a yellow robe and has a red halo; in His hand He is carrying a white scroll. Illustrations of this apocryphal story from the *Evangiles de l'Enfance* are rare, except in this region at this time (*cf.* the Child-hood window in the church of Sankt Dionysius at Esslingen).

The window has three lights with ten registers each. The Marian cycle begins with the Genealogy of the Virgin Mary and continues to the Baptism of Christ. Scenes such as the Birth of the Blessed Virgin occupy a number of panels. Two scenes from the windows are preserved in the Staatliche Galerie Moritzburg at Halle.

The spindle-shaped compartments are set against a damask ground composed of ivy scrolls. The framing strips decorated with plants are similar in arrange-ment to Strasbourg stained glass from the beginning of the 14th century. The damask ground in the scenes accentuates the detailing in the glass. A stylistic kin-ship can be seen with the windows in the south aisle of Strasbourg Cathedral; however, there are few close parallels with earlier local workships such as those at Saint-Denis. The range of colors is intense but restric-ted. State of preservation: excellent.

WENTZEL, *Die Glasmalereien*, pp. 153–58, ill. 305.

5 MÖNCHENGLADBACH, St-Vitus-Münster: apse, bay 0, right light, 5th register
Typological window (*Bibelfenster*): *The Adoration of the Magi* (Pl. 183)
Dimensions (light): H. ca. 9.70 m.; W. 0.60 m.
ca. 1275

This is one of the most characteristic examples of a *Bibelfenster* ("biblical window"), in which Old Testa-ment scenes, set in the left light, prefigure New Testa-ment events, set in the right one; this follows a typological formula developed by Honorius Augus-tudonensis. Accordingly, the Queen of Sheba before Solomon on the left corresponds to the Adoration of the Magi on the right.

The arrangement and the decoration of the lights differ, though each has fourteen scenes. On the left, at the top of each light, is Christ giving His blessing; on the right, the Virgin orante.

In the New Testament light, each scene is enclosed in a richly framed octafoil. Furthermore, a wide encir-cling stem unifies all the historiated compartments. In the foliated scrolls beneath the scene are busts of Moses and Aaron pointing towards the scene. These prophets' names are inscribed on scrolls.

The handling is characteristic of the *Zackenstil* ("hard, or jagged style"): angular and abrupt. This is an intermediate type of window between the typologi-cal window in the Three Kings Chapel in Cologne Cathedral (1260) and that from the church of the Dominicans, now installed in the chapel of Saint Stephen in Cologne Cathedral (*cf.* cat. 2).

State of preservation: good, despite some restored pieces. It was restored most recently in 1975, by Dr. G. Frenzel.

H. OIDTMANN, *Die rheinischen Glasmalereien vom 12. bis zum 16. Jahrhundert*, vol. I, Düsseldorf, 1912, pp. 109–15, ill. 156–64 and pl. IX; WENTZEL, 1954, p. 91, ill. 87; J. CLADDERS, H. RODE, H. BANGE, *Das Gladbacher Bibelfenster, Gefährdung, Restaurierung*, Mönchengladbach: Städtisches Museum, 1976.

6 WIENHAUSEN (Lower Saxony), Cistercian abbey: cloister, south side, bay 4, tympanum
Christ's Entry into Jerusalem (Pl. 205)
0.71 m. square
1330–1340

Christ, in red and green, is shown riding a grey donkey and followed by a crowd. A yellow tree in front of Him follows the oblique form of one side of the compart-ment—a canted square—in which the scene is set.

The cloister windows retain in large part their orig-inal Passion cycle. The most innovative scene is Christ Crucified accompanied by the Virtues and a group of apostles and saints (St. Benedict of Nursia, St. Bernard of Clairvaux). The panels occupy either the amortize-ments of each of the two lights in the bay or the center of the tympanum above them, as in the case of the Entry into Jerusalem. (The lower parts of the lights were probably closed with wooden shutters.)

In his recent study of this stained glass, U.D. Korn pointed to the influence of Parisian models from the years around 1300. These windows may have been made at Lübeck or, more likely, at Lüneburg. Stylistic similarities can be drawn to the panel with Christ set between the Wise and Foolish Virgins, made by a Lüneburg workshop for the abbey at Isenhagen in 1327 and now preserved at the Niedersächsisches Lan-desmuseum in Hannover.

State of preservation of the panel: good.

WENTZEL, 1954, p. 92, ill. 126; U.D. KORN, *Kloster Wienhausen*, Vol. 5: *Die Glasmalereien*, n.d.; n.p.

7 WIMPFEN AM BERG (Baden-Württemberg), church of the Dominicans: chevet, bay 0, left light (?), 3rd register (?)
Typological window (*Bibelfenster*): *Moses and the Burning Bush* (Pl. 196)
Dimensions (panel): H. 0.88 m.; W. 0.67 m.
Between 1299 and 1310
Preserved at the Württembergisches Landesmuseum, Stuttgart

According to Wentzel, the scene of Moses and the Burning Bush was considered a prefiguration of the Nativity. The window originally contained three lights with thirteen scenes each. Old Testament episodes were represented in the left light and New Testament scenes in the center. A cycle of the life of Saint Domi-nic was set in the third light, paralleling the biblical and Christological events in the other two.

Only twenty historiated panels from this window survive. In the 19th century they were installed in the Neo-Gothic castle of Odenwald belonging to the counts of Erbach. Eight panels are from the Old Tes-tament light; eight are from the New Testament, and four are from the light dedicated to Saint Dominic. At the church, some decorative panels remain in the lan-cet heads and in the tracery. The glass can be dated by the arms of the family of Conrad of Weinsberg, the church's founder, between 1299 and 1310.

The spindle-shaped medallion contains a hexafoil with pierced corners. The handling is refined and includes the use of silver stain (yellow). The coloring used for the clothing is pale, but the background colors are rather brutal.

The figural style is analogous to Strasbourg models but surpasses them in line, color and the mastery of composition. The oak-leaf decoration against which the medallions are set has a formal similarity to the windows in the Dominican church at Colmar.

The original background of the medallion has been lost; there are restored areas in Moses' cloak.

WENTZEL, *Die Glasmalereien*, pp. 234–43 [esp. p. 241, ill. 592].

Austria

8 HEILIGENKREUZ, Cistercian abbey: cloister, wash house, bay 6, 2nd light, 4th register
Babenberg Window: Margrave Leopold III (Pl. 207)
ca. 1280

Margrave Leopold III (1095–1136), arrayed with sym-bols of his power, is represented frontally in a poly-foil frame inscribed: + LEOPOLD [US] MARCHIO AUS-TRIE FUNDATOR HORUM CENOBIORUM. Canonized in 1485, the margrave founded the abbeys of Heiligen-kreuz and Klosterneuburg, which are represented in the lancet heads of this window that commemorates the members of his illustrious family.

The reconstruction of this wash house dates to the end of the 13th century. Its stained glass decoration included "portraits" of the Babenbergs. The two lights of the third window contain original figures. Other original elements are scattered among the seven other bays. The monastery was partly destroyed by the Turks in 1683. Missing areas were restored in 1884 in accordance with a description of 1640.

The effect of the window is precious. The rigid treatment of folds and drapery anticipates the series of prophets in the choir; however, the faces, especially that of the margrave, retain a Romanesque quality.

State of preservation of the figures: good; the bor-ders are modern.

FRODL-KRAFT, 1972, pp. 124–25, pl. 364; J. HAYWARD, "Glazed Cloisters and their Development in the Houses of the Cistercian Order," *Gesta* XII (1973): 100–4; P. NIEMETZ, *Die Babenberger-Scheiben im Hei-ligenkreuzer Brunnenhaus*, Heiligenkreuz, 1978.

9 KLOSTERNEUBURG, Cistercian abbey: cloister, west side, bay 9 (IX)
Christ Healing the Man Born Blind (John IX) (Pl. 212)
H. 0.98 m.; W. 0.57 m.
ca. 1330
Reinstalled at Klosterneuburg: chapel of Saint Leo-pold, bay 2 (II), 4th light, upper register

The scene illustrates the beginning of chapter nine of the Gospel of Saint John, in which Christ cures a man born blind. The blind man is seated in the foreground, with two witnesses behind him. Christ, followed by a disciple, holds a double scroll reading: + QUID. PEC-CAVIT. HO[MO]/NEQ[.] HIC. PECCAVIT. NEQUE. PARENTES. EIUS (John IX: 2–3). The frame of complicated foils and cusps is composed of a wide fillet on which is written: DE. QUO. CULPATUR. HIC. QUOD. CECUS. GENERATUR.

Like the ambo by Nicholas of Verdun at Kloster-neuburg (now an altarpiece), the windows in the west and north sides of the cloister once had a typological cycle. In the perforations of the tympanum were the portraits of the Babenbergs, founders and benefactors of the abbey from the 11th to the 13th century, as well as portraits of monastic dignitaries and Marian scenes.

Today the majority of the panels have been regrouped in the east windows of this chapel.

Though the frame follows a glazing tradition dating from 1280 in this region, the composition and the handling of the design have become Gothic. Simpli-fied treatment: beak folds in the drapery.

State of preservation: excellent.

FRODL-KRAFT, 1972, pp. 165–98 [esp. pp. 187–88, ills. 564, 581–84, and fig. 44].

10 SAINT WALPURGIS (near Saint Michael, Styria), chapel of ease: apse, bay 3 (north II), 1st light, 2nd register
Wise Virgin (Pl. 209)
Dimensions (panel): H. 0.97 m.; W. 0.41 m.
1295–1297

The virgin, holding a chalice in her hand, is seen in three-quarter view, dressed in a white robe beneath a red mantle lined in yellow. A festooned yellow halo frames her long hair. The figure is set in a polyfoil frame against a ground covered with small blue foliated scrolls.

This church was founded by Abbot Henri d'Admont (1275–1297) and dedicated to Saint Walpurgis. Four of its apse windows have been reconstructed.

The theme of the Wise and Foolish Virgins, from the Last Judgment, appeared in the decoration of religious buildings from the mid-12th century, for instance on the central portal of the west facade of Saint Denis.

The style of this virgin places her in the final phase of the *Zackenstil* in Styria. Certain aspects such as the pose of the young virgin augur Gothic art.

State of preservation: poor, for the painting has been partially lost.

E. BÄCHER, "Frühe Glasmalerei in der Steiermark" (exh. cat.), Graz, 1975, p. 15; *idem, Die mittelalterlichen Glasgemälde in der Steiermark, CVMA*: Austria, vol. III/1, Vienna, Cologne and Graz, 1979, pp. XXIV–XXVII [introduction].

Spain

11 LEÓN, cathedral: nave clerestory, north side, bay 225
The Hunt Window (Pl. 179)
H. 10 m.; W. ca. 4 m.
3rd quarter of the 13th century

This composite window with four lights representing different subjects is datable to the second half of the 13th century. There are two main groups:
1) Musical Angels and representations of the Liberal Arts;
2) a Royal Hunt, from which the window takes its name. Among the dogs and hares in the latter window, thirteen horsemen are riding, some sounding the trumpet, while others hold a falcon or carry a standard bearing the arms of Castile. The figures, different in scale and presentation from those in the first group, may have been in a window of the royal palace of Alfonso X, the Wise, before being remounted in the cathedral in the 14th century.

The scale is monumental. The awkward construction is compensated for by the liveliness of the linework. Blue and red predominate, as they do in the French tradition of the first half of the 13th century.

State of preservation: mediocre.

M. GÓMEZ-MORENO, *Catálogo monumental de España, Provincia de León*, Madrid, vol. I, 1925–26, pp. 263–64; vol. II, pl. 356; J. FERNÁNDEZ ARENAS and J.C.F. ESPINO, *Las vidrieras de la catedral de León*, León, 1983, pp. 78–80.

France

12 AMIENS, cathedral of Notre Dame: chevet, axial chapel, bay 1
Border of Birds with Confronted Heads (Pl. 15)
H. 0.65 m.; W. 0.25 m.
ca. 1240
Preserved at Champs-sur-Marne, storage depot of the Monuments Historiques

The border is from a two-light window illustrating scenes from the Acts of the Apostles. Despite the efforts made by Coffetier and Steinheil from 1853, these panels form a barely coherent iconographic ensemble. They were already very altered when G. Durand described them in his monograph on the cathedral. Taken down at the beginning of the First World War, the glass was heavily damaged by a fire that destroyed the workshop of master glazier Socard, where it was being restored; nevertheless, most of the border panels were saved. Inventoried several years ago by J.J. Gruber, they will be reinstalled in a bay of the cathedral.

This zoomorphic motif, with delicate line-work, was also used in the 13th century for a window of the collegiate church at Saint-Quentin and was very fashionable in the 14th century, especially in Normandy, for example in Saint Ouen at Rouen.

State of preservation: mediocre.

G. DURAND, *Monographie de l'église Notre-Dame, cathédrale d'Amiens*, Vol. II: *Amiens and Paris*, 1903, pp. 564–65, fig. 257.

13 AMIENS, cathedral of Notre Dame: chevet, axial chapel, bay 2
The Tree of Jesse: King (Pl. 102)
H. 0.60 m.; W. ca. 0.50 m.
ca. 1245
Preserved at Champs-sur-Marne, storage depot of the Monuments Historiques

This window, like cat. 12, also burned in the fire at Socard's glass restoration workshop (1921), but a few panels were saved and inventoried some years ago by J.J. Gruber. His workshop is currently restoring them for reinstallation at Amiens Cathedral.

The format is the standard one: the kings are shown in the middle panel at the center of a mandorla formed by the branches of the tree. They sit on thrones of leaves. The lateral compartments, two per register, are reserved for the prophets, who are represented in profile.

The scale is not monumental. The glass has been cut into geometric shapes. The painting was rapidly but very precisely done. The drapery and folds are angular. The lively facial expressions are rendered by only a few lines. The decoration has been confined to sleek fillets ending in schematically drawn leaflets. There is a narrow border of the "arch" type. The lively color is characteristic of French glass in the 13th century.

State of preservation of this panel: good, though the others that survived the fire are more altered.

DURAND, *Monographie*, vol. II, pp. 369–72; F. PERROT, "Franse Kerkramen—Vitraux de France", exh. cat., Amsterdam: Rijksmuseum, Dec. 1973–Mar. 1974, pp. 59–61.

14 ANGERS, cathedral of Saint Maurice: choir clerestory, bay 108, left light, lower registers
Life of Saint Thomas Becket: Pursuit of Thomas Becket by Knights on Horseback, then in a Boat (?) (Pl. 49)
Dimensions (two registers): H. ca. 2 m.; W. 1.50 m.
1235–1240

The border contains two armorial shields of the Beaumont family. Two members of that family occupied the episcopal see of Angers between 1203 and 1240, so that the window can be dated between those years. Unfortunately, the state of preservation is defective, and the eight scenes, which read from bottom to top, do not follow in logical order.

The first shows three armed knights in coats of mail carrying shields and surely represents the Pursuit of Thomas Becket, ordered by King Henry II. The second shows two knights and a man in a boat and may be the continuation of the same scene. Third is the Appearance of Christ to Thomas Becket, who is praying before an altar; it is a modern panel. Fourth is the Engagement of Henry of England to Marguerite of France. Fifth is the Meeting of King Henry II and Thomas Becket; sixth, the Burial of Thomas Becket. The seventh scene represents Thomas Becket as a child being saved from the millstones of a mill, and again, it is a modern panel. The eighth scene depicting the Murder of Thomas Becket is likewise modern.

The original emphasis, though difficult to reconstruct with certainty, must have been on the struggle between the English prelate and King Henry II. Conceived only a few decades after the annexation of Anjou by King Philip Augustus of France, the work had evident political import.

The composition remains Romanesque, with one quatrefoil per register. Similarly, the ornament is faithful to the traditions of Angers at the end of the 12th century: spandrels filled with bracketed bouquets of palmettes enclosed in large spindle-shaped leaf borders. On the other hand, the figural style has evolved towards non-monumental pieces of glass. It has a formal dryness and favors contour at the expense of modeling.

The glass was restored by the Gaudin workshop in 1892 and removed from the neighboring window.

L. DE FARCY, *Monographie de la cathédrale d'Angers*, Vol. I: *Les immeubles*, Angers, 1910, pp. 171–72; HAYWARD and GRODECKI, 1966, pp. 36–39; C. BRISAC, "Thomas Becket dans le vitrail français au début du XIIIᵉ siècle," *Actes du Colloque international Thomas Becket–Sédières 1973*, Paris (1975): 230–31.

15 AUXERRE, cathedral of Saint Etienne: ambulatory, bay 12, lower register, right medallion
The Apocalypse: The White Horseman (Pl. 110)
Overall dimensions of the cycle: H. 1.90 m.; L. 2 m.
1230–1235

Only ten medallions of an original seventeen survive. Nine have been reunited, but the arrangement has been confused; the tenth is now set in another window (bay 21). Originally the window was composed of groups of four medallions connected by a wide *fermaillet*, or boss, two in each register, as opposed to three as seen now.

This is the sole example in 13th-century French stained glass of a narrative cycle about the Apocalypse. The iconographic sources are close to manuscript illuminations of that text, in which episodes of the Apocalypse frequently include the apostle John (e.g., Paris, Bibl. Nat., ms. fr. 403).

The drawing is bold and the handling energetic: powerful silhouettes making sweeping gestures. This workshop was also responsible for the Saint Eligius window and, according to Virginia Raguin, for the monumental figures of Saint Stephen and Saint Germanus in bay 102. These craftsmen would then have traveled to Saint-Julien-du-Sault and to Saint-Fargeau to work. This is probably the most original style in Burgundian stained glass from the first half of the 13th century.

State of preservation: mediocre.

ABBÉ BONNEAU, "Description des verrières de la cathédrale d'Auxerre," *Bulletin de la Société des Sciences historiques et naturelles de l'Yonne* 34 (1885): 296–308, 338–39; L. FOURREY, "Les verrières historiées de la cathédrale d'Auxerre," *Bulletin de la Société des Sciences historiques et naturelles de l'Yonne,* 83 (1929): 59–61; J. LAFOND, "Les vitraux de la cathédrale Saint-Etienne d'Auxerre," *C. Arch.* 116 (1958): 66–67; V. CHIEFFO RAGUIN, *Stained Glass in Thirteenth Century Burgundy,* Princeton, 1982, pp. 34–35, figs. 67, 70, 77.

16 AUXERRE, cathedral of Saint Etienne: ambulatory, bay 20, 3rd and 4th registers
Legends of Abraham, Noah and Lot: (from left to right) The Sacrifice of Abraham (Gen. XXII: 9–12); Abraham Offers Food to the Angels (Gen. XVIII: 1–15); Angels Announcing the Destruction of Sodom (Gen. XVIII: 16–22); the Intercession of Abraham (Gen. XVIII: 23–33); Lot Greets the Angels (Gen. XIX: 1–2); Lot's Wife Welcomes the Angels (Gen. XIX: 3) (Pl. 107)
Overall dimensions: H. 4.80 m.; W. 1.90 m.
ca. 1230–1235

Under the impetus of Bishop Guillaume de Seignelay (1207–1220), building on the Gothic cathedral of Auxerre was undertaken in 1215, but the windows of the ambulatory were not installed until after 1230. In 1567, the Huguenots sacked the building, and the stained glass sustained great damage. The original program was irredeemably altered, and the glass mutilated. Between 1866 and 1873, L. Steinheil undertook an important restoration with the participation of the Veissière brothers, who were local craftsmen. After Fourrey's article was published in 1929, a large number of panels were regrouped by subject, but without significant result.

The scenes, read from bottom to top. The story of Lot is told in the two upper registers, while that of Noah occupies the six lower compartments.

The narrative is overabundant. The illustration, divided into small hexagonal compartments (three per register), is quite extensive. The frame is restricted to two sleek fillets. The use of a rinceau ground is perpetuated here, beginning at the outside framing strip and coiling up into the spandrels. The narrow border has scanty, schematized plant motifs.

The scale of execution is small, but the compositions are dynamic. The silhouettes are thin and taut; the faces small and lively, with surprised expressions. The stiffness of the shapes results in a stiffening of posture and gesture, which contrasts with the freedom of the composition. These characteristics can be found in the majority of the windows in the ambulatory at Auxerre—the Creation, Samson, St. Mary of Egypt, Mary Magdalene, etc. The sources are local and do not seem to derive from the Ile-de-France.

The window is incomplete; state of preservation: mediocre.

BONNEAU, "Description des verrières," pp. 296–348; FOURREY, "Les verrières historiées," pp. 21–24, 92; LAFOND, "Les vitraux," 1958, pp. 66–67; CHIEFFO RAGUIN, *Stained Glass,* pp. 107, 120, 160–61, figs. 12–14.

17 BAYE (Marne), chapel of the castle: bay 1
The Tree of Jesse: The Virgin Mary (Pl. 32)
Overall dimensions: H. ca. 4 m.; W. 1.50 m.
ca. 1210–1220

This chapel is the earliest part of the castle and has been rebuilt and transformed many times since its foundation. Archeological analysis shows that the chapel was built at the beginning of the 13th century. It is one of the rare examples of this type of building from this age in France and the only one which still has its original glass. The five windows fill the lights in the north side and the apse. From north to east, they represent the Tree of Jesse, the Life of Saint John the Evangelist, the Childhood of Christ, a sequence on the Resurrection of Lazarus and the Passion.

The iconographic scheme of the Tree of Jesse is traditional, with two ancestor-kings, the Virgin Mary and Christ surrounded by Seven Doves. The prophets are set in the lateral panels. The panel containing Jesse, however, is lost.

The slender, hieratic figure of the seated Virgin, set against a red ground, is surrounded by white palm branches that enclose her in a kind of mandorla, outlined with a narrow blue fillet. Nimbed and crowned, she wears a pale green gown and a long blue veil that forms a mantle. On her knees she holds a book.

The strict agreement between figure and frame is reinforced by the linear play of thin, parallel folds. The type of figure and the treatment of the elongated face with fixed features, enlivened only by a dimple in the chin, is similar to work from Soissons such as the figure of the Blessed Virgin (destroyed in 1944) that was in the Kunstgewerbemuseum in Berlin.

State of preservation of this panel: good, but the other panels have numerous pieces of modern glass.

LASTEYRIE, 1852–57, vol. I, p. 198; D. DAGUENET, "La chapelle de Baye et ses vitraux," *C. Arch.* 135 (1977): 629–46.

18 BOURGES, cathedral of Saint Etienne: ambulatory, bay 3
The New Alliance:
1) Christ Carrying His Cross (4th register, lower circle, central quatrefoil, right side) (Pl. 43)
2) Moses and the Brazen Serpent (6th register, middle group, left trefoil) (Pl. 63)
Overall dimensions: H. 6 m.; W. 2.20 m.
ca. 1210–1215

The theological density of the iconographic program of the lower windows in the chevet at Bourges was rarely equaled. Major themes of Christian doctrine are set next to the Parables, intensifying certain commentaries. In the three bays of the radiating chapels the lives of the most popularly venerated saints of the time are depicted. The New Alliance and its pendant, the Last Judgment, are the central elements around which the other subjects are articulated.

In the New Alliance, episodes from the Passion of Christ—the Carrying of the Cross, the Crucifixion and the Resurrection—are compared with Old Testament scenes that, according to medieval exegesis, prefigured them. Accordingly, Moses and the Brazen Serpent (Pl. 63) accompanies the Crucifixion. Butchers at

work are shown at the bottom, for their guild donated the window.

The sophisticated composition is divided in two large quadrants, each composed of a central quatrefoil with four radiating lateral compartments. A medallion flanked by two trefoils is set between the two quadrants.

The spatial distribution is exceptional for the time: the main characters are strongly individualized. The elegant drapery suggests the volume of the elongated bodies. These pictorial qualities indicate that the master glazier came from the north. This is one of the most accomplished achievements of the 1200 Style in stained glass.

The glass was excessively restored in the 19th century; since 1970 it has become opaque and deteriorated alarmingly. The cleaning and restoration undertaken by Jean Mauret under the direction of the Research Laboratory of the Monuments Historiques have restored most of the glass's translucence, but three panels of the lower quadrant had to be replaced by copies because of their poor condition; however, they will be returned to the cathedral shortly.

CAHIER and MARTIN, 1841–44, pp. 1–132, pl. I; MÂLE, 1910, pp. 171–77; GRODECKI, "A Stained Glass 'Atelier' of the Thirteenth Century," *Journal of the Warburg and Courtauld Institutes,* 11 (1948): 87–111; idem, "The 'Maître du Bon Samaritain' de la cathédrale de Bourges," in *The Year 1200: A Symposium,* New York, 1975, pp. 348–49; C. B. BRISAC and J. M. BETTEMBOURG, "La vie mystérieuse des chefs-d'œuvre," exh. cat., Paris: Grand-Palais, 1980, pp. 130–31; *Recensement,* II, p. 170.

19 BOURGES, cathedral of Saint Etienne: ambulatory, bay 4, 4th register, middle quatrefoil
The Last Judgment: The Damned Being Driven toward Leviathan (Pl. 42)
Overall dimensions: H. 6 m.; W. 2.20 m.
ca. 1210–1215

Like its counterpart, the New Alliance window (cf. cat. 18), the formal system is conceived as a theological lesson. In the center are three, large, pierced quatrefoils, divided into five compartments encircled by irons. On the sides, the scenes are "sewn" to the mosaic ground with diagonal leading and lozenges decorated with crossettes. The border has acanthus bouquets set perpendicular to the window's axis and enclosed in "arches."

Reading from bottom to top the scenes are
1) the Death of the Pious Man and of the Unbeliever;
2) the Resurrection of the Dead: the Risen Dead Leaving their Tombs, Angels Sounding the Trumpet, the Elect Being Led toward the Bosom of Abraham, the Damned Being Driven toward Leviathan and the Weighing of Souls;
3) Christ in Glory, enthroned on a rainbow and surrounded by angels carrying the instruments of the Passion, and by the Virgin Mary, Saint John and the heavenly host;
4) at the top, angels and the Holy Spirit as a dove.

The handling shows an exceptional mastery. The faces are finely and carefully painted, and there is a balance between the rendering of contour and modeling. The spatial organization of the Damned is similar to that of the People of Reims in the Saint Nicasius window from the cathedral of Soissons, now in the Isabella Stewart Gardner Museum in Boston (cf.

Pl. 26). The glazing was done by the same workshop as the New Alliance window.

Restored in 1853 by N. Coffetier and more recently by Jean Mauret (1976–1981); state of preservation since the latter effort: satisfactory.

CAHIER and MARTIN, 1841–44, pp. 171–78, pl. X; F. QUIÉVREUX, "Les vitraux du XIIIᵉ siècle de l'abside de la cathédrale de Bourges," *Bull. Mon.* 101 (1943): 255–75; GRODECKI, "Le 'Maître du Bon Samaritain' de Bourges," pp. 348–49, figs. 12–13.

20 BOURGES, cathedral of Saint Etienne: ambulatory, bay 5, 4th register
The Parable of the Prodigal Son: the Prodigal Son Leaving his Father's House (Pl. 69)
Overall dimensions: H. 6 m.; W. 2.20 m.
ca. 1210–1215

Represented as a young noble, the Prodigal Son, mounted on his horse and holding a falcon in his hand, wears a purple gown and has a fur-lined mantle over his shoulders. A servant accompanies him.

The parable from Luke XV: 11–32 was often represented in French stained glass during the first half of the 13th century—at Auxerre, Chartres, Sens and Coutances. Here its choice is a metaphor of salvation. The tanners, the guild which donated the window, are represented in the three lower compartments.

The window is composed of two large quatrefoils, each divided into five historiated compartments and separated by a band composed of a circle and semicircles (compare with the neighboring New Alliance window, cat. 18). The mosaic ground has diagonal leading and small medallions each containing the bust of a king. The border consists of knotted acanthus leaves.

The compositions are open and often rest on "bridges". The figures are slim, with large, characteristic heads: low foreheads, long aquiline noses and receding chins. The folds and drapery provide an ornamental effect.

The window was made by the principal workshop of the Bourges ambulatory, run by the "Master of the Relics of Saint Stephen," who was responsible for eleven of the surviving twenty-two windows in the ambulatory and radiating chapels.

Restored after 1853 by N. Coffetier, and more recently by Jean Mauret in 1982–83; state of preservation: good (one head is now in the Yale University Art Gallery).

CAHIER and MARTIN, 1841–44, pp. 179–88, pl. VI; GRODECKI, "Le 'Maître du Bon Samaritain' de Bourges," pp. 341–43.

21 BOURGES, cathedral of Saint Etienne: ambulatory, bay 6, 3rd register
The Passion of Christ: The Last Supper (detail): The Head of Christ (Pl. 71)
Overall dimensions: H. 6 m.; W. 2.20 m.
ca. 1210–1215

The medallions are distributed in two parallel rows, following a Romanesque principle that persisted in western France (Poitiers). The medallions are not joined by the classic type of leading, but by wide vertical lines composed of several fillets. The corners have a barely legible damask ground that follows the Romanesque tradition of removing the paint by stick-lighting.

The scale is small, in contrast to nearby windows such as the Apocalypse (bay 14), which is nevertheless by the same workshop.

The donors—the furriers—are represented in the lower register. The scenes read from bottom to top in a well-developed iconographic program that begins with two scenes of the Entry of Jesus into Jerusalem, followed by the Miracles of Christ, the Last Supper, the Washing of the Disciples' Feet, the Agony in the Garden, the Kiss of Judas, the Raising of the Cross, Christ before Pilate, the Flagellation, the Crucifixion, the Descent from the Cross, the Entombment and the Descent into Limbo.

The hieratic position of Christ contrasts with the supple, flowing lines of His hair and beard. The colors are bright; the window was made by the workshop of the "Good Samaritan Master."

Restored after 1853 and, more recently, by Jean Mauret in 1982; state of preservation: excellent.

CAHIER and MARTIN, 1841–44, pp. 189–90, pl. V; J. HAYWARD, "Techniques of Stained Glass," *The Bulletin of The Metropolitan Museum of Art* (Dec. 1971–Jan. 1972): 105; GRODECKI, "Le 'Maître du Bon Samaritain' de Bourges," pp. 343–45, fig. 9.

22 BOURGES, cathedral of Saint Etienne: nave clerestory, south side, bay 216, tympanum rose
The Coronation of the Blessed Virgin (Pl. 116)
Diam. ca. 1.20 m
Middle of the 13th century

Enough of the original glass from the nave clerestory remains to suggest that most of the windows were decorated with grisaille lights. Subjects in full color, such as this Coronation, were reserved for the tracery roses. Whether this formal choice of simplified decoration (in comparison with the clerestory windows in the chevet and choir) was dictated by economic necessity or by esthetic choice remains an open question, especially since these medallions, with their varied iconography, are probably not in their original location.

The Coronation is in the same style as another medallion in bay 220, the Annunciation. The scale of the cut pieces of glass is small. The drawing is abrupt and dry. The handling is simplified and makes use of oblique and beak folds. The formal evolutionary stage of the figure is the same as that of the windows by the principal workshop responsible for the middle period of glass painting at the cathedral of Le Mans (cf. Pls. 118, 121).

State of preservation: mediocre; there are numerous repair leads.

K. HASELHORST, "Die gotischen Glasfenster der Kathedrale von Bourges," Munich, 1974, p. 43 [thesis]; *Recensement*, II, p. 180.

23 CARCASSONNE, church of Saint Nazaire and Saint Celse: south transept, chapel of the Holy Cross, bay 10, middle registers
The Tree of Life: Christ on the Cross (Pl. 165)
H. 12.50 m.; W. 3.50 m
ca. 1310

This three-light window illustrates a Franciscan theme popularized by Saint Bonaventura's treatise, *Lignum Vitae*. The cross has been transformed into a symbolic tree. Birds forage among the leaves and flowers on its trunk. The branches consist of bracketed scrolls

giving the chapter titles of the work, which glorifies successively the Life, the Death and the Resurrection of Christ. Prophets are set in trefoil niches on the sides, in a scheme resembling that of the Tree of Jesse. At the top are the Seven Gifts of the Holy Spirit. The lower panels (not shown here) were poorly restored in the 19th century by Alfred Gérente, who did not understand the origin and meaning of the composition. According to J.P. Suau, the composition must have been copied from a manuscript.

Each of the three lights is composed of twenty-three narrow registers. The tracery in the tympanum is filled with floral motifs.

Despite the size of the window, the scale of execution is small. The composition is confused, and the colors dense.

State of preservation: imperfect, with much modern glass.

G. J. MOT, "Les vitraux de Saint-Nazaire de Carcassonne," *Mémoires de la Société archéologique du midi de la France* 22 (1954): 52–4; J.P. SUAU, "L'iconographie du Christ et de la Vierge dans le vitrail gothique méridional," University of Paris-X, Nanterre, 1983, vol. I/2, pp. 176–270 [Unpublished thesis].

24 CHARTRES, cathedral of Notre Dame: ambulatory, bay 7
The Story of Charlemagne:
1) Voyage of Charlemagne to Constantinople (lower registers) (Pl. 54)
2) Building a Church in the Presence of Charlemagne (Pl. 55)
Overall dimensions: H. 8.11 m.; L. 2.38 m.
ca. 1220–1225

This window is one of the most famous in the cathedral. The furriers, who donated it, are represented in a half-medallion at the bottom of the piece.

The composition consists of alternating circles and lozenges, the latter flanked by semicircles divided in half horizontally and set parallel to the border. There are twenty-four historiated compartments and an oyster-shell mosaic. The border is composed of acanthus leaves connected by broken bars. The armature has been forged into the shape of the historiated compartments.

As the stake, from the second quarter of the 12th century, in a political conflict between the Capetian kings and the emperors of the Holy Roman Empire, Charlemagne was not canonized until 1165. However, his iconography had already developed, notably at Saint Denis in France, where a window from the period of Abbot Suger (now lost) glorified his legend. The lost windows from Saint Denis and the scenes at Chartres have a common inspiration.

Reading from bottom to top, the first part of the window is inspired by Charlemagne's trip to the Orient, the second by his Spanish "Crusade".

1) Charlemagne Receives Constantine's Envoys: Constantine's Vision; Battle against the Infidels; Constantine Offers Three Reliquaries to Charlemagne, Who Takes Them to Aachen.

2) Charlemagne and his Advisers Watch the Sky; Saint James Appears to Charlemagne in a Dream; the Departure for Spain; the Taking of Pamplona; the Building of a Church; the Miracle of the Flowering Lances; the Battle against the Saracens; six scenes from the Legend of Roland; the Mass of Saint Giles; Censing Angels. Many of the scenes have bands inscribed: CAROLUS or CARROLUS.

The compositions are full and often set on "bridges". The figures are symmetrically placed. The background is open and airy, making even the liveliest actions very easy to read. The colors are light and even. The work has been quickly but carefully done. This is the most accomplished work of the "classical workshop," responsible for many of the windows in the choir—the Saint Stephen and Saint James windows, for example—and for later commissions such as the Lady Chapel at the cathedral of Le Mans.

The Lorin studio was responsible for the most recent restoration in 1921. State of preservation: good, despite recent, progressive blackening of the glass.

DELAPORTE and HOUVET, 1926, pp.313-19, pls. CIV-CX; E.G. GRIMME, "Das Karlfenster in der Kathedrale von Chartres," *Aachener Kunstblätter des Museumsvereins* 19-20 (1960-61): 11-24; R. LEJEUNE and J. STIENNON, *La légende de Roland dans l'art du Moyen Age*, vol. I, Brussels, 1966, pp.192-99, pls. VII-XVIII; F. GARNIER, *Le vitrail: XIIIe siècle, L'histoire de Charlemagne*, Paris, 1969; P. POPESCO, *Chefs-d'œuvre du vitrail européen: la cathédrale de Chartres*, Paris, 1970, p.139, fig.38; C. MAINES, "The Charlemagne Window at Chartres Cathedral: New Considerations on Text and Image," *Speculum* 52 (1977): 801-23.

25 CHARTRES, cathedral of Notre Dame: ambulatory, 1st north radiating chapel, bay 15
Legend of Saint Chéron (4 lower registers) (Pl. 58)
Overall dimensions: H. 8.90 m.; W. 2.10 m.
ca. 1220-1225

1) In the lower register, the donors are shown at work. In the left compartment, two workmen verify that a building is plumb; in the three others, sculptors complete a statue for the splay or porch that is in a style similar to those that were being set in the transept of the cathedral at the time.
2) 2nd-4th registers, Legend of Saint Chéron: 2nd register: at the left, Saint Chéron as a child is being taken to school by his parents. The inscription reads: ARAUNUS. At the right, the saint recites a lesson to a teacher. 3rd register: Saint Chéron Refuses to Marry. 4th register: Having Become a Priest, the Saint Goes to Italy and Exorcises a Young Woman Possessed by the Devil. The rest of the window represents the martyrdom of the saint, his death, the translation of his relics, and the pilgrimage and cure of the son of Clothair.

Veneration of Saint Chéron, a young 5th-century patrician, hardly extended beyond the diocese of Chartres. There, however, he was greatly venerated because of the miracles that took place at his tomb. An abbey dedicated to him was built over his tomb, which is not far from the city.

The window is conceived in groups of two or four rectangular compartments under trefoil arcades resting on little columns. There is no background. The composition is open, the figures independent of one another, thus increasing their legibility and formal autonomy. The drapery is rigid; beaks and broken folds sometimes occur. The faces are small, with strong features and a decided look.

The sustained color is restricted to the dominant blue and red. White is confined to small areas, mostly the framing fillets.

The border is still wide, but its decoration has been simplified, usually to one daisy per motif.

State of preservation: relatively good until recent years; browning of the glass has now made it difficult

to read this most representative example of the "hardened" style of the "Master of Saint Chéron".

DELAPORTE and HOUVET, 1926, pp.337-43, fig.38, pls. CXXIII-CXXVI; GRODECKI, 1978, pp.52-61.

26 CHARTRES, cathedral of Notre Dame: choir, bay 30, lower register, right compartment
Our Lady of the Belle-Verrière: The Public Life of Christ: The Temptation of Christ on the Mountaintop (Matt. IV:8-11) (Pl. 56)
Overall dimensions: H. 7.50 m.; W. 2.40 m.
1210-1215

A figure of the Virgin and Child, probably executed around 1180, occupied an important place in the cathedral of Bishop Fulbert (perhaps the window in the axial chapel?). Saved from the fire of 1193/1194, it was reused around 1210-1215 in a bay in the newly constructed south aisle. To it was added a series of figures and scenes that expanded the original meaning and gave it a liturgical and typological significance as the Virgin-Tabernacle, reflecting exegesis of the first quarter of the 13th century. Set in the upper part of the bay, the Blessed Virgin was surrounded by angels, with the Holy Spirit as a dove over her head. A cycle from the Public Life of Christ filled the three lower registers. In the lowest register were three panels showing the Temptation of Christ (Matt. IV:1-11); the second and third registers contained the Marriage at Cana (John II:1-12). The development of this episode, the only miracle in which the Virgin played an intercessory role, could serve as a link between the two parts of the window. (The name *Belle-Verrière*, or "Beautiful Window", which appeared in texts of the 15th century, refers above all to the Romanesque Virgin).

The composition of the Christological cycle follows the "star" scheme, often used for the low ambulatory windows at Chartres.

The spatial effect is already Gothic because of the open, symmetrical compositions. The figures are independent of one another. The treatment of the figures is close to that found in Chartrain sculpture, notably the Job and the Confessors portals. There is a verticality to the drapery and folds, and a fullness of pose and gesture. This master was probably trained in the Sens region during the first decade of the 13th century. The colors are strong.

State of preservation of the 13th-century cycle: not heavily restored, but much of the glass has blackened and degenerated. The last restoration was carried out by Félix Gaudin in 1906.

DELAPORTE and HOUVET, 1926, pp.216-22, col. pls. IV-V, black and white pls. XL-XLII; C. BOUCHON, C. BRISAC, C. LAUTIER and Y. ZALUSKA, "La Belle-Verrière de Chartres", *Revue de l'art* 46 (1979): 16-24.

27 CHARTRES, cathedral of Notre Dame: nave, bay 43, 2nd register
Life of Saint Eustace: Saint Placidas Hunting (Pl. 14)
Overall dimensions: H. 8.05 m.; W. 2.40 m.
ca. 1210

The window illustrates one of the most popular 13th-century legends. During a hunt in the forest (shown here), a Roman general named Placidas saw an image of Christ Crucified between the horns of the stag he was pursuing. He immediately converted to Christianity, along with his wife and two children, and

adopted the name Eustace. As a Christian, he was persecuted and eventually martyred with his family. They were placed in a vat and boiled, but their bodies were later found intact (*Acta Sanctorum*, September, 1900, VI, pp.123 ff). The donors, the furriers' guild, are shown at work in the four medallions of the second register.

The composition is unusual for Chartres. Superimposed in the center are canted squares; on each side are medallions of different diameter, grouped in twos or fours and independent of one another and of the middle compartments. The most important compartments have armatures that follow their shape; the smaller ones are encircled with lead.

The decoration is rich and inventive in the ground, composed of "classical" acanthus scrolls, in the framing fillets, the friezes of short palmettes or small quatrefoils, and in the Romanesque border. While the border can be compared to the Saint Peter window in the chevet of Poitiers Cathedral (about 1160-1165), it is treated in a manner characteristic of the 1200 Style.

The compositions are harmonious and balanced, despite crowding (as here) and the frequently asymmetrical distribution of the central figures. These figures are elongated and have noble, elegant faces; their gestures are calm, in spite of drama inherent in some scenes. The drapery is supple and linear. The sharp delicate colors are atypical for Chartres.

The work is extremely meticulous, with careful modeling and numerous boldly drawn areas.

This window is the sole work at Chartres of a master probably responsible for numerous windows in the Lady Chapel of the collegiate church at Saint-Quentin.

State of preservation: generally good. The most recent restoration was by Gaudin in 1923.

DELAPORTE and HOUVET, 1926, pp.398-404, fig.5, col. pls VII, XVII-XVIII; black and white pls CLXVII-CLXXIX; L. GRODECKI, "Le 'Maître de saint Eustache' de la cathédrale de Chartres," *Gedenkschrift Ernst Gall*, Berlin, 1965, pp.174-80.

28 CHARTRES, cathedral of Notre Dame: nave, side aisle, bay 44
Parable of the Good Samaritan (Pl. 53)
H. 8.16 m.; W. 2.43 m.
ca. 1205-1210

The composition is analogous to the contemporary Prodigal Son window at Bourges. There are three large quatrefoils divided into five historiated compartments and three bands composed of a medallion and two half-quatrefoils. The mosaic background has trellis leading. The border contains bouquets of palmettes, joined by broken bars. The armatures adopt the shape of each historiated compartment.

Unlike the windows in Bourges and Sens cathedrals, where the illustration of this parable is accompanied by its commentary, at Chartres the two stories follow each other. In the lower compartments the shoemakers, who donated the window, are depicted. In the lateral scenes they are shown at work; kneeling at the center, they offer their window. The next ten medallions are dedicated to the parable (Luke X: 25-28): Christ recounting the parable; the traveler leaving the city; robbers attacking the traveler; the priest passing by, then the Levite; the Samaritan stopping and aiding the traveler; taking the traveler to the inn where he is cared for. The rest of the window treats traditional exegetical commentary, using the story of Genesis: the Creation of Adam and Eve; Original Sin;

the Labors of Adam and Eve; Cain's murder of Abel. At the top, flanked by two angels, the true Samaritan–Christ the Redeemer–is seated on a rainbow, holding the globe and giving a benediction.

The composition is dynamic and crowded, the postures of the figures energetic. There is tension in the faces, but ease in the treatment of drapery.

State of preservation: generally good, despite recent and progressive blackening.

DELAPORTE and HOUVET, 1926, pp. 168–70, pls XVIII–XXI; P. POPESCO, "La verrière du Bon Samaritain de la cathédrale de Chartres," *Cahiers de la Céramique et des Arts du Feu* 38 (1966): 119–40; *idem*, *Chefs-d'œuvres du vitrail européen*, pp. 132–35.

29 CHARTRES, cathedral of Notre Dame: south transept, east face, bay 116, right light
Saint Dionysius (Denis) Hands the Banner of the Abbey of Saint Denis to Jean Clément du Mez (Pl. 59)
H. 6.60 m.; W. 2.50 m.
1228–1231

At the left, under an architectural canopy, Saint Dionysius stands behind an altar, holding a book and giving the banner of the Abbey of Saint Denis to Jean Clément du Mez, marshall of France from 1225. Under the saint is a banderole inscribed: S[ANCTUS] DIONISIUS. At the right under a lower canopy is the figure of Jean Clément du Mez; he is turned toward Saint Dionysius and wears a hauberk and breeches, a surcoat of armor and a balerick. In his right hand he grasps the staff of the banner. The image is adapted from the transmission of the *labarum*, an iconographic theme that had been used since the 4th century in Byzantium and the West. Revived here in the context of feudalism, the symbolism is obvious: Saint Dionysius was the protector of the Capetian monarchy and the patron saint of the abbey where the brother of Jean Clément du Mez—Eudes'—was abbot from 1228 to 1231. Thus the stained glass must have been made within the period of Eudes's abbacy. The arms of Jean Clément du Mez are represented in a shield below, between two candlesticks.

The border is of the Chartrain type, with superimposed bouquets of palmettes linked by a vertical stem.

The work is remarkable, not only for the monumental scale of the cut pieces of glass and its energetic, sculptural workmanship, but also for the powerful effect of its chromatic variation: the purple face of the knight, his eyes leaded in virtuoso style, harmonizes with the red ground but contrasts with the blue ground against which Saint Dionysius is set. The saint's face is pale, and his eyes are leaded in the same manner as the knight's. The glass was produced by the workshop of the "Master of Saint Chéron".

The most recent restoration was done by the Gaudin studio in 1920. State of preservation: satisfactory, despite recent blackening of the glass.

DELAPORTE and HOUVET, 1926, pp. 439–44, pls CCXVIII–CCXI; POPESCO, *Chefs-d'œuvre du vitrail européen*, pp. 140–1, fig. 41; GRODECKI, 1978, pp. 52–61.

30 CHARTRES, cathedral of Notre Dame: south transept, bay 122
Ensemble Donated by the Dreux-Bretagne Family:
1) five lights, at the top, the Donors (Pierre de Mauclerc and his family), the Virgin and Child Flanked by Four Tall Prophets Carrying an Evangelist (H. [each light] ca. 6.35 m.; W. 1.70 m.) (Pl. 11)

2) Rose: The Glorification of Christ (Diam. 10.55 m.) (Pl. 11)
1221–1230

The ensemble, homogeneous in its iconography and its style, was given by the Dreux-Bretagne family whose arms fill the lower register of the central light. In the lower registers of the adjoining lights, the kneeling donors themselves appear. At the right is the head of the family, Pierre de Mauclerc, and his son Jean le Roux. To the right is Pierre's wife, Alix de Thouars, and their daughter, Yolande. Events in the life of this family allowed Delaporte to date this window to between 1221 and 1230.

Above is a standing Virgin and Child. Crowned and nimbed, she represents Ecclesia. Following an unusual iconography, she is flanked by four prophets (their names on bands beneath their feet) and by the four Evangelists, whose names appear on the semicircular arch or on a band at face level. From left to right, they are IHEREMIAS-S[ANCTUS] LUCAS; YSAIAS-S[ANCTUS] MATH[EU]S; EZECHIEL-S[ANCTUS] IOH[ANNES]; DANIEL-S[ANCTUS] MARCUS.

The rose has a multifoil central oculus with the Enthroned Christ, holding a globe and giving a blessing. In the inner circle is the Tetramorph and eight censing angels. In the second and third circles are the twenty-four Elders of the Apocalypse holding chalices or musical instruments. Between the two circles are twelve quatrefoils with the Dreux-Bretagne arms.

The monumental power of this glass has seldom been equaled. The style of drawing and the handling are vehement. The expressionism of the figures in the lights is exaggerated. The drapery with broken folds is emphasized by the massiveness of the figures. This is one of the most important works by the workshop of the "Master of Saint Chéron".

The glass was restored by N. Coffetier between 1875 and 1877. State of preservation: very altered. Much of the glass has blackened, making it hard to read, especially the figures in the lights.

MÂLE, 1910, pp. 9–10; DELAPORTE and HOUVET, 1926, pp. 431–36, col. pl. VIII; black and white pls CIC–CCII; J. VAN DER MEULEN, "Recent Literature in the Chronology of Chartres Cathedral," *Art Bull.* XLIX (1967): 153–56; GRODECKI, 1978, p. 58, fig. 29.

31 CHARTRES, church of Saint Pierre: nave clerestory, bay 222, right light, 2nd register
Life of Saint Dionysius (Denis): Saint Dionysius Is Attacked by a Crowd while Preaching in Paris (detail): head of a clergyman (Pl. 153)
Dimensions (light): H. 8 m.; W. 1.80 m.
ca. 1305–1310

The window has six registers, each with a scene extending over the full width of the light and crowned by three similar trefoil arcades; each arcade corresponds to a panel. The border is adorned with castles of Castile and quatrefoils.

The choice of the Life of Saint Dionysius underscores the connections between the Chartrain abbey and the royal family, which dedicated many windows to the saint at this time. The Life of Saint Dionysius begins in the lower register of the neighboring light, dedicated to Saint Clement, with Pope Clement sending Saint Dionysius and his companions to preach in Gaul. The right light begins in the heavily restored lower register with the prediction of Saint Dionysius. The second register shows Saint Dionysius preaching with his companions to the crowd in Paris which

assails him; the third register is the scourging of the saint and his companions. In the fourth register, Saint Dionysius is spared by the dogs, and at the left he is thrown into the furnace. The fifth register represents Saint Dionysius and his companions holding their heads after their decapitation. (The decapitation itself is not shown and must be lost.) The sixth register is modern. In the second register and some other scenes, two episodes are telescoped, a practice that was frequent in the 14th century.

The style of drawing is simple but effective; the lines are light and supple. Expressive liveliness is one of the stylistic hallmarks of this Chartrain workshop, which was responsible for most of the historiated windows in the nave clerestory. The palette of the ensemble is lively.

State of preservation of the head: good, despite browning of the glass. The window, however, is heavily restored, with many modern panels by the Lorin studio. Additional restoration was done in 1980 by the Hermet-Juteau studio of Chartres.

M. LILLICH, *The Stained Glass of Saint-Père de Chartres*, Middletown, Conn., 1978, pp. 135–42.

32 CHÂTEAUROUX (Indre), former church of the Grey Friars: chevet, bay 0, tympanum, central oculus
The Last Judgment: Christ the Judge (Pl. 70)
Diam. ca. 2.40 m
ca. 1230–1240

Little remains of the original glass of this church, built after 1225: the Last Judgment, in its original position, and some historiated panels—mostly from the Childhood of Christ—installed in the lights of the large axial bay.

The monumental figure of the seated Christ is shown frontally, centered against a blue ground with large rosettes. Flanking Him are the kneeling figures of the Virgin and Saint John as intercessors, each accompanied by an angel carrying an instrument of the Passion. Christ the Judge is showing His wounds—His arms are wide apart, His palms open and bleeding, His feet resting on a rainbow—He is presiding over the Resurrection of the Dead, who rise from their tombs as four angels sound their trumpets.

The wide, simply cut glass panels are held by straight-bar armatures. The strong, sustained color and the heaviness of the pictorial execution accentuate the monumental effect of this composition. While the glass at Châteauroux is iconographically and stylistically simpler than at Bourges, these qualities are also found in the products of one of the workshops active in the clerestory of the ambulatory of the cathedral at Bourges, especially in the right light of the axial bay.

State of preservation: mediocre, due to treatment in the 19th century. The glass was taken down in 1876 and exhibited first at the Musée du vitrail at the Palais de l'Industrie and then at the Trocadéro. Not until 1924 was it given back, along with other panels, to the Musée de Châteauroux.

GRODECKI, in "Vitraux de France," Paris, 1953, no. 18, p. 56; pl. 12; J. and V. CHAUSSÉ, "Les vitraux de l'Indre," *Revue de l'Académie du Centre*, 104th year (1978): 53–59.

33 DOL-DE-BRETAGNE (Ille-et-Vilaine), former cathedral of Saint Samson, bay 100
Scenes from the Old and New Testaments and from the Lives of the Saints

1) *The Passion of Christ*: Washing the Disciples' Feet (detail): head of Saint Peter (4th light from the left, 3rd register) (Pl. 157)

2) *Life of Saint Samson*: Saint Samson Cures the Daughter of Prince Privatus (6th light, 4th register) (Pl. 158)

Overall dimensions: H. 9.50 m.; W. 6.50 m.

After 1280

The window is composed of eight lights and a large tympanum. Its seven different subjects concern the traditions of this powerful church, the foremost in Brittany during the Middle Ages.

In the first light is the Life of Saint Margaret, of whom Dol possessed a relic.

The second light represents the Legend of Abraham.

The third light depicts the Childhood and Public Life of Christ.

The fourth and fifth lights show the Passion of Christ.

The sixth light relates the Life of Saint Samson, founder of the church at Dol and legendary archbishop of York.

In the seventh light, the early archbishops of Dol are shown surrounded by their suffragans—the bishops of Saint-Pol-de-Léon, Tréguier, Saint-Brieuc, Aleth, Vannes and Quimper.

The eighth light relates the Life of Saint Catherine; one of her teeth was venerated at Dol.

The Last Judgment is shown in the tracery.

A similar arrangement is used for all the lights: four pierced quatrefoils, placed one above the other, set against a two-colored mosaic ground. There are several borders with heraldic motifs such as castles of Castile and fleurs-de-lis; this decoration is repeated in the shapes within the tracery.

Though different hands can be distinguished, the handling is generally heavy, the painting done in thick, simplified lines. The compositions are crowded and symmetrical. The palette is still dark.

The glass has been restored heavily and often. In the first documented restoration, undertaken during the bishopric of Mathurin de Plédran in 1509, many compartments were completely remade. Further restoration was carried out in the 19th century, the most important and most recent being done by Oudinot in 1870. After the Second World War, a new campaign of restoration was undertaken by J.J. Gruber. The glass has been taken down and is currently being restored again.

C. ROBERT, "La grande verrière du XIIIᵉ siècle de la cathédrale de Dol," *Mémoires de la Société archéologique d'Ille-et-Vilaine* XXII (1843): 1–29; COMMISSION BRETAGNE DE L'INVENTAIRE GÉNÉRAL DES MONUMENTS ET RICHESSES ARTISTIQUES DE LA FRANCE, "Le vitrail en Bretagne," exh. cat., Rennes, 1980, pp. 16–18.

34 DONNEMARIE-EN-MONTOIS (Seine-et-Marne), church of Notre Dame: chevet, bay 100, rose
The Last Judgment: Resurrection of the Dead (Pl. 78)
Diam.: 0.51 m
ca. 1225
Preserved at Bryn Athyn, Pennsylvania: The Glencairn Museum (03.SG.211)

Only nine historiated medallions of the original glass from this rose survive: one in the Pitcairn Collection at Bryn Athyn, and eight others still *in situ*. Those remaining at the church no longer occupy their original position; they have been enlarged by wide mod-ern strips and set into medallions in the inner circle of the rose. This arrangement, completed by floral medallions in the outer circle, dates to the 1840s, when the American medallion is said to have been removed.

The overall iconographic program cannot be reconstructed. Five medallions, including the one at Bryn Athyn, show the resurrected dead rising from their tombs, always two per compartment and in varying poses. In two other medallions angels are depicted: one greeting the Elect, the other guiding them. The last two medallions show the crowned Elect, looking toward the central oculus, where Christ the Judge would surely have been placed.

The theme of the Last Judgment was often used for rose windows in the 13th century, especially for the inside of west facades (at Braine, Chartres and Mantes). It was likewise frequently represented on portal tympana in Romanesque sculpture.

The compositons are simple and symmetrical. The style of drawing is heavy yet dynamic, contrasting with the precise rendering of the faces. The drapery is supple but repetitive. The range of colors is restricted.

Despite numerous stopgaps, the Pitcairn medallion is in better condition than the medallions that are still in place and which have lost much of their translucence and even their paint. They were taken down in the autumn of 1982 for restoration and repair.

AUFAUVRE and FICHOT, *Les Monuments de Seine-et-Marne*, Paris, 1858, p. 146; F. PERROT, "La rose de l'église de Donnemarie-en-Montois," *Bulletin de la Société d'Histoire et d'Archéologie de Provins* 124 (1970): 55–63; "Radiance and Reflection," New York, 1982, no. 62, pp. 166–68, col. pl. X.

35 DREUX, church of Saint Pierre (?)
The Childhood of Christ: Herod Receives the Magi (Pl. 6)
Diam.: 0.31 m
ca. 1220–1225
Preserved at Dreux, Musée municipal d'Art et d'Histoire

This fragment is one of seventy-one panels found in 1938 in the flamboyant tracery in the bays of the nave in the church of Saint Pierre at Dreux. In the absence of archival documents, their provenance remains problematic. Two hypotheses have been advanced. According to L. Grodecki, they may have come from the glazing of the ambulatory of Saint Pierre and have been reused during the reconstruction of the nave in 1498. Alternatively, V. Chaussé has suggested that the panels came from the collegiate church of Saint Etienne, which was destroyed during the French Revolution; their reuse, then, would only date to the beginning of the 19th century. After being removed in 1937, they were restored by F. Lorin; since 1976 they have been exhibited at the Municipal Museum at Dreux.

The surviving glass is not homogeneous in either date or iconography. The famous series of the Life of Saint Eustace, a Tree of Jesse, the Legend of Theophilus and a Life of Saint Nicholas are from the first quarter of the 13th century. From the Childhood of Christ twelve panels survive, having numerous stopgaps and odd pieces. The figure of Herod from the scene illustrated here is in another panel.

The paint has been applied in two layers. The style already shows a certain "hardening," similar to the work of the "classic" workshop at Chartres.

State of preservation of this fragment: good, but the condition of the others varies considerably.

Y. DELAPORTE, "Vitraux anciens récemment découverts dans l'église Saint-Pierre de Dreux," *Bull. Mon.* 97 (1938): 425–30; V. MORÉCHAND-CHAUSSÉ, "Les vitraux du XIIIᵉ siècle de l'église Saint-Pierre de Dreux," *L'Information d'Histoire de l'Art*, no. 5 (1975): 214–17; *Recensement*, II, pp. 66–67.

36 EVRON (Mayenne), church of Notre Dame de l'Epine: choir clerestory (?), south side (?)
Two Bishops (Pls 155–56)
1) H. 1.22 m.; W. 0.49 m.
2) H. 1.20 m.; W. 0.48 m.
After 1320
Preserved at Bryn Athyn, Pennsylvania, The Glencairn Museum (03.SG.28, 03.SG.29)

The provenance of these figures is confirmed through early photographs. A third figure is also at Bryn Athyn, and the upper part of a fourth is in the Philadelphia Museum of Art. One piece from this series remains *in situ*; it was recently withdrawn from public sale (*Vente après décès: Ancienne collection de M.M. Acezat, Vitraux français, Hôtel Drouot*, Paris, November 24–25, 1969, no. 31) and returned to Evron. The bishops in the Pitcairn Collection at Bryn Athyn were probably sold as early as the beginning of the 19th century. For a good part of the 1800s they were installed in the Neo-Gothic chapel of an English manor house (Costessey Hall in Norfolk). Raymond Pitcairn did not acquire them until 1923.

The original location and disposition of the figures remain in dispute, because the Gothic glass of this former Benedictine abbey church has been altered on numerous occasions since it was first installed at the end of the 13th century. These figures belonged to the program of the choir clerestory, the remains of which have been regrouped in five windows. The bishops were probably placed opposite the earlier series of apostles, now located in the second bay of the choir clerestory, north of the transept crossing. Even the identity of the bishops is uncertain, and numerous suggestions have recently been advanced that relate to the prestigious history of the abbey: Saint Hadouin, founder of the first church on the site (cf. cat. 43); Saint Julian, bishop of Le Mans, of whom Evron possessed a relic; Saint Martin (?) or Saint Nicholas (?).

The figures standing in a hip-shot stance are set under a finely worked architectural canopy. The heavy, expressive style of drawing is reinforced by a restricted but violent palette in which yellow is dominant. The strong treatment of the faces contrasts with the simple rendering of the clothing. Certain details, like the earlobes, show sophisticated stylization, reminiscent of glass in the cathedral at Sées. M. Lillich believes that this series is the product of a monk who worked earlier in the abbey church of La Trinité at Vendôme and in other abbeys in western France. However, there are notable differences in the handling of these figures, and a workshop composed of a number of painters seems more likely.

The occasional use of silver stain, especially to accent the mitres, precludes a date before 1320 for this series.

State of preservation of the two figures: satisfactory, despite numerous repair leads and loss of paint. The architectural canopies, on the other hand, contain many restored pieces.

"Radiance and Reflection," New York, 1982, pp. 240–43, col. pl. XIV; M. LILLICH, "Bishops from Evron: Three Saints in the Pitcairn Collection and a Fourth in the Philadelphia Museum," *Actes du XIe colloque international du Corpus Vitrearum, New York, 1982*, New York [forthcoming]; *idem*, "Stained Glass from Western France (1250–1325) in American Collections," *Journal of Glass Studies* 25 (1983): 126–28.

37 FÉCAMP, church of La Trinité, "first" Lady Chapel (?) (destroyed)
Life of Edward the Confessor: Edward the Confessor and his Wife Edith Take Vows of Chastity (Pl. 166)
H. (with the architectural canopy): 1.30 m.; W. 0.45 m
After 1308
Now in the present Lady Chapel, bay 1, left light, 2nd register

J. Lafond has dated this window (of which only eleven scenes remain) to the year following the marriage in 1308, in Paris, of Isabella of France (daughter of King Philip IV, the Fair) to King Edward II (r. 1307–1327) of England. The window has "political" significance, since the cult of Edward the Confessor was part of the saga of the Anglo-Norman monarchy from its beginnings (cf. most recently, M. M. Gauthier, *Les routes de la foi*, Fribourg, 1983, pp. 83–86). Furthermore, Fécamp was the ideal spot to revive the memory of Edward the Confessor, the last Anglo-Saxon king of England, who died in 1066; this exemplary monarch spent part of his childhood at the court of the duke of Normandy and was one of the benefactors of the abbey.

M. Harrison Caviness has shown that the iconographic sources for the window were English. They are taken from *La Estoire de seint Aedward le Roi*, illuminated by Matthew Paris and his atelier around 1250 for the wife of King Henry III, Eleanor of Provence, who chose Edward as her patron saint. The marriage scene illustrated here, however, may have been copied directly from the text of *La Estoire*, for it was not illustrated by Paris's atelier.

The glass is from a window in the "first" Lady Chapel, the westernmost bay of which is still standing. Although they are now blocked up, the width of the lights corresponds to that of the panels of the Life of Edward the Confessor and of the Hermit Saints.

The original arrangement is not known. Architectural canopies are used, enriched with pinnacles and flying buttresses. The scale of execution is small. The elongation of the figures compensates for the dense composition necessitated by the narrow dimensions of the lights. The pictorial treatment is precise and refined. The style is a blend of Parisian conventions and English influence, a mixture often seen in Normandy in this period. The palette is pale and subtle.

State of preservation of this scene: good; the condition of the others varies.

J. LAFOND, "Les vitraux de l'abbaye de la Trinité de Fécamp," in *L'Abbatiale bénédictine de Fécamp, Ouvrage scientifique du XIIIe centenaire 658–1958*, vol. III, Fécamp, 1961, pp. 102–5; M. HARRISON CAVINESS, "A Life of St. Edward the Confessor in Early Fourteenth-Century Stained Glass at Fécamp, in Normandy," *Journal of the Warburg and Courtauld Institutes* 26 (1963): 22–37; P. VERDIER, "L'Art et la Cour, France et Angleterre, 1259–1328," exh. cat., vol. I, Ottawa: The National Gallery of Canada, 1972, pp. 173–75, n. 98.

38 FÉCAMP, church of La Trinité: "first" Lady Chapel (?) (destroyed) or Chapel of the Virgins (destroyed)
Life of Saint Catherine of Alexandria: Saint Catherine Discoursing with Two Philosophers (Pl. 137)
Overall dimensions: H. 7 m.; L. ca. 1.20 m.
Dimensions (panel): H. 0.60 m.; L. 0.57 m.
ca. 1275
Now in the present Lady Chapel, bay 5, right light, 3rd register

This life of Saint Catherine, divided between the two lights of the bay, has suffered considerably over the centuries. Today it is almost incomprehensible because of its poor state of preservation. Reused in the Lady Chapel (which was rebuilt between 1498 and 1504), the Saint Catherine cycle is incomplete today. Originally it was much more developed and included twenty-eight scenes, mostly focusing on the passion of the saint. Furthermore, the scenes are out of sequence, and many have losses or have become illegible. Even the provenance is uncertain, though the cycle probably comes from the Chapel of the Virgins, which was destroyed in 1682.

The legendary window has superimposed medallions composed of pierced quatrefoils. The mosaic with oblique leading, decorated with small crosses, perpetuates a tradition of the mid-13th century. The border is very narrow and adorned with superimposed leaves. The scale of execution is small and the composition free. The glass displays ease of drawing and knowledgeable handling.

The palette is fairly pale, with new color harmonies such as green and pinkish purple.

This is one of the best-preserved panels from the window, despite the opacity of the glass. There are wide areas of paint loss. The last restoration was carried out by J. J. Gruber in 1957.

J. LAFOND, "Le vitrail en Normandie de 1250 à 1300," *Bull. Mon.* 111 (1954): 340–44; *idem*, "Les vitraux de Fécamp," vol. III, pp. 99–101.

39 GERCY or JARCY (Essonne), abbey church (destroyed)
Life of Saint Martin: The Miracle of the Pine Tree (Pl. 79)

Diam.: ca. 0.65 m
ca. 1220
Preserved in Paris, Musée de Cluny, on deposit from the Monuments Historiques

Saint Martin, a halo around his head, dressed in episcopal garb and holding the crozier that symbolizes his pastoral power, raises his right hand to move a pine tree, a huge branch of which has fallen on pagan peasants. Two witnesses appear to the left in the background. This miracle, which took place after the elevation of the saint to the see of Tours (*The Golden Legend*, November 11), is also represented in 13th-century windows (at Angers, Auxerre, Chartres, Bourges, Le Mans and Tours), which were dedicated to this most popular of French saints.

The medallion has been enlarged by a wide, grisaille border. Originally it was part of a window from which two other scenes survive. The first—the Appearance of Christ to the Sleeping Saint Martin—occupied two medallions in the two registers above the miracle illustrated here; the second—a Charity of Saint Martin—after being transformed into a rectangular panel, stands alone.

Originally these panels and two others—fragments of a Tree of Jesse—were intended for the church at Gercy, which became an abbey church in 1269. Subsequently they were moved to the church at Varennes. Removed in 1882 and purchased by the State in 1885, they were exhibited by Lucien Magne at the Palais de l'Industrie as early as 1886, at the Exposition universelle in 1900 and finally at the Musée de Sculpture comparée at the Trocadéro from 1910 to 1934. Since 1950, they have been stored at the Musée de Cluny by the Monuments Historiques.

The individual pieces of glass are small. The figures have slender, elongated proportions, but squarish heads. Modeling has been replaced by strong contour lines. There are simple scooped folds, and the colors are bright.

State of preservation: good; there are modern pieces in the tree.

L. MAGNE, "Les vitraux de Varennes provenant de l'ancienne abbaye de Gercy," *Département de Seine-et-Oise, Commission des Antiquités et des Arts* (Commission de l'inventaire des Richesses d'art), 7 (1887): 76–77, 80, 90–93; *idem, Palais du Trocadéro, Musée de Sculpture comparée. Galerie de vitraux anciens. Notice sommaire*, Paris, 1910, nos. 48–49; F. PERROT, "Catalogue des vitraux du Musée de Cluny à Paris," Dijon, 1975, fasc. II, pp. 55–62 [unpublished thesis].

40 LAON, former cathedral of Notre Dame: chevet, bay 0
The Passion of Christ:
   1) Overall view with the east rose (Pl. 12)
   2) Overall view with the two other windows in the chevet (Pl. 23)
Overall dimensions: H. ca. 9 m.; W. 2 m.
1210–1215

According to F. Deuchler, the Passion of Christ and the two lateral windows in the chevet were created as windows for the ambulatory, which was replaced around 1210 with the present flat chevet. Consequently this work can be dated to the years around 1200, especially since it shows strong iconographic and stylistic connections with the Ingeborg Psalter (Chantilly, Musée Condé, ms. 1695), created between 1193 and 1213.

The composition consists of five large medallions linked by five small historiated quatrefoils. The scenes

in the medallions occasionally extend over two compartments. The background has trellis leading, and there is a leafy border.

The scenes reading from bottom to top are the Entry into Jerusalem; the Washing of the Disciples' Feet; Christ in the Garden of Olives; the Kiss of Judas; Jesus before Caiphus; the Carrying of the Cross; the Crucifixion; the Entombment; the *Noli me tangere*; Saint Peter and Saint John at the Tomb; the Supper at Emmaus and the Ascension.

There is great variety in the arrangement of scenes —some are crowded (the Washing of the Disciples' Feet); some are airy and open, prefiguring Gothic spatial qualities (the Carrying of the Cross). The handling is clear and precise, and modeling plays an important role. The figures are elongated yet sculptural. Their poses are noble, their gestures lingering. The drapery is supple and fluid, and the fold lines fall in troughs. The palette is characteristic of the beginning of the 13th century: light blue, red and green and a considerable amount of white. Of the three windows in the chevet, this one is the closest to the east rose (cf. cat. 12), perhaps indicating that this work was originally conceived for the bay in which it is located.

State of preservation: imperfect. The lower register is partly modern; the glass is blackening progressively.

A. DE FLORIVAL and E. MIDOUX, *Les vitraux de la cathédrale de Laon*, Paris, 1882-1890, chap. IV; F. DEUCHLER, "Die Chorfenster der Kathedrale in Laon: Ein ikonographischer und stilgeschichtlicher Beitrag zur Kenntnis der nordfranzösischen Glasmalerei des 13. Jahrhunderts," Bonn, 1956 [thesis]; GRODECKI, "Le 'Maître de saint Eustache,'" pp. 188–89; F. DEUCHLER, *Der Ingeborgpsalter*, Berlin, 1967, pp. 155–60.

41   LAON, former cathedral of Notre Dame: chevet, bay 2
The Childhood of Christ with Typological Scenes
    1) Overall view with east rose (Pl. 12)
    2) Overall view with the two windows of the chevet (Pl. 23)
    3) The Flight into Egypt (7th register; H. [two panels together] 0.67 m.; W. ca. 1.45 m.) (Pl. 21)
Overall dimensions: H. 9 m.; W. 1.90 m.
1210-1215

The composition is similar to that of the left window: it has the same background, the same border and the same number of historiated compartments; however, like the axial window, it has several scenes extending over two medallions.

The scenes reading from bottom to top are
1) the Annunciation;
2) the Visitation;
3 and 4) the Birth of Christ;
5 and 6) the Annunciation to the Shepherds;
7 and 8) the Adoration of the Magi;
9 and 10) the Presentation of Jesus in the Temple;
11) the Fleece of Gideon;
12) Moses and the Burning Bush;
13 and 14) the Flight into Egypt;
15) the Sleeping Magi;
16) the Journey of the Magi;
17 and 18) the Fall of the Idols;
19) the Sacrifices of Cain and Abel;
20) the Presentation of the Virgin Mary in the Temple;
21 and 22) the Massacre of the Innocents;
23 and 24) Angels.

The Childhood cycle and the corresponding typological scenes are no longer in logical order. While some of these changes may be due to early restoration, F. Deuchler has suggested that the incoherence could be indicative of the reuse of glass originally intended for the ambulatory bays (cf. F. DEUCHLER, *Der Ingeborgpsalter*, Berlin, 1967, pp. 153–54, esp. n. 263).

The iconography is close to that of the illuminations in the Ingeborg Psalter, where the formula was often influenced by Byzantinizing models from Sicily. For instance, the Flight into Egypt is almost identical to the manuscript: the nimbed Virgin, her head and part of her gown covered by a maphorion, is seated side-saddle on an ass led by a servant. Her hands extended, she looks at her Son, who is being held by Joseph in the next medallion. Behind them is a servant.

The figural style is close to that seen in the axial window.

In addition to the disorder of the scenes, there are numerous modern pieces.

FLORIVAL and MIDOUX, *Vitraux de Laon*, chap. IV; L. GRODECKI, "Les vitraux soissonais du Musée Marmottan et des collections américaines," *Revue des Arts* X (1960): 175–76; DEUCHLER, *Der Ingeborgpsalter*, pp. 150–51, 158.

42   LE MANS, cathedral of Saint Julien: inner ambulatory, bay 103, central light, 3rd register
The Childhood of Christ: The Nativity (Pl. 121)
Overall dimensions: H. 4 m.; W. 3.30 m.
ca. 1250–1255

Though begun in 1217 or 1218, the Gothic choir of the cathedral at Le Mans took many decades to complete, due to the extent of construction involved in building beyond the Gallo-Roman walls. The new sanctuary was given a double ambulatory; the inner one set under the clerestory windows had thirteen bays, each composed of three to five lights (plus two smaller ones at the transept entrance). Except for the axial bay, the bays contained legendary windows with small compartments, a single window often containing subjects from the Life of Christ and the lives of the Virgin and various saints (depending on the personal devotions of the donors, clergymen or guilds).

The glass is arranged in tangent half-medallions joined to a border of rosettes. The background has been reduced to a faint pattern of squares.

The scenes, reading from bottom to top are
1) the Annunciation;

2) the Visitation and the Annunciation to the Shepherds;
3) the Nativity;
4) the Adoration of the Magi;
5) the Massacre of the Innocents.

The lateral lights illustrate the Life of Saint Paul. In the spandrels between the lights are an Enthroned Christ (at the right), and a Censing Angel (at the left).

The scale of the cut pieces is very small; the handling is hasty, emphasizing the contour lines, and the modeling has been restricted to areas that do not correspond with the shape of the pieces. The figures are slender; their gestures seem rapid. The folds of the drapery are simplified and straight.

State of preservation: imperfect, principally because of the restorations by N. Coffetier at the end of the last century. There are inversions in the sequences of the scenes and numerous repair leads. The application of an artificial patina has brought about a recent blackening of the glass due to silicate formation.

E. HUCHER, *Calques des vitraux peints de la cathédrale du Mans*, 1864, fol. II [2nd delivery]; A. LEDRU, *La cathédrale Saint-Julien du Mans, ses évêques, son architecture, son mobilier*, Mamers, 1900, p. 428; L. GRODECKI, "Les vitraux de la cathédrale du Mans," *C. Arch.* 119 (1961): 85; C. BRISAC, "Les vitraux du chœur," *La cathédrale du Mans*, Paris, 1981, pp. 113–15.

43 LE MANS, cathedral of Saint Julien: inner ambulatory, bay 105, 2nd light to the left, 1st–5th registers
Founding the Abbey at Evron (Pl. 120)
Dimensions (light): H. 2.50 m.; W. 0.70 m.
ca. 1255

The five-light window was given by Abbot Ernaud (1241–1258) of Evron, probably between 1255 and 1258. One light is dedicated to the miraculous foundation of this Benedictine abbey (illustrated at left below), one of the most important in the diocese of Le Mans during the Middle Ages. Reading from bottom to top, the scenes are as follows:
1) A seated pilgrim brings back a relic of the Virgin from the Holy Land;
2) He places it in a tree, from which it cannot be removed;
3 and 4) People come to see it;
5) The bishop of Le Mans, Saint Hadouin, comes to the tree and orders the foundation of a monastery on the site.

The style is completely different from the other windows on this level: it avoids the tendencies of the Rayonnant style.

The compositions are awkward, the drawing naive. The figures are proportionately short with large heads. The folds are straight, yet broken by numerous beaks. The decoration is simple and unpolished.

State of preservation: satisfactory.

HUCHER, *Calques des vitraux peints*, fol. II, pl. LXXXVII [2nd delivery]; LEDRU, *La cathédrale Saint-Julien du Mans*, p. 428; GRODECKI, "Les vitraux du Mans," pp. 84–85, 88; BRISAC, "Vitraux du chœur," pp. 117–18; M. LILLICH, "The Consecration of 1254: Heraldry and History in the Windows of Le Mans Cathedral," *Traditio* XXXVIII (1982): 346, fig. 3.

44 LE MANS, cathedral of Saint Julien: chevet clerestory, bay 201, right light, 3rd–6th register
The Scourging of Saint Gervase (Pl. 122)
Figure dimensions: H. 2 m.; W. 0.80 m.
Dimensions (two-light window): H. 9 m.; W. 1.70 m.
ca. 1254

The nimbed Saint Gervase, in a yellow gown and with a book in one hand, remains resigned while he is being struck by the whip of his torturer who is standing behind him, arms poised against the border. The two figures are set in an architectural frame.

In the cathedral of Le Mans it is apparent that a profound veneration for the cathedral's first patron saints—Gervase and Protase—was maintained; they are frequently represented in both its Romanesque and Gothic windows.

The other figures in the window are also martyrs. Above Saint Gervase is the Decapitation of Saint Protase. The other light (the product of a different workshop) represents, from bottom to top: Saint Vincent on the Grill; the Scourging of Saint Vincent and the Stoning of Saint Stephen. In the lower registers are the donors, who may not be in their original positions; at the right is a woman; at left, the woodcutters or innkeepers (?).

The martyrdom has been innovatively adapted to the narrow light. The style of drawing is violent; the handling energetic; the colors strong. An almost "Expressionist" effect is achieved by this exceptional master, who was also responsible for the axial window in the clerestory, which was donated for the cathedral's consecration on April 24, 1254, by Bishop Geoffroy de Loudun. It is likely that the light with the Martyrdom of Saint Gervase and Saint Protase was also in place for that event. The style, which developed out of the work of the Master of Saint Chéron at Chartres, may have been very influential in the formalistic and chromatic elaboration of this second "school" of western France.

There is a heraldic border with fleurs-de-lis.

State of preservation: fairly good.

HUCHER, *Calques des vitraux peints*, fol. III [4th delivery]; LEDRU, *La cathédrale Saint-Julien du Mans*, p. 424; GRODECKI, "Les vitraux du Mans," pp. 90–92; BRISAC, "Vitraux du chœur," p. 125; LILLICH, "The Consecration of 1254," pp. 344, 350–51.

45 LIVRY (Nièvre), church of Notre Dame: bay 1
Virgin and Child (Pl. 112)
H. 0.50 m.; W. 0.60 m.
3rd quarter of the 13th century

The panel has been reused and set in a 19th-century decorative window.

The Virgin holding the Child is seated on an altar-shaped throne between two chandeliers. The Child Jesus is giving His blessing with one hand and holding an apple in the other, an iconographic detail that can also be seen in the Virgin and Child in the rural church at Orçay (Loir-et-Cher). The inscription, MATER DEI, runs in a narrow band under the Virgin's feet.

The handling is heavy, perpetuating the tradition of Berry glass in the first half of the 13th century.

This interesting work testifies to the activity of second-rank workshops on the fringe of the main currents.

State of preservation: mediocre, with numerous stopgaps and modern pieces of restoration in the crown and drapery of the Virgin; the heads, however, are authentic.

46 LYONS, cathedral of Saint Jean: chevet, bay 0
The Redemption (Pl. 76)
H. 6.95 m.; W. 1.50 m.
1215–1220

This important window is filled with typological glass depicting the Redemption, the fundamental dogma of the Church. The scenes from bottom to top are the Annunciation; the Nativity; the Holy Women at the Tomb, illustrating the Resurrection; the Crucifixion and the Ascension, which covers two octafoils. Following contemporary exegesis, the complementary scenes—typological or drawn from the Bestiary—are placed opposite the Christological ones in cartouches that enliven the border. The Annunciation is accompanied by the Prophecy of Isaiah at the left (Isaiah VII: 14); at the right, by a maiden riding a unicorn; the Nativity is flanked by Moses and the Burning Bush (Exodus III: 1–5) and by the Fleece of Gideon (Judges VI: 36–40). The Crucifixion is shown with the Sacrifice of Abraham (Gen. XV: 9–13) and with Moses and the Brazen Serpent (Numbers XXI: 6–9); the Holy Women at the Tomb, with Jonah Expelled by the Whale and a lioness with her young. The apostles witnessing the Ascension are accompanied by the healing calandrius and by an eagle flying around the sun—subjects taken from the Bestiary; Christ flanked by the Virgin Mary and Saint John is shown with two white angels who will announce His Second Coming to the apostles. On a scroll is the inscription: VIRI GALILEI.

The iconographic schemes are archaic, often following Early Christian or Carolingian models but including numerous Byzantinizing motifs as well.

The composition is still Romanesque, with a single medallion per register. The elongated figures have small shoulders, long, sad faces and flat drapery that falls in nested folds. These traits underscore the Byzantine style of this workshop, which also produced three of the seven other windows in this series: Saint Cyprian, Saint John the Evangelist and Lazarus.

The glass was dramatically restored by E. Thibaud between 1842 and 1844. While the original composition was not altered, many modern pieces were added. Furthermore, the left-hand part of the lower border was removed at the beginning of the 20th century and is now in The Glencairn Museum at Bryn Athyn, Pennsylvania (03.SG.127, cf. "Radiance and Reflection" [exh. cat.], New York: The Metropolitan Museum of Art, 1982, pp. 180–82).

CAHIER and MARTIN, 1841–44, pp. 127–32; *idem*, "Explication d'une verrière de l'apside de Saint-Jean de Lyon," *Revue du Lyonnais* XIX (1844): 217–21; L. BÉGULE, *Monographie de la cathédrale de Lyon*, Lyons, 1880, pp. 115–25; MÂLE, 1910, pp. 52–57, 190–96, 317–18; C. BRISAC, "Les vitraux de l'étage inférieur du chœur de Saint-Jean de Lyon," vol. I, University of Paris IV, 1977, pp. 177–86, 253–71; and vol. II, (cat.) pp. 57–68 [unpublished thesis]; *idem*, "Byzantinismes dans la peinture sur verre à Lyon pendant le premier quart du XIII⁰ siècle," *Il medio Oriente e l'Occidente nell'arte del XIII secolo (Atti del XXIV congresso C.I.H.A., Bologna, 1979)*, Bologna, 1982, pp. 219–28, pls 204–14; M. CHAUSSÉ and M. PABOIS, "Objectif Vitrail Rhône-Alpes," exh. cat., Lyons, 1982, pp. 23–26.

47 LYONS, cathedral of Saint Jean: chevet, bay 1
Life of Saint John the Baptist (Pl. 77)
H. 6.96 m.; W. 1.50 m.
After 1225

Like all the windows in this series, this work retains the Romanesque manner of composition: one medallion per register. Seven large ovals are linked by *fermaillets*, or bosses, and by a wide border with superimposed bouquets of palmettes. The mosaic background is composed of two-colored circles linked by yellow pearling. The bars are straight.

The lower medallion (now very much restored) contains an image of Archbishop Raynaud de Forez, primate of Lyons from 1193 to 1226, who continued construction of the present cathedral, which was begun around 1170. This representation of the archbishop kneeling before an altar is not a donor portrait, but rather a posthumous gift from his clergy.

The iconographic cycle of the patron saint of the cathedral has been restricted to six scenes:
1) an angel announces the forthcoming birth of a son to Zachariah and his wife;
2) the birth of John the Baptist;
3) Zachariah inscribes the name of his son;
4) the dance of Salome;
5) the beheading of John the Baptist;
6) Salome carrying the head of John the Baptist.

Despite the small number of scenes, two peculiarities can be noted: the announcement of the birth of John the Baptist adopts an unusual format, showing both elderly parents together; furthermore, the Baptism of Christ is missing. To our knowledge, only one other cycle bypasses this event: that in Saint Jean at Müstair (Graubünden, Switzerland) dated to the 1160s.

251

Monumentality is achieved by using large pieces of glass. The uncrowded compositions have already attained a Gothic sense of space. The figures are massive, the drapery supple and flowing. The light bright colors contrast with the dark ones in the neighboring windows. The glazing represents an experimental approach to stylistic innovations from the north, but it had no formal sequel at Lyons.

The dramatic restoration by E. Thibaud in 1844–1845 did not affect the general composition or ornament; however, there is much modern glass.

CAHIER and MARTIN, 1841–44, pp. 278–79, study pl. VII; BÉGULE, *Cathédrale de Lyon*, pp. 113–15; BRISAC, "Les vitraux de l'étage inférieur du chœur," vol. I, pp. 197–200, 250–70; vol. II (cat.), pp. 59–75; *idem*, "La peinture sur verre à Lyon au XIIᵉ et au début du XIIIᵉ siècle," *Les Dossiers de l'Archéologie* 26 (Jan.–Feb. 1978): 40; CHAUSSÉ and PABOIS, "Objectif Vitrail," p. 26, no. 16.

48 MANTES-GASSICOURT (Yvelines), church of Saint Anne: bay 3
The Childhood of Christ:
1) The Visitation (H. 0.48 m.; W. 0.36 m.) (Pl. 135)
2) The Nativity (H. 0.59 m.; W. 0.37 m.) (Pl. 136)
Preserved in the United States in a private collection in New England
ca. 1270–1280

These two panels were probably removed from the Childhood cycle in 1861 during the restoration entrusted to E. Didron the Younger. Subsequently they belonged to various private collectors in France; for more than half a century they have been in the United States. Another panel—part of the Adoration of the Magi—was published in the catalogue of the Homberg sale in 1908; its present location is unknown.

Only six panels remain *in situ*: the Sleeping Magi; two of the Magi (perhaps from an Adoration of the Magi); the Voyage of the Magi; the Massacre of the Innocents; Herod and a Soldier; two Armed Soldiers. They were placed in the lateral lights of the bay in 1960 during the restoration by J. J. Gruber (*Recensement*, I, p. 132).

The historiated compartments are ovoid and indented, characteristics of the second half of the 13th century. The framing is restricted to two thin fillets. The scale is small. The compositions are distinct and set against grounds that are still dark. The figures are elongated and gracile. The palette has been lightened: the faces are done on uncolored glass.

The American panels have been mutilated. The original right side and the lower part of the Visitation medallion are missing and have been replaced by 12th-century border pieces; the left part of the Nativity panel is also missing. Nevertheless, the number of modern pieces remains small. The paint has a tendency to scale off, for instance in the profile of Elizabeth's face next to the Virgin's in the Visitation panel.

C. S. HAYWARD, "Medieval and Renaissance Stained Glass from New England Collections," exh. cat., ed. by M. CAVINESS, Cambridge, Mass.: Harvard University, Busch-Reisinger Museum, 1978, nos 12a, b.

49 MANTES-GASSICOURT (Yvelines), church of Saint Anne: bay 4, left light, 7th register
Lives and Martyrdoms of Deacons Vincent, Stephen and Lawrence: Saint Vincent on the Grill

Overall dimensions (bay): H. 4.80 m.; W. 2.40 m.
Dimensions (panel): H. 0.57 m.; W. 0.53 m.
ca. 1270

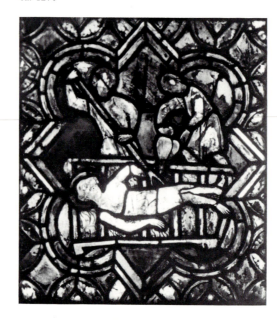

The window is incomplete. The original panels occupy only the upper part—five of nine registers of the three-light window. Each is dedicated to one of the canonized deacons most venerated in the Middle Ages: Saint Vincent at the left, Saint Stephen in the center and Saint Lawrence at the right. The scenes that remain *in situ* mostly concern the passion and martyrdom of these saints. The lives of these saints probably filled the lower registers, which now contain a creation by J. J. Gruber (1960) made to accompany the originals above. Two panels from the window, now in the United States in the same collection as the Childhood panels, illustrate events preceding the passion of these saints (cf. "Medieval and Renaissance Stained Glass from New England Collections," exh. cat., ed. by M. CAVINESS, Cambridge, Mass.: Harvard University, Busch-Reisinger Museum, 1978, nos 13, 14, pp. 35–37).

Each light now has five scenes enclosed in pierced quatrefoils. In the uppermost panel is Christ in Glory, testifying to the universality of the event below. In the tracery are three trefoils with a canonized deacon in the central medallion of each, a book in hand and his name inscribed on a wide band.

The scale of execution is small. The compositions are animated. The pictorial treatment is rapid but precise. The figures are narrow, with round and expressive heads, despite a concise style of drawing. The postures are supple and natural, in spite of the zigzag arrangement of folds and drapery.

The fresh and bright colors are characteristic of the last third of the 13th century.

State of preservation: poor, with many restored pieces. The paint has been partly lost. In many places the patina is artificial.

L. GRODECKI, "Cathédrales," exh. cat., Paris: Musée du Louvre, 1962, pp. 160–62, no. 157; *Recensement*, I, p. 132.

50 MUSSY-SUR-SEINE (Aube), church of Saint Pierre lès liens: chevet clerestory, bay 200, central light, middle registers
Calvary: Christ on the Cross (Pl. 164)

Dimensions (figure): H. ca. 2 m.; W. 0.70 m.; (light): H. 5 m.; W. 0.70 m.
After 1300

Christ is shown according to a formula that was popular from the third quarter of the 13th century: His arms curving far below the arms of the cross, His head falling, His body forming an arabesque with the feet crossed and held by a single nail. The placement of the Crucifixion in front of a protecting architectural niche, however, is original. The branches of the cross extend the full width of the light. In the lateral lights, on the other hand, the Virgin Mary and Saint John are placed within the niches. These three figures and the multi-level canopy over them fill the middle registers and are framed by panels of largely colorless grisaille with diagonal strips and ivy leaves. At the center of each decorative panel is a brightly colored *fermaillet*, or boss. A border of superposed leaves frames the central light, while the lateral ones are decorated with castles of Castile and fleurs-de-lis.

The drawing is supple, but the handling is heavy. The restricted palette is dominated by yellow.

Extensive restoration was carried out by E. Didron in 1893.

ARBOIS DE JUVAINVILLE, *Répertoire archéologique du département de l'Aube*, Paris, 1861, p. 77; J. J. GRUBER, "Technique," in *Vitrail français*, 1958, pp. 66–67.

51 MUTZIG (Bas-Rhin), church of Sankt Mauritius (destroyed): apse, bay 0
The Crucifixion (Pl. 190)
H. 4.09 m.; W. 1.72 m.
ca. 1310
Preserved at Strasbourg, Musée de l'Œuvre Notre-Dame (MAD. no. LXV. 70)

The window is composed of three long and narrow lights, each of which is divided into six registers. In each of the lower registers is a saint in a curved architectural canopy, outlined with a leafy rope. From right to left are depicted: Saint Peter Carrying a Key; Saint Mauritius, patron of the church; Saint Oswald on Horseback and in Armor; followed by a raven, and a Virgin and Child from another window, which replaces the figure of Saint Paul. A Calvary appears in the upper niches.

The composition, decoration and typology of the architectural niches are characteristic of a group of windows that includes, among others, the one from Klingenberg in the cathedral of Freiburg im Breisgau (1315–1317) and the Crucifixion (1310) at the Cistercian abbey of Kappel am Albis, in the canton of Zurich, Switzerland. These similarities testify to the stylistic connections of Alsatian glass with workshops in the Constance area from the beginning of the 14th century.

The figural style is close to a window of about 1325 in the south aisle of Strasbourg Cathedral, with the Life of the Virgin and the Childhood of Christ.

The parish church at Mutzig, which had a Romanesque nave, and a Gothic choir from the beginning of the 14th century, was demolished in 1879. The glass was restored by Ott Brothers in 1881.

There are numerous old stopgaps that do not detract from the overall effect.

R. BRUCK, *Die elsässische Glasmalerei*, Strasbourg, 1902, p. 67, pl. 40; H. WENTZEL, "Das Mutziger Kreuzigungsfenster und verwandte Glasmalereien der 1. Hälfte des 14. Jh. aus dem Elsass, der Schweiz und

Süddeutschland," *Zeitschrift für schweizerische Archäologie und Kunstgeschichte* 14 (1953): 159–79; *idem*, 1954, p. 92, ill. 122; Becksmann, 1967, pp. 142–44, ill. 34; L. Grodecki, "L'Europe gothique," exh. cat., Paris: Palais du Louvre, 1968, pp. 126–27, no. 209; V. Beyer, *Les vitraux des Musées de Strasbourg*, Strasbourg, 1978, 3rd ed. with additions by M. J. Forte, p. 38, no. 40, pls 6–7.

---

52 PARIS, cathedral of Notre Dame: north transept, rose, medallion of the 2nd circle
The Glorification of the Virgin: Moses the Judge (Pl. 97)
Diam. (rose): 12.90 m.
ca. 1250–1255

The north rose of Notre Dame was built by Jean de Chelles after 1245, like the ensemble of the north transept facade. It developed out of the earlier experiences of the first half of the century at Laon, Chartres and Reims but surpasses them, especially in the spandrels opened beneath the rose. The rose's structure is spectacular: sixteen mullions emerge from a multifoil rose, develop and divide into sixteen more, and then into thirty-two shapes in accordance with the architectural principles of the time. There are trefoils in the outer circle and a historiated medallion in each shape.

The iconographic program is the same as that of the north rose at Chartres (cf. cat. 30) but more developed. Around the Virgin are ninety-six Old Testament figures: prophets in the inner circle, judges and kings in the second, other kings and high priests in the outer trefoils. Here Moses is included with the judges, as indicated by the inscription on the tablets of the Law—JUDICES on one, MOYSES on the other. He is depicted in the traditional manner, with two yellow horns emerging from his hair, and is dressed in a green gown and purple mantle; sitting majestically, Moses holds a rod, one of his habitual attributes.

The large-scale decoration of the background that accompanies the figurative medallions is varied.

The style of drawing is energetic, but the handling is hasty. The pieces composing the figures have been cut into geometric shapes. The reuse of the same cartoons is masked by variation in color. The figural style is close to that of the Sainte Chapelle. The classic blue-red palette has been tempered by the addition of new colors: white, yellow and green.

Most of the panels are old but have been subjected to varying amounts of restoration; furthermore, there is much paint loss, which is especially noticeable in this medallion.

Lasteyrie, 1853–57, pp. 134–38, pl. XXI; Lafond, 1959, pp. 35–51, pls 5–8; P. Cowen, *Roses médiévales*, Paris, 1979, p. 135.

---

53 PARIS, cathedral of Notre Dame: inside of the west facade, rose
The Virgin in Glory Surrounded by Prophets, the Signs of the Zodiac, the Labors of the Months, the Virtues and the Vices:
1) Kindness (Pl. 40) (H. 1.10 m.; W. 1.10 m.)
2) Cowardice (Pl. 41) (Diam.: 0.70 m.)
Diam. (rose): 9.60 m.
ca. 1220

The composition is difficult to see from ground level because of the cathedral's organ. At the center is a modern Virgin and Child, surrounded by twelve seated prophets. In the upper half of the outer circle is Psychomachia with the Virtues and the corresponding Vices. In the lower half of the circle are the Signs of the Zodiac, accompanied by the Labors of the Months. The cosmological program (Signs of the Zodiac and Labors of the Months) and the didactic one (Virtues and Vices) emphasize the universality of the Mother of Christ. This was one of the most popular iconographic themes at the beginning of the 13th century, taking up the Laon formula from the end of the 12th. The Virtues are represented as seated noblewomen, holding a lance and having their emblem in a round shield. (Kindness holds a lamb.) The Vices, on the other hand, are treated picturesquely: Cowardice, for example, is illustrated by a soldier throwing down his sword and fleeing from a rabbit.

While the style is comparable to northern French work from the first two decades of the 13th century, the painterly execution is more masterful, the lines very firm and the colors more subtle.

Extensively restored in the 16th century (many historiated compartments date from that period) and in the 19th century (in particular the ornamental sections), the composition today includes only eleven old medallions; their state of preservation is relatively good.

Lafond, 1959, pp. 23–33, col. pl. 1, black and white pls 2–4.

---

54 PARIS, former abbey of Saint Germain des Prés: Lady Chapel (destroyed)
The Life of the Virgin:
1) Saint Ann Waiting for Joachim (Pl. 86). (Preserved in London: Victoria and Albert Museum [1233–1864]. H. ca. 0.70 m.; W. ca. 0.40 m.
2) The Marriage of the Virgin (Pl. 82). (Reused in Paris: church of Saint Germain des Prés, 1st south radiating chapel, 4th bay, 3rd register, left compartment. H. ca. 0.70 m.; W. ca. 0.40 m.)
1240–45

The original series must have had an extensive narrative, judging from the vast iconographic field of the surviving panels, which are dispersed among numerous museums, collections and depots. In the former abbey church of Saint Germain des Prés, three scenes remain, remounted in the first south radiating chapel: the Annunciation (?); the Marriage of the Virgin, and Ann and Joachim. A lancet head with two censing angels is in storage at the Monuments Historiques, Champs-sur-Marne. The other panels are in museum collections: the Victoria and Albert Museum, London; the Germanisches Nationalmuseum, Nuremberg and the Museum of Fine Arts, Montreal. Some scenes are no longer in their original framework and have yet to be identified.

The original composition must have involved a series of "quadrants" in groups of four joined by wide *fermaillets*, or bosses.

The execution is heavy; the paint has been applied in thick trace lines. The figures are short and squat, but the heads are very expressive. The quality of the decorative background, with its diagonal leading and circles decorated with flower-shaped ornaments, contrasts with the rather careless treatment of the figures. The style is far from that found in the glass from the Sainte Chapelle workshops or even from that in the Saint Vincent window or in the "historical series" done at the same time for the Lady Chapel or the refectory at Saint Germain des Prés.

State of preservation of these two panels: satisfactory.

B. Rackham, *Victoria and Albert Museum: A Guide to the Collections of Stained Glass*, London, 1936, p. 30; L. Grodecki, "Stained Glass Windows of Saint-Germain-des-Prés," *The Connoisseur* (March 1957): 34–35; *idem*, "Les vitraux de Saint-Germain-des-Prés," *Bulletin de la Société historique du VIᵉ arrondissement de Paris* new series (1977–78): 12.

---

55 PARIS, former abbey of Saint Germain des Prés: Lady Chapel (?) (destroyed)
Life of Saint Vincent: Saint Vincent and Bishop Valerius in Chains. (Pls 83–84)
H. 0.62 m.; W. 0.51 m.
1240–45
Preserved in New York: The Metropolitan Museum of Art, George D. Pratt Bequest (24.167)

A large chain around their necks, Saint Vincent and the bishop are being led by an executioner to Governor Dacian, who is represented in the facing medallion. This episode, which preceded the torture of the young deacon, was part of his passion.

Only seventeen panels from the original window, which must have comprised at least forty, remain. Eight are in The Metropolitan Museum of Art, New York; eight others in the Walters Art Gallery, Baltimore, and one is in the Victoria and Albert Museum, London. The memory of Saint Vincent who, along with the Holy Cross and Saint Stephen, was one of the first patron saints of the Parisian abbey, was revitalized by the gift of a relic—the saint's jaw—carried off from Castres in 1215 by the future King Louis VIII. Such royal bounty was sufficient to justify placing such an important cycle in this privileged location. This provenance, however, touched off a controversy between P. Verdier and L. Grodecki. Verdier maintains that the cycle was intended for the refectory built by Pierre de Montreuil between 1235 and 1244. Grodecki, on the other hand, believed it was destined for the Lady Chapel, constructed a little later, contemporary with the Sainte Chapelle. (Both the Lady Chapel and the refectory were destroyed between 1802 and 1805).

Enough panels survive to suggest that the composition consisted of a series of quadrants—assembled in spindle-shaped compartments—with semicircles side by side, clasped together. The trellis leading is decorated with rosettes. The narrow border is composed of the superimposed half-leaves typical of the second quarter of the 13th century.

The delicate treatment of faces, the features carefully painted with tiny lines and highlighted with smear, contrasts with the geometric outline of the drapery, characterized by straight folds falling rigidly.

State of preservation of the panel: good.

J. J. Rorimer, "Recent Reinstallations of Medieval Art," *The Bulletin of The Metropolitan Museum of Art* (1948): 201–04; Grodecki, "Stained Glass of Saint-Germain-des-Prés," pp. 36–37; P. Verdier, "La verrière de saint Vincent à Saint-Germain-des-Prés," *Mémoires de la Fédération des Sociétés historiques et archéologiques de Paris et Ile-de-France* IX, (1957–58): 69–87; *idem*, "The Window of Saint Vincent from the Refectory of the Abbey of Saint-Germain-des-Prés (1239–1244)," *The Journal of the Walters Art Gallery* XXV–XXVI (1962–63): 33–99; Grodecki, "Vitraux de Saint-Germain-des-Prés," pp. 11–13.

56 PARIS, former abbey of Saint Germain des Prés: Lady Chapel (?) (destroyed)
Seated King and a Soldier (Pl. 85)
ca. 0.70 m. square
1240–1245
Preserved in London: Victoria and Albert Museum (5461–1858)

The panel was part of a "historical group," discovered by P. Verdier. Other known vestiges can be found in a window of the first south radiating chapel at the abbey church of Saint Germain des Prés (bay 2); in a composite window installed by J. Formigé at Saint Denis in 1958 (bay 15) and in museum collections outside France (New York: The Metropolitan Museum of Art and London: Victoria and Albert Museum).

The iconography, about which there have been numerous theories, remains a mystery. Most of the scenes represent royal cavalcades, acts of donation, noblewomen in the company of monks or performing acts of charity. They may represent the expedition of Childebert against the Visigoths, or the foundation of the abbey by the king and Saint Germanus, and Queen Ultrogoth's gifts to the abbey in the 6th century, or perhaps the translation of the relics and tunic of Saint Vincent preserved at Saragossa. It is possible that one window included all the important events in the history of the Parisian abbey up to the time of the Albigensian Crusade, when a relic of the jaw of the martyr was obtained. The placement of the window has also been the subject of different interpretations. L. Grodecki believed it to have been in the Lady Chapel, while P. Verdier attributes it to the refectory.

The pieces of glass are geometrically cut and often angular, and the scale is not monumental. The handling is hasty. The gestures are rapid and the expressions lively. The style is close to that of the Passion Master of the Sainte Chapelle. The ornament is carefully done, as in the series of the Life of the Virgin. The background has diagonal leading decorated with a square pane filled with fleurons.

State of preservation: mediocre. The paint is scaling and has been lost on the face of the king. There are some stopgaps, especially at the bottom of the scene where pieces from the background of the Saint Vincent window have been reused.

R. LENOIR, *Statistique monumentale de Paris*, atlas, Vol. 1: *Abbaye de Saint-Germain-des-Prés*, Paris, 1867, pl. XXIII and *Explication des planches*, pp. 103–4; RACKHAM, *Guide to the Collections*, p. 30; RORIMER, "Recent Reinstallations of Medieval Art," pp. 201–4; GRODECKI, "Stained Glass of Saint-Germain-des-Prés," pp. 36–37; VERDIER, "La verrière de saint Vincent," pp. 72–79; *idem*, "The Window of Saint Vincent," pp. 83–89; GRODECKI, "Vitraux de Saint-Germain-des-Prés," p. 12.

57 PARIS, Sainte Chapelle: Upper Chapel
Overall view (Pl. 7)
Between 1242 and 1248

Saint Louis ordered the two-storied Sainte Chapelle to be built at the royal palace (now the Palais de Justice) to house the relics of Christ's Passion acquired from Emperor Baldwin II. The construction took place between 1242 or 1243 and 1248. While there is no longer any 13th-century glass in the lower chapel, that in the upper chapel is original, except for the western rose, which dates from the end of the 15th century. This series of fifteen windows, often restored under

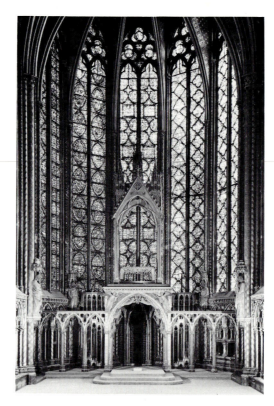

the French monarchy, suffered when the chapel was turned into a depository for legal archives at the beginning of the 19th century. A plan for restoring the building was put into effect in 1837. Despite some excesses, the work (which continued until 1855) was exemplary. Almost two-thirds of the nearly 1,100 panels are in large part authentic. Some were eliminated, but a good number of others survive in museums and private collections, both in France and abroad.

The glazing program is an immense glorification of the Passion of Christ, the central event in the history of mankind. The iconographic program can be divided into a number of cycles: 1) in the nave, nine windows are dedicated to Old Testament themes that underscore the continuity between biblical royalty and the Capetian kings; 2) a cycle of the Life of Christ occupying several windows is framed by a cycle of Saint John the Baptist, the last of the prophets, and Saint John the Evangelist, a witness to Christ's life and the author of the Apocalypse, which was originally set on the inside of the west facade; 3) the adjoining windows are dedicated to the great prophets and serve to link the Passion with biblical events; 4) a last window (the first to the south of the entrance to the nave) illustrates the history of the relics, from their discovery to their arrival at the remarkable Sainte Chapelle.

The glass is described in order, beginning with the first north window and following around the building: Genesis (bay 13 or 0); Exodus (bay 11 or N); Numbers (bay 9 or M); Deuteronomy-Joshua (bay 7 or L). Judges (bay 5 or K); Isaiah and the Tree of Jesse (bay 3 or J); Saint John the Evangelist and the Childhood of Christ (bay 1 or I): the Passion of Christ (bay 0 or H); Saint John the Baptist and Daniel (bay 2 or G); Ezekiel (bay 4 or F); Jeremiah and Tobit (bay 6 or E); Judith and Job (bay 8 or D); Esther (bay 10 or C); Kings (bay 12 or B); History of the Relics of the Passion (bay 14 or A).

The lateral windows, with four lights, are set in tracery pierced by three roses and by spandrels. The

double-light choir and chevet windows, set under a tracery of triple trefoils, are lower (about 13 meters as opposed to approximately 15 meters). All the windows are of the "legendary" type, composed of numerous scenes between which are set ornamental panels. The number of scenes per window and the forms vary, as was standard practice from the beginning of the 13th century. The ornament remains traditional, especially the background motifs, which are still painted with precision. The borders, on the other hand, are quite narrow and conform for the most part to the "half-border" type. Plant motifs run along the length of the inner fillet of the frame, a simplification by comparison with models from the first half of the century. There is a great variety of heraldic and royal decoration in the backgrounds of some windows, in the bosses and the borders, which often are adorned with three-towered castles of Castile and fleur-de-lis motifs.

Although the overall conception was the responsibility of a single master glazier, the realization was divided among a number of workshops whose individual characteristics as well as those of their principal assistants can be recognized. The workshop of the principal master was responsible for ten windows—the four lateral ones on the north side, the five in the chevet and the light to the left of bay 2 (G), dedicated to Saint John the Baptist. The second workshop produced the Ezekiel window, the Kings window, as well as the light to the right of the one cited above: this is the Ezekiel Master's workshop. The third, the Master of the Judith and Esther windows, produced only the windows for which he is named. The Relics window is the collaborative effort of the principal master's and the Ezekiel Master's workshops.

A recent renovation of the chapel necessitated the repair of many windows on the south side by Sylvie Gaudin's studio.

GRODECKI, 1959, pp. 71–349 [contains the entire earlier bibliography on these windows].

58 PARIS, Sainte Chapelle: Upper Chapel, bay 0 (H), left light, 5th register, central section
The Passion of Christ: the Crowning with Thorns (Pl. 89)
Dimensions (2 lights): H. 13.56 m.; W. 2.26 m.; (square panel): 0.66 m. a side
Between 1242 and 1248

The entire window comprises one hundred and thirty panels, fifty-seven of which—or more than a third—are historiated. Squares alternate with four quarter-circles set laterally and linked by a boss decorated with flower-shaped ornaments. Most of the scenes are set in the sides, since the square panels are reserved for major events. The panel arrangement is sophisticated, with armatures forged into the shapes of the compartments and linking them together. Next to the scenes is the plant border; it is similar in decoration to that in the Numbers, Deuteronomy, Saint John the Evangelist, Childhood of Christ and Relics windows. The diagonal leading of the background has heraldic decoration composed of the two royal emblems.

The iconographic program is rather original, with special emphasis on the events preceding the Passion and those pertaining to the Death of Christ. Of course, the choice of subject was dictated by the function of the building itself, which was meant to house the relics of the Passion.

The window is characteristic of the style of the master of the principal workshop, known as the Passion Master because of the high quality of this window, the most beautiful one in the ensemble. The scale is fairly large. The compositions are harmonious; the colors are balanced but lively; the paint has been applied with rapid, straight strokes, and the modeling reduced to large areas of wash, which in some instances have been purposely smeared.

State of preservation: good, despite some iconographic errors in the lower registers due to 19th-century restoration. The paint has become fragile and has a tendency to flake.

GRODECKI, 1959, pp. 195–206, pls 49–52.

59   PARIS, Sainte Chapelle: Upper Chapel, bay 4 (F), left light, 4th register
Book of Ezekiel: Vision of the Four Beasts and the Four Wheels. (Ezekiel I: 4–25; III: 22–25) (Pl. 92)
Overall dimensions (2 lights): H. 13.45 m.; W. 2.12 m.; (quatrefoil): H. 0.66 m.; W. 0.68 m.
Between 1242 and 1248

The window ensemble includes one hundred and twelve panels, only thirty-three of which are historiated, since the composition of each light is traditional: superimposed quatrefoils along the windows' axis. The armature assumes the shape of the historiated compartments; therefore, the ornamental panels are isolated. The border adjoining the ornamental panels has a pattern of leafy bouquets in "arches," a simplified version of a type already used in the Romanesque period. The ground has diagonal leading and heraldic decoration composed of castles of Castile. In the head of each light is a large yellow fleur-de-lis in a quatrefoil.

The iconographic program is clearly inspired by the *Bibles moralisées*, the accent more on the Parables than on the visions of the prophets, one of which is illustrated here. In a lilac mantle and a conical red hat, the prophet Ezekiel stands surrounded by the Tetramorph. Three concentric circles are at his feet, and four superimposed wheels over his head. A comparison with the *Bible moralisée* (Paris, Bibl. Nat., ms. lat. 11 560, fol. 184–189ᵛ) shows a close iconographic relationship.

The style is distinct from the other windows, both in its lively colors and its treatment of paint. The compositions are very symmetrical, often enclosed by architectural canopies or resting on "bridges". The figures are elongated, with small heads, wide eyes, and delicate noses. The angularity of the folds and drapery underscores the almost abstract shapes into which the pieces have been cut. This workshop, whose origin remains uncertain, was also responsible for the Kings window (bay 12 or B).

State of preservation: poor.

GRODECKI, 1959, pp. 218–28, pls 57–60.

60   PARIS, Sainte Chapelle: Upper Chapel, bay 8 (D), 3rd light from the left, 13th register
Judith and Job:
   1) Job Has his Head Shaved (Job I:20) (Diam. 0.68 m.) (Pl. 95)
   2) The Army of Holofernes Crossing the Euphrates (preserved at the Philadelphia Museum of Art [30–24.3], Diam. 0.63 m.) (Pl. 93)
Overall dimensions (4 lights): H. 15.35 m.; W. 4.57 m.
Between 1242 and 1248

Of a total of one hundred and eighty-four panels, only fifty-six are historiated. Thus, the area of illustration in this window is less extensive. The composition with superimposed medallions is traditional, but the ornament is original: a ground of oblique leading forming lozenges decorated with fleurs-de-lis and a plant border of coiled leaves and clusters of grapes.

Judith and Job are shown together because of the similarity of their lives: their emphasis on family, on helping their people and their devotion to God. Reference should be made to moral interpretations of the Bible as defined in exegesis of the first half of the 13th century. The Judith cycle fills the lower part of the window, that of Job the upper registers. While the Judith story was often illustrated in the 13th century, its development over forty scenes is exceptional. Old inscriptions in French explain certain scenes.

The Job cycle is more restricted, with the accent on the beginning and end of his life. The account of his afflictions is abbreviated; it may be that it was eliminated during an early restoration and not reused in the 19th century, which would account for the lack of balance between the two cycles. The panel illustrated here comes from the middle of Job's life, when, as a sign of his distress after Satan has destroyed his children's house, he has his hair shaved off by a servant.

The execution is very meticulous, and the scale of the individual pieces is tiny. The paint is laid down with mannerist preciousness, especially in the details. Blue is dominant in the dark palette. This is a characteristic example of the style of work from the Judith Master's workshop.

State of preservation: mediocre (nineteen historiated medallions are modern), but the 19th-century restoration largely respected the original arrangement.

GRODECKI, 1959, pp. 241–57, col. pl. VI, black and white pls 65–70; M. HARRISON CAVINESS and L. GRODECKI, "Les vitraux de la Sainte-Chapelle," *Revue de l'Art*, nos 1–2 (1968): 13–4, ill. 11.

61   PARIS, Sainte Chapelle: Upper Chapel, bay 10 (C), 3rd light, 8th register, upper part of the right panel
Book of Esther: Esther and Ahasuerus at the Feast (Pl. 88)
Overall dimensions (4 lights): H. 15.35 m.; W. 4.72 m.; (right panel): H. 0.77 m.; W. 0.51 m.
Between 1242 and 1248

The proportion of historiated panels in this window—one hundred and twenty-nine out of two hundred and twenty-one—is one of the highest in the Sainte Chapelle. The composition is characteristic of the mid-13th century, with quarter-ovals arranged laterally, set in fours and linked by a large heraldic boss. Each ornamental panel is decorated with a heraldic medallion set against a mosaic of two-colored circles in blue and red. The border with fleurs-de-lis and castles of Castile is identical to that of the axial window.

This is the most extensive illustration of the Book of Esther; even secondary events are shown in one or more scenes; for instance the Feast of Esther (Esther V: 6–8) is told in six compartments. Wearing a green gown, her right hand grasping the clasp of her mantle, Esther holds Ahasuerus by the hand; he is dressed in a red robe and a mantle lined with fur.

The compositions are simple and open. The figures are elongated and graceful, and the drapery and folds are linear. The thin faces, often set on long necks, are strongly individualized, as are decorative details in the scenes such as trees, architecture, etc. The master of

this workshop was also responsible for the Judith and Job window, for which he is named. It may be that he was not just a master glazier, for despite the difference of supports, his handling is close to the illuminations in a group of "royal" manuscripts, especially the Old Testament miniatures in the Pierpont Morgan Library (New York, m. 638; see most recently, H. STAHL, "Old Testament Illustrations during the Reign of St. Louis: The Morgan Picture Book and the New Biblical Cycles," *Il medio Oriente e l'Occidente nell'Arte del XIII secolo, Atti del XXIV congresso C.I.H.A., Bologna, 1979*, Bologna, 1982, pp. 79–83).

Overall state of preservation: mediocre. The paint is fragile and tends to flake. The glass has recently been restored by Sylvie Gaudin's studio.

GRODECKI, 1959, pp. 258–74, pls 71–76.

62   PARIS, Sainte Chapelle: Upper Chapel, bay 14 (A), 4th light, 12th register, inverted trefoil
History of the Relics of the Passion: Displaying the Crown of Thorns (Pl. 87)
Overall dimensions (4 lights): H. 15.35 m.; W. 4.60 m.; (trefoil): H. 0.75 m.; W. 0.84 m.
Between 1242 and 1248

The window is composed of one hundred and ninety-four panels, of which only sixty-seven—less than a third—are historiated. The composition is similar to the Deuteronomy and Joshua window, with armatures that follow the shape of the historiated medallions. The half-border is of a type analogous to the Deuteronomy, Numbers and Passion windows. The circles in the background are decorated with fleurs-de-lis and castles of Castile—the only mosaic using both these heraldic motifs.

The iconographic program can be divided into two cycles. The first illustrates the discovery of the relics by Saint Helena, their capture by Chosroes II and, finally, their recapture by Heraclius I. These tales occupy the lower registers. The second cycle concerns the acquisition of the relics by Saint Louis and their transport to the Sainte Chapelle. The medallion illustrated here shows an archbishop (probably Guillaume Cornut of Sens) presenting the Crown of Thorns, set on a yellow cushion, to the king and his entourage. Guillaume Cornut recorded the history of this translation of the relic in *Historia Susceptionis Coronae Spinae Jesu Christi*; his text has provided the key to the images in this window.

The style of the window is fairly mixed; Louis Grodecki has established that it is the work of numerous painters from the workshop of the Ezekiel Master and the principal master.

State of preservation: poor, both because of the large number of modern panels and because of paint loss. It has been restored recently by Sylvie Gaudin's studio.

GRODECKI, 1959, pp. 295–309, pls 83–88.

63   POITIERS, cathedral of Saint Pierre: bay 107, 6th register, right compartment
The Story of Isaac: The Sacrifice of Isaac (detail), An Angel Prevents Abraham from Killing his Son (Pl. 46)
Overall dimensions: H. ca. 4 m.; W. ca. 1.40 m.
ca. 1210–1215

In the center, dressed in a white robe, Abraham raises a long knife and prepares to kill his son Isaac, who is kneeling on a pyre in the form of an altar. At the right is an angel who, with raised arm, stops Abraham and indicates with the index finger of his other hand the ram that should be sacrificed in place of the boy. The animal is placed outside the scene, in the lower right-hand spandrel of the panel.

The window, reading from top to bottom and left to right, represents the Birth of Isaac; Abraham Banishing Hagar and Ishmael; Abraham and Isaac Leaving for Mount Moria; the Sacrifice of Isaac (illustrated here); Abraham Sending Eliezer to Find a Wife for Isaac; the Departure of Eliezer; Rebecca and Eliezer; the House of Bethuel and Laban (this scene is in disorder); Rebecca Admitting Eliezer into the House of Her Brother; Laban and Bethuel Dining; Eliezer Asking for Rebecca's Hand in Marriage. The lower register is modern and was restored by F. Chigot in 1948.

The two vertical rows of oval medallions are interrupted in the middle of the window by a circle divided into four compartments. The composition recalls the windows with the Funeral of the Virgin Mary and with Saint Vincent in the cathedral of Angers, dated around 1180.

The drawing is nervous. The "dancing" pose of Abraham, with his legs crossed, is still Romanesque. The faces are long and have strong features. The drapery is flat.

State of preservation of the panel, one of the best-preserved in the window: mediocre. There are numerous stopgaps, especially in the figure of Abraham. While there are modern pieces, the two heads are original.

ABBÉ AUBER, *Histoire et description de la cathédrale de Poitiers*, vol. I, Poitiers, 1848, pp. 351–52; GRODECKI, "A Stained Glass 'Atelier,'" pp. 87–111; *idem*, "Les vitraux de la cathédrale de Poitiers," *C. Arch.* CIX (1951): 151–52, 160–62.

64 POITIERS, church of Sainte Radegonde: nave clerestory, north side, bay 111, lower register
The Life of Saint Radegunda: Saint Radegunda Washing the Feet of the Poor (detail), the Poor (Pl. 159)
Overall dimensions: H. ca. 8 m.; W. 1.40 m.
ca. 1270

This is the most original example of mixed glazing, for the full-color figures are set off by a field of painted grisaille. Though rarely used in the second half of the 13th century except in rural churches, for example at Saint Antoine de Sommaire (Eure), this formula enjoyed a certain popularity in the 14th century, notably in Saint Ouen at Rouen. The grisaille motifs can be dated to the 1260s.

The iconography is also very interesting. The cycle must be based on an 11th-century *libellus* illustrating the Life of Saint Radegunda, as recorded by Saint Venatius Fortunatus in the 6th century (Poitiers, Bibl. mun., ms. 250). The sequence of events, however, is now confused, owing to efforts by the restorer H. Carot, in the late 19th century, to give the work a coherence it lacked. As a result, only some parts, like the scene illustrated here (no longer in its original position), are still authentic.

Saint Radegunda, wife of King Clothair I, retired to the monastery of Poitiers, which became the site of a popular pilgrimage in her honor.

The silhouettes are short and naive, but the facial expressions are lively and accented. The treatment is fairly sophisticated, especially in the multiplication of details.

The scene has been reinstalled backwards. The paint has a tendency to scale off.

B. FILLON, "Notice sur les vitraux de Sainte-Radegonde," *Mémoires de la Société des antiquaires de l'Ouest* 11 (1844): 490–95; E. MÂLE, "La peinture sur verre en France à l'époque gothique," in *Histoire générale de l'Art (A. Michel)*, vol. II/1, Paris, 1906, p. 384; J. J. GRUBER, "Quelques aspects de l'art et de la technique du vitrail en France, dernier quart du XIIIe siècle, premier quart du XIVe," in *Travaux des étudiants du groupe d'Histoire de l'art de la Faculté des Lettres de Paris*, Paris, 1927, pp. 80–81; J. BIDAUT, "Eglise Sainte-Radegonde de Poitiers," *C. Arch.* 109 (1951): 113.

65 POITIERS, church of Sainte Radegonde: nave clerestory, north side, bay 113
The Childhood and Public Life of Christ: the Visitation (Pl. 160)
H. 0.77 m.; W. 0.60 m.
1270–1280
Preserved at Bryn Athyn, Pennsylvania: The Glencairn Museum (03.SG.43)

This panel, still in place in the mid-19th century, was removed from a window at Sainte Radegonde by master glazier Henri Carot, under the pretext of restoring order to the church's Gothic glass, which had been in disarray since attacks by the Huguenots in 1562. Six scenes from the Childhood (the Nativity, the Annunciation to the Shepherds, the Adoration of the Magi, the Journey of the Magi, the Flight into Egypt, the Presentation at the Temple) and two from the Public Life of Christ (the Temptation of Christ and Christ with the Pharisees [?]) remain in place. These scenes, each composed of two half-medallions, are currently distributed along the lower register of the eight-light window. The tympanum contains a rose window with the Last Judgment, a gift from Alphonse de Poitiers (1269–1271), while the head of the lancets represents Christ's Passion. The Childhood and Public Life cycles are missing numerous scenes such as the Annunciation. Originally they may have occupied one or two semicircular bays on the south side of the nave. They were set two by two, following a glazing tradition used in western France since the Romanesque period. The borders, however, were "sewn" onto the panels without any separating armature.

The composition is balanced. The form of the compartment and its frame (beading inside and a smooth narrow fillet outside) grew out of the Angevine tradition. The figural style is close to that of the Childhood series in Saint Martin at Tours (1260), now in the cathedral at Tours. The drawing and arrangement of the grisaille show analogies with the colorless windows in the nave clerestory of the cathedral at Poitiers, datable to the 1270s. The medallion and border are characterized by saturated colors.

There is much modern glass; for instance, the head of the Virgin at the left.

"Radiance and Reflection," New York, 1982, no. 86, pp. 221–23; LILLICH, "Stained Glass from Western France," pp. 124–25.

66 REIMS, cathedral of Notre Dame: choir clerestory, bay 103, left light
The Church at Châlons Upholding the Apostle Philip (Pl. 104)

Dimensions (light): H. 9.50 m.; W. 1.85 m.
1240–1250

In the lower part of the light is a symbolic representation of the church at Châlons: a schematic two-story facade, each story crowned with a pediment and pierced openings that are often Gothic in character. At the top is an angel sounding the trumpet. There is an inscribed band. Enthroned above, in frontal position, is a figure of the apostle Philip. The inscription over his head reads: PHILIPPUS.

The program of the choir clerestory in the cathedral, glorifying the Church at Reims, includes ten windows also composed of a bishop and a representation of a church that was part of the Church or province of Reims. To the north are the churches at Laon, Châlons, Senlis, Amiens and Morinie (Thérouanne); to the south those at Soissons, Beauvais, Noyon and Tournai. Reims itself is represented in the axial bay with Archbishop Henri de Braisne (1227–1240). In the other light of the axial bay is a Virgin and Child, symbolizing the Church, and a Crucifixion.

The effect is monumental. The supple rendering of the figures contrasts with the schematic, almost abstract treatment of the churches. The colors are vivid.

The glass has been much restored, making it—like all the windows in the choir clerestory—difficult to read.

L. GRODECKI, "De 1200 à 1260," in *Vitrail français*, 1958, p. 140; H. REINHARDT, *La cathédrale de Reims*, Paris, 1963, pp. 183–87; E. FRODL-KRAFT, "Zu den Kirchenschaubildern in den Hochchorfenstern von Reims—Abbildung und Abstraktion," *Wiener Jahrbuch für Kunstgeschichte* 25 (1972): 59–60, fig. 3.

67 ROUEN, cathedral of Notre Dame: Lady Chapel, bay 7, 1st light to the right
Saint Ouen (Pl. 167)
Dimensions (light): H. 10.50 m.; W. 1.80 m.
1310–1320

Saint Ouen (641–684), twentieth bishop of Rouen, is shown under a high canopy, wearing his sacerdotal robes and holding a cross and a book. The inscription in the trefoil arcades over his head reads: S.[ANCTUS] OUEN. This elegant figure is set against a damascene ground composed of small pierced quatrefoils, in which are set a leopard or two confronted parrots. The latter motif is repeated in the border. In the other three lights of the window are other bishops of Rouen from the 6th and 7th centuries—Saints Ansbert, Godard and Filleul. The original decoration of this chapel (built after 1302) focused on the prestigious history of this church and was illustrated by figures of Rouen's bishops and archbishops. From this program, only sixteen figures survive; they are set, like Saint Ouen, under an architectural canopy, following a popular 14th-century formula. The technique is refined and makes use of silver stain to enliven hair, beards, etc. Elegant and sophisticated modeling is achieved by brushwork, often emphasized by designs scratched with a needle. The rendering of folds attempts to imitate the fall of heavy fabric.

There are numerous innovations in the decoration, which copies floral and plant elements. The grisaille is decorated with oak-leaf scrolls. The exceptional style manages to combine two naturally opposed effects —detailing and monumentality. The colors are pale and subtle.

This is one of the best preserved panels in an imperfect series.

RITTER, *Les vitraux de Rouen*, 1926, p. 69, pl. XLIV; F. PERROT, *Le vitrail à Rouen*, Rouen, 1972, pp. 18–20.

68 ROUEN, cathedral of Notre Dame: ambulatory, bay 11, lower register, right panel
Story of the Patriarch Joseph: signature of Clement of Chartres (Pl. 18)
Dimensions (panel): 0.65 m. square
ca. 1235

It is the inscribed banderole that makes this panel interesting. One of the rare signatures by a master glazier of the 13th century preserved in France, it reads: CLEMENS VITREARIUS CARNOTENSIS M[E] [FECIT]. The panel is set in the lower right-hand corner of the window. It represents part of Joseph's Judgment by Potiphar who, acting on the false accusations of his wife, had the patriarch thrown in jail. Potiphar is seated; he is wearing a conical hat and holding a scepter in his hand. The exemplary story of Joseph's life, often interpreted as a lesson in salvation, was frequently represented in glass during the 13th century (Bourges, Chartres, the Sainte Chapelle, Poitiers, Tours); at Rouen it occupies two windows.

The pieces of glass are cut into geometrical shapes. Potiphar's pose is dynamic and complex; the contour lines have been accentuated, but the modeling is still very flowing. The folds in the clothing are full and fall straight.

State of preservation of the panel: poor. There are numerous stopgaps in the lower parts of the figure's garments. The paint has scaled off and been retouched in places.

LASTEYRIE, 1852–57, vol. I, p. 180; RITTER, *Les vitraux de Rouen*, 1928, pp. 43–45, pl. XIV; GRODECKI, in "Vitraux de France," Paris, 1953, no. 22, p. 60, pl. 15; PERROT, *Vitrail à Rouen*, p. 15.

69 ROUEN, cathedral of Notre Dame: transept, Chapel of Saint Jean jouxte les fonts, bay 27
Azon le Tort and the Members of his Family Offering Windows to the Virgin Mary (Pl. 148)
Overall dimensions: H. 8 m.; W. 1.80 m.
ca. 1266

Five full-color figural panels are set in the middle of this grisaille window. Two registers are occupied by a Virgin and Child, standing in a slightly hip-shot stance under a canopy with three-cusped arches inside, the rampant arches decorated with a leafy rope. She receives homage from three kneeling donors in the three other colored panels; the red ground behind them, decorated with circular motifs, "subdues the backgrounds and brings out the figures" (J. J. Gruber). The central donor is dressed as a pilgrim; the other two—a woman at the left and a man at the right—are offering a "Rayonnant" type of window. Next to the man at the right is a scroll inscribed: GE SUIS CI POR ACE LE TORT, identifying him as Azon le Tort, a citizen of Rouen: in his will (1126), he endowed a chantry in this chapel. The pieces of glass are still cut geometrically. The painting is simplified, but there are numerous projecting beak folds.

The organization of the grisaille into circles or quatrefoils crossed by oblique colored fillets and the drawing of the leaves, which often end in acorns, are reminiscent of models from 1230–1240. It is possible that the figural panels were added at the time the chantry was endowed or slightly before.

Today the grisaille panels are modern recreations after the original motifs. The state of preservation of the figures, which were taken down in 1939, is fairly good.

RITTER, *Les vitraux de Rouen*, 1926, p. 51, pl. XXXIII; GRUBER, "Quelques aspects du vitrail en France," pp. 87–88; LAFOND, "Vitrail en Normandie," p. 336; PERROT, *Vitrail à Rouen*, p. 17.

70 ROUEN, cathedral of Notre Dame: (nave?)
Legend of the Seven Sleepers of Ephesus:
1) Messengers before Emperor Theodosius (preserved in Worcester, Mass.; Worcester Art Museum [1921.X60]; H. 0.62 m.; W. 0.58 m.) (Pl. 39)
2) Head of a Sleeper (currently stored at the Champs-sur-Marne storage depot of the Monuments Historiques; H. 0.08 m.) (Pl. 38)
ca. 1205–1210

From this legendary series, only a dozen more or less complete panels survive. They were probably originally set in the nave in a window demolished during the arrangement of the lateral chapels around 1270. Many have been recently reinstalled in a window of the north radiating chapel in Rouen Cathedral. The most beautiful, however, are in American museums and private collections. M. Cothren has recently suggested a reconstruction of this window, with two medallions per register, linked by bosses into ensembles of four compartments. The Rouen cycle depicts an Eastern legend introduced into the West in the 6th century by Gregory of Tours (*PL*, LXXI, col. 787–89). Beginning in the 11th century, the story spread, particularly in Normandy. Seven young Christians from Ephesus who had been buried alive at the order of the pagan Emperor Decius were found alive two centuries later during the reign of Theodosius II. In the scene illustrated here, three messengers, two of them wearing Phrygian caps, come to tell the emperor about this resurrection.

The pictorial execution is firm and precise. The fluid drapery is close to that seen in the Laon-Soissons group, but the treatment of the faces with high, hollow cheekbones can be compared to glass by the Good Samaritan workshop in the nave at Chartres (cf. Pl. 53). Stylistic analogies with panels in the Life of Saint John the Baptist, reinstalled in the *Belles-Verrières*, are strong enough to suggest that they are the work of the same master.

The panel has been reduced in width, the two beaded borders dating from an early restoration. The lower part is modern and reuses much glass. A semicircular arch and mosaic surmounting the scene have been added later. The figures are well-preserved, but the paint has scaled off in places.

"Art Through Fifty Centuries from the Collections of the Worcester Art Museum," exh. cat., Worcester, 1948, p. 86, fig. 48; "The Year 1200," New York, 1970, vol. I, pp. 202–4, no. 207; J. LAFOND, "La verrière des Sept Dormants d'Ephèse et l'ancienne vitrerie de la cathédrale de Rouen," *The Year 1200: A Symposium*, vol. III, New York, 1975, pp. 399–411; M. CAVINESS, in "Stained Glass from New England Collections," pp. 17–19, fig. 5.

71 ROUEN, castle of Philip Augustus (?) (destroyed): chapel (?) (destroyed)
Saint Peter (Pl. 149)
H. 0.70 m.; W. 0.56 m.
ca. 1260–1270
Preserved in Paris: Musée de Cluny (22727)

Saint Peter is seated sideways on a pale purple throne ending in lion-head terminals; the saint is holding a white key in his hand. The inscription reads: S[ANCTUS] PETRUS. The heraldic border consists of three-towered castles of Castile.

This panel is presented in bands; the grisaille panels (not illustrated) flank the colored ones but blend poorly with them. It may be that the decorative panels were not originally intended for this window. The floral motifs are composed of unidentifiable leaves and ivy leaves, indicating a date in the 1260s. The Musée de Cluny, Paris, has three other figures of apostles from this series—Saint John the Evangelist, Saint Paul and Saint James the Greater. The Metropolitan Museum of Art, New York, has a number of the grisaille panels (69.236.2–9 and 10, cf. J. HAYWARD, "Stained Glass Windows," *The Bulletin of The Metropolitan Museum of Art*, [Dec. 1971–Jan. 1972]: 118), and the Corning Museum of Glass, Corning, New York, has about sixty fragments (cf. M. LILLICH, "Three Essays on French Thirteenth-Century Grisaille Glass," *Journal of Glass Studies* XV [1973]: 73–5).

J. Lafond suggested that this series came from one of the chapels in the royal castle of Philip Augustus (1180–1223), built or decorated subsequently during the reign of Saint Louis, after his captivity. The castle was destroyed in the 17th century, and some of the windows were reused in a convent chapel before passing into a private collection at the beginning of the century, and then to the Musée de Cluny.

The outlines of the figure are emphatic. The effect is not monumental; the handling is precise and harsh. There are numerous beaks, which emphasize the folds. The colors are strong and dominated by green.

State of preservation: good.

LAFOND, "Vitrail en Normandie," pp. 337–41; PERROT, "Catalogue des vitraux religieux," fasc. II, pp. 111–14.

72 SAINT-FARGEAU (Yonne), church of Saint Ferréol: nave (?)
The Passion of Christ: The Kiss of Judas (Pl. 111)
Dimensions (panel): H. 0.63 m.; L. 0.43 m.
1250–1255
Preserved in Geneva: Musée d'Art et d'Histoire (D76)

None of the Gothic glass in this church (built after 1240) remains *in situ*. Badly damaged in the 15th century, the chevet was rebuilt and decorated with glass from the nave, which was recut for use in the new windows. In poor condition by the end of the 19th century, the windows were removed and replaced by the work of E. Didron. Some years later, after 1880, twenty-two panels—some remade using foreign elements—were acquired by G. Revilliod for the Musée Ariana in Geneva through the intervention of the painter C. Töpffer. In 1960, they were transferred to the Musée d'Art et d'Histoire.

In recent years, two other fragments from the glazing have been identified:
1) a Christ and Apostles at Wellesley College in Wellesley, Massachusetts (cf. M. CAVINESS, "Medieval and Renaissance Stained Glass from New England Collections," exh. cat., Cambridge, Mass.: Harvard

University, Busch-Reisinger Museum, 1978, pp. 28–29, no. 10;

2) a Last Supper in The Glencairn Museum, Bryn Athyn, Pennsylvania (cf. "Radiance and Reflection," exh. cat., New York, 1982, pp. 211–13, no. 81).

According to J. Lafond, the various fragments belonged to six different windows—the Life of the Virgin, the Childhood of Christ, the Passion of Christ, the Last Judgment and the Lives of Saint Blaise and Saint Vincent. V. Raguin has recently discovered another subject (the Life of Saint Francis of Assisi), which would be one of the first examples in French glass (cf. *Actes du XIᵉ colloque international du Corpus Vitrearum, New York, 1982*, December 1984).

The panel illustrated in Pl. 111 is from the Passion window. At the left, Christ, His feet slightly offset and His hands held by a jailer, is being kissed by Judas, who is shown in profile with the cast of features traditional for an executioner. Saint Peter, seated at the left and recognizable by his tonsure, prepares to cut off the ear of Malchus, who was set in the left part of the window, which is now destroyed. Behind him are two guards.

The composition is crowded, but the arrangement of the figures in a circle suggests depth. The drapery, on the other hand, has been flattened. The silhouettes are bulky, the faces not very expressive. The handling is heavy. According to V. Raguin, the workshop responsible for this ensemble worked first in the cathedral at Auxerre (between 1230–1240), then in the collegiate church at Saint-Julien-du-Sault and finally at Saint-Fargeau.

The panel is mutilated at the bottom; originally it must have been joined to the border and set tangentially to another half-medallion, where the scene would have continued. The leading is modern; there are many repair leads and stopgaps.

W. DEONNA, *Catalogue du Musée Ariana*, Geneva, 1983, pp. 173–75; J. LAFOND, "Les vitraux français du Musée Ariana et l'ancienne vitrerie de Saint-Fargeau (Yonne)," *Genava* 26 (1948): pp. 115–32; S. PELISSIER, "L'ancienne vitrerie du XIIIᵉ siècle de l'église de Saint-Fargeau," *Bulletin de la Société des Sciences historiques et naturelles de l'Yonne* 112 (1980): 71–84; CHIEFFO RAGUIN, *Stained Glass*, pp. 58, 64–67, 114, figs 95–96, 98–100; C. LAPAIRE, *Vitraux du Moyen Age*, Geneva: Musée d'Art et d'Histoire, n. d., p. 25, pl. 5.

73 SAINT-GERMAIN-LÈS-CORBEIL (Essonne), church of Saint Vincent: chevet, bay 0, upper quatrefoil, central medallion
The Passion and Ascension of Christ: Head of an Apostle Witnessing the Ascension (Pl. 81)
Overall dimensions: H. 4.50 m.; W. 1.60 m.
ca. 1220–1225

The scenes are distributed in three quatrefoils, each composed of five medallions. Between the quatrefoils are historiated half-medallions abutting the border. The ground is decorated with small quarries. The leaves in the narrow border are set perpendicular to the window's axis.

In the lower quatrefoil, only the medallion of the Crowning with Thorns is original; the others are modern. In the center, the central medallion depicts the Crucifixion, with Ecclesia in the left foil and Synagoga in the right. In the upper foil are two half-length angels. One is nimbed with the disk of the Sun; the other has a feminine face and the crescent moon above

his head. The lower foil contains a representation of the Flagellation.

The Holy Women at the Tomb and the Ascension occupy four compartments in the upper quatrefoil.

In the half-medallions at the sides are Christological scenes that have not been properly identified: the Appearance of Christ to His Mother (?) and the Incredulity of Saint Thomas (?).

The compositions are dense and lively. Though varied, the proportions of the figures are often short. The faces are round, expressive and animated by nervous linework and detailed handling. The drapery is supple and smooth. The range of colors is rich and strong.

The paint has a tendency to flake. Much of the glass has blackened despite recent restoration.

L. VOLLANT, *L'église de Saint-Germain-lès-Corbeil*, Paris, 1897, pp. 31–32, pl. IX; "L'Europe gothique," p. 116, no. 94; V. RAGUIN, "Windows of Saint-Germain-lès-Corbeil: A Travelling Glazing Atelier", *Gesta* XV (1976): 265–72, nos 1–2; *Recensement*, I, p. 83.

74 SAINT-QUENTIN (Aisne), former collegiate church of Saint Quentin: apse, axial chapel, bay 1, 5th register
The Childhood of Christ: The Nativity (Pl. 30)
Overall dimensions: H. 3.50 m.; W. 0.90 m.
ca. 1220

This Lady Chapel retains only two windows from its original glass on both sides of the axial bay. Both present a similar arrangement: six canted squares linked together by lateral compartments of quarter-circles. The iron bars are forged in the shape of the medallions; the armature is composed of straight bars.

The left window reads from top to bottom; the middle compartments illustrate the Childhood of Christ from the Annunciation to the Flight into Egypt. In the medallions at the side are scenes from the Old Testament (prefigurations of Christological scenes), a pattern already seen in the left window of the chevet in Laon Cathedral (cf. cat. 41).

The iconographic treatment of the Nativity is original for the time and makes use of numerous sources; for instance, the Presentation of the Christ Child in a grotto (shown here as a number of hillocks), guarded by two angels, is Byzantine in origin. Moreover, the Nativity is combined with the more unusual scene of the Adoration of the Shepherds, who are represented by the lone Shepherd at the left behind Joseph.

The composition is made legible by the clever arrangement of the protagonists in tiers around the cradle. The ease of the figures' outlines is augmented by that of the drapery, with its profusion of linear folds that flatten the bodies' bulk. The pictorial technique is elegant and precise, with a balance between modeling and line.

The window has an acanthas-scroll ground. The border is composed of bouquets set perpendicular to the axis of the bay, which is typical of the Laon-Soissons region at this time (cf. the axial window in the upper choir of Soissons Cathedral). The colors of the ensemble are pale; much of the glass is purple, yellow and green, while there is little ruby glass.

State of preservation: mediocre, varying considerably from one panel to the next. While there are a number of restorations in the Nativity, they do not affect the composition.

GRODECKI, "Le 'Maître de saint Eustache,'" pp. 180–88, figs 110, 112–14.

75 SAINT-SULPICE-DE-FAVIÈRES (Essonne), church of Saint Sulpice: bay 0, right light
The Adoration of the Magi (Pl. 134)
Dimensions (panel): H. 1.05 m.; W. 1.10 m.
ca. 1280

The scene is composed of two panels; only half of the left one remains. The presentation of the figures is identical: they are placed under three-cusped arches. Crowned and nimbed, the Virgin seated at the right holds a large lily as a scepter in one hand and her Son in the other. The Christ Child is holding a bird and giving a blessing; He receives homage from the first king, who is kneeling with his crown on his knee and offering a goblet. At the left, there is only one other king, who is standing with his crowned head facing backward, as he points forward, with hand raised, to the star. The only other scene to survive from this Marian cycle is a poorly preserved Nativity set under the Adoration of the Magi. It provides no additional indication as to the origin and proper placement of the panels, which were used as stopgaps in the axial windows, along with other elements from lost windows of various dates and diverse provenance (in the left light: five scenes from the Passion of about 1235; in the right one, in addition to the Marian cycle, two scenes from the Life of Saint Sulpicius, patron of the church, of about 1250).

The scale of execution is small, the compositions open, and the poses relaxed. There is a refined treatment of folds that even takes the quality of the fabrics into account. The style is closer to non-monumental Parisian sculpture than to illumination, despite a handling of the drapery similar to the full-page illuminations in Parisian manuscripts such as the missal for the use of the abbey of Saint Denis (Paris, Bibl. Nat., ms. lat. 1107). The palette is bright and light.

There are few modern pieces, but the paint has been obliterated. J. J. Gruber did the last restoration between 1956 and 1958.

P. SALIN, *L'église de Saint-Sulpice-de-Favières*, Paris, 1865, pp. 25–30; "Vitraux de France," Paris, 1953, pp. 64–65, no. 26; F. GATOUILLAT, "A Saint-Sulpice-de-Favières, des vitraux témoins de l'art parisien au temps de Saint Louis," *Dossiers de l'archéologie*, no. 26 (1978): 56–57.

76 SAINT-SULPICE-DE-FAVIÈRES (Essonne), church of Saint Sulpice: south aisle, bay 6
The Life of the Virgin and the Childhood of Christ:
    1) Overall view (Pl. 131)
    2) The Presentation in the Temple: the Virgin Mary Holding the Christ Child and Accompanied by a Serving Maid (right light, 2nd register, left compartment) (Pl. 133)
    3) One of Saint Ann's Neighbors Is Surprised That She Is Pregnant (central light, lower register) (Pl. 132)
H. 8.40 m.; W. 4.60 m.
1255–1260

This cycle contains no fewer than thirty historiated compartments set in three lights in the bay. The arrangement in the central light differs from those at the sides: it has a single medallion with a blue ground per register; the lateral lights each contain two abutting half-quatrefoils with red grounds. The scenes read from left to right and from bottom to top and ignore the mullions. The events prior to the Marriage of the Virgin occupy the two lower registers; the third register is dedicated to events preceding the Annunciation. The three remaining registers are concerned with the

Childhood of Christ up to the Fall of the Idols. Some scenes (the Adoration of the Magi) occupy two compartments. The iconographic sources are varied, blending traditions from the gospels and apocrypha.

In the tympanum are the Virgin and Child flanked by kneeling angels. Saints Peter and Paul enthroned occupy the trefoils above the lateral lights.

There is abundant heraldic decoration: a fleur-de-lis border in the lateral lights and castles of Castile in the axial one. The damask background in the lateral lights contains gold fleurs-de-lis and blue lozenges. Only the ground of the central light lacks this type of decoration; it is composed of red and blue oblique leading, punctuated with blue dots.

The scale of execution is tiny and carefully worked; the pictorial treatment is refined, even in the smallest details. The figures are very legible. There is balance and subtlety in the distribution of colors, thanks to a rich palette which abounds in pale tones such as yellow and white.

There have been interpolations in many panels: the Presentation of Jesus in the Temple, having been misinterpreted, is not in its original location. The extent of restoration varies from panel to panel but does not affect the general arrangement of the window. The last restoration was done by J.J. Gruber in 1956.

GATOUILLAT, "A Saint-Sulpice de Favières, des vitraux témoins," pp. 58-62.

77　SÉES (Orne), cathedral of Notre Dame: chapel of Saint Augustine, bay 24
Canons Listening to Saint Augustine Explain His Rule (Pl. 151)
H. 0.60 m.; W. 0.55 m.
1270-1280
Preserved at Bryn Athyn, Pennsylvania: The Glencairn Museum (03.SG.50)

Five half-length figures of canons, turned toward the right with their hands raised or joined, are looking at Saint Augustine as he explains his rule to them. The panel with Saint Augustine and the one with the lower part of this group are still in place in the other light of the axial bay in the chapel dedicated to this Father of the Church. Another window in the chapel shows Saint Augustine seated at his desk, writing his rule (cf. J. LAFOND, "Les vitraux de la cathédrale de Sées," *C. Arch.* 111 [1954]: 70-72). The American panel was probably removed during the restoration carried out by Steinheil, and later by Leprévost, after the reconstruction work in the choir was finished at the beginning of the 20th century. The panel was originally surmounted by an architectural canopy; it was replaced by a composition slightly different from the original.

This chapel, like all those in the choir, was decorated with "mixed" windows—brightly colored historiated panels set against decorative grisailles, many panels of which are also in the United States now (The Corning Museum of Glass, Corning, New York [51.3.228]).

The figural style is one of the most original of the "school" of western France, with its arrangement of protagonists in tiers, which creates a certain depth, its violent coloring and, above all, its simplified handling of drapery and brutal treatment of faces. The exceptional size of the figures' hands underscores the panel's expressive character.

The border is very narrow and restricted in decoration, with small stylized motifs.

State of preservation: poor, with numerous repair leads and scaling paint.

"Radiance and Reflection," New York, 1982, pp. 223-25, no. 87; LILLICH, "Stained Glass from Western France," pp. 125-26.

78　SÉES (Orne), cathedral of Notre Dame: 1st north radiating chapel (?)
Grisaille with Columbine-Leaf Decoration (Pl. 142)
H. 0.57 m.; W. 0.62 m.
ca. 1280
Preserved in Bryn Athyn, Pennsylvania: The Glencairn Museum (03.SG.53)

At Sées today, the majority of grisaille panels associated with figural and historiated scenes have been replaced by modern pieces copying the authentic decorative motifs. The substitutions were made during the restoration carried out by master glazier Leprévost in 1880. Many of these panels, deemed unuseable because of their poor condition, were then sold and are now to be found in museums and private collections outside France (cf. cat. 77), as well as in the storage depot of the Monuments Historiques at Champs-sur-Marne. The latter were exhibited by L. Magne at the Musée de Sculpture comparée in the Palais du Trocadéro between 1910 and 1934 (cf. "Vitraux de France," Paris, 1953, p. 63, no. 25).

The glass illustrated here probably accompanied historiated panels dedicated to Saint Nicholas in the chapel named for him (cf. LAFOND, "Les vitraux de Sées," pp. 68-70).

The leading defines a central quatrefoil set against a rectangular panel. Forms from the main motif are repeated in the corners. The columbine-leaf decoration belongs to the "transitional" phase defined by M. Lillich. This symmetrical composition is based on a central, vertical branch from which four similar scrolls emerge. Between them the ground is woven with *cage à mouches* ("crosshatched fly screen"). The decoration is heraldic.

State of preservation: excellent.

"Radiance and Reflection," New York, 1982, pp. 225-27, no. 88.

79　SEMUR-EN-AUXOIS (Côte d'Or), church of Notre Dame: chevet, axial chapel, bay 3, 2nd register
Life of Saint Peter: Saint Peter Awakened by an Angel (Pl. 113)
Dimensions (panel): 0.52 m. square
after 1240 (?)
Currently stored at Champs-sur-Marne: storage depot of the Monuments Historiques

In 1847, Eugène Viollet-le-Duc had the Gothic glass of Notre Dame at Semur regrouped in the windows of the axial chapel in the chevet. Consequently, the Saint Peter window is not in its original location, nor is its arrangement now correct. The cycle must have had even more scenes, since two figures belonging to it have been reused in the neighboring window dedicated to Mary Magdalene. The medallions may not be in their original shapes.

The subjects revolve almost entirely around the arrest and imprisonment of the apostle. From bottom to top, they are Peter before Nero; a Guard throws Peter into Prison; Peter Talks to his Jailers; Peter Escaping from Prison; Peter Awakened by an Angel (illustrated); Peter in the House of Mary (Acts XII:12).

The figures are placed on two levels. The prison is suggested by a crenellated fillet that follows the shape of the compartment. The silhouettes are squat, and the drawing is nervous. The contour lines have been reinforced at the expense of the modeling. The palette is contrasting but restricted, and white has been used extensively. V. Raguin's theory that these medallions were made by the same workshop as the windows at Saint-Germain-lès-Corbeil is difficult to accept. The date of this panel is not firm.

State of preservation: satisfactory, except for the blue ground, which is made up of glass from different periods.

"Histoire et Description de l'église Notre-Dame de Semur-en-Auxois," *Commission des Antiquités du département de la Côte d'Or,* 1832-33, p. 63; CHIEFFO RAGUIN, *Stained Glass,* pp. 164-65, figs 58-59.

80　SENS, cathedral of Saint Etienne: ambulatory, bay 15, lower and middle quatrefoils
Parable of the Good Samaritan (Pl. 74)
Overall dimensions: H. ca. 4 m.; W. 2.50 m.
ca. 1210-1215

The composition has been adapted to demonstrate a theological argument. The parable is outlined in the three middle compartments, composed of canted squares set in iron bars. Reading from top to bottom the scenes are as follows:

1) The Traveler Is Attacked on the Road to Jericho. The inscription reads: HIC INCIDIT MAN(IBUS) LA-[TRO]NUM.

2) The Traveler, symbolizing Christ, lies on the ground, a cruciform halo around his head. The inscription reads: HOMO.

3) The Samaritan, having put the traveler on his horse, guides him to the innkeeper. The inscription reads: (PER)EGRINUS SAMARITANUS above, and STABULA[RIUS] (mutilated) below. The four side medallions accompanying each scene of the parable are in keeping with standard commentaries of the time. At the top are scenes from the Creation; in the middle are scenes from Exodus and, at the bottom, events from the Passion. At the very top is the image of the Heavenly Jerusalem, bearing the inscription: CIVITAS IHERUSALEM.

The background is restricted to ornamental bosses that fill the spandrels between the scenes. The bouquets of palmettes in the border are perpendicular to the window's axis.

The stylistic principles are similar those in the neighboring Prodigal Son window: the compositions are stable and rest on "bridges". The silhouettes are heavy and strongly modeled, yet the drapery is supple. The colors are lively, and white is used extensively, especially in clothing.

The window was heavily restored in the 19th century; the glass is much corroded.

L. BÉGULE, *La cathédrale de Sens, son architecture, son décor,* Paris, 1929, pp. 52-54, figs 63-67.

81　SENS, cathedral of Saint Etienne: ambulatory, bay 19, 4th register, right medallion
Life of Saint Thomas Becket: Thomas Becket Preaching to the People (Pl. 75)
Diam.: ca. 0.65 m.
ca. 1210-1220 (?)

The primate, accompanied by his clergy, preaches from an ambo to the faithful seated in a group below. The partly reworked inscription reads: PREDICATIO S[ANCTI] TOME AD POPULUM.

Thirteen scenes make up this "political" cycle, which originally emphasized the role of the king of France in the temporary reconciliation between Thomas Becket and the Plantagenet King Henry II. The following scenes illustrate Becket's return to Canterbury and the dramatic circumstances of his death. At the top is the Enthroned Christ giving a blessing, signifying the universality of the scenes below.

The composition is symmetrical and unfolds on two levels, punctuated by the colonnettes of the ambo, with the inscription acting as a "bridge". The drapery is supple and archaizing. The colors are lively.

WESTLAKE (1881-84, vol. I, pp. 110-13, pl. LXII) and subsequent historians have often compared the Sens ambulatory windows, especially the Becket window, to those in Canterbury. It is chiefly in the composition and the quality of the ornament that links can be seen. According to the findings of M. Caviness, the similarity results from the fact that the same cartoon maker worked at Canterbury and at Sens.

The dating has not been clearly established. The two hypotheses are that the glass was done after the fire of 1207, or that it was made to commemorate the translation of the martyr's relics to Canterbury in 1220.

Extensive restoration has accentuated the peculiarities of this original style.

ABBÉ BRULLÉE, "Description des verrières de la cathédrale de Sens," *Bulletin de la Société archéologique de Sens* VII (1876): 165-69; BÉGULE, *La cathédrale de Sens*, pp. 44-47, figs 52-54; T. BORENIUS, *Saint Thomas Becket in Art*, London, 1932, p. 45; BRISAC, "Thomas Becket dans le vitrail français," pp. 224-26; M. CAVINESS, *The Early Stained Glass of Canterbury Cathedral (circa 1175-1220)*, Princeton, 1978, pp. 92-96, figs 135, 160, 166, 176, 202.

---

82   SOISSONS, cathedral of Saint Gervais et Saint Protais: chevet, axial chapel, bay 1, 5th and 6th registers
Life of Moses (from left to right, and bottom to top): Jethro Giving his Daughter to Moses (Exodus II: 21); the Hebrews Marking the Lintels with the Blood of a Lamb (Exodus XII: 7); Moses Climbing the Mountain (Exodus XIX: 20); Pharaoh's Daughter Finding Moses (Exodus II: 5-6) (Pl. 96)
H. 1.40 m.; W. ca. 1.90 m.
ca. 1250

During the renovation of the choir in 1772, much of the glass from the nave was transferred to the three bays in the axial chapel, resulting in some incoherent scenes and confusion in the biblical narrative. The corresponding window, where this cycle continued, has been lost; it had been dismantled with the other two during the First World War in 1915. The story of Judith is represented in the axial window. Over the years, other elements of what seems to have been an important program, perhaps copied from that of the Sainte Chapelle in Paris, have been identified in museums and collections outside France (M. CAVINESS and V. CHIEFFO RAGUIN, "Another Dispersed Window from Soissons: a Tree of Jesse in the Sainte-Chapelle Style," *Gesta* XX, no. 1 [1981]: 191-98). Thus these panels must be considered as mere vestiges, in as much as the restorations of Tournel (in 1913) accentuated their false character under the pretext of restoring order.

The workshop responsible for the glass developed close to that of the Passion Master of the Sainte Chapelle.

State of preservation: average; most of the heads are original. There are numerous repair leads in the background, which is made of disparate pieces.

L. GRODECKI, "Les vitraux soissonnais du Louvre, du Musée Marmottan et des collections américaines," *Revue des Arts* X (1960): 168, 172-73; J. ANCIEN, "Vitraux de la cathédrale de Soissons," vol. I, Soissons, 1980, pp. 136-53 [typewritten].

---

83   SOISSONS, cathedral of Saint Gervais et Saint Protais: chevet, bay 100
Tree of Jesse: Ancestor-King (Pl. 25)
H. 0.77 m.; W. 0.80 m.
ca. 1200-1210
Preserved at Bryn Athyn, Pennsylvania: The Glencairn Museum (03.SG.229)

It was probably during the restoration by master glazier E. Didron that this panel and the figure of the Blessed Virgin in two panels were taken from the original window, probably donated by King Philip Augustus of France. The Virgin, purchased by the Kunstgewerbemuseum in Berlin, was destroyed in the bombings of 1944. The bust of the Ancestor-King, acquired by an American collector, was dated to the 12th century and first attributed to Bourges by Kingsley Porter. In 1953, L. Grodecki discovered its true provenance. The Jesse-Tree window now *in situ* at the cathedral of Soissons, was restored between 1923 and 1927 after the bombings of the First World War. It must be considered a poor and inaccurate reconstruction, notably because of the chromatic disharmony between the original panels and the modern ones, numbering thirteen out of a total of thirty-six.

The king, crowned and with a halo, folds his hand across his chest and holds the clasp of his mantle. He is presented frontally against an "antique" ground of acanthus scrolls with carefully wrought terminating leaflets. The rigorously outlined face and the rectilinear folds of the mantle contrast with the monumentality of the decoration. Yet there is extraordinary invention in the disposition and treatment of the scrolls that form the tree.

State of preservation: good, but there are numerous repair leads, especially in the face.

A. K. PORTER, "Le Roi de Bourges," *Art in America* VI (1918): 264-73; L. GRODECKI, "Un vitrail démembré de la cathédrale de Soissons," *Gazette des Beaux-Arts* 42, no. II (1953): 169-76; ANCIEN, "Vitraux de Soissons," vol. I, pp. 100-12; "Radiance and Reflection," New York, 1982, pp. 140-42, no. 52.

---

84   SOISSONS (?), cathedral of Saint Gervais et Saint Protais (?): placement unknown
Legend of Saint Nicholas:
   1) Three Knights Appear before a Roman Consul (Pl. 28)
   2) Saint Nicholas Intercedes on Behalf of the Three Knights (Pl. 27)
Dimensions (panel): H. 0.54 m.; W. 0.39 m.
ca. 1210-1215
Preserved in New York: The Metropolitan Museum of Art, The Cloisters Collection (1980.263.2 and 3)

Nothing is known of the history of these panels, which are not mentioned by either the Soissons historians or

---

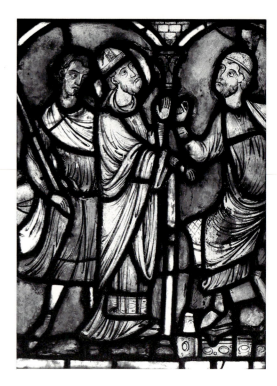

by F. Guilhermy. Their attribution to the glazing of Soissons Cathedral is based purely on stylistic analysis but is quite plausible. First, the windows of that building have suffered so many losses since the 18th century that the panels may well never have been inventoried. Second, the second radiating chapel south of the axis was dedicated to Saint Nicholas until 1768, and one or more windows may have been dedicated to its patron saint, as often happened in the 12th century.

The Legend of Saint Nicholas was frequently represented in Romanesque glass, the panels at Troyes being one example. This episode from the *Golden*

Legend, however, is rarely seen. In the first panel, three innocent knights appear before a consul. The inscription—[N]icolaus-Preces Milites—does not correspond to this scene. In the second panel, Saint Nicholas intercedes with the consul on behalf of the knights, in a composition that is the reverse of the first. The second scene carries no inscription.

Because of the composition, line-work and handling of these two panels, they have been attributed to Soissons Cathedral, rather than to another church in the Laon-Soissons group. The figures' gestures, their relationship to one another and their placement in scenes defined by arches correspond closely to that seen in the Soissons panels in the Musée Marmottan in Paris and the Corcoran Gallery of Art in Washington, D.C.

While the panels have been mutilated both in width and height, the state of preservation is good.

"Radiance and Reflection," New York, 1982, pp. 137–39, no. 51, pls VI–VII; S. Childs, "Two Scenes from the Life of Saint Nicholas and Their Relationship to the Glazing Program of the Chevet Chapels at Soissons Cathedral," *Studies on Medieval Stained Glass, CVMA*: United States, *Occasional Papers 3,* New York, 1985 [in press].

85   STRASBOURG, cathedral of Notre Dame: triforium, north side, western bays (?)
Genealogy of Christ: Melchi (Pl. 187)
H. 0.43 m.; W. 0.31 m.
ca. 1260 (?)
Preserved in Strasbourg: Musée de l'Œuvre Notre-Dame (MAD LXV.64)

Only the upper part of this ancestor of Christ survives—the head framed by the inscription: Qui Fuit Melchi, identifying the figure. Melchi has blond hair, a short beard and a blue zucchetto on his head. On his neck at the left is a flower-shaped brooch that holds his mantle.

The triforium lights in the nave represented the Genealogy of Christ, according to both Luke and Matthew. The ancestors were represented standing, from east to west on the south side and then from west to east on the north. Only a few original elements survive *in situ* on the north side. The work was done by workshops from different traditions between 1245 and 1275, the date of the completion of the nave.

The figure of Melchi is stylistically similar to sculptures from the former rood screen at Strasbourg (before 1261 [?]), now also preserved in the Musée de l'Œuvre Notre-Dame, executed by a sculptor trained at Reims (cf. the Passion cycle on the archivolts at the left of the cathedral's west portal).

The paint is flaking and has been lost completely in some parts, especially in the beard. A repair lead now cuts across the face.

J. Schweighäuser, *Wegweiser der Stadt Straßburg,* Strasbourg, 1768, p. 37; V. Beyer, *Chefs-d'œuvre du vitrail européen: La cathédrale de Strasbourg,* Paris, 1970, p. 34, pl. IX; idem, *Les vitraux des Musées de Strasbourg,* 3rd ed., Strasbourg, 1978, (with amendments by M. J. Forte), p. 34, no. 22, pl. 4.

86   STRASBOURG, church of Saint Thomas: apse
Solomon and the Queen of Sheba. (I Kings X: 1–10)
(Pl. 186)
H. 0.53 m.; W. 0.63 m.
ca. 1270
Preserved in Strasbourg: Musée de l'Œuvre Notre-Dame (MAD LVII, 5)

The Queen of Sheba with a bluish-grey face, accompanied by a serving maid, approaches the enthroned and crowned Solomon, who is holding a scepter in his right hand, to offer him a cup.

The panel is from one of the lateral apse windows of the church of Saint Thomas at Strasbourg (now a Protestant church). The glass was removed and dispersed during the installation of the marshal of Saxony's mausoleum by J. B. Pigalle (1775/1776). Seven panels have been recovered and are now preserved in the Strasbourg museum. An eighth now belongs to the Württembergisches Landesmuseum at Stuttgart (see H. Wentzel, *Die Glasmalereien in Schwaben von 1250-1350 CVMA*: FRG I, Berlin, 1958, pp. 266–67, ill. 621). Except for one panel devoted to Saint Thomas, the church's patron, they all illustrate Old Testament events.

The multifoil medallion is set within a circle against a background of yellow and green lozenges adorned with small quatrefoils.

Despite the reduced scale of execution, the series follows in the tradition of the Strasbourg workshop responsible (for the historiated tracery in the side aisles of the cathedral's nave and in the Dominicans' windows [1254–1260]), but makes use of more relaxed line-work.

The lower area is modern in parts.

V. Beyer, "Les roses du réseau des bas-côtés de la cathédrale de Strasbourg et l'œuvre d'un atelier strasbourgeois du XIIIᵉ siècle," *Bulletin des Amis de la Société de la Cathédrale de Strasbourg,* no. 7, 2nd series (1960): 82–86, ill. 20; Grodecki, in "L'Europe gothique," pp. 120–21, no. 200; Beyer, *Les vitraux de Strasbourg,* 3rd ed., p. 36, no. 32.

87   TOUL (Meurthe-et-Moselle), church of Saint Gengoult: chevet, bay 0, left light, 7th register
Life of Saint Gangolfus: The Adulterous Behavior of Gangolfus's Wife Ganea (Pl. 139)
Overall dimensions: H. 16 m.; W. 2.70 m.
1260–1270

The collegiate church of Saint Gengoult, founded by Saint Gerard, bishop of Toul from 963 to 994, was first rebuilt in the 11th century and then in the mid-13th. The window dedicated to the church's patron saint dates soon after the reconstruction, which began in the chevet.

The edifying life of Saint Gangolfus—told here in fifteen medallions—was very popular in the Middle Ages. A military governor, the saint was assassinated by his wife's lover, a clergyman. Saint Gangolfus's cult extended beyond the territories of the ancient kingdom of Burgundy, where he lived in the 8th century, into other regions such as Picardy and Lorraine. This is one of the rare 13th-century hagiographic windows to occupy such a prestigious place in the church—the axial window, which it shares with a Life of Christ in the right light. In the rose window of the tympanum is Christ in Glory surrounded by Evangelist symbols and numerous figures alluding to the Passion of Christ and to the Last Judgment.

The arrangement is simple and archaic: a single medallion in each register flanked by wide borders. The compositions are open, and the scale of execution is small. The colors are still dark, despite the heavy use of white.

State of preservation: barely satisfactory. There is much restored glass in the canopy over the adulterous couple.

Abbé Balthasar, "La collégiale Saint-Gengoult de Toul," *Revue archéologique* (1853): 14–29; Abbé J. Choux, "Lorraine," *Vitraux de France du Moyen Age à la Renaissance,* Colmar and Ingersheim, 1970, pp. 120–21; idem, "Le vitrail lorrain au Moyen Age et à la Renaissance," "Le vitrail en Lorraine," exh. cat., Nancy, 1983, pp. 36, 357, no. 147.

88   TOURS, cathedral of Saint Gatien: chevet, triforium, bay 103, 3rd light from the left
Apostle (H. ca. 2 m.; W. 0.80 m.) (Pl. 124)
Overall dimensions (bay): H. 3.80 m.; W. 2.70 m.
1255–1260

The triforium level of Tours Cathedral on the right side of the choir is one of the earliest glazed with colorless grisaille windows. The colored figures of apostles around the Blessed Virgin, who is being venerated by two angels, are in the five bays of the apse. Each bay has three short lights containing one figure, a format that became widespread in the second half of the 13th century, especially in western France (cathedral of Sées, La Trinité at Vendôme, etc.).

The donors' arms in the tracery (bay 102) were found by M. Lillich to be those of one of Saint Louis's knights, Guillaume Ruffin de Binaville and his wife; accordingly, the glass can be dated to around 1255.

This apostle is of interest since he is the only one in the series to be shown in profile, a formula often used after 1260 (Saint Pierre at Chartres and Saint Urbain at Troyes).

The outlines of the figures and folds are done with vigor and simplicity, though the folds are still angular. The style is probably one of the sources of the second "school" of western France.

The chromatic distribution is still traditional in the backgrounds of the lights—alternately blue and red; it is enlivened in the figures by widespread use of yellow and, in the drapery, green. The decoration is restricted to a floral border that is identical throughout.

State of preservation of the apostle: fairly good, despite a large number of repair leads; the state of preservation in the other panels varies.

J. Bourrassé and R. Manceau, *Verrières du Chœur de l'église métropolitaine de Tours,* Tours, 1849, p. 74, pl. XVII; Canon H. Boissonot, *Les verrières de la cathédrale de Tours,* Paris, 1932, p. 132; M. Lillich, "The Triforium Windows of Tours," *Gesta* XIX, no. 1 (1980): 29–35.

89   TOURS, cathedral of Saint Gatien: choir clerestory, bay 206
The Canons of Loches (Pl. 128)
H. 10.50 m.; W. 3.20 m.
After 1259

This four-light window was given by the canons of the collegiate church of Notre Dame (now Saint Ours) at Loches, after the castle at Loches was integrated into the French royal domain in 1259. In that year, King Henry III of England finally renounced his claims to the county of Touraine, which Philip Augustus of France had annexed in 1204 and 1205. Occupying the lower register of the light farthest to the right is an image of the castle, its crenellated encircling wall surmounted by two French standards of azure blue decorated with fleurs-de-lis. Below is a band signaling the donors: Presbiteri Lochenses.

Standing in profile, alone or in pairs, beneath trefoil or ogee arches and wearing priestly vestments, the canons who donated the window have been positioned in two bands separated by panels of grisaille and are paying homage to their patron saint, the Virgin Mary, who is shown holding her Son in the upper registers of the light farthest to the left. In the rose of the tympanum Christ in Glory is depicted.

This is the earliest preserved example—with the facing window devoted to the bishops of Tours (bay 205)—of a band-window, i.e. one in which full-color panels, usually with figures, alternate with panels of colorless grisaille. Here a formal and chromatic balance has been achieved between the vividly colored panels, covering two registers, and the grisailles, highlighted solely by a few ornamental bosses, which form two panels in three registers. The border motif is three-towered castles of Castile.

The drawing is nervous and dry, the silhouettes elongated; the palette light and restricted in color.

Although the glass has not been very much restored, it is now blackening.

Bourrassé and Manceau, Verrières de Tours, pp.24–25, 49, pl.V; Boissonnot, Les verrières de Tours, pp.36–37; M. Lillich, "The Band-Window: A Theory of Origin and Development," Gesta IX, no.1 (1970): 26–33; L. Papanicolaou, "Stained Glass Windows of the Cathedral of Tours," New York: New York University, Institute of Fine Arts, 1979, pp.63–65 [unpublished thesis].

90   TOURS, cathedral of Saint Gatien: choir clerestory, bay 207, 4th light from the left, 2nd register
Genesis: The Fall of Adam and Eve (Pl.125)
H.10.50m.; W.13.20m.
ca. 1255–1260

Each of the window's four lights contains six superimposed compartments: elongated quatrefoils linked by ornamental bosses. In the lower register are the donors: farm workers. The twenty other scenes recount the first four books of the Bible, from the Creation to the chastisement of Lamech, who killed Cain (Gen. IV: 23–24). The iconography is original, often taking its inspiration from the Histoire scholastique by Pierre le Mangeur, one of the basic theological teaching manuals of the 13th century. The moralizing intention is clear. The Creation story is reduced to two scenes: the Creation of the World and the Creation of Eve. However, the Fall and subsequent events such as the Labors of Adam and His Family and the story of the fratricidal strife between Cain and Abel occupy numerous compartments. In the three oculi in the tympana of the rose windows standing bishops are depicted.

The glazing of this "legendary" type of window is an adaptation that was meant to be seen at a distance: the medallions are large, and the number of people in each scene is restricted. The handling is rapid and summary. Modeling is often sacrificed in favor of trace line. The pieces of glass are cut to a large scale.

The silhouettes of the figures are elongated, with refined, even sophisticated poses and gestures. The style is close to that of Parisian manuscripts dating after the captivity of King Louis IX (1250).

The traditional balance between blue and red has been modified by the frequent use of green and light purple. There is some use of yellow.

Like all the windows in this series, this one has deteriorated and become opaque.

Bourrassé and Manceau, Verrières de Tours, p.65, pl. XII; Mâle, 1910, pp.206, 325; Boissonnot, Les verrières de Tours, pp.25–28; Papanicolaou, "Stained Glass Windows of Tours," pp.65–66; idem, "The Iconography of the Genesis Window of the Cathedral of Tours," Gesta XX, no.1 (1981): 179–89.

91   TROYES, cathedral of Saint Pierre: ambulatory, axial chapel, bay 0, 3rd register
The Life of the Virgin Mary: The Presentation of Christ in the Temple (tracing by Lisch, ca. 1850) (Pl.34)
H.0.60m.; W.0.45m.
ca. 1210

The present arrangement of the window may not be authentic. The panels were placed in this window during restoration by master glazier Vincent-Larcher in the 19th century. They had previously served as stopgaps in the 18th century and were dispersed among several bays in the radiating chapels. In fact, they may come from a window in the collegiate church of Saint Etienne, which was destroyed at the beginning of the 19th century. At the time of his intervention (around 1853), Vincent-Larcher created an artificial unit by bringing the panels together and imposing an "archeological" composition. He forged new armatures shaped to the medallions and recreated the background and the border.

The iconographic scheme of the Presentation in the Temple is somewhat problematic, though the pose of the Infant Jesus being held at the altar by the high priest is customary. At the left are two women, one carrying the standard basket with two sacrificial doves; however, there is no woman with a halo to represent Mary. Joseph, who is usually included in the scene, is also absent here. It may be that the original window included a panel—now lost—with the parents of Jesus.

The composition is open, and the scale of execution is small. The proportions of the figures are short; the heads are small and finely drawn. The drapery is supple but has many massed folds, similar to the "classic" sculpture of the Champagne region in the same period. In formal qualities, the panel is also comparable to work seen in the Laon and Soissons areas around 1200.

This panel has been enlarged in situ by the addition of a fillet at the left; however, most of the pieces are original. The light glass has browned, above all in the faces.

J. Lafond, "Les vitraux de la cathédrale Saint-Pierre de Troyes," C. Arch. 113 (1957): 35–36; J. Ledit, Cathédrale de Troyes: vitraux, Troyes and Paris [1972], pp.100–1.

92   TROYES, cathedral of Saint Pierre: choir, bay 14, 6th register
Life of Saint Peter: "Quo Vadis Domine"
H. ca.6m.; W.1.60m.
ca. 1205–1210

The cathedral at Troyes preserves two legendary windows devoted to its patron saint. They are found in the second south radiating chapel, which was originally dedicated to Saint Peter and Saint Paul.

While the first window focuses on the miracles of Saint Peter, the second shows the episode of Simon the Magician, above which is the apocryphal scene of

the Quo Vadis Domine. At the top is the Crucifixion of Saint Peter. The order of the scenes is questionable.

The style is not monumental. The treatment is delicate and metallic, but the drapery is fluid. The colors are dark.

State of preservation: mediocre. A number of scenes have not been conclusively identified. Much of the old glass has been repainted.

Lafond, "Les vitraux de Troyes," p.30.

93   TROYES (?), cathedral of Saint Pierre (?): axial chapel (?)
Tree of Jesse: the Prophet Daniel (Pl.36)
H.0.64m.; W.0.30m.
1210–1215
Preserved in London: Victoria and Albert Museum (5–1881)

The axial window of the third south radiating chapel contains a Tree of Jesse, reconstituted by Vincent-Larcher in the 19th century. It includes only the figures of Jesse and six others, four of which are original: the Virgin Mary, Christ and two kings. It is likely, however, that the ten panels with prophets in the Victoria and Albert Museum—some in very good condition—are the missing lateral figures of the window. Jean Lafond has suggested that the glass was originally placed in the axial bay of the Lady Chapel.

Each nimbed prophet is wearing a robe covered by a mantle and is barefoot; they hold scrolls, often bearing their names—in this case DANIEL.

The line-work is elegant and vigorous. The treatment of the face is archaizing. The poses are noble, and the colors lively.

State of preservation: excellent.

RACKHAM, *Guide to the Collections*, p. 34, pl. 4; LAFOND, "Les vitraux de Troyes", pp. 42–43.

94 TROYES, church of Saint Urbain: chevet and choir, south side
Overall view of the windows (Pl. 9).
Overall dimensions (triforium): H. 5; W. 3 m.; (clerestory) H. 12 m.; W. 3 m.
ca. 1270

The collegiate church of Saint Urbain was founded by Pope Urban IV (1261–1264) in 1262 on the site of the house in which he was born at Troyes. His work was continued by his successor Pope Clement IV; partial consecration took place in 1266, and mass was celebrated there in 1277, though building was not complete. Construction then slowed, and the west facade was not finished until the beginning of the 19th century after a radical restoration. Consolidation efforts are currently underway to stabilize the chevet.

This relatively small building illustrates perfectly the changes in Gothic architecture after 1260. All the windows mix colorless grisaille with full-color historiated or figural panels. The use of the latter in an architectural context is the most innovative aspect of the stained glass from the last quarter of the 13th century, not only in France but also in Europe. The earliest panels were probably made from about 1265 to 1270, at the time of the first building campaign. Thibaud V of Champagne, king of Navarre, left money in his will, in 1270, for their manufacture. The glazing program, however, has suffered losses and replacements over the centuries, and removals during 19th-century restorations. Most of the early glass from the last quarter of the 13th century or the beginning of the 14th is found in the following areas:

1) In the choir and the apse.

A series of fifteen scenes from the Passion can be found at the triforium level, enclosed in cusped quatrefoils and framed with grisaille panels accented by numerous colored fillets. The very narrow colored border contains stylized motifs. On the clerestory level, in the nine three-light windows of the chevet and choir, Old Testament patriarchs and prophets surround a Calvary in the axial bay that contains a modern Christ. Wide heraldic borders in the apsidal windows show the arms of Pope Urban IV, Thibaud V, etc., producing an effect comparable to that of the destroyed windows from Saint Nicaise at Reims (1287–1297). There are seven grisaille designs for the nine windows and numerous colored fillets and ornamental bosses. The tracery roses in the tympana have historiated medallions surrounded by grisaille.

2) In the chapels.

In the northern one, three of the eight scenes from the Childhood are original: the Visitation, the Annunciation and the Massacre of the Innocents. Until 1874, two panels with Saint Nicholas, now in the United States, were also there (cf. M. CAVINESS, "Medieval and Renaissance Stained Glass from New England Collections" [exh. cat.], Cambridge, Mass.: Harvard

University, Busch-Reisinger Museum, 1978, pp. 38–41, nos 15–16). These elements may have come from the Saint Nicholas Chapel, founded in 1286.

On the south side, the only early panels are the grisailles decorated with ornamental bosses adorned with grotesques, which are assembled in the southernmost windows and are later in date (about 1300).

3) Some early grisaille elements in the windows of the side aisles.

The state of preservation varies considerably. Most of the modifications are due to 19th-century restorations (1842–1846 and 1876–1906). At present, the five windows in the apse have been removed.

O. F. JOSSIER, *Monographie des vitraux de Saint-Urbain de Troyes*, Troyes, 1912; L. GRODECKI, "Les vitraux de Saint-Urbain de Troyes," *C. Arch.* 113 (1957): 122–38.

95 TROYES, church of Saint Urbain: chevet, glazed triforium, bay 5, right light
The Passion of Christ: Washing of the Disciples' Feet (Pl. 162)
H. 0.52 m.; W. 0.55 m.
ca. 1270

The triforium level is decorated with grisaille panels punctuated by colored fillets framing "miniatures in glass," one per light. They illustrate the Passion in fifteen scenes, beginning at the north: Christ Preaching; the Entry into Jerusalem; the Washing of the Disciples' Feet (illustrated); the Kiss of Judas; Christ before Pilate; the Carrying of the Cross; the Flagellation; the Crucifixion; the Descent from the Cross; the Resurrection (modern); Christ Appearing to Mary Magdalene; Dinner in the House of Simon; the Descent into Limbo; the Gathering of the Apostles and the Ascension. (The last three scenes are very restored.)

That the draughtsmanship is precise can be seen, especially, in the damascene ground against which the compositions are set. They are enclosed in cusped quatrefoils, a form that enjoyed new popularity at the end of the 13th century (the Life of Saint Catherine at Fécamp, and so on).

The compositions are balanced. The line-work is harmonious, yet nervous and strongly marked. The effect is not monumental and is similar to that found in Parisian manuscripts of 1260 to 1270. The colors are lively but subdued by the damascene ground.

Despite the evidence of numerous restorations, this series has been considered, since the 19th century, one of the major works of Gothic stained glass.

E. VIOLLET-LE-DUC, "Vitrail," *Dictionnaire raisonné de l'architecture française*, vol. IX, Paris, 1858, p. 432; WESTLAKE, 1881–84, vol. I, pp. 132–33; JOSSIER, *Vitraux de Saint-Urbain de Troyes*, pp. 73–75; GRODECKI, "Les Vitraux de Saint-Urbain," pp. 132–35; *idem*, in "L'Europe gothique," p. 120, no. 199.

96 TROYES, church of Saint Urbain: choir clerestory, bay 103, left light
The Prophet Zachariah (Pl. 163)
Dimensions (figure): H. 2.40 m.; W. 0.85 m.
ca. 1270

The windows on this level represent a group of Old Testament figures, identified by scrolls bearing their names and arranged one per light around the Calvary

scene in the axial window. (The Christ at its center is almost completely modern.) The figures are set in bands, but they are placed very high in the windows.

The iconographic program is no longer coherent, and it is likely that it originally extended beyond the choir. At the center of the tympana are historiated medallions in the rose windows, most of which are no longer in their original location.

The figures are set beneath architectural canopies that are still small. By contrast, the poses have great freedom: some prophets and patriarchs are shown in profile as if walking. The figure of Zachariah, while more traditional in its presentation, is one of the most striking because of its energetic line-work, which is almost metallic in the hair and white beard. The emaciated face, on the other hand, is painted on brown glass, while the eyes (cut out separately and inset) are as white as the hair and beard, giving the prophet a visionary expression. The color of the clothing set against a dark blue ground reinforces this impression. The beak folds are comparable in effect to contemporary sculpture from the Champagne region, which differs from Parisian art of the third quarter of the 13th century.

The grisaille decoration is also carefully worked and varied: nine different models are used in the ensemble. The wide heraldic borders are almost abstract in conception.

The figure is well-preserved, but the scroll and some parts of the red mantle are modern. While the figures are generally in good condition, Abraham in bay 101 is modern; the grisaille panels have been sufficiently restored. Some were removed by E. Didron during restoration at the end of the 19th century and are now in American collections (see "Radiance and Reflection," New York, 1982, pp. 215–17, no. 83).

JOSSIER, *Vitraux de Saint-Urbain de Troyes*, pp. 55–60; GRODECKI, "Les vitraux de Saint-Urbain," pp. 126–32; *idem*, in "L'Europe gothique," p. 119, no. 198.

97 VENDÔME (Loir-et-Cher), church of La Trinité: north transept, east wall, bay 23
The Virgin in Glory (Pl. 62)
Dimensions (panel): H. 0.59 m.; W. 0.71 m.
ca. 1215

Only a little more than twenty-five years ago, this panel with the remains of a majestic figure of the Virgin was returned to the church from which it came and installed in this bay.

Its monumentality and iconographic type place it in line with Chartrain Virgins such as the Virgin in the *Belle-Verrière* at Chartres. Under a trefoil arch, seated on a throne, crowned and nimbed, this Virgin undoubtedly held the Infant Jesus in front of her, in a formula often represented at Chartres.

The large scale and the pictorial treatment, which emphasizes line-work over modeling, indicate that this figure was meant to be seen from a distance and was placed in a high window. The style is also derived from Chartres, especially from that of the workshop responsible for the axial window in the choir, where a Virgin and Child is also represented.

State of preservation of the ensemble: good. There are few new pieces; however, the glass in the Virgin's and the angels' faces has turned brown due to corrosion.

GRODECKI, in "Vitraux de France," pp. 4–5, no. 11, pl. 8; *Recensement*, II, p. 155, fig. 132.

98 VENDÔME, church of La Trinité: chevet clerestory, bay 202, middle registers
Pierre d'Alençon Giving the Holy Tear to the Abbot of La Trinité (Pl. 154)
Dimensions (scene): H. 2.80 m.; W. 2.35 m.; (window): H. 8 m.; W. 2.35 m.
ca. 1280

In the left light, Pierre d'Alençon (1258–1284), fifth son of Saint Louis, is represented with one knee on the ground, dressed in a hauberk of mail over which he is wearing a surcoat with a fleur-de-lis pattern. He carries a sword in his belt. His hands are veiled as a sign of respect as he offers a rectangular coffret with four trefoil arches, which is meant to hold the Holy Tear—a remarkable relic given to the abbey by its founder, Geoffroy Martel, count of Vendôme and Anjou (1006–1060). In the central light is the abbot of La Trinité, surrounded by two clerics. Wearing priestly vestments and holding a crozier, the abbot receives the homage of the prince. At the right, a cleric and laymen witness the event. The scenes have a background of small flowers. The lateral lights have a fleur-de-lis border; in the central one, border motifs are three-towered castles of Castile (partially modern).

The figures were probably originally set in bands, as they are today; however, changes made in the 16th century make the original arrangement uncertain, especially the placement of the scene within the grisailles. The lancet heads and tympanum are filled with partly original grisaille panels. The architectural canopies are not yet fully developed; the niche has a trefoil arch on the inside and a leaf cable on the outside.

The drawing and poses are elegant, despite rather simplified handling. The style is still within the Rayonnant tradition like the windows at the cathedral of Tours, and others. As this glass was probably given by Pierre d'Alençon, who died in 1284, the window and others by the same workshop (such as the axial window) can be dated around 1280. Archeological and archival evidence concerning the choir clerestory, which was rebuilt after 1270, corroborates this theory.

State of preservation of the figures: fairly good, but there are restorations in the architectural niches.

M. LILLICH, "The Choir Clerestory Windows of La Trinité at Vendôme: Dating and Patronage," *Journal of the Society of Architectural Historians*, 34, no. 3 (1975): 243, 245–47; J. B. DE VAIVRE, "Une représentation de Pierre d'Alençon sur les verrières de La Trinité de Vendôme (circa 1280)," *Bull. Mon.* 140 (1982): 305–13.

England

99 CANTERBURY, cathedral: Trinity Chapel, bay 15 (n. IV)
Life of Thomas Becket. Ornamental panel with foliated scrolls (Pl. 13)
H. 0.80 m.; L. 0.45 m.
1190–1205
Preserved in London: Victoria and Albert Museum (C. 2-1958).

This ornamental panel consists of a rich foliated scroll with four volutes set against a red ground. The principal volute ends in an acanthus bouquet, which acts as a decorative ground or plant frieze between the historiated medallions and the framing fillets of the historiated compartments. M. Caviness has proven that this panel comes from a window in Trinity Chapel that is dedicated to Thomas Becket.

This is one of the most remarkable examples of backgrounds of a type often used in windows in the 1200 Style, when plant scrolls (*rinceaux*) were an important decorative element in sculpture, painting, manuscript illumination and stained glass. In Burgundian glass of the middle of the century, such scrolls were used again, but the decoration seems dry and atrophied in comparison (cf. cat. 16).

State of preservation: excellent.

"The Year 1200," New York, 1970, p. 224, no. 228; CAVINESS, *Early Stained Glass of Canterbury*, p. 68, fig. 115; *idem, The Windows of Christchurch Cathedral Canterbury, CVMA*: Great Britain, vol. II, London, 1981, p. 314, no. 6.

100 DORCHESTER (Oxfordshire), abbey church of Saint Peter and Saint Paul: bay 3, 2nd register
Saint Birinus Receiving his Archepiscopal Cross (Pl. 172)
Diam.: 0.37 m.
Middle of the 13th century

In the middle, his crozier in one hand, Saint Birinus receives from a pope's hands the other symbol of his pastoral power—his archepiscopal cross. The saint wears a red chasuble, a green dalmatic and a white mitre. The pope is wearing a mitre similar to the saint's, making his identification difficult. Behind Saint Birinus is a deacon with folded hands. Below is the inscription: BERNIUS, which acts as a "bridge" to the scene.

The translation of the relics of Saint Birinus, the first Saxon bishop, to this abbey southwest of Oxford took place in 1142.

The composition is simple, the line-work rigid, almost dry. There are interlocking V folds.

The scene is the unique survivor of a Life of Saint Birinus (though the former abbey church has a later one datable to the 14th century). The panel no longer retains its original form. There are numerous stopgaps from different eras, and the glass is significantly corroded.

P. NEWTON with J. KERR, *The County of Oxford: A Catalogue of Medieval Stained Glass, CVMA*: Great Britain, vol. I, London 1979, pp. 84–85, pls 31 a–b.

101 LINCOLN, cathedral
Parable of the Prodigal Son: Banquet Celebrating the Return of the Prodigal Son (Luke XV: 21–24) (detail), Musician and Guest (Pl. 171)
Dimensions (medallion): unknown
ca. 1210–1220
Reused at Lincoln cathedral: south transept, gallery under the rose window, 2nd light from the left, 2nd register

The inscription (not illustrated) "bridging" the bottom of the scene identifies it: [HIC] [E] PULAN[TUR] REVERSO FILIO—("they celebrate the return of the son"). The other scenes from the window have disappeared.

The present arrangement of the light dates from the 18th century. The five other medallions also come from destroyed windows dateable to the first decades of the 13th century.

The faces are elegant and noble. The ample treatment of folds and drapery is difficult to discern today because of the fragmentary state of this Gothic window.

The original composition of the medallion has been altered. The head of the guest and face of the musician are original. There are numerous restored pieces.

J. LAFOND, "The Stained Glass Decoration of Lincoln Cathedral in the Thirteenth Century," *Archeological Journal* CIII (1946): 132; N. MORGAN, *The Medieval Painted Glass of Lincoln Cathedral, CVMA*: Great Britain, *Occasional Papers 3*, London, 1983, pp. 23, 30–31, pl. 3.

102 OXFORD, Merton College: chapel, choir
Saint Stephen (Pl. 177)
H. 0.91 m.; L. 0.6 m.
Between 1298 and 1311

The saint is represented traditionally, as a young deacon holding a stone, symbol of his martyrdom, in one hand. The figure is set in an architectural canopy, the uprights formed by superimposed miniature bays decorated with a leafy cable. The saint is identified by an inscription on a banderole at the bottom of his robe: S[ANCTUS] [ST]EPHANUS. This is a band-window, i. e. the figure is set between grisaille panels.

Merton College was founded in 1264. Twelve of the fourteen windows in the choir have three lights. They are decorated with colorless grisaille panels, with the figure of an apostle or a saint at the center of each light. At both sides kneels the donor: Henry de Mamesfeld, Chancellor of Oxford University in 1311. He holds an inscription reading: MAGISTER HENRICUS DE MAMESFEL[D]M[E] FECIT.

The treatment of the subject is refined: the scale of execution small, the colors lively. The workshop responsible for this ensemble seems to have been very active in this part of England and to have worked at Checkly (Staffordshire) and Stanford-on-Avon (Northamptonshire).

State of preservation: satisfactory.

J. D. LE COUTEUR, *English Medieval Painted Glass*, 1st ed., London, 1926, p. 92; R. W. GARROD, *Ancient Painted Glass of Merton College*, Oxford, 1931; GRODECKI, in "L'Europe gothique," pp. 123–24, no. 204.

Italy

103 ASSISI, Upper Basilica of San Francesco: apse, bay 2 (VIII), left light, 6th register
Typological Window of the Passion and the Appearances of the Risen Christ: Eliseus and the Sunamitess (?) (4 Kings IV: 27) (Pl. 213)
Dimensions (light): H. 7.50 m.; W. 0.98 m.
Middle of the 13th century

The nine Old Testament scenes in this light are typologically linked to parallel scenes from the Passion of Christ and his post-Resurrection appearances. This panel corresponds to the *Noli me tangere*. The New Testament scenes occupy the right light and, like German typological windows, they have a different arrangement from the Old Testament ones. In a recent article, R. Haussherr has questioned the identification

of this medallion, suggesting that it represents Song of Songs III:4.

The other two windows have an arrangement similar to Rhenish typological windows. Though these were generally limited to the axial bay, the Assisi cycle extends over three windows. Its unusual iconography can only be deciphered thanks to works such as the *Biblia Pauperum*.

This series of windows was probably executed by a German workshop that gradually abandoned its own traditions to become more Italian.

The border has "Kufic" decoration.

State of preservation of the panel: good.

G. GRISTOFANI, L'iconographie des vitraux du XIIIe siècle de la Basilique d'Assise," *Revue de l'Art chrétien* 62 (1912): 111-16; H. WENTZEL, "Die ältesten Farbfenster in der Oberkirche von S. Francesco zu Assisi," *Wallraf-Richartz Jahrbuch* 14 (1952): 42-74; BEYER, "Les roses de réseau," pp. 87-88; G. MARCHINI, *Le vetrate dell'Umbria, CVMA*: Italy, vol. I, Rome, 1973, pp. 31-38; R. HAUSSHERR, "Der typologische Zyklus der Chorfenster der Oberkirche von S. Francesco zu Assisi," *Kunst als Bedeutungsträger: Gedenkschrift für Günter Bandmann*, Berlin, 1981, p. 112, fig. 114.

104 SIENA, cathedral of Santa Maria: apse, bay 100, rose
The Glorification of the Virgin Mary (Pl. 215)
Diam. ca. 2.80 m.
1287-1288

This rose window is divided into nine compartments by rectilinear bars. Depicted in the middle register, from bottom to top, are the Dormition of the Virgin; the Virgin in Majesty, set in a mandorla carried by four angels, and the Coronation of the Virgin. On each side of the panel are two saints standing side by side in multifoil frames reminiscent of German formulae. The three patrons of the city (Saints Ansanus, Crescentius and Savinus) appear with the apostle Bartholomew. In the four remaining panels are the four Evangelists writing at their desks, accompanied by their symbols.

The rose window is no longer in its original location. Executed for the former apse of the cathedral, it was moved to its present location in 1365.

The composition is close to panel painting. The austerity of the line-work recalls the tradition of Cimabue. The drapery treatment, however, is soft. The colors are luminous, but their range is restricted. Perspective has been used.

E. Carli and then G. Marchini have maintained that the design for this work is by Duccio, but other art historians have disagreed.

State of preservation: mediocre.

E. CARLI, *Vetrate duccesca*, Florence, 1946; G. MARCHINI, *Le vitrail italien*, Paris, 1955, pp. 27, 223, note 31, pls 17-19; B. TOSATTI SOLDANO, *Miniature e vetrate senesi del secolo XIII*, Genoa, 1978, pp. 83-124; F. DEUCHLER, *Duccio*, Milan, 1984, p. 196.

105 SIENA, Oratory of the Madonna della Grotta (?)
Virgin and Child (Pl. 214)
H. 0.65 m.; W. 0.63 m.
ca. 1280
In storage at the Pinacoteca Nazionale, Siena

The enthroned Virgin is enveloped in an ample, light purple *maphorion*. The Christ Child, seated on her left arm, clenches a scroll in one hand. While the Virgin is of a type that is still Byzantine, her attitude and refined colors prefigure early 14th-century stylistic innovations at Siena. The drapery and folds are still stereotyped, despite an effort toward softness around the low neckline.

The origin of this work remains problematic. The oratory was not built until the 15th century.

State of preservation: precarious, following poor restoration. These efforts have partially destroyed the coherence of this "incunabulum". The paint on the Virgin's face has been lost.

E. CARLI, *Dipinti senesi del contado e della Maremma*, Milan, 1955, pp. 35-38; E. CASTELNUOVO, "Vetrate italiane," *Paragone* IX (1958): 21; "L'Art gothique siennois," exh. cat., Avignon: Musée du Petit Palais, June-Oct., 1983, pp. 34-35, no. 1.

Switzerland

106 KÖNIGSFELDEN (Aargau), former Franciscan abbey church: chevet
Overall view of the windows (Pl. 197)
Dimensions (each window): H. 10.20 m.; W. 1.70 m.
1325-1330

By order of the Hapsburg Queen Elizabeth and her daughter, Princess Agnes, a chapel was built on the site where Albert I was assassinated on May 1, 1301, by Duke John of Swabia. Then, in 1310-1312, the two women endowed a double Franciscan monastery. The building, constructed in two stages, became the mausoleum of the Hapsburgs from 1316. The building was consecrated in 1320; the choir was then built by the Master of Berne. The glass that decorated the eleven windows was installed between 1325 and 1330 by a workshop headed by an exceptional "international" master, who was cognizant of the most recent developments in painting such as the Italian innovations. All the windows were donated by direct descendants of Albert I; the years of their marriages and deaths usually allow us to date each of the works.

The overall plan, of great theological depth, links a Franciscan program to Hapsburg traditions. Bay 0 shows the Passion of Christ; bay 1, His post-Resurrection appearances; bay 2, the Childhood of Christ. Bay 3 represents the Life of Saint Paul and the Death of the Virgin; bay 4, The Life of Saint John the Baptist and the Martyrdom of Saint Catherine of Alexandria. Bay 5 has six of the apostles and bay 6, the remaining six; bay 7, Saint Nicholas; bay 8, the Life of Saint Francis of Assisi. Bay 9 illustrates the Life of Saint Clare; bay 10 the Life of Saint Ann. The earliest windows are those in the chevet; the most recent those in the straight bays of the choir.

Formally, these windows correspond to two types of compositions:

1) Scenes or figures under architectural canopies set against damascene grounds. In the case of scenes, each light generally contains one of the protagonists. There are two historiated windows, each with five scenes, and they frame the axial window. The historiated and architectural panels are each the size of a register. The figurative windows contain apostles, each with two series of three superimposed apostles.

2) Superimposed medallions or quatrefoils, four per window, fill the entire width of the bay. The registers, however, are the same as in the first type of window, creating a remarkable formal unity.

Between the compartments are figures and architectural elements. The rich ornament uses the formulae of Strasbourg and Swabian glass from the beginning of the 14th century.

There is an extraordinary mastery of execution. The compositions are open and legible, with Italian perspective. The colors are lively.

State of preservation: varies among the windows; some have lost part of their scenes. Extensive restoration work was done between 1896 and 1900. At present they have been taken down for additional restoration.

W. LÜBKE, *Über die alten Glasgemälde der Schweiz*, Zurich, 1866, pp. 19-22; F. ZSCHOKKE, "Alte Glasmalerei der Schweiz," exh. cat., Zurich: Kunstgewerbemuseum, 1945-46, pp. 26-40; E. MAURER, "Das Kloster Königsfelden," *Die Kunstdenkmäler des Kantons Aargau*, vol. III, 1954, pp. 74-234; *idem*, "Hapsburgische und franziskanische Anteile am Königsfelder Bildprogramm," *Zeitschrift für schweizerische Archäologie und Kunstgeschichte* 19 (1959): 220-25; *idem*, "Die Glasmalereien," in *Königsfelden*, Zurich, Olten, Freiburg im Breisgau, 1970, pp. 53-165.

107 KÖNIGSFELDEN (Aargau), former Franciscan abbey church; choir, bay 2, 5th and 6th registers
The Childhood of Christ: Adoration of the Magi (detail): King Gaspard (left light) (Pl. 199)
H. 1.65 m.; W. 1.70 m.
1325-1330

The scene extends over three lights. At the right is the Enthroned Virgin with her Son, in a yellow robe, standing on her knees. A rose—a Marian symbol—decorates her green gown, which is covered with a red-lined purple mantle. Above them is a star and a yellow drapery that forms a canopy. In the central light, Balthasar kneels with his crown set on his knee, following an iconographic tradition dating back to the end of the 12th century, while Melchior stands. In the left light is Gaspard, dressed as a young prince. All three carry a gold cup as a present for the Child. Over their heads are half-length figures of angels. The ground is blue, with quatrefoil decoration. The architectural canopies are set against a red ground decorated with small lozenges. The richer central canopy is surmounted by two small figures of the prophets Malachi and Tobit: their names are written on scrolls.

The other scenes, from bottom to top, are 1) the Annunciation, 2 and 3) the Nativity, and the Annunciation to the Shepherds, 4) the Presentation in the Temple and 5) the Baptism of Christ. There is openwork plant decoration in the tympanum.

The formal relationship with the workshops in Alsace and the area around Lake Constance is clear.

State of preservation of this register: fairly good; the bottom of the Virgin's gown is modern.

MAURER, "Das Kloster Königsfelden," vol. III, pp. 106–121; BECKSMANN, 1967, pp. 94–95; *idem*, "Die Glasmalereien," pp. 80–81, 117.

108   KÖNIGSFELDEN (Aargau), former Franciscan abbey church: choir, bay 8, 6th register, central panel
Life of Saint Francis of Assisi: Saint Francis Preaches to the Birds (Pl. 198)
H. 0.83 m.; W. 0.42 m.
1325–1330

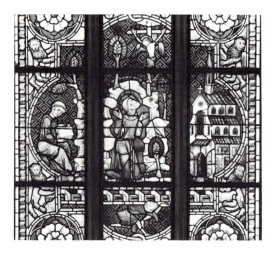

This panel occupies the central part of the third medallion in the window given by Duke Otto of Hapsburg (1301–1339) and his wife, Elizabeth of Bavaria, who died in 1330.

The work consists of five compartments tracing the most important events in the life of the *Poverello*. Reading from bottom to top, they are

1) Saint Francis leaves his father and goes to find Bishop Guido of Assisi;
2) Saint Francis presents his rule to Pope Innocent III;
3) Saint Francis preaches to the birds;
4) Saint Francis receives the Stigmata;
5) the death of the saint.

The scenes are set against a red ground decorated with quatrefoils. They rest on "bridges" formed by a series of beams seen in perspective and supported by atlantes in imitation of the grotesques in contemporary manuscripts.

Between the compartments are white roses in medallions, and lions—both heraldic symbols of the house of Hapsburg.

The composition is very legible; the birds are naturalistically rendered. The palette is rich and bright.

The lower part of the saint's gown is modern.

A. SCHMARSOW, *Das Franziskusfenster in Königsfelden und der Freskenzyklus in Assisi*, Leipzig, 1919; MAURER, "Das Kloster Königsfelden," vol. III, pp. 176–93; *idem*, "Habsburgische und franziskanische Anteil," pp. 220–25; *idem*, "Die Glasmalereien," pp. 121–23.

109   LAUSANNE, cathedral of Notre Dame: south transept, rose
Image of the World:
1) Overall view (diam. ca. 9 m.) (Pl. 114)
2) *Luna* (inscription: LUNA; Diam. 0.58 m.) (Pl. 115)
3) *May* (inscription: MAIVS; Diam. 0.58 m.
ca. 1235

The present cathedral at Lausanne was begun in the 1160s, but the rose window dates from the episcopate of Boniface of Brussels (1231–1239). The bishop was a Flemish theologian, a friend of Albertus Magnus and Thomas de Cantimpré, author of the encyclopedia *De natura rerum*. There is a clear link between the scholastic philosophy of Boniface and the iconographic theme of the rose—a symbolic image of the world. The window was executed by Pierre d'Arras, active in Lausanne between 1217 and 1235.

In the central ensemble was the figure of Annus (god of the year), surrounded by the Sun; Luna (the Moon) represented on a chariot with a torch in hand; Day and Night. Then, arranged in four semicircles, are the Seasons and the Months. In four circles are the Elements, the Signs of the Zodiac, and the Arts of Divination (*Aerimancia* and *Piromancia*). Finally, the

Rivers of Paradise, the mythological peoples of the ends of the earth, and the eight winds on the compass rose are represented. The program uses antique models revived by the Carolingians and betrays a strong French influence, especially in the composition of the months, like May (illustrated).

The glass has been cut to medium scale. Dry linework is used for the faces, but the lines of drapery are sometimes soft. The handling is heavy and sometimes accentuated. The colors are bright. The glass retains connections with the stylistic principles of northern France in the first half of the century.

The glass was restored between 1894 and 1899 by Edouard Hosch, who remade and displaced close to twenty medallions, among them the central one.

J. RAHN, "Die Gemälde in der Rosetten der Kathedrale von Lausanne," *Mitteilungen der antiquarischen Gesellschaft Zürich* XX (1879): 29–58; E. J. BEER, *Die Rose der Kathedrale von Lausanne und der kosmologische Bilderkreis des Mittelalters*, Berne, 1952; *idem*, *Die Glasmalereien der Schweiz vom 12. Jahrhundert bis zum Beginn des 14. Jahrhunderts*, CVMA: Switzerland, vol. I, Basel, 1956, pp. 28–58, pls 2–40; J. LAFOND, "Les vitraux de la cathédrale de Lausanne," *C. Arch.* 110 (1953): 116–32; GRODECKI, in "L'Europe gothique," pp. 121–22, no. 201; E. BEER, "Les vitraux du Moyen Age de la cathédrale," *La cathédrale de Lausanne*, Berne, 1975, pp. 221–49, figs 278–99.

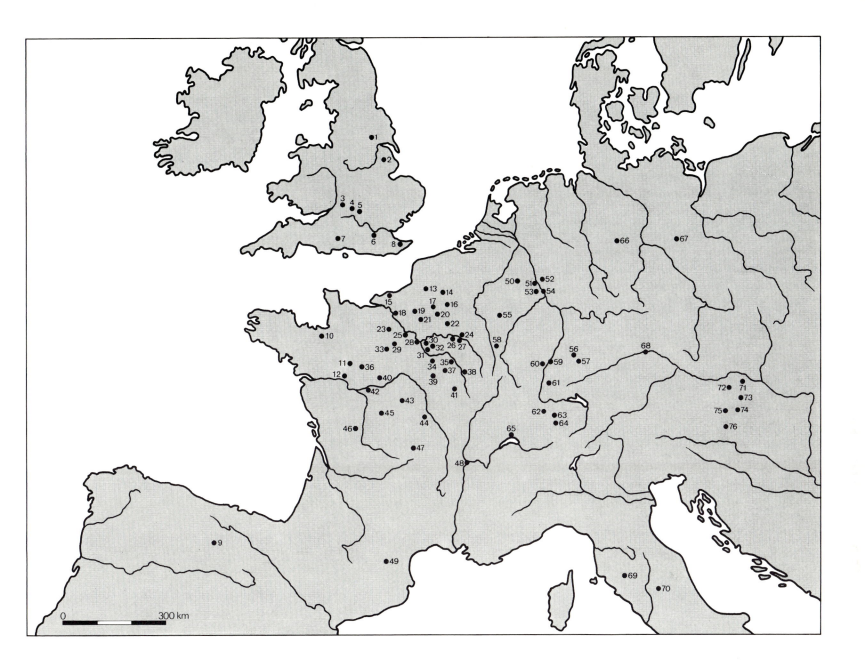

Map with the Location of the Works Illustrated

Bibliography

This bibliography is not an exhaustive list of all works or articles consulted, nor of those cited in the chapter notes and catalogue entries. It includes only books (and occasionally, articles) that are of general interest—inventories or studies of ensembles, attempts at synthesis and proposed theories. We have omitted general histories, which are sometimes of use in the study of stained glass, and works on iconography, whether general or specialized.

1. Bibliography

CAVINESS, M. HARRISON with STAUDINGER, E.R. *Stained Glass before 1540. Annotated Bibliography.* Boston, 1983.
GERÓ, J. *Bibliographie du vitrail français.* Paris, 1983.

2. General Works

BOOM, A. VAN DER. *Die Kunst der Glazeniers in Europa (1100-1600).* Amsterdam and Antwerp, 1960.

COWEN, P. *Rose Windows.* London, 1979. [Trans. into French: *Roses médiévales.* Paris, 1979; and into German: *Die Rosenfenster der gotischen Kathedralen.* Freiburg im Breisgau, Basel and Vienna, 1979].

DAY, L.F. *Windows: A Book about Stained and Painted Glass.* 3rd Ed. London, 1909.

FISCHER, J.L. *Handbuch der Glasmalerei.* 2nd Ed. Leipzig, 1937.

FRODL-KRAFT, E. *Die Glasmalerei: Entwicklung, Technik, Eigenart.* Vienna and Zurich, 1970.

LAFOND, J. *Le Vitrail.* Paris, 1966; 2nd Ed. 1978 [coll. *Je sais, je crois*].

LASTEYRIE, F. DE. *Histoire de la peinture sur verre en France d'après ses monuments.* 2 Vols. Paris, 1852-57.

LEE, L.; SEDDON, G. and STEPHENS, F. *Stained Glass.* London and New York, 1976 [Trans. into French: *Le Vitrail.* Paris, 1977].

MÂLE, E. "La peinture sur verre en France à l'époque gothique." In *Histoire générale de l'art* (A. Michel). Vol. II, Part 1, Paris, 1906, pp. 372-96.

OIDTMANN, H. *Die rheinischen Glasmalereien vom 12. bis 16. Jahrhundert.* 2 Vols. Düsseldorf, 1912-29.

– *Die Glasmalerei.* 2 Vols. Cologne, 1892-98 [Vol. I: *Die Technik der Glasmalerei;* Vol. II: *Die Geschichte der Glasmalerei*].

OTTIN, L. *Le Vitrail, son histoire ses manifestations à travers les âges et les peuples.* Paris, n.d. [1896].

WESTLAKE, N.H.J. *A History of Design in Stained and Painted Glass.* Vols. 1 and 2. London, 1881 and 1882.

3. Technique, Problems of Origin and of Function

A. Technique

CHESNEAU, G. "Contribution à l'étude de la technique des vitraux du Moyen Age." *Bull. Mon.* 92 (1933): 265-94.

DODWELL, C.R. (ED.). *Theophilus: De Diversis artibus/ Theophilus, The Various Arts.* London, 1961.

FRODL-KRAFT, E. "Le vitrail médiéval, technique et esthétique." *Cahiers de Civilisation médiévale* X (1967): 1-13.

GRUBER, J.J. "Technique." In *Vitrail français,* Paris, 1958, pp. 55-80.

HAWTHORNE, J.G. and SMITH, C.S. (EDS.). *On Divers Arts: The Treatise of Theophilus.* [Chicago, 1963]; reprint: New York, 1979.

KNOWLES, J.A. "The Technique of Glass Painting in Medieval and Renaissance Times." *Journal of the British Society of Arts* LXII (1914): 567-85.

LAFOND, J. *Pratique de la peinture sur verre à l'usage des curieux: suivie d'un essai historique sur le jaune d'argent; et d'une note sur les plus anciens verres gravés.* Rouen, 1943.

L'ESCALOPIER, C. DE (ed.). *Theophili presbyteri et monachi libri III. Seu Diversarum Artium Schedula.* Paris, 1843; reprint: Nogent-le-Roi, 1977.

LEVIEIL, P. *L'Art de la peinture sur verre et de la vitrerie.* Paris, 1774.

NEWTON, R.G. *The Deterioration and Conservation of Painted Glass: A Critical Bibliography and Three Research Papers.* CVMA: Great Britain, *Occasional Papers 1.* London, 1974.

VIOLLET LE DUC, E. "Vitrail." In *Dictionnaire raisonné de l'architecture française du XIᵉ au XVIᵉ siècle.* Vol. IX. Paris, 1858, pp. 372-462.

WENTZEL, H. "Glasmaler und Maler im Mittelalter." *Zeitschrift für Kunstwissenschaft* 3 (1949): 53-62.

B. Problems of Origin and of Function

BECKSMANN, R. *Die architektonische Rahmung des hochgotischen Bildfensters. Untersuchungen zur Oberrheinischen Glasmalerei von 1250 bis 1350.* Berlin, 1967.

ENGELS, M.T. *Zur Problematik der mittelalterlichen Glasmalerei.* Berlin, 1937.

GRODECKI, L. with BRISAC, C. and LAUTIER, C. *Le Vitrail roman.* Fribourg: Office du Livre, 1977; 2nd Ed. 1983.

– "Le vitrail et l'architecture au XIIᵉ et au XIIIᵉ siècle." *Gazette des Beaux-Arts* 33 (1949): 5-24.

GRUBER, J.J. "Quelques aspects de l'art et de la technique du vitrail en France; dernier quart du XIIIᵉ siècle, premier quart du XIVᵉ siècle." In *Travaux des étudiants du groupe d'histoire de l'art de la Faculté des Lettres de Paris.* Paris, 1928, pp. 71-94.

SCHMARSOW, A. "Kompositionsgesetze frühgotischer Glasgemälde." *Abhandlungen der philologisch-historischen Klasse der sächsischen Gesellschaft der Wissenschaften* 36, no. 3 (1919).

4. Bibliography by Country

Austria

Corpus Vitrearum Medii Aevi:
BÄCHER, E. *Die mittelalterlichen Glasgemälde in der Steiermark.* Part 1. *CVMA:* Austria, vol. III/1. Vienna, Cologne and Graz, 1979.

FRODL-KRAFT, E. *Die mittelalterlichen Glasgemälde in Niederösterreich.* Part 1. *CVMA:* Austria, vol. II/1. Vienna, Cologne and Graz, 1972.

– *Die mittelalterlichen Glasgemälde in Wien. CVMA:* Austria, vol. I. Vienna, 1962.

FRODL, W. *Glasmalerei in Kärnten.* Klagenfurt and Vienna, 1950.

KIESLINGER, F. *Gotische Glasmalerei in Österreich bis 1450*. Vienna, 1928.

France

AUBERT, M. *Le Vitrail en France*. Paris, 1946.

– *et al. Vitrail français*. Paris, 1958 [collective work, notably: GRODECKI, L. "De 1200 à 1260"; pp. 115–62; and AUBERT, M. "De 1260 à 1380"; pp. 163–78].

Corpus Vitrearum Medii Aevi:
AUBERT, M.; GRODECKI, L.; LAFOND, J. and VERRIER, J. *Les Vitraux de Notre-Dame et de la Sainte-Chapelle de Paris. CVMA*: France, vol. I. Paris, 1959.

Recensement des vitraux anciens de la France. 2 Vols. *CVMA*: France, complementary series, Paris, 1978 and 1981. [Vol. I (windows from Paris, the region around Paris, Picardy and Nord-Pas-de-Calais); Vol. II (windows from central France and the Loire valley)].

———

GRODECKI, L. "Les problèmes de l'origine de la peinture gothique et le 'Maître de saint Chéron de la cathédrale de Chartres.'" *Revue de l'Art*, nos 40–41 (1978): 43–64.

LAFOND, J. "Le vitrail du XIVᵉ siècle en France: étude historique et descriptive." In LEFRANÇOIS-PILLION, L. *L'Art du XIVᵉ siècle en France*. Paris, 1954.

– "Le vitrail en Normandie de 1250 à 1300." *Bull. Mon.* 111 (1953): 317–58.

"Vitraux de France du XIᵉ au XVIᵉ siècle." Exh. cat. by GRODECKI, L. Paris: Musée des Arts Décoratifs, 1953.

Germany

BECKSMANN, R. "Fensterstiftungen und Stifterbilder in der deutschen Glasmalerei des Mittelalters." *Vitrea dedicata: Die Stiftbilder in der deutschen Glasmalerei*. Berlin, 1975, pp. 65–85.

Corpus Vitrearum Medii Aevi:
BECKSMANN, R. *Die mittelalterlichen Glasmalereien in Baden und der Pfalz ohne Freiburg in Br. CVMA*: GFR, vol. II/1. Berlin, 1979.

DRACHENBERG, E. *Die mittelalterliche Glasmalerei im Erfurter Dom. CVMA*: GFR, vol. I/2. Berlin, 1979.

– MAERCKER, K.J. and SCHMIDT, C. *Die mittelalterliche Glasmalerei in den Ordenskirchen und im Angermuseum zu Erfurt. CVMA*: GFR, vol. I/1, Berlin, 1976.

RODE, H. *Die mittelalterlichen Glasmalereien des Kölner Domes. CVMA*: GFR, vol. IV/1. Berlin, 1974.

WENTZEL, H. *Die Glasmalereien in Schwaben von 1200–1350. CVMA*: GFR, vol. I. Berlin, 1958.

———

DRACHENBERG, E.; MAERCKER, K.J. and RICHTER, C. *Mittelalterliche Glasmalerei in der Deutschen Demokratischen Republik*. Berlin, 1979.

SCHÜRER VON WITZLEBEN, E. *Farbwunder deutscher Glasmalerei aus dem Mittelalter*. Augsburg, 1965; 2nd Ed. 1967.

WENTZEL, H. *Meisterwerke der Glasmalerei*. Berlin, 1951; 2nd Ed. 1954.

Great Britain

BAKER, J. *English Stained Glass*. Intro. by H. READ. London, 1960 [Trans. into French: *L'Art du vitrail en Angleterre*. Paris, 1961].

Corpus Vitrearum Medii Aevi:
CAVINESS, M. *The Windows of Christ Church Cathedral Canterbury. CVMA*: Great Britain, vol. II. London, 1981.

MORGAN, N. *The Medieval Glass of Lincoln Cathedral. CVMA*: Great Britain, *Occasional Papers 3*. London, 1983.

NEWTON, P. with KERR, J. *The County of Oxford: A Catalogue of Medieval Stained Glass. CVMA*: Great Britain, vol. I. London, 1979.

———

NELSON, P. *Ancient Painted Glass in England, 1170–1500*. London, 1913.

READ, H. *English Stained Glass*. London, 1926.

Italy

CASTELNUOVO, E. "Vetrate italiane." *Paragone* 8, no. 103 (1958): 3–24.

Corpus Vitrearum Medii Aevi:
MARCHINI, C. *Le vetrate dell'Umbria. CVMA*: Italy, vol. I. Rome, 1973.

———

MARCHINI, G. *Le vetrate italiane*. Milan, 1955 [Trans. into English: *Italian Stained Glass Windows*. London and New York, 1957; and into French: *Le Vitrail italien*. Paris, 1957].

TOSATTI SOLDANO, B. *Miniatura e Vetrate senesi del secolo XIII*. Genoa, 1978.

Scandinavia

Corpus Vitrearum Medii Aevi:
ANDERSSON, A.; CHRISTIE, S.M.; NORDMAN, C.A. and ROUSSELL, A. *Die Glasmalereien des Mittelalters in Skandinavien. CVMA*: Scandinavia, Stockholm, 1964.

Spain

FERNÁNDEZ ARENAS, J. and ESPINO, J.C.F. *Las vidrieras de la catedral de León*. León, 1983.

Switzerland

Corpus Vitrearum Medii Aevi:
BEER, E.J. *Die Glasmalereien der Schweiz aus dem 14. und 15. Jahrhundert, ohne Königsfelden und Berner Münsterchor. CVMA*: Switzerland, vol. III. Basel, 1965.

– *Die Glasmalereien der Schweiz vom 12. bis zum Beginn des 14. Jahrhunderts. CVMA*: Switzerland, vol. I, Basel, 1956.

———

MAURER, E. *Das Kloster Königsfelden (Die Kunstdenkmäler des Kantons Aargau)*. Vol. III. Basel, 1954.

ZSCHOKKE, F. *Mittelalterliche Bildfenster der Schweiz*. Basel, 1946 [Trans. into English: *Medieval Stained Glass in Switzerland*. London, 1947; and into French: *Vitraux du Moyen Age en Suisse*. Basel, 1947].

Photo Credits

We are grateful to the photographers who were responsible for photographing the illustrations and to the museums and institutions that gave us access to the photographic material reproduced in this book. The numbers refer to plate numbers.

Ingrid de Kalbermatten, working with Catherine Brisac, was responsible for the photo documentation.

Aargauische Denkmalpflege, Aarau 200 (photo Hiller); cat. 108 (photo Heim); 197, 198, 199
Didier Alliou, Le Mans 121
Archives Photographiques, Paris/S.P.A.D.E.M. 12, 21, 74, 89, (photos J. Feuillie); 7, 9, 10, 11, 18, 20, 23, 29, 30, 31, 35, 37, 40, 43, 45, 47, 48, 49, 52, 57, 59, 60, 62, 64, 65, 66, 67, 68, 70, 72, 73, 75, 80, 90, 91, 92, 95, 96, 97, 99, 101, 103, 104, 107, 108, 112, 116, 118, 119, 120, 122, 124, 125, 127, 134, 137, 138, 139, 140, 141, 144, 146, 147, 148, 154, 158, 159, 162, 165, 166, 167; cat. 40, cat. 43, cat. 49, cat. 57, cat. 92
Bibliothèque nationale, Paris 16, 17, 22, 94, 126
Bildarchiv Foto Marburg 182
Bulloz, Paris 8
Bundesdenkmalamt, Vienna 206, 207, 208, 209, 210, 212
Madeline Caviness 69, 135, 136
Véronique Chaussé 61; cat. 35
Corpus Vitrearum Medii Aevi, Germany, Freiburg-en-Breisgau 181, 201 (photos D. Rentsch); 185, 194, 195, 203 (photos R. Harling); 205 (photo R. Becksmann); 181
M. Cothren 71
CRDP, Beauvais 100 (photo Roussel)
CRDP, Clermont-Ferrand 129
Draeger 5, 6, 55
Dr. Gottfried Frenzel, Nürnberg-Fischbach 183
Françoise Gatouillat 131, 132, 133
Editions Gaud, Moisenay 110
Sylvie Gaudin 81, 87, 88
G.E.M.O.B., Beauvais 145
Giraudon, Paris 2, 14, 50, 53, 54, 56, 58, 161, 168, 169, 187, 188
The Glencairn Museum, Bryn Athyn (Penn.) 151
Sonia Halliday & Laura Lushington, Weston Turville 3, 170, 171, 177, 178
André Held, Lausanne 114, 115; cat. 109
Gérard Hermet, Chartres 152
Hessisches Landesmuseum, Darmstadt 193, 202
Fritz Hummel, Nuremberg 211
Institut für Denkmalpflege, East Berlin 204
Inventaire Général des Pays de Loire 19, 123 (photo P. Giraud); 117
Inventaire général, B. Cougnassout, Lyons 76, 77
Joly, Paris 41
L. Mary, Reims 32
Mas, Barcelona 179
The Metropolitan Museum of Art, New York 27, 28, 44, 78, 83, 84, 155, 156; cat. 83, cat. 84

Monuments Historiques, Research Laboratory of the 4, 15, 24, 33, 51, 63, 82, 109, 113, 143, 153, 157, 163
Musée d'Art et d'Histoire, Geneva 98, 111
Musée National Suisse, Zurich 192
Musée de l'Œuvre Notre-Dame, Strasbourg 186, 190
National Monuments Record, London 173, 174, 175
Pasquino, Paris 38
Philadelphia Museum of Art 93 (photo Eric E. Mitchell)
Réunion des Musées Nationaux, Paris 79, 149
Rheinisches Bilderarchiv, Cologne 184
Jean Rollet, Paris 105, 164
Georges Routhier, Studio Lourmel, Paris 102
Sacro Convento di S. Francesco, Assisi 213
Secrétariat Régional de l'Inventaire Poitou-Charentes/Alain Chamboutard, Poitiers 46
Soprintendenza per i Beni Artistici e Storici, Sienna 214 (photo Grassi, Sienna); 215; cat. 104
Strasbourg, City museums of 189
Thomas, Saint-Michel-de-Volangis (Cher) 42
Eileen Tweedy, London 36; cat. 93
J.-C. Vaysse 128, 130, 176
Victoria and Albert Museum, London 13, 85, 86
Worcester Art Museum, Worcester (Mass.) 39
Württembergisches Landesmuseum, Stuttgart 196
H. Zakin 25, 142, 160
Author's and publisher's archives 1, 34, 150, 191

Index

The words in small capitals are place names and proper names. Those in italics refer to techniques and methods; those in normal typeface to iconographic themes. The numbers in italics refer to plate numbers.

This book was printed in August, 1985, by the Imprimeries Réunies S.A., Lausanne. It was set by Typobauer Filmsatz GmbH, Ostfildern, FRG. The photolithographs (color) are the work of cooperativa lavoratori grafici, Verona, and of E. Kreienbühl + Co AG, Lucerne (black and white). The book was bound by Mayer & Soutter, Renens. Editorial coordination: Barbara J. Perroud-Benson. Design: Ronald Sautebin, Fribourg. Production: Marcel Berger.

Printed in Switzerland